Other A to Z Guides from Scarecrow Press

The A to Z of Buddhism by Charles S. Prebish, 2001.
The A to Z of Catholicism by William J. Collinge, 2001.
The A to Z of Hinduism by Bruce M. Sullivan, 2001.
The A to Z of Islam by Ludwig W. Adamec, 2002.
The A to Z of Slavery & Abolition by Martin A. Klein, 2002.

HISTORICAL DICTIONARIES OF RELIGIONS,
PHILOSOPHIES, AND MOVEMENTS
Edited by Jon Woronoff

The A to Z of Slavery and Abolition

Martin A. Klein

The Scarecrow Press, Inc.
Lanham, Maryland, and Oxford
2002

SCARECROW PRESS, INC.

Published in the United States of America
by Scarecrow Press, Inc.
A Member of the Rowman & Littlefield Publishing Group
4720 Boston Way, Lanham, Maryland 20706
www.scarecrowpress.com

PO Box 317
Oxford
OX2 9RU, UK

British Library Cataloguing in Publication Information Available

Library of Congress Cataloging-in-Publication Data

Klein, Martin A.
  The A to Z of slavery and abolition / Martin A. Klein.
    p. cm.
Rev. ed. of: Historical dictionary of slavery and abolition, 2002.
Includes bibliographical references.
  ISBN 0-8108-4559-8 (pbk. : alk. paper)
  1. Slavery—History—Dictionaries. 2. Antislavery movements—History—Dictionaries. 3. Abolitionists—History—Dictionaries. I. Klein, Martin A. Historical dictionary of slavery and abolition. II. Title.
  HT861 .K54 2002b
  306.3'62'03—dc21

                                              2002011953

CONTENTS

ACKNOWLEDGMENTS

The history of slavery is a long and brutal one. The history of abolition is short and incomplete. It has been challenging to try to cover both tales in a single volume, and in particular, to cover the different forms slavery has taken and the different places in which it has developed. In trying to do so, I have depended on the advice of a number of fellow scholars. Many colleagues and students have helped, but Joseph C. Miller, Michael Wayne, Peter Blanchard, and Suzanne Miers have been particularly generous of their time and knowledge and have kindly read relevant parts of this volume. They have saved me from some grievous errors, both factual and grammatical. In particular, they have tried to save me from the sin of oversimplification. If they have not been completely successful, it is largely due to my stubbornness.

I also have a debt of respect. Most writers on abolition stress the actions of people of generous and humane values. I would not denigrate these, but I have tried to give equal attention to the struggle of slaves and former slaves to assert their dignity and get some control over their work and family lives. The student of slavery does not always see human beings at their best. Our somber task is lightened somewhat by those moments in which the oppressed assert themselves to establish their right to live free from the control of others. They did so not only by violent resistance, but also by taking advantage of the limited opportunities a harsh life offered them. I have tried to write not only about slavery, but also about the slaves and their quest for autonomy and self-respect.

Finally, I owe a special debt to my wife, Suzanne Silk Klein. She has long been my most perceptive critic. She has put up patiently with the periods of distraction that my writing has caused and has been, even though her name is not on the title page, a generous companion and a very rewarding collaborator.

CHRONOLOGY

Slavery

c. 3200 BCE   Evidence of slavery in Sumer

c. 2500 BCE   Evidence of Egyptian enslavement of war prisoners

c. 1790 BCE   Hammurabi's Code regulates slavery in Babylon

c. 1500 BCE   Hittite law code regulates slavery; there is also evidence of slavery in ancient China, Assyria, Babylonia, and Crete

c. 1220 BCE   Moses leads ancient Israelites out of Egypt to freedom

c. 650 BCE   Messenian helots begin 20-year revolt against Sparta

c. 600 BCE   Intensive use of slave labor in Persia

c. 590 BCE   Solon abolishes debt slavery in Athens and recognizes landless Athenians as citizens; this leads to development of Athens as a slave society

c. 500 BCE   Slavery is common in ancient India; evidence of slavery in Meso-America

c. 464-455 BCE   Helots revolt against Spartan rule

453 BCE   Twelve Tables include slave law in Roman Republic

c. 300 BCE   The *Arthashastra* explains law of slavery in ancient India

241 BCE   Rome defeats Carthage and begins accumulation of slaves in Italy

c. 200 BCE   Roman conquests bring massive numbers of slaves to Italy

136-132 BCE   Slave revolts in Sicily

73-71 BCE   Spartacus leads slave revolt against Rome

17 Wang Mang, who usurped Chinese throne, abolishes slavery, but it is re-established on his death six years later

c. 300   Roman slavery is in decline

c. 500   German invasions temporarily revive slavery in Europe

622 Prophet Muhammed flees to Medina; beginning of Islam

c. 700   Islam develops law of slavery

701   Taiho Code regulates condition of slaves in Japan

726   *Ecloga* regulates slavery in Byzantine Empire

c. 800   Establishment of Cambodian Empire with massive use of slave labor

c. 862   Foundation of Kievan state; Vikings sell slaves to Byzantium

883   Zanj slaves revolt in southern Mesopotamia

c. 1000   Dublin is founded by Vikings, becomes an important slave market; development of institution of military slavery in Muslim world

c. 1150   Slavery disappears in England and France

1206   Foundation of Delhi Sultanate, often called the "slave sultanate" because it was dominated by Turkish *mamlukes*

1265   Spanish law code *Siete Partidas* regulates slavery

c. 1300   Beginning of main period of Korean slavery; Italians develop sugar cultivation on Cyprus and Crete

1314   All remaining slaves are freed in Sweden

1341 Portuguese navigators reach Canary Islands

1443 Portuguese navigators reach Senegal River in West Africa

1444 Sale of slaves from West Africa in Portugal

1452 Pope Nicholas V issues a bull authorizing Portuguese to enslave people taken prisoner in a "just war"

1453 Constantinople falls to the Ottoman Turks

1482 Portuguese navigator Diogo Cao establishes contact with Kongo kingdom

1485 Portuguese begin developing sugar cultivation on São Tomé

1492 Christopher Columbus discovers island of Hispaniola

1495 Christopher Columbus sends large shipment of slaves to Spain

1500 Pedro Alvares Cabral claims Brazil for Portugal

1502 First African slaves arrive in West Indies

1518 Spanish king Charles I establishes the *asiento*

1521 Slave revolt on Hispaniola

1526 King Afonso I of Kongo protests enslavement of his subjects

1538 First African slaves introduced to Brazil

1552 Bartolomé de Las Casas publishes *Brief Relation of the Destruction of the Indies*

1553 Dutch enter Atlantic slave trade

1562 First British slave trading voyage to Africa

1571 French King Charles IX decrees that any person setting foot on

French soil was free

1576 Portuguese establish slave trade post at Luanda

1602 Dutch East India Company established

1610 Brazilian maroons form settlement of Palmares

1618 Company of Royal Adventurers of London is first British slave trade company

1619 First African slaves landed at Jamestown, Virginia

1621 Dutch West India Company founded

1627 English settle Barbados; French settle St. Kitts

1630 Dutch invasion of Brazil

c. 1640 English settlers on Barbados shift in to sugar

1648 Brazilians under Salvador de Sa recapture Angola from the Dutch

1652 Dutch East India Company founds Capetown

1654 Dutch are driven out of Pernambuco in Brazil

1627 English colonists found Barbados

1672 Royal African Company founded in England

1685 French enact *Code Noir* to regulate slavery in colonies

1694 Destruction of maroon state of Palmares in Brazil

1702 Asantes become dominant power on Gold Coast

1705 Virginia enacts a harsh slave code

1715 French occupy island of Mauritius, introduce slaves

c. 1720   Slaves in Virginia and Maryland achieve positive rate of reproduction

1733   James Oglethorpe founds Georgia and prohibits slavery there

1739   Stono rebellion in South Carolina; colony passes a harsh slave code; British sign treaty with Jamaican Maroons, ending 80 years of conflict

1749   Trustees of Georgia colony repeal the prohibition of slave imports

1760   Tacky's rebellion on Jamaica

1763   Slave revolt on island of Berbice

1772   Slave revolt in Demerara region of Guiana

1780   French sign a treaty with Maroons on Saint Domingue

1793   Invention of cotton gin by Eli Whitney leads to spread of slavery; passage of first Fugitive Slave Law in United States

1794   Led by Richard Allen, a group of African-Americans found the Mother Bethel Church, which becomes the African Methodist Episcopal Church

1795   Julien Fédon leads slave revolt on Grenada; slave revolt on Curaçao

1800   Gabriel's rebellion in Virginia

1806   Said ibn Sultan comes to power in Oman and Zanzibar

1811   German Coast slave revolt in Louisiana

1822   Denmark Vesey leads slave revolt in South Carolina

1831   Nat Turner leads slave revolt in Virginia; slave revolt in Jamaica

1834   Slave revolt in Cuba

1835   *Male* slave revolt in Bahia province of Brazil

1836 American settlers in Texas revolt against a Mexican constitution that contained an anti-slavery clause

Abolition

1511 Father Antonio Montesinos attacks exploitation of native people on Hispaniola

1514 Bartolomé de Las Casas begins to attack enslavement of Indians

1542 The New Laws proclaimed by Charles I of Spain prohibit enslavement of Indians

1549 Charles I prohibits holding of Indians as slaves

1573 Bartolomé de Albornoz attacks enslavement and sale of Africans

1576 French jurist Jean Bodin criticizes morality of slavery

1648 Society of Friends (Quakers) founded in England

1688 A group of Quakers in Germantown, Pennsylvania sign a statement that slavery was contrary to Christian principles

1700 Judge Samuel Sewall publishes an anti-slavery tract, *The Selling of Joseph*

1712 Pennsylvania bans further import of slaves

1741 Pope Benedict XIV condemns the slave trade as practiced in Brazil

1748 Montesquieu, *The Spirit of the Laws*, criticizes slavery

1754 Philadelphia Yearly Meeting of Quakers decides that slavery is a sin

1765 The *Encyclopédie* speaks of liberty as a natural right

1772 Lord Mansfield rules in Somerset case that slaves brought to England cannot be forced to return to slave colonies

1775 The Earl of Dunmore, governor of Virginia, offers to free male slaves joining British forces opposing the American rebels

1776 Philadelphia Yearly Meeting of Quakers is closed to slaveowners; Second Continental Congress calls for an end to the import of slaves

1777 New Vermont constitution prohibits slavery

1780 Pennsylvania passes gradual emancipation statute; new Massachusetts constitution abolishes slavery; Condorcet's *Reflexions sur l'esclavage de nègres* is published

1782 British ships take almost 15,000 black Loyalists to Nova Scotia and the West Indies

1784 Organization of the Pennsylvania Abolition Society; Connecticut and Rhode Island pass abolition laws

1786 New Jersey adopts a gradual emancipation law

1787 Creation of Sierra Leone as a colony for freed slaves; British abolitionists create the Association for the Abolition of slavery; U.S. Congress prohibits slavery in the Northwest Territory

1788 *Société des Amis des Noirs* founded in France; Northwest Ordinance in the United States prohibits slavery in territories north of the Ohio River

1791 Haitian Revolution begins

1792 Denmark abolishes the slave trade

1794 France abolishes slavery

1799 Gradual emancipation law passed in New York; George Washington dies; his will frees his slaves

1801 Korean government frees agricultural slaves belonging to state

1802 Napoleon reestablishes slavery and slave trade in French colonies

1804 Haitian independence

1807 Great Britain abolishes slave trade

1808 United States ends slave imports

1811 Chile approves a "free womb" emancipation law

1816 Simón Bolívar and José San Martín promise freedom to all slaves who support the struggle for liberation from Spain; African Methodist Episcopal Church founded in the United States; American Colonization Society founded

1817 Portugal ends the slave trade, but only in lands north of the equator

1820 Missouri Compromise establishes balance between slave and free states in the United States; Spain abolishes slave trade south of the equator

1821 Congress of Cucutá approves gradual abolition in Gran Colombia. José San Martín decrees gradual emancipation in Peru; it was not completely enforced

1822 Liberia is founded by repatriated American slaves

1823 Formation of British Anti-Slavery Society

1824 Slaves were freed in the United Provinces of Central America; end of slavery in New York

1829 Mexico abolishes slavery

1831 William Lloyd Garrison founds the American Anti-Slavery Society; France abolishes the slave trade

1831-1832 Virginia state convention debates abolition and rejects it

1833 Great Britain abolishes slavery

1835 Georgia enacts death penalty for publication of abolitionist tracts

1837 Abolitionist editor Elijah P. Lovejoy murdered by mob

1837-1838 Great Britain signs a series of treaties with other nations which allowed the Royal Navy to search their ships for slaves

1838 Frederick Douglass escapes from slavery

1839 Formation of British and Foreign Anti-Slavery Society

1840 Great Britain frees the *Hermosa*, which was shipwrecked in the Bahamas; Liberty Party runs James G. Birney for president of the United States

1841 U. S. Supreme Court rules that Africans on *Amistad* were illegally enslaved

1842 Paraguay approves a gradual emancipation law

1843 East India Company ends legal recognition of slavery in India; Vermont and Massachusetts bar state officials from aiding efforts to remove fugitive slaves

1844 Arab slave traders found Unyamwezi as base in western Tanzania

1845 Annexation of Texas opens new areas of United States to slavery; Mexican-American War arouses conflict over extension of slavery

1846 Congressman David Wilmot proposes exclusion of slavery from lands acquired in Mexican War

1847 Liberian independence; Frederick Douglass starts publishing *North Star* in Rochester, NewYork

1848 France abolishes slavery in all its colonies; Liberty Party merges into new Free Soil Party

1849 John Beecroft appointed consul to Bights of Benin and Biafra

1850 Compromise of 1850 includes second Fugitive Slave Act; Brazil prohibits import of slaves

1851   British occupy slaving port of Lagos in West Africa; Christiana, Pennsylvania abolitionist mob disperses band of slave catchers

1852   Ecuador liberates all remaining slaves; publication by Harriet Beecher Stowe of *Uncle Tom's Cabin*

1854   Kansas-Nebraska Act opens two years of civil conflict in Kansas; Peru abolishes slavery; completion of gradual emancipation in Argentina and Venezuela; formation of Republican Party

1854-1855   Many northern states pass personal liberty laws to block enforcement of Fugitive Slave Law

1857 Supreme Court rules in Dred Scott case that federal government could not restrict slave owner's rights over slave; Ottoman Empire prohibits slave imports

1859   John Brown leads raid on Harper's Ferry

1860   Election of Abraham Lincoln as president of the United States

1861   Formation of Confederate States of America; American Civil War begins with bombardment of Fort Sumter; Confiscation Act authorizes freeing of slaves in areas under Union army control; Russian Czar Alexander II frees the serfs

1862   Congress frees slaves in District of Columbia

1862-1863   Peruvian "blackbirding" expeditions in the Pacific

1863   Emancipation Proclamation frees slaves in areas under Confederate control; the Netherlands abolishes slavery in its colonies

1864 Reelection of Abraham Lincoln to the United States presidency.

1865 Unionist legislatures in Missouri and Tennessee abolish slavery; Thirteenth Amendment to U.S. Constitution abolishes slavery; United States Congress sets up Freedmen's Bureau

1866 Civil Rights Act makes freed slaves citizens

1867 Last slave ship from Africa arrives in Cuba; Reconstruction Acts send Union troops back into South to protect rights of freed slaves

1868-1878 Ten Years' War begins emancipation of slaves in Cuba

1870 Ratification of Fourteenth and Fifteenth Amendments to the United States Constitution; Moret Law enacts gradual emancipation in Cuba

1871 Brazilian law provides for emancipation of unborn children

1873 Zanzibar agrees to end slave trade; Spain abolishes slavery in Puerto Rico

1874 King Chulalongkorn (Rama V) of Thailand begins reforms that lead to abolition of slavery

1877 Egypt prohibits import of slaves

1880 Formation of Brazilian Anti-Slavery Society; Spain enacts Law of Patronato, which begins abolition of slavery in Cuba

1884 French colonial government abolishes slavery in Cambodia; provinces of Amazonas and Ceara in northern Brazil abolish slavery

1886 Abolition of slavery in Cuba

1888 Golden Law ends slavery in Brazil; Pope Leo XIII supports struggle of slaves for emancipation

1889-1890 Brussels conference takes weak measures against African slave trade

1890 Pope Leo XIII attacks slavery in encyclical *Catholicae Ecclesiae*

1895 Abolition of slavery in Korea

1905 France abolishes all transactions in persons in Africa; this involves sale, gift, or exchange; Thailand abolishes slavery

1909 Chinese emperor orders that all slaves be released and given the status of commoners

1915 British colonial government abolishes slavery in Malaya

1924 League of Nations creates Temporary Slavery Commission

1926 League of Nations Slavery Convention is approved; British colonial government abolishes slavery in Burma

1927 British colonial government abolishes slavery in Sierra Leone

1932 League of Nations appoints Standing Committee of Experts on Slavery

1936 British colonial governments abolish slavery in Nigeria and the Anglo-Egyptian Sudan

1942 Emperor Haile Selassie abolishes slavery in Ethiopia; establishment of a slave labor system in Nazi Germany

1948 United Nations Universal Declaration of Human Rights

1949 Communist China proclaims abolition of slavery in China

1950 United Nations establishes Ad Hoc Committee on Slavery to continue anti-slavery work of the League of Nations

1956 United Nations Supplementary Convention on the Abolition of Slavery, the Slave Trade and Institutions and Practices Similar to Slavery

1962 Saudi Arabia and Yemen abolish slavery

1970 Muscat and Oman abolishes slavery

1980 Mauritania abolishes slavery, but allegations of slavery continue

1980s Resurgence of slavery as a result of Sudanese civil war

1990 Bonded Labor Liberation Front organizes National Workshop on the Eradication of Child Labor in the Carpet Industry; Korean group demands reparations from Japan for Korean women forced to serve as sexual slaves during World War II

1990s   Allegations of slavery in Brazil, Dominican Republic, and Ghana

1993   Anti-Slavery International begins campaign against child prostitution in Asian sex industry

INTRODUCTION

For almost 4,000 years, men and women with power have figured out ways to get people to work for them. The exploited have been slaves, serfs, helots, tenants, peons, bonded laborers, and forced laborers, among others. They have built pyramids and temples, have dug canals, and have mined the earth for its minerals. They have built the palaces and mansions in which they powerful have lived, have been their servants, and have fed and clothed them. They have also produced commodities for market and provided profits for their masters. Slavery is one of the most common forms of exploitation and one of the most profitable.

Slavery is separated from the other kinds of exploitation by the complete nature of the slave's subjugation. The slave is owned. He or she has no family. The slave can be forced to do any kind or work. His body, or more often, her body can be used in any way her owner wishes. Modern religions have often tried to limit the exercise of the master's rights, but not always effectively. Slaves have often found ways to protect themselves, but slavery leaves them few options. Slavery is a system of total control by some persons over the bodies and labor power of others. Masters have not always pushed that control to the limit. They have sometimes been more interested in service than in labor and have sometimes been interested in absorbing slaves into their communities and even their families, but always as inferiors.

Emergence of Slavery

The origins of slavery lie far back in the mists of prehistoric time. Most pre-agricultural societies were egalitarian. They had few status distinctions and did not have enough of a surplus to have slaves. Many of these societies rarely engaged in war. When they did fight with or raid their neighbors, they could easily absorb female captives, but usually as wives. Occasionally such societies absorbed male prisoners, but also as full members. Among the Woodland Indians of North America, a male prisoner could either be tortured and killed or absorbed. If absorbed, it was usually as a replacement for someone who died in war or from disease and the prisoner took on that person's identity. Male and female prisoners could also be ransomed.

Some writers have seen women as the original slaves, but they were usually not absorbed as inferiors, but as wives. The crucial moment of transition to slavery was probably the point at which the successful warriors decided that they could exploit the labor of prisoners if they made them into a permanently degraded part of the society that labored for others. The status of the first slaves was not necessarily hereditary, but as the institution developed, slave status became permanent. The emergence was usually coterminous with the emergence of a state. For egalitarian societies, it always involved an end to equality. Not only were slaves a distinct social group, but the existence of slaves involved the presence of an elite. Someone controlled the slaves. Either they were owned by persons, perhaps those who took them prisoners, or they were owned by the group and exploited by its chiefs.

In most complex preindustrial societies, some form of servitude existed, but forms of slavery differed and slavery was only one kind of social domination. Human societies have known a wide range of servile statuses. Ancient Sparta was not interested in selling the prisoners it took, but rather in exploiting their labor in place. They were helots, who maintained their own religion and family life, but owed labor to Spartan masters. Serfdom later developed as a system in which the dominated people were attached to the land and owed various dues to lords. They were, however, part of a community and like the helots preserved their own family life. In medieval Europe, serfs existed within a relatively self-sufficient manorial economy, but in other areas, for example, early modern Eastern Europe and China, a similar relationship provided goods for market.

In many parts of the world, debt slavery or pawnship was common. These were often societies where commercial relations were developed but not private property in land. The only security a borrower could give for a loan was himself or a member of his family. In most cases, the person and his or her family could be redeemed if the debt were repaid, though sometimes the relationships became permanent. Debt has also been important in post-slavery societies, where bondage in India or peonage in the Americas were used to tie cultivators to landowners. Often those so bound were former slaves or the descendants of slaves and the debt merely confirmed the dependence of the bondsperson. In many cases, these debts were inheritable, and thus, the bondsperson's status was passed on to offspring.

Scholars have long debated both the boundaries between these different kinds of servitude and the nature of slavery. The term slavery includes a range of relationships. Slaves work in different ways. Slaves in some societies have rights. In others, they have none at all. Some slaves were highly privileged servants of those who wielded power. A slave concubine could become very influential if her son inherited power. Other slaves were condemned to the misery of unremitting labor in mines or on plantations. Generally, definitions of slavery have stressed three variables. First, the most frequently stressed characteristic of the slave is that he or she is property and therefore can be sold. The slave belongs to someone else. Thus, H. J. Nieboer defines the slave as "the property of another" and James Watson argues that the property relationship "is what distinguishes slavery from all other forms of dependency and involuntary labour."

Others stress the second variable, that the slave was always an outsider, a person who had no place in the kinship system. Thus Orlando Patterson writes: "Not only was the slave denied all claims on, and obligations to his parents and living blood relations, but by extension, all such claims and obligations on his more remote ancestors and on his descendants." For Suzanne Miers and Igor Kopytoff, the African slave was defined by his or her marginality, but this marginality decreased as he or she was gradually integrated into the kinship system. For Claude Meillassoux, by contrast, the slave remained outside the kinship system, a kind of permanent anti-kin. But all these writers agree that without kinship ties, the slave was power-less. Watson differentiates between open societies, within which gradual integration took place, particularly among those born into the society, and closed societies, where slaves and their descendants were kept forever outside the kinship system. In fact, these two variables, the property relationship and absence of kinship, were intimately related. They were the opposite faces of the same coin. The property relationship made it possible to keep slaves marginalized and made it easier to exploit their labor. The marginality made it possible for them to be bought and sold, and thus, to be property.

The third variable is that the slave originated in an act of violence, the violence of war or of the slave raider or the legal violence of the criminal law. The slave was torn from a network of social relations in which he or she lived and inserted in a new one in which he or she was completely powerless. The potential of violence also kept the slave subservient. It made possible the exploitation of the slave's labor and kept the slave in an enforced marginality. Some slaves were well off. A slave could be a military leader or a royal official and could enjoy great wealth, but this wealth was always dependent on the slave being the instrument of another human being. The privileged slave could always be stripped of his wealth and status because he enjoyed them only because of his dependence. The most privileged were often eunuchs, who were physically incapable of forming families.

Within most slave situations, there was a tension between the desire to keep the slave marginal and the fact that the slave was a human being. Law and culture often treated the slave as a thing, an instrument of another's will. In fact, slaves had wills of their own and intelligence. Masters were also interested in productivity. This could often be best achieved by recognizing the slave's humanity. Thus, slaves were allowed and even encouraged to live in family units and while the law denied the slave the rights free persons had in their offspring, slaves built family structures. Slaves were often given private plots because it was the most efficient way to have them, but these plots often made it possible for them to engage in petty commerce. Many slave-owning societies had a paternalistic ideology. Institutions like the Catholic Church tried to protect family and religious life. In spite of this, a child could be sold away from his parents and an adult away from his or her spouse. Furthermore, the slave rarely had any protection against a brutal master or one who was irrational in his exploitation of his slaves.

The slave family was usually strong, though slavery posed problems. The slave family was mother centered, and with parents spending long hours at work, a child was usually raised by an extended family. Slaves in many parts of the world clung to their religion and culture. African possession rituals were common in both the Muslim and Christian worlds. In both Christian and Muslim worlds, the religion of African slaves has often shaped the beliefs and practices of the larger societies. American evangelical cults have practices rooted in Africa. In Brazil, white Catholics often attend *candomble* ceremonies and in North Africa, *bori* and *gnauwa*, African possession cults, have been incorporated within Muslim Sufism. Though slave owners often prohibited drumming, for fear it could be used to send messages, African music survived in the Americas and contributed to jazz, blues, calypso, and other American musical idioms.

There was also within most slave systems a certain amount of amelioration and manumission. Amelioration meant that even the newly acquired slave could aspire to an improvement in his or her well-being and the slave born in the society, the Creole in the Americas or in West African slave societies, the slave "born in the house," could expect somewhat better treatment and higher status. If nothing else, the Creole slave spoke the master's language and was rooted in his culture. Manumission was possible in almost all slave-owning societies and directed the energies of many abler slaves toward their own liberation. Only in some American jurisdictions was manumission prohibited, and even there legal fictions often gave abler slaves considerable autonomy. For example, Simon Gray, a Mississippi slave, controlled a fleet of barges on the Mississippi River and was able to purchase his wife and children, but could not purchase his own freedom. Of course, even the Creole slaves worked long hours, and a minority of slaves was manumitted, in most societies a small minority.

The importance of manumission meant that most slave-owning societies were marked by a significant "flow-through," by which slaves acceded over a lifetime first to some kind of clientship and eventually to freedom. A large percentage of those freed were the female lovers of rich and powerful men and their offspring — and in Muslim law, the child of a slave concubine inherits his father's status and is thus born free. Others were loyal retainers, but there were often mechanisms by which a clever or ambitious slave could win his own freedom either through valor on the battlefield or by earning the money to do so. This meant that most slave societies had a large population of freed persons, usually clients of their former masters. In the Americas, racial difference kept these people in a kind of social middle ground. Many were poor, but many played a middleman role.

Slavery and the Growth of the State

Slavery was often important in the development of states. Slaves were important objects in the process of accumulation and their existence was a major factor in political centralization. Slaves were often the major prize of war. They were controlled by rulers and by those the rulers sought to award. Slaves could be distributed after a victory to those who served the ruler well, particularly on the field of battle, or they could be put to work producing commodities for sale or food for the elite. Roman military commanders often became wealthy landowners. The surplus slaves produced was often used to feed the court, and therefore made it possible for the ruler to support more dependents. Slaves were important in another way. In most early states and many more recent ones, royal power was established in a struggle between royal and aristocratic power. To increase his power, the king needed loyal dependents, men who identified with him and who could not become rivals. In early modern Europe, rising monarchies used commoners, but no group has been more important over time than slaves.

In slave-owning societies, the rich and powerful were often surrounded by servants and retainers. Being a "big man" often involved having an entourage ready to do the big man's bidding. The ablest in this band were often entrusted with major responsibilities. If the big man was a king or a potential king, the quality of the men around him was crucial to his success. Such slaves could have wealth, privilege, and power, but only by guaranteeing that their man was successful. In some societies, like the Ottoman Empire or the Hausa states of West Africa, there were mechanisms for male slaves to be chosen young and trained for bureaucratic or military service. The abler among them could rise to the highest offices in the empire. Slave soldiers like the Ottoman Janissaries were usually the elite troops and often were the cavalry or had the best weapons. In 19th century West Africa, slave soldiers were often the first armed with late-model rifles. Not surprisingly, the ruler's closest advisors were often chosen from these privileged slaves. They were the group most committed to him.

We can see two different models of how the state used other slaves and of how the use of slaves impacted on state power. In China, population densities were high for well over two thousand years. This meant that slaves were not needed to work the land, though for long periods land was worked by tenant farmers who had a serflike relationship to landowners. Even when conquered people were enslaved, they were rather quickly transformed into a kind of tied peasantry. Slaves were found primarily in courts and in the households of the wealthy and powerful. They were predominantly concubines and servants, though some, particularly the eunuchs, often became officials. We see a similar evolution in the Arab world, which was an important market for slaves from both eastern Europe and Africa. Slaves were primarily concubines, servants, and soldiers and after the ninth century were not heavily used for agricultural labor.

By contrast, in Southeast Asia lands were fertile and well-watered, but population densities were low. In China, wars were fought to defend frontiers or to conquer new areas. Land was sought. In Southeast Asia, wars were fought to get control over people. It was common for victors to move large numbers of conquered people to areas they controlled. This may in turn have kept population densities low. The difference between these two areas is explained partly by Nieboer's theory that slavery is most likely to develop in areas where land is freely available, labor in short supply, and technology simple. Of course, slavery was important in China, but in a very circumscribed way. Low population densities were also a reason for the importance of slavery in Africa, and the slave trade, by keeping population densities low, assured the importance of slave labor.

Slavery was important wherever complex political institutions existed. Slavery existed in Sumer by 3200 BCE. It was regulated in most subsequent Middle Eastern law codes. By 1500 BCE, and probably much earlier, ancient Egypt was procuring slaves from Nubia. They were present in ancient India at least as far back as the Aryan conquests, which began in about 1750 BCE. Slavery was present in China during the first millennium BCE and probably in Mesoamerica during the same period. Slavery was a factor in processes of political evolution in all parts of the world.

Emergence of Slave Societies

Even though slavery had a very long history, slave societies or slave modes of production did not exist until relatively recently. These are societies where slaves were the major source of productive labor and slavery shaped all aspects of life. Moses Finley argues that there are three preconditions for the creation of a slave society: private ownership of land; commodity production and the existence of markets in which surplus could be sold; and the lack of adequate supplies of labor at home. They are thus societies with a substantial market economy. Societies have followed different paths to the creation of a slave society. The first community we can identify as a slave society was Athens during the fifth century BCE. The trigger was the reforms of Solon. Near the beginning of the fifth century, Athens was faced with a social crisis that resulted from the spread of debt slavery and involved much popular discontent. Solon resolved the crisis by abolishing debt slavery and granting citizenship to peasants and artisans. The poorer Athenians thus participated in political life and became rowers for the Athenian fleets, which then dominated the seas of the eastern Mediterranean. Landowners solved the resultant labor shortage by purchasing slaves from Asia Minor, the Balkans, and the shores of the Black Sea or absorbing captives taken in various wars. Slavery thus underwrote both Athenian democracy and its rapid economic growth.

Rome followed another path. From the third century BCE, the conquest of southern Italy and the defeat of Carthage brought increasing numbers of captives back to Rome. Two parallel developments took place. Lands were available because more and more male peasants were away serving in the Roman legions. Rich Romans were able to acquire these lands and work them with slaves acquired elsewhere. Southern Italy and Sicily were major centers of slave-based production. The success of Roman legions meant that for more than four centuries captives were being brought back to Rome in large numbers and were providing the basis for economic activity. During some periods, captives arrived in such great numbers that revolts like that of Spartacus became a problem. Slaves were numerous but less important elsewhere in the empire. Roman law was also to provide a framework for the treatment of slaves in later European empires.

Greece and Rome never had a slave majority. That did not happen until European expansion and the spread of capitalist plantation agriculture introduced more intensive forms of slavery in the Americas, in Africa, and on the islands of the Indian Ocean and Southeast Asia. Sugar was first domesticated in India or Southeast Asia, but Europeans discovered it as a result of the Crusades. Venetian and Genoan entrepreneurs realized that they could produce sugar using Arab technology and slave labor on Cyprus and Crete. Here they improved the technology and developed the plantation. Slaves came mostly from the Black Sea and eastern Europe, but also from Arab prisoners and Africans. With an increasing European demand for sugar, which was at first a luxury crop, sugar cultivation spread first to Sicily and the western Mediterranean and then, as Portuguese and Spanish navigators discovered new places, onto the Atlantic islands.

The Portuguese started planting sugarcane on Madeira in about 1455. The Spanish introduced sugar on the Canary Islands in the same period. Capital for both areas was provided largely by Genoan financiers. By 1500, Madeira was the most important source of sugar for Europe, and land was being granted by Portugal for plantations on São Tomé. Here the technology for grinding sugarcane was improved. Though briefly important as a source of sugar, with the development of sugar plantations in Brazil, São Tomé became more important as an entrepôt for slaves from Central Africa. There was also a problem of security on São Tomé as Maroon settlements in the mountainous interior harassed the plantations. This problem was to recur elsewhere. By the end of the 16th century, Brazil was the world's largest sugar producer.

Some islands, like Madeira, were unpopulated, but on others there was a common pattern of development. Often the first Europeans enslaved and sold native peoples. The Guanche of the Canary Islands were heavily raided during the 14th century. In Hispaniola, Columbus sent a shipment of about 500 slaves back to Spain in 1495. Europeans usually moved quickly to using enslaved native labor rather than selling it. This was the pattern on the Canaries, on Hispaniola, in Brazil, and in the British American colonies, but enslavement and European diseases so reduced the population of native peoples that would-be entrepreneurs had to find other sources of labor. Sugar planters were the first to be squeezed by this demographic crisis. Sugar offered them a good return, but only if they could find a source of labor.

The only place they could find enough labor was Africa. Before the middle of the 15th century, the major source of slaves for the Mediterranean was eastern Europe. Then, when the Turks took Constantinople in 1453, they reduced Mediterranean access to Slavic sources at the very time that Portuguese navigators were opening up African sources for slaves. The first Atlantic producers of sugar were close to Africa and looked to nearby areas of Africa for slave labor. By the time sugar plantations developed in the Americas, the Portuguese had a regular ongoing trade with various African states that was capable of expansion. The quest for slaves was not the major motive for the Portuguese voyages, but the slave trade was the major result. The Portuguese not only provided slaves for their own sugar producers, but also for the Spanish under contracts called *asientos*.

The Northern European Challenge

In the late 16th century, the nations of northern Europe began challenging the Iberians. The first were the Dutch. The wealthiest part of an empire ruled by the Spanish Hapsburgs, the Protestant Netherlands revolted against Catholic Spain in 1569. When the Spanish and Portuguese crowns were united in 1580, the Dutch saw the far-flung Portuguese empire as the most vulnerable place to attack Spain. After some success raiding Iberian fleets, the Dutch East India Company was chartered in 1602 and began seizing parts of Portugal's Asian empire and developing more intensive forms of exploitation. In 1621, the Dutch West India Company was chartered and began seizing Portuguese positions in Africa. In 1630, it seized Pernambuco, a sugar-producing province of northeastern Brazil. Dutch control did not last long. In 1648 a Brazilian force reconquered Angola, and by 1656 the Dutch had been pushed out of Brazil.

By this time, however, the Dutch had learned a lot about sugar and were teaching what they knew to others. The English and French were colonizing both the American mainland and the Caribbean. The West Indies were particularly inviting because they were underpopulated and potentially fertile. The English settled Barbados and the French St. Christopher in 1627. After experimenting with other crops, both islands switched to sugar by the 1640s. The Dutch were major agents of this transformation, providing slaves from their West African posts, technology, know-how, and credit. Sugar brought large profits and spread rapidly. By the end of the century, six European nations were cultivating sugar in the West Indies. For Britain and France, the West Indies was by far the most important overseas source of wealth during the 18th century. West Indian markets for food and timber were also important to the growth of British and French colonies on the mainland.

The sugar-slave complex lay at the heart of European expansion. A similar but smaller sugar system developed on the Indian Ocean islands of Mauritius and Réunion. Slave labor was also used elsewhere. Slaves cultivated spices for the Dutch in Indonesia. Slave concubines and servants inhabited the households of many of the Europeans who built empires in

Asia and in the Atlantic. Slaves cultivated tobacco in Virginia and Maryland, spices on Granada, and rice in South Carolina. Slave labor was important in cities that sprang up on both sides of the Atlantic and in Asia to service the new imperial economy. Nevertheless, at the end of the 18th century, most slaves in the Atlantic economy were cultivating sugar. Then in 1793, Eli Whitney developed a machine, the cotton gin, that could cheaply remove the seeds from cotton. The British Industrial Revolution had just begun and was based in its first phase almost exclusively on cotton textiles. There was thus a tremendous demand for cotton. Cotton spread quickly to new states west of the Appalachian mountains. By 1860, two-thirds of the slaves in the United States were growing cotton.

The effects of the trade were disastrous for Africa. Many parts of the world have been exposed to a demand for slaves from wealthier and more powerful societies, but none has been exposed to such a sustained demand as Africa and none has provided so many people to labor for others. Slavery existed in Africa as it did elsewhere in the world, but no African society in the mid-15th century specialized in the production of slaves. The first slaves were procured in relatively small numbers from areas near the coast. The first society to be influenced by the demand for slaves was the Kongo kingdom, which was eager to learn from the Portuguese and to modernize, but by the 1520s, King Afonso was unable to control slave raiding and civil conflict within his kingdom. More successful slave producers were careful to control the conditions of the trade and not to allow Europeans to maintain permanent residences within their kingdoms. Trade was conducted at coastal ports or specialized markets, which could be controlled by the African trading state.

The steadily increasing demand for slaves on the coast and increasingly effective resistance by potential victims led merchants to push trade routes farther and farther into the interior and influenced military leaders to focus their efforts on taking prisoners who could be sold. In the 16th century a quarter of a million slaves were exported across the Atlantic. The sharpest increase came after the middle of the 17th century, when demand for the expanding sugar complexes of the West Indies led to an increase in prices along the West African coast. The period from 1660 to 1725 saw the creation of a series of powerful states in the interior of Africa, which were all capable of producing large numbers of slaves. Over 6 million slaves were exported across the Atlantic in the 18th century, and others were shipped across the Sahara. Many decentralized and stateless societies resisted the lure of the slave trade at first, but often found themselves dependent on goods like iron and weapons that could only be procured by selling slaves. Slave merchants slowly developed social institutions like the

Aro network in eastern Nigeria, which were capable of moving slaves through decentralized areas in the interior to the coast. For every slave shipped across the Atlantic, the Sahara, or the Indian Ocean, it is probable that several died in the wars, on the harsh caravan trail to the coast, or while being held for sale.

The safest places in western Africa were at the center of the large slaving kingdoms. Elsewhere, slave merchants managed to stimulate conflict and create needs that could only be met by selling slaves. For example, young men chafed at the control of their elders, who often made them work for years before allowing them to marry. Kidnapping or raiding gave young men revenues they could use to marry. The slave trade thus turned people against each other. It also made slaves available for African users. During the 18th century, Africa probably kept as many slaves as it sold. Most of those kept were women and children, who were easier to assimilate. The European traders preferred men, who made up two-thirds of the adults exported. African purchasers preferred women. In the interior, however, the price of women of all ages was always higher than the price of men of the same age. Wherever the demand for labor existed, slaves were sought. They were particularly important in the desert-side areas, where the transhumant cycles of the pastoralists brought them south every dry season. They were also important in Saharan oases, in market towns across the region, and in the heart of many powerful kingdoms.

Slave Labor

The work regimes within different kinds of slave economy varied radically. The harshest was sugar. Sugar has to be into the presses within hours of being cut or less of the sweet liquid can be squeezed from the cane. The harvest was long, anywhere from five to eight months, and planters usually had more sugar planted than they were capable of harvesting. The field work was harsh, but the presses and the boiling rooms were often kept running all day. Men working there often had 18- to 24- hour shifts. A man who was not alert could easily be maimed or killed if his arm got caught in the press. Sugar colonies had a high mortality, both because of the harshness of the labor and because planters preferred to buy men, knowing that it was cheaper to buy a new slave than to raise one. Labor was also highly regimented. Mines also often had a high mortality, especially where workers had to work underground.

Rice farms also had a high mortality, though for a different reason. Rice was grown in swampy lowlands. Workers often worked in water and were exposed to malaria and various water-borne diseases. The work regime on tobacco farms was more benign and the diversified agriculture of the Chesapeake made for a better diet. The units of production were small and the work diversified. By 1720, the slave population was increasing in Virginia and Maryland by natural reproduction. Cotton involved long work days and unpleasant stoop labor, but slaves were well fed and slave populations also saw a natural increase there.

In all slave societies, a large percentage of the slaves, at least 10 percent and up to 25 percent, worked within the household. This involved cooks, butlers, seamstresses, and child care. The work was less harsh, but the hours were long and supervision constant. Slaves had the greatest freedom in the cities. Imperial cities were often new cities and were frequently populated largely by slaves. Whether in coastal Africa, the American South, Latin America, or the West Indies, many slaves did skilled work and slaves were often allowed autonomy. They had their own social and religious life and were capable of learning new skills. They often worked for wages and paid their masters a percentage of their income. Many were able to develop remunerative sidelines and sometimes used income from these sidelines to purchase their freedom.

Slaves resisted in many ways. Slave revolts were not numerous, and with the exception of the Haitian Revolution, were usually put down quickly and brutally. Invariably, the vast number of those killed were slaves, often people merely suspected of being involved. Slave societies are almost by definition paranoid societies. Within them, slave owners were surrounded by a servile majority that did not want to be there. The hostility of the slaves was most intense where there were large numbers of the newly enslaved. In ancient Rome, as in South Carolina or Jamaica, these were the people most likely to revolt. As a result, slave societies were marked by law codes that applied cruel punishments to anyone involved in revolts. There were usually patrols to keep an eye on slave movements and passes were often required for slaves leaving plantation or household. Justice was swift and often arbitrary. Slave patrols usually had the authority to deal out instant punishment. The slave still had options. Some ran away if there was somewhere to run to, though they often had to outrun professional slave catchers. Where there were mountains or forests, slaves formed Maroon settlements, some of which sustained themselves. There were also subtle forms of day-to-day resistance like sabotage or work slowdowns.

Religion and Slavery

There is no evidence of a systematic attack on slavery as an institution in any society before the 18th century. Many of the universal religions had reservations about slavery and sought to control both who could be enslaved and how they were treated. In Christian thought, there was a strong belief that a person could be enslaved only in a just war. Such a belief was also characteristic of Islam, which permitted enslavement only in a jihad or holy war and restricted the type of wars that could be called jihads. Buddhism condemned warfare and the Buddha forbade his followers from engaging in the slave trade. All three also regarded slaves as human beings and sought to convert them. All three also saw slaves as worthy of divine concern and all insisted that masters treat their slaves humanely. In Buddhism, slaves were people being punished for the sins of an earlier life, and like other human beings, were amenable to reform.

In spite of this, all of these religions accepted the legitimacy of enslavement, though all criticized the enslavement of coreligionists. This was also true of the Zororastrians. All of the universal religions rose at times when slavery was widespread and would not have succeeded if they taught otherwise. Paul counselled slaves to serve their masters faithfully, seeking their reward in the afterlife. Muhammed also counselled obedience and the Buddha asked slaves not to envy the wealth of their masters. Perhaps most important, slave raiders and slave dealers ignored the teachings of their respective religions on just war and jihad, and even used religion as a justification for enslaving nonbelievers. Slave masters also ignored many religious teachings. The Catholic Church, for example, tried to protect the sanctity of the sacraments, particularly the sacrament of marriage. Many slave masters could not accept the idea that they should not have sexual relations with their slaves, or that they could not separate a slave from his or her spouse or parent. Buddhist temples often had large slave holdings.

Slavery did decline in many places, though rarely because anyone saw the institution as immoral. Often the decline was linked to an increasing inability to procure new slaves, but the most important reason was usually that changes in social or economic structure made other ways of exploiting labor more attractive. The decline of slavery could be linked to economic decline or to an increase in population that facilitated other means of acquiring labor. The best studied decline was in medieval Europe. The decline began when Roman conquests ceased and Roman legions stopped bringing home captives. With the collapse of the commercial economy and increasing insecurity, other means of organizing labor became more efficient and serfdom replaced slavery. By the 12th century, slavery had disappeared in Britain, France, and Germany. It persisted in the Mediterranean, but no longer as a major source of agricultural labor.

Other areas saw similar declines. Slavery seems to have disappeared from Japan by the 12th century, though Tokugawa Japan (1602-1867) bound peasants to the land. In China, people enslaved during periods of conquest were often quickly transformed into peasants, sometimes with serflike obligations. Slavery was very important in medieval Korea, probably more important than any other East Asian country, but by the 16th century, population growth was making slavery unnecessary. In 1775, the king established a policy of gradual emancipation and, in 1895, Korea abolished slavery altogether. In Scandinavia, the Vikings were very effective slavers, but as population built up, slaves were no longer sought and slavery declined between the 12th and 14th centuries. Other forms of labor organization were more useful. Christianity seems to have also been a factor in the decline in Scandinavia and perhaps elsewhere. In Russia, slavery declined in the 17th century, but serfdom was tightened up to the point where it was as restrictive as many forms of slavery. In Mesopotamia, the massive use of slaves to revive irrigation systems led to the Zanj revolt of 883 CE and probably convinced Arab rulers to limit the use of slave labor.

Early Christian teaching accepted that slaves had eternal souls and were equal to free persons in the eyes of God, but it saw the Christian life as the only true liberty. Convinced that earthly life was meaningless, it counselled obedience. Nevertheless, from early on, the Church fathers imposed two restrictions on the rights of the slave owners. First, they accepted the validity of marriage between slaves, which meant the legitimacy of relations between spouses and between parent and child. Second, they condemned extramarital sexual relations between master and slave. Some popes also protested against Christians holding fellow Christians as slaves, and in the late Middle Ages the Church was responsible for reintroducing Roman law, which afforded slaves important protections and encouraged manumission. There were also dissident voices. The 13th-century theologian, John Duns Scotus, condemned the enslavement of prisoners of war and argued that enslavement was only justified as a punishment of crime. In the 16th century, the French Renaissance political theorist Jean Bodin was critical of Aristotle's notion that some men were slaves by nature. He also attacked the ways people were enslaved and used.

Catholic missionaries in the Americas were forced early to confront the harsh realities of exploitation in the new imperial economy. Almost from the beginning Spanish priests like Antonio de Montesinos and Bartolomé de Las Casas and Portuguese priests like Manuel da Nobrega protested against enslavement and cruel treatment of Indians. They attacked legal justifications of slavery and persuaded Pope Nicholas III to issue *Bulla Sublimus Deus* (1537), which asserted the rationality of the Amerindians and their potential for Christian life. They also persuaded King Charles I to issue his New Laws (1542) prohibiting the enslavement of Amerindians and their exploitation in the *encomiendas*. In order to reduce the demands on Amerindians, Las Casas at first advocated the import of African slaves, but in his later years he was critical of African slavery. Other missionaries like the Spaniards Tomás de Mercado and Bartolomé de Albornoz picked up the African cause later in the century. In Brazil, missionaries like the 17th-century Jesuit Antonio Vieira tried to play the same role. Catholic thinkers were often divided on the legitimacy of slavery and the slave trade, but many were critical of the conduct of the trade and the harshness of slave life. In all of the Spanish and Portugese colonies, there were laws requiring that slaves be baptized, given religious education, the opportunity to worship, and the right to marry. Catholic priests and bishops often attacked the sexual exploitation of slave women.

Abolition

Few of the Catholic missionaries advocated the abolition of slavery. The systematic attack on slavery began in the middle of the 18th century and had two sources. The first was the European Enlightenment. The French political theorist, Montesquieu, rejected traditional justifications of slavery though he shied away from attacking French colonial slavery. Others were not so cautious. Philosophers like Jean-Jacques Rousseau and the authors of the influential *Encyclopédie* argued that all human beings were endowed with certain natural rights, including the right to liberty. The Scotch political economist, Adam Smith, argued that slavery was not as efficient as free labor. Though many Enlightenment thinkers invested in slaving enterprises, and some, like Thomas Jefferson, owned slaves, Enlightenment thought influenced educated public opinion and shaped the ideas of leaders of the American, French, and Spanish American Revolutions. A belief in an inalienable human right to liberty found expression in the American Declaration of Independence and the French Declaration of the Rights of Man, though many supporters of both declarations thought that these rights were only held by white people.

The other source, Protestant religion, turned out to be more potent. It started with the Quakers. Based on a belief in equality and a rejection of violence, Quakers had reservations about slavery from their establishment in about 1650. By the second half of the 18th century, many Quaker meetings accepted that slavery was sinful and were closed to slave owners. Quakers were influential in forming the first anti-slavery society in Philadelphia in 1775 and soon became important in other such societies. Other Christians also got involved. Granville Sharp used the courts to assist runaway slaves who did not want to be returned to the West Indies. When Lord Mansfield decided in 1772 that James Somerset, a former Virginia slave, was not property under English law, this meant that slaves could not be forced to return to the colonies against their will and could no longer, in fact, be considered slaves in England. Soon after that, another Anglican, Thomas Clarkson, began doing research on the slave trade. In 1787, they came together with other British abolitionists to form the Society for the Abolition of the Slave Trade under the leadership of the Anglican William Wilberforce. A year later, French abolitionists joined to form the *Société des Amis des Noirs*.

Abolition registered rather speedy successes. In the United States, all northern states passed some form of abolition law between 1780 and 1804. Mostly, these were gradual emancipation laws, often free womb laws which freed slaves born after a certain date. Some were quite slow. In New Jersey, there were still 18 slaves in 1860, but in general, northern slavery was insignificant by 1830. Slavery issues were important at the Constitutional Convention of 1787. One of many compromises protected the import of slaves until 1808, but authorized an end to the trade after that. In Europe, only the French debated slavery itself, and there the issue was forced by the Haitian Revolution, which began in 1791. In 1794, with ex-slave armies in control of most of the island of Saint-Domingue, slavery was abolished. Eight years later, slavery and the slave trade were reestablished by Napoleon, but the army sent to Saint-Domingue failed to reconquer the island. Denmark abolished the slave trade in 1792.

In Great Britain, then the world's largest slave trader, the abolitionists faced a strong West Indian lobby, but they became skillful at mobilizing public opinion. They used the churches, held meetings all over the country, and used petitions to put pressure on Parliament. Finally in 1807, Britain abolished the slave trade. From 1807, British diplomatic pressure was used to put pressure on other European powers and the British navy tried to block the export of slaves from Africa. The continuation of the slave trade by other nations soon persuaded the abolitionists that the trade would exist as long as there were slaves. In 1823, they organized the Anti-Slavery Society and, in 1833, after a very effective campaign, the British Parliament voted to abolish slavery. The French agreed reluctantly to abolish the trade after the defeat of Napoleon, but they did not enforce the abolition of the trade until 1831. In 1848, a new revolutionary government abolished slavery in all French colonies. The Dutch were slower, abolishing slavery in the Dutch West Indies only in 1863. This did not touch Indonesia. Portugal abolished the slave trade in 1836 and slavery itself in 1869, but both slavery and disguised versions of the slave trade existed in Africa until the 20th century.

In Spanish America, the issue of slavery became a central one during the wars of liberation. Both sides recruited slaves and former slaves and promised them their liberty. Leaders like Simón Bolívar and José San Martín were convinced that they could only throw off the colonial yoke if they were willing to offer liberty to the slaves. The abolition of the slave trade by Chile and Venezuela in 1811 was followed by abolition of the trade elsewhere, and in many cases, by abolition of slavery itself. In most cases, these were gradual emancipation laws, usually "free womb laws." With the victory of the Patriot cause, some states reestablished slavery, but by midcentury liberals all over Hispanic America were becoming influential. Many of them were convinced by the experience of Great Britain and the northern United States that economic development would be more rapid if based on free labor. Only Brazil and Cuba stood against the tide. Brazil became independent from Portugal in 1822 while Cuba remained under Spanish rule. Though isolated voices in both countries opposed slavery, Brazil and Cuba increased their imports of slaves, expanded the production of sugar and, when British sugar production declined, took over much of Great Britain's market share.

In the United States, the divide between North and South led to a bloody confrontation over slavery. In the early years of the new republic, leaders like Benjamin Franklin and George Washington feared that the slavery issue would divide the Union and often were careful not to push it. That did not prevent the issue from surfacing. Before the invention of the cotton gin in 1793, some Southerners were concerned about the region's large slave population and favored gradual emancipation and, sometimes, resettlement in Africa. After 1793, the Deep South moved heavily into cotton. In the cotton South, there was a strong sense that the region's wealth was based on slavery and that abolition threatened that wealth. The end of the slave trade in 1808 did not seriously hinder the cotton boom because of the rapid natural increase of slave population, especially in Virginia and Maryland. With the decline in tobacco production, they had more slaves than they needed. The surplus slaves were either sold off or moved to the Deep South with their owners.

In the North, there was a more broad-based economic growth fueled by industrialization, immigration and free labor. The North soon became wealthier, more urban, and more populous than the South. Both North and South spread west and as new states entered the Union, they did so as either slave or free. This required intermittent compromises, the first being the Missouri Compromise of 1820. Though there was little abolitionist pressure during the first decades of the new century, the divide was there. In the South, intermittent slave revolts both at home and in the West Indies, and a sense of increasing isolation fostered a pro-slavery militancy. Both the northern states and Great Britain were convinced that their growth and prosperity resulted from the use of free labor. This belief was shared by workers and farmers who feared competition with slave labor. There were also increasingly self-conscious African-American communities hostile both to the slavery and to a political order in the North that denied them the vote and gave them few rights. They organized within their own churches and social organizations. They soon found allies. In 1831, William Lloyd Garrison began publishing a newspaper called the *Liberator*. Garrison provided a focus for people, most of them deeply committed Christians, who were convinced that slavery was a sin.

The immediate abolition advocated by Garrison was never popular, but abolition societies began springing up all over the North. The abolitionists were marked by the intensity of their commitment. A lecture circuit developed. Like their British counterparts, abolitionists organized petition campaigns and, in numerous publications, publicized the evils of slavery. They also provided a platform for African-American leaders, founded schools and training programs for African-Americans, and provided assistance to slaves fleeing the South. The involvement of abolitionists in other causes, particularly women's rights, split the movement but did not dull its vehemence. For many early feminist activists, the causes of slaves and women were linked. In 1840, the more moderate abolitionists organized the Liberty Party, which ran James G. Birney for the presidency. An increasingly eloquent African-American leadership emerged in the 1840s, many of them former slaves like Frederick Douglass, Henry Highland Garnet and William Wells Brown, who were able to talk about their experiences with slavery.

The annexation of Texas in 1845 and the resultant war with Mexico was strongly supported in the South, which was looking for places where slavery could expand. This contributed to northern fears of a slave hegemony. In 1848, the Liberty Party was replaced by the Free Soil Party, which called not for the abolition of slavery but for stopping its extension. It had greater success at the polls, but was still a third party. The Compromise of 1850 was an effort to settle the increasing divide between North and South. It included a Fugitive Slave Act, which provided for federal enforcement and heavy penalties for interfering with federal officials. The law had the opposite effect. While many runaways fled to Canada or Great Britain, where they attracted support for the abolitionists in the northern United States, there were confrontations all over the North where crowds tried to prevent the enforcement of the law, and in many cases state authorities interfered to keep federal officials from carrying out the law.

Then, in the Kansas-Nebraska Act of 1854, Congress suggested that the fate of any states in the territory be decided by popular sovereignty. This meant that the settlers were to decide themselves whether the state was to be slave or free. "Bleeding Kansas" was the result as militants from both sides poured into the state. The best known figure to emerge from this prelude to the Civil War was John Brown, who became a martyr when he was executed after the Harper's Ferry raid of 1859. Also in 1854, the Republican Party was formed by a merger of the Free-Soilers and sympathetic Whigs. In the 1856 elections, the Republicans replaced the Whigs as the second party and carried much of the North. In the subsequent years, events pushed the Union toward war. In 1857, the Supreme Court in the Dred Scott case negated all previous compromises when it held that Congress could not limit the right of a slave owner to take his slave anywhere in the United States. This angered the North while the South was disturbed by John Brown's attack on Harper's Ferry, by sympathy with Brown, and by the continuing inability the federal government had in enforcing the Fugitive Slave Law.

In 1860, the Republican candidate, Abraham Lincoln, swept the North and was elected president without the support of a single slave state. In spite of Lincoln's assurances that he had neither the right nor the intention of interfering with slavery where it already existed, all but four of the slave states seceded and formed the Confederate States of America. While Lincoln carefully limited federal objectives, slaves took matters in their own hands, crossing federal lines in massive numbers. Under pressure from abolitionists and African-American leaders, in January 1863 Lincoln issued the Emancipation Proclamation, which freed slaves in all areas in rebellion. This and the increasing use of African-American troops, recruited at first by local commanders and finally with Lincoln's authorization, changed the nature of the war. What began as a war to save the Union ended up being a war to end slavery. In 1865, the Thirteenth Amendment to the United States Constitution abolished slavery throughout the Union. The Fourteenth and Fifteenth Amendments, which followed soon thereafter, gave the freed slaves citizenship and defined their rights.

A Continuing Struggle

By 1865, slavery was illegal in all areas settled by Europeans except Cuba, Puerto Rico, and Brazil. In Cuba, the intensification of slavery and an increase in imports led to several slave revolts and an effort to find other sources of labor. During the Ten Years' War (1868-1878), both sides tried to recruit slaves. By the end of the war, former slaves and free people of color were a majority of the liberation army. Slavery was ended in Puerto Rico in 1873. In Cuba, it was done in small steps, but final abolition came in 1886, by which date there were few slaves left. In Brazil, the import of slaves was abolished in 1851. An abolitionist movement was formed during the 1850s. In 1871, a gradual emancipation statute was passed, but emancipation moved slowly until after 1880, when under pressure from an increasingly vigorous abolition movement, individual provinces began to act. In the last stages, as in the United States and Cuba, slaves simply started leaving the plantations in large numbers. In 1888, slavery was abolished in Brazil.

Throughout the 19th century, British naval and diplomatic pressure was used in countless areas. By 1839, Great Britain had treaties with all major maritime powers except the United States providing the right to stop and search each other's vessels. These treaties were valuable to the British navy in its efforts to stop the trade. British ships cruised off Brazil, Cuba, and the Atlantic and Indian Ocean coasts of Africa. Britain also put pressure on various Muslim states. British efforts produced a resistance in some parts of the Muslim world because slavery was seen as an institution legitimated by the prophet Muhammed. Nevertheless, many Muslim states were amenable to British pressure. In 1846, Tunisia abolished the slave trade and, a year later, the Ottoman Empire closed the Constantinople slave market and banned the slave trade in the Persian Gulf. Egypt closed its slave markets in 1854 and signed an anti-slavery treaty with the British in 1877. In 1873, an anti-slavery treaty was signed with Zanzibar, and in 1876 the slave market was closed. Others areas resisted British blandishments. The pilgrimage to Mecca remained the occasion of a clandestine slave trade well into the 20th century.

By the late 19th century, the notion that slavery was immoral was widely accepted in Europe and America, as was a belief in the superiority of free labor. In a little over a half century, slavery had been abolished throughout the European world. The Catholic Church, once at the forefront of efforts to limit slavery, had resisted involvement in this movement throughout the 19th century. The Church had been stunned by the French Revolution and the role in various progressive movements of anticlericals and it identified abolition with those movements. In Europe, most active abolitionists were anticlerical. Late in the 19th century, Pope Leo XIII moved the Catholic Church away from this fear of progressive movements. Cardinal Charles Lavigerie persuaded the pope to authorize the organization of anti-slavery movements and, in 1888, he toured Europe doing so. In 1890, the pope condemned slavery.

At this time, European nations were creating new colonial empires in Africa, Asia, and the Pacific. Many of these were areas where slavery was important, but the slave owners were indigenous people, not Europeans. Colonial regimes often had limited funds and military forces, and as a result, often ruled through local elites. These elites were often slaveholders. Many of the colonial armies were also made up of slaves, and some were rewarded partly by booty, which often included women and children taken prisoner. Colonial regimes often stopped slave raiding, which was a barrier to their economic plans, and slave trading, which was crucial to the slave economy. They were reluctant to attack slavery itself, and in fact many colonial military and civil officials enjoyed the services of slaves themselves. The regime, however, received its appropriations from democratically elected parliaments and thus had to justify themselves to a public opinion that opposed slavery. In many cases too, their plans for economic development depended on creating a free labor market.

The British abolitionists did not rest on their laurels. In 1839, they organized the British and Foreign Anti-Slavery Society, now known as Anti-Slavery International. One of their first concerns was India. India had not been affected by the Abolition Act of 1833 because it was ruled not by the Crown, but by the East India Company. In 1843, under pressure from Parliament and the abolitionists, the company proclaimed Act V, which held that under Indian law there could be no recognition of slavery. This meant that slave owners could neither use the courts nor the coercive power of the state to maintain their control over slaves. It also meant that colonial officials had no obligation to either compensate slave owners for their losses or to intervene to encourage emancipation.

The Indian formula was useful to many other colonial regimes. It was used first in the Gold Coast in 1874, though the law proclaimed there only had effect in areas near the coast. In other parts of Africa, colonial power was slower to act. The issue was also important in Asia. The Dutch began a step-by-step emancipation of slaves in Indonesia in 1878. In Cambodia, the French abolished slavery in 1897. The British abolished slavery the same year in Zanzibar. In French Africa, an effort was made to distance the colonial state from slavery. Administrators applying a new law code in

1903 were told not to receive complaints from masters, and two years later, a law prohibited all transactions in persons. Within a year a massive exodus from slavery had begun that culminated with about a million slaves leaving their masters. In Northern Nigeria, Lord Frederick Lugard acted to prevent such an exodus. He told administrators to free only slaves who had been abused and asked others to use a Muslim process called *murgu* to enable slaves to purchase their freedom. Slavery was only abolished in Nigeria in 1936, but in the interim many slaves freed themselves. In Malaya, slavery was abolished piecemeal, state by state, and was not complete until 1915. During the interwar period, pressure was placed on the colonial regimes and on countries like Liberia and Ethiopia by League of Nations committees. In Burma the process of emancipation was completed only in 1926. In Sierra Leone, slavery was abolished in 1928.

The European discourse on slavery increasingly shaped other areas. In many areas, reformers interested in modernizing their own societies looked to what European states had done. Sometimes edicts were issued only to placate British public opinion. Menelik, the powerful emperor of Ethiopia, issued countless anti-slavery edicts between 1887 and 1908, while the sale of captives from his military campaigns in southern Ethiopia was increasing. Others, however, became convinced that free labor was more productive than slave labor and essential to any effort to copy European modernization. In Thailand, anti-slavery policies were part of an effort to fend off the French and British appetite for empire, but emancipation was facilitated by the increasing importance of wage labor. The Ottoman Empire was also anxious to avoid imperial partition, but anti-slavery also became part of reform agendas. In the years just before World War I, a reform regime ended the slave trade, and after the war, Kemal Ataturk abolished all forms of slavery. In China, slavery was abolished in 1910; when the empire fell the following year, there was no government capable of enforcing emancipation. In the Arabian peninsula, slavery was abolished in 1962 in Saudi Arabia and in 1970 in Oman.

Emancipation

In the last stages of various slave systems, it was often the slaves who acted to destroy slavery. They did so sometimes by revolting, but usually by just walking away from the site of their servitude. In Haiti, the revolt of the slaves in 1791 put pressure on French revolutionary assemblies uncertain about what to do about slavery. In the British Caribbean, the expectation of emancipation led to slave revolts in Jamaica and Barbados. When emancipation finally came, the British set up a transitional phase called apprenticeship. It did not work and was ended by Parliament in 1838. In the United States, during the early years of the Civil War, Abraham Lincoln opposed any action against slavery because he was trying to convince the South to return to the Union. Slaves, however, forced his hand, crossing Union lines wherever possible. In Brazil, anti-slavery measures during the 1880s aroused the expectations of slaves and led many to simply walk away from the plantations. By the time abolition was finally approved in 1888, most of the slaves were gone. In French West Africa, those slaves who remembered an earlier home went there. Elsewhere in Africa, many other slaves also left.

The abolition of slavery did not necessarily end slavery. It generally led to a struggle for the control of the labor of the former slaves. Often slaves had nowhere else to go and the post-slavery situation involved a complex process of negotiation. In this, the question of mobility and the question of land were important to former slaves. Mobility existed where slaves could withdraw their labor and go elsewhere. Where slave owners controlled most of the land or remained dominant in the state, they were often able to substitute other forms of control. In India, bondage based on debt became a way to tie peasant farmers to landowners. In parts of Latin America, peonage remained important. In the United States, where pro-slavery elements controlled state governments after the Civil War, southern states passed the so-called Black Codes to force the freed slaves to continue working for their masters. Congress intervened to give citizenship and protect the rights of the former slaves. A 10-year period called Reconstruction followed, which carried out many profound changes in southern life, but full citizenship involved a struggle that lasted a century. Few former slaves, however, accepted a return to plantation labor in the United States or anywhere else.

Everywhere, freed slaves were concerned about two things above all. The first was control over their family life. This meant the right to chose their spouses. It meant that women no longer had to submit to the sexual demands of masters, sons of the masters, and their visitors. It meant that people could no longer be sold away from their families. It meant that they could plan for themselves and that whatever they accumulated could be passed on to their offspring. The second thing former slaves sought was the right to work for themselves. For artisans with a marketable skill, this was usually easy. They often already worked for wages part-time, or in the case of some urban slaves, worked full-time for wages. With farm slaves, autonomy generally depended on the availability of land. On the island of Mauritius in the Indian Ocean, the whole slave population left the plantations and moved into mountainous areas in the center of the island not suited to plantation crops. In less than a decade, they were completely replaced by indentured labor from India. Similar, in Jamaica and other Caribbean islands with mountainous areas, freed slaves often moved onto their own lands. The men would work on the plantations, but never the long and abusive hours of slavery. The women were withdrawn from the labor force, creating a crisis for Caribbean sugar producers and necessitating the import of Indian indentured laborers. In the American South, white control of land forced the freed slaves to submit, but they worked as sharecroppers rather than submitting to the hated discipline and gang labor of the plantation.

Heritage of Slavery

Strictly speaking, slavery exists nowhere today, but the impact of slavery remains wherever it was important. The most important part of this heritage is racism. People of all colors and from all parts of the world have been slaves, but the largest source of slaves over the last 500 years has been Africa. Africans were the victims in the largest forced migration in history. In the period up to 1800, more people crossed the Atlantic in slave ships than as free persons. The numbers were so massive that native people who had been enslaved earlier were largely absorbed within an African mass. During this period, Europeans did not enslave each other except as a punishment for crimes. They often killed each other in wars, but never sold those taken prisoner or sent them to the Americas to do plantation labor. Europeans thus had to explain why it was right to enslave Africans and not Europeans. The only way they could do so was to argue that these Africans were somehow inferior to other peoples. This belief in racial inferiority in turn underlay segregation and racial discrimination and has been a major source of conflict wherever African slavery was important and has been used to deny people of African descent the full development of their potential. The abolition of slavery was often only the beginning of the struggle for equality and against discrimination.

The stigma of slave descent remains important even in areas where the slaves are not physically distinct. In areas where the former slaves did not remain a distinctive group, they disappeared, melting into the general population, often migrating to other places where they could make a fresh start. Elsewhere, for example, in parts of Africa, the stigma of slave descent remains powerful and is underpinned by the belief that people of slave descent lack honor. Often people of free descent will not marry them and they are ineligible for certain Muslim offices. Sometimes, however, they are better off economically than those of free ancestry because they are more entrepreneurial and more willing to do kinds of work that lack status.

There are also many new kinds of servitude. The United Nations regularly investigates different contemporary forms of slavery. These involve mostly children and women. Children are particularly valued in industries like rugmaking where their small fingers can work faster than those of adults. They are also sought for the sex industries of some Third World cities. For adult women, the most important form of slavery is coerced prostitution. It involves women from Eastern Europe, Asia, and Africa, who are sold and can be moved to wherever the market for sex seems attractive. Many are women who sought other kinds of work, but once out of their home countries found themselves controlled by criminal syndicates. There are other examples. Domestic service in some countries often involves people who are hereditary retainers, the children of slaves who remain clients of wealthy families. It also involves poor young women who contract to work for wealthy families and find themselves virtual slaves when they arrive at their destination. In some parts of the world, male farm workers also live in conditions of virtual servitude. All of these people are not slaves strictly speaking because they are not in a permanent relationship, but all are forced to do a job that they do not seek and are denied the freedom to leave.

These contemporary forms of slavery exist primarily in the poorer parts of the world, though prostitutes are virtual slaves in some of the world's most prosperous cities. Contemporary forms of slavery exist because of poverty. They exist also because criminal syndicates can coerce those they control. They exist because those syndicates and unscrupulous employers can profit by paying low wages to unwilling workers. These operations are essential neither to the global economy nor to the well-being of the countries where the new forms of slavery exist. Rugs are produced by both free labor and coerced labor. Landowners are prosperous in those parts of India where bonded labor has disappeared. The struggle against such forms of exploitation is a constant one, and probably one that will never be ended.

There is, however, no part of the world where formal slavery exists and where human beings are freely traded. The end of slavery is not easily explained. At the time it took place, slave plantations were still prosperous. Sugar, cotton, coffee, cloves, and other spices were being grown profitably. Furthermore, the late 19th century saw unprecedented demands for labor for sugar plantations in the West Indies, Fiji, and South Africa, to shovel guano on islands off the Peruvian coast, and to construct railroads in all parts of the world. Labor had to be enticed to areas that need it. Why then was slavery abolished? More than anything else, it was because of the rapid economic progress of a handful of countries, first Great Britain and the United States, then Western Europe, later Japan. These were all nations where labor was free and where people believed that free labor was more efficient and better motivated than servile labor. These were by the end of the 19th century all democratic nations where most people believed that human beings had the right to freely chose where and how to work and how much. People are often pushed to migrate and seek work elsewhere by poverty, but most of those seeking work today make their own choices about when, where, and how. They are often exploited and not always well treated, but they are no longer marched in chains and kept at work by the threat of whipping.

In the dictionary, bold face terms indicate cross-references to other articles.

THE DICTIONARY

-A-

ABLEMAN v. BOOTH. This was a case that involved conflict between federal and state law in the United States. The genesis of this important case was the capture of a runaway slave, Joshua Glover, in Racine, Wisconsin, by his master and United States Marshall Steven Ableman in 1854. The local sheriff immediately arrested Ableman and the master for assault and battery, and a mob freed the slave. Charges were brought in federal court against the leaders of the mob, Sherman Booth and John Rycraft, but a state judge freed them. They were then rearrested and convicted, but a state court again intervened, holding that the **Fugitive Slave Law** of 1850 was unconstitutional. When the case reached the Supreme Court, Chief Justice **Roger Taney** held that state courts could not use writs of habeas corpus to free federal prisoners. He also held the Fugitive Slave Act to be constitutional. The case ended state court resistance to the act, but within two years the nation was at war.

ABOLITION, BRAZIL. The first steps toward emancipation came not from an abolition movement, but from British pressure, first from 1810 on Portugal, and then, after Brazilian independence in 1822, on Brazil. In 1831, the Brazilian parliament passed a law ending the import of slaves and freeing those introduced illegally. This law was widely ignored for 20 years. During this period half a million slaves entered Brazil. By the 1850s, an abolition movement had emerged led by José Tomas Nabuco de Araujo, and later by his son, **Joaquim Nabuco de Araujo**. An 1851 bill abolished the African **slave trade**. An 1871 bill gave freedom to the newborn and set up a fund to free children. During the Triple Alliance War (1865-1870) in which Brazil, Argentina, and Uruguay fought Paraguay, Brazil freed slaves willing to enlist in its army.

In 1880, Nabuco and fellow reformers, disappointed by the slow pace of progress on the issue of slavery, organized the Brazilian Anti-Slavery Society and began an active propaganda campaign. The next few years were a period of intense debate. A number of provincial movements developed and proved effective. There was also support from members of the royal family. In 1886, Parliament responded to the brutal whipping of two slaves to death by passing a law prohibiting whipping. Soon after, there was a massive flight of slaves from São Paulo coffee **plantations**. Masters responded by offering conditional freedom, but that proved inadequate. In May 1888, recognizing that slavery had collapsed, parliament voted to end slavery. Brazil was the last country in the Americas to do so. The slaves succeeded where neither British pressure nor the eloquence of humanitarian elites had been effective. One ironic effect was the overthrow of the empire in November 1889 by conservative elements unhappy about the support members of the imperial family had given the abolitionists. The new regime, however, did not try to reinstitute slavery. *See also* BRAZIL-IAN SLAVERY.

ABOLITION, FRANCE. In France, abolition was part of the heritage of the **Enlightenment** and of the **French Revolution**. The first French abolition society was the **Society of the Friends of Blacks** founded in 1788. This was later than in Great Britain or the United States and it differed from those in being very elitist. Its membership was small but influential. It did not engage in appeals to public opinion and was not rooted in the churches. Nevertheless, the French Enlightenment had seriously questioned slavery and the assemblies of the French Revolution were sympathetic both to the rights of free blacks and to anti-slavery. In 1791, the National Assembly extended citizenship to mulattoes in the Caribbean. This act increased tensions in St. Domingue, where the **Haitian Revolution** was in its first stages. This event, in turn, pushed France to take further action. In 1794, it abolished slavery throughout the empire and barred slave owners from bringing their slaves to France. In 1802, Napoleon reinstituted colonial slavery. In 1817, defeated in the Napoleonic wars and under pressure from the British, the French agreed to end the **slave trade**. The Restoration monarchy in France did little to fulfill its commitments and suppress the illegal slave trade until 1831.

By this time, the abolition movement had reemerged. It was still very elitist in organization and methods. Though most of its members were Catholics, it lacked the support of the **Catholic Church**, which had been alienated by the activities of many leading abolitionists, most

Catholic clergy. One of its members was the Duke of Orleans, who became King Louis Philippe after the July Revolution in 1830. The July Monarchy was not, however, interested in going beyond the ending of the slave trade. In 1834, the French Society for the Abolition of Slavery was organized. The most important abolitionist, however, was **Victor Schoelcher**. Many members of the Society wanted gradual abolition, but Schoelcher advocated immediate and total abolition. In 1848, when the July Monarchy was replaced by the Second Republic, Schoelcher was part of the government that abolished slavery in all French colonial domains.

With the total end of slavery in the French colonial empire, the abolition movement disappeared only to re-surface in the 1870s when slavery once again became an issue in the new French colonies of Africa. Both Schoelcher and West Indian deputies like Alexandre Isaac raised the question of toleration of slavery in these new African colonies. Then, in 1888, the Cardinal-Primate of Algeria, **Charles Lavigerie** won the support of Pope Leo XIII for the creation of a Catholic anti-slavery movement. He made a tour of Catholic Europe, which resulted in the creation of a series of anti-slavery organizations. In 1903, the colonial state ordered the courts to stop considering slave status in legal cases. This application of the "Indian formula" meant that masters could no longer go to the courts to reclaim slaves. In 1905, a new law abolished all transactions in persons: sale, gift, bequeathals, or exchange. It was followed by a massive exodus, as many slaves left their masters to return to earlier homes or to create a new life for themselves. *See also* BANAMBA; EMANCIPATION, INDIA.

ABOLITION, GREAT BRITAIN. Over the centuries, there were many critics of slavery, but before the late 18th century, there was never a movement to abolish it. The movement that took form in Great Britain in the 1780s was rooted in **Enlightenment** philosophy, in economic theories that proclaimed the superiority of free labor, and in British Protestantism's belief that slavery was immoral. Its most dramatic success was the abolition by the world's largest slave trader of the **slave trade** in 1807 and of slavery itself in 1833. Though faced with a powerful entrenched West Indian lobby, the abolitionists had a speedy success. The movement can be traced to the middle of the 18th century, when many meetings of the Society of Friends (**Quakers**) decided that no slave dealer could be a member of the Quakers. Slavery had not existed in Great Britain since the Middle Ages, but with the development of great wealth in the Americas, planters began returning to Britain with slave servants. A young Anglican, **Granville Sharp**, began to use the courts to seek freedom for slaves in Britain. In 1772, in the case of James Somerset, a Virginia slave who had fled his master, Lord Justice Mansfield ruled that Somerset could not be returned to Virginia against his will. Nevertheless, until the 1780s, such movement as existed was largely among the Quakers and a few other Christian supporters like Sharp.

Then, in 1787, the **Society for the Abolition of the Slave Trade** was formed. Major roles were assumed by non-Quakers, **William Wilberforce**, who led the parliamentary campaign, and **Thomas Clarkson**, who was in charge of organization and research. Strongly based in the Protestant churches, the movement was speedily able to create local societies in all parts of Britain. In 1792, a petition signed by 400,000 individuals persuaded the House of Commons to approve a gradual end to the trade. Then, for over a decade, war with France took priority over abolition. Finally, in 1807, the British Parliament approved abolition of the slave trade. This satisfied those supporters of abolition called ameliorationists, who assumed that treatment of slaves would improve when imports were no longer possible. They founded the **African Institution** to monitor enforcement of abolition laws and create alternative sources of income for those societies that had participated in the slave trade.

By this time, however, the abolitionists had learned to exploit their support in the churches to mobilize public opinion. With the end of the Napoleonic wars, Great Britain put pressure on other European powers to follow Britain's lead in abolishing the trade, and then, later, to accept treaties giving the British navy the right to search ships suspected of being slavers. The **Africa Squadron** of the Royal Navy pursued slavers in the Atlantic and Indian Oceans for over half a century. At the same time, the abolitionists realized that ending the trade would have little impact on slavery itself. In 1823, a new organization, the Anti-Slavery Society was formed. William Wilberforce yielded the parliamentary leadership to **Thomas Fowell Buxton**, but Thomas Clarkson still played a key role. The abolitionists were at first successful in providing more opportunity for religious instruction for slaves, in removing barriers to manumission, and in regulating flogging. In 1831, an aggressive group of younger abolitionists organized the Agency Committee, which sent itinerant preachers and lecturers around Britain to whip up support. In 1833, Parliament finally abolished slavery throughout the British

Empire. To win support from gradualists, Buxton approved a transitional phase in which the slaves would become apprentices. When it became evident that slave owners saw apprenticeships as a form of slavery, the abolition movement attacked again and apprenticeship was ended in 1838.

Even then, abolitionists were aware that millions of people were in slavery and that the trade was continuing in many parts of the world. In 1839, they reorganized as the **British and Foreign Anti-Slavery Society**. One of their first victories was in India, which was not affected by the 1833 act because it was property of the East India Company and not of the British Crown. In 1843, slavery was abolished in India. The abolitionists continued to put pressure on Britain to use its influence to end slavery elsewhere in the world, and in particular, in British colonies. The successor of the British and Foreign Anti-Slavery Society, **Anti-Slavery International,** is still actively fighting slavery and slavery-like institutions in all parts of the world. *See also* EMANCIPATION, INDIA; SOMERSET v. STEWART; STURGE, JOSEPH.

ABOLITION, UNITED STATES. In 1758, the annual meeting of the Philadelphia Society of Friends voted to exclude members who traded in slaves. This was the first act of what became an active abolition movement. Abolition in the United States took its strength from three sources. First, the **Quakers** and other Protestants became convinced that slavery was opposed to Christian teachings. Second, many American thinkers were strongly influenced by the **Enlightenment** critique of slavery and emphasis on universal human rights. Finally, the ideology of the **American Revolution** stressed equality and the struggle for liberty. These ideas came together in **Thomas Jefferson**'s writing of the Declaration of Independence, which stressed the right of all persons to "life, liberty and the pursuit of happiness." A slave holder himself, Jefferson freed only eight of his own slaves, and then only in his will.

Slavery at this time existed in all parts of the United States, but was more limited in the North. There, abolitionist societies persuaded one state after another to abolish slavery. The Massachusetts constitution of 1780 effectively ended slavery there. Pennsylvania in 1780, Connecticut and Rhode Island in 1784, and New York in 1789 followed with emancipation acts. By 1804, every northern state had approved some form of emancipation, though in some cases emancipation was very gradual. Many slaves were also freed by the British during the **American Revolution** for supporting the royal cause and resettled in Nova

Scotia, Britain, and Jamaica after the war. Many others freed themselves or were freed for military service. At the Constitutional Convention of 1787, there was a heated debate when abolitionists attacked the slave trade. The compromise approved authorized Congress to end the import of slaves after 1808. By that time, the slave trade had been abolished in all states except South Carolina. Congress then followed suit. Thus, the United States ended the import of slaves the same year as Great Britain.

At the Constitutional Convention, some Southerners like Jefferson were sympathetic with abolition, but with the development of the cotton gin in 1793, **cotton** became the major commercial crop in the South. Heavily dependent on slave labor to pick the cotton, the South dug in, developed its slaveholding culture and determined to protect it. In the North, resettlement of slaves in Africa, advocated by the **American Colonization Society**, was the most popular approach to abolition, especially among those who believed that African-Americans were not ready for liberty. A more militant abolitionism emerged with the formation of the **American Anti-Slavery Society** under the leadership of **William Lloyd Garrison** in 1833. Garrison also published the *Liberator*, an anti-slavery newspaper. Abolitionists believed strongly that human progress was based on free labor. Many also believed that slavery was a sin.

Abolitionists split over a number of issues. A western wing led by **Theodore Dwight Weld** favored a more gradual approach than that of Garrison. They differed on violence, an issue that came to a head with Bleeding Kansas in 1854 and **John Brown**'s raid on Harper's Ferry in 1859. Others differed on race. As the free black population grew and competed with white immigrants for jobs, racial discrimination increased. Some abolitionists felt that the movement should seek equal rights for those it freed. By contrast, the **Free Soilers** only wanted to limited the expansion of slavery and often even wanted to exclude free Blacks from the new western states. At the same time, African-Americans like **Frederick Douglass** and **Henry Highland Garnet** increasingly played a strong role in the movement.

The abolitionists remained a minority. The abolitionist **Liberty Party** was successful mostly in spreading ideas. The passage of the **Fugitive Slave Act** in 1850 made it possible for slave owners to reclaim runaway slaves in the North and provided a crucial issue for the abolition movement. At the same time, abolitionist activity convinced Southerners that they could not accept the election of **Abraham Lincoln**. Lincoln did not advocate abolition of slavery, but he opposed its extension and for the South, protection of Southern interests depended on North-South parity in the Senate. Many leading abolitionists played an active role in the American Civil War and in the **Reconstruction** period that followed. In the earliest stages of the Civil War, Lincoln was reluctant to abolish slavery because he hoped to persuade Southerners to return to the Union. In 1863, the **Emancipation Proclamation** ended slavery in areas still in rebellion against the Union and in 1865, the **Fifteenth Amendment** to the **Constitution of the United States** ended slavery elsewhere. *See also* CIVIL WAR; QUACO WALKER CASES.

ADAMS, JOHN QUINCY (1767-1848). After serving as President of the United States from 1825 to 1829, John Quincy Adams was elected to the House of Representatives. Though he personally found slavery morally repugnant, Adams was reluctant as Secretary of State and President to push anti-slavery ideas that would strain the American union. In Congress, however, he became more outspoken. A popular abolitionist tactic was the submission of petitions to Congress. The majority in the House of Representatives responded by passing the gag rule, which prohibited the presentation of anti-slavery petitions to Congress. This was a violation of the First Amendment to the U.S. Constitution, which guaranteed the right to petition. Week after week, for years, Adams rose in the house to read petitions sent to him, often facing abuse from pro-slavery colleagues. Finally in 1844, the gag rule was rescinded. In 1841, in the important *Amistad* case, Adams represented the mutineers before the U.S. Supreme Court and won the case.

AFONSO I, KING OF THE KONGO (DIED C. 1545). Nzinga Mbembe was a Kongolese price born shortly after the arrival of the Portuguese in the Kingdom of the Kongo in 1482. He was one of the first converts to Catholicism, and with Portuguese support, became the Mani Kongo in about 1506. Afonso was eager to absorb European technology and modernize his kingdom. To that end, he corresponded with King Manuel I of Portugal, who offered him advice and promised assistance. In exchange, Afonso sold slaves. As the **slave trade** developed, it turned out to be disastrous for the Kongo. Slave traders from the Portuguese island of **São Tomé** encouraged warfare, provided aid to Afonso's vassals, who increasingly broke free from Afonso's control. Young men sent to Portugal for training disappeared into the slave trade. In 1526, Afonso wrote King John III to complain of the slavers' practices. Finally, he tried to stop the trade, but was unable to do so. The trade eventually destroyed the unity of the Kongo kingdom. *See also* KONGO.

AFRICAN INSTITUTION. After the abolition of the British **slave trade** in 1807, the African Institution was founded to monitor compliance with the new law and to lobby for abolitionist objectives. It was also concerned to disseminate information about Africa and to encourage the growth of new forms of commerce in Africa. Some of its leading members were involved with mission activities and with the colony of **Sierra Leone**, which was the base of Britain's **African Squadron**. It also corresponded with American abolitionists and maintained a central slave registry that documented harsh treatment of slaves. It operated primarily by lobbying the powerful, but by 1823 many abolitionists wanted to attack slavery itself and were convinced that popular mobilization was necessary. In that year, the members of the African Institution voted to become part of the British Anti-Slavery Society. *See also* ABOLITION, GREAT BRITAIN.

AFRICAN METHODIST EPISCOPAL CHURCH (AME). In 1787, the African Methodist Episcopal Church began when a group of free blacks in Philadelphia, who objected to being seated in the gallery of the Methodist church they attended, broke away and created their own church, today known as the Mother Bethel Church. Under the leadership of an ex-slave named **Richard Allen**, they started worship in a black-smith shed, but soon constructed their own building. Their example convinced other black Christians offended by racial discrimination in white churches to form their own. In 1816, a group of these churches united and formed the African Methodist Episcopal Church. Soon, there were AME churches in almost every sizable African-American community.

From the first, the AME Church gave a voice to African-Americans denied the vote and mobilized black support for their brothers and sisters in slavery. The Mother Bethel Church was also a way station on the **Underground Railroad**. Members like **William Still** played a key role in feeding and clothing refugees from slavery. Leading abolitionists like **Frederick Douglass** often spoke at AME churches. AME members like **Denmark Vesey** were sometimes involved in revolts, which led to efforts to suppress the church in the South. Beginning with the establishment of Wilberforce University in Ohio in 1856, the AME Church created six institutions of higher learning, which played a major role in educating former slaves.

The AME Church has also played an important role in missionary work in Africa. Today, it contains over 2,000 churches in the United States, Canada, Africa, Great Britain and the West Indies.

AFRICAN SLAVERY. Slavery has long existed in Africa, but often in forms very different from the Americas. Traditionally, most slaves came from capture in war, though there was probably some kidnapping. The majority were women, who were incorporated into families as junior wives. Slaves were generally part of a household economy and often worked alongside free members of the household. They did more work than others, but not necessarily different work. They often lived in the same compound and ate with free-born family members. Children young enough to be initiated with the captor's children often became virtually full members of society as did the children of those captured.

In these societies, slaves differed from the free-born in that they had no kin to whom they could turn for help. Lacking kin, they were powerless and were seen as lacking **honor**. They also remained lifetime dependents. In most African societies, no slave could become a chief or the head of a household. A slave remained indefinitely under the authority of others, dependent on others for the grant of land or for the arrangement of a marriage and always with lower status.

Slavery began to change wherever centralized states emerged and a market economy developed. Here, slavery became a hereditary status, though manumission was always possible and was encouraged in Muslim societies. In centralized states, the bulk of slaves taken prisoner were often kept by the king and the more powerful nobles. Attractive women became concubines of the rich and powerful. Some male slaves became soldiers and servants and were relatively well off. Powerful men were often surrounded by a large retinue made up largely of slaves. Some slaves exercised power and enjoyed privilege, though always as the agents of other men.

In these societies, most slaves were settled in special slave villages, where they produced food that fed the court. Where markets were important, slaves were also put to work producing commodities for exchange. Such an area was, for example, the desert-side area, where Saharan nomads descended every year into the savanna during the dry season. They exchanged salt, copper and animals for grain and cloth. The grain and cloth were often produced by slaves. Slaves also did most of the labor on oases, and some nomads had slave villages that provided them with grain.

Where **mining** developed slaves often did much of the dangerous underground labor. Slaves in such areas usually had precisely defined labor obligations, though those born within the society often were allowed once married to practice a kind of sharecropping in which they worked their own land and made fixed annual payments to the masters. When European nations abolished the export **slave trade**, many slaves were put to work producing commodities for European markets. *See also* AFRICAN SLAVE TRADE; ASANTE; CENTRAL AFRICA; ELITE SLAVES; ISLAM; SAHARA; WEST AFRICA.

AFRICAN SLAVE TRADE. The major effect of the export of slaves to the Americas, the Mediterranean, and the Middle East was the development of slavetrading and slave production within Africa. In the early years, slaves were often provided from areas close to the coastal export centers, but as demand increased and as local people proved effective at defending themselves, routes penetrated farther and farther into the interior and professional slave traders emerged to move slaves long distances.

The long-distance slave trade also stimulated slaving activities and the development of professional slave traders. Wars became more frequent and were increasingly directed to taking slaves. Kidnapping became a serious problem in many areas and enslavement increasingly became a penalty for wrongdoing. The large-scale slave trade also stimulated the use of slaves. Particularly important was the use of slave soldiers. They were generally assumed to be loyal, but some regimes like Bambara Segou were dominated by their slave soldiers. The **Atlantic slave trade** generally preferred men, but women were preferred within Africa. Some were incorporated within the harems of the rich and powerful. Others became the wives of the slave soldiers. A large number also became farmers, working alongside male slaves. Some slave farmers produced to feed the elite, but the greatest expansion was among merchant families, who marketed the slaves and provided the weapons and commodities the military elites needed. Increasingly, they used slave labor to produce goods for sale.

After the closing of the Atlantic slave trade, there was a dramatic increase in the use of slaves within Africa to produce goods like palm oil, peanuts, and cloves for European and Asian markets. Because of the insecurity engendered by slaving, it was not easy to recruit free labor in most parts of Africa. As a result the labor needs of areas that were producing for export were met by the slave trade. Only with the emergence of free porters on East African trade routes and the growth of diamond and gold mining in the late 19th century South Africa did a free labor migration develop. Elsewhere, the period after the closing of the Atlantic trade saw an increased demand for slaves. With newer and better weapons available, areas hitherto isolated from the slave trade experienced its ravages in a particularly brutal manner. This was particularly true in the southern Sudan and in the interior of east and central Africa. The generation before the partition of Africa in the late 19th century was probably the bloodiest in the history of the continent. *See also* AFRICAN SLAVERY; CENTRAL AFRICA; EAST AFRICAN SLAVE TRADE; MILITARY SLAVES; MIDDLE PASSAGE; SUDAN; ZANZIBAR.

AFRICA SQUADRON. After Great Britain abolished the slave trade, ships of the Royal Navy were sent to the coast of **West Africa** to enforce the law. With the end of the Napoleonic wars, Britain signed treaties with other European powers providing a mutual right to stop and search ships believed to be slavers. Only the British, French and briefly the Americans and Portuguese ever had ships doing this. The most important was the British Navy, which maintained a squadron in West African waters until 1869.

The British squadron was based in Freetown, **Sierra Leone**, which was also the location of the Prize Court. British ships also operated in the Indian Ocean and off the coasts of Brazil and Cuba. When a slave ship was captured on the high seas, the ship and its cargo had to be taken to Freetown, where the slaves were freed. If the Prize Court condemned the ship, the Captain of the British ship received prize money. Over 1,600 ships were stopped, more than 85 per cent by the British Navy. The African Squadron stopped the trade on large stretches of the West African coast and raised the cost of slaving, but only a little over 160,000 slaves were freed. More than 2.5 million made it across the Atlantic. The squadron also often intervened in African affairs both in the struggle against the slave trade and in protection of British commercial interests. *See also* EAST AFRICAN SLAVE TRADE; RECAPTIVES; SIERRA LEONE.

AFRO-BRAZILIANS. The Afro-Brazilians were descendants of slaves shipped to Brazil from **Dahomey**, who returned to the Benin coast during the 19th century as merchants and petty traders. Many of the European slave-trading nations abandoned their forts during the

Napoleonic wars, but with most of the slaves going to Brazil, Brazilian merchants were in a strong position. Domingo Martins in Porto Novo controlled much of the slave trade to Cuba. **Felix Francisco De Souza** built a string of trading posts along the Bight of Benin and helped King Ghezo to seize power in Dahomey in 1818. He was rewarded with the title of *chacha* and put in charge of customs collection, a position that enabled him to dominate the **Whydah** trade. Then, after a slave revolt at Bahia in 1835, the Brazilian government began deporting free Blacks to Africa. Over a 40-year period, about 3,000 settled at points along the coast, most of them engaging in trade. They were Portuguese speaking, had Portuguese names, and were Catholic. Many of the Brazilian families were important under French colonial rule and have remained important up to this day. *See also* BAHIAN SLAVE REVOLTS.

ALBORNOZ, BARTOLOMÉ DE (?-1575). Albornoz was a theologian and the first professor of law at the University of Mexico. He was one of the first Spaniards to criticize the enslavement of Africans. His major work, *Arte de los contratos* (1573), contained an essay, "De la esclavitud," which attacked the **Atlantic slave trade** as sinful. Enslavement was in theory based only on capture in a just war, but Albernoz argued that purchasers had no way of knowing whether the slaves they bought originated in a just war. Furthermore, even the theory of just war did not justify the enslavement and sale of women and children. He also took issue with the idea that conversion to Christianity justified enslavement and suggested that if conversion were the goal sought, the church should send missionaries to Africa. Finally, though he did not call for emancipation of slaves, he argued that Africans had a natural right to liberty. He criticized slave merchants as sinful and urged them to get out of the trade. Albornoz's book was not translated into other languages, and in later years it was banned by the Inquisition. *See also* CATHOLIC CHURCH.

ALLEN, RICHARD (1760-1831). Born a slave, Richard Allen converted to Methodism as a teenager and then converted his master. Working as a bricklayer, woodcutter and wagon driver, he persuaded his master to let him purchase his freedom at the age of 20. It took him five years to do so. Though self-educated, Allen became an itinerant preacher. In 1786, he was invited to preach to Black members of Philadelphia's St. George Methodist Episcopal Church. A year later, he formed the Free African Society to fight both slavery and racism. Later the same year, Allen and other black members of the church were ordered to sit in a segregated gallery. They refused and left together to form the Mother Bethel Church. After worshipping for seven years in an empty blacksmith shed, they dedicated their own church. Allen then had to fight to win recognition for Mother Bethel as a separate church. After the Pennsylvania Supreme Court gave them independent church status in 1816, a meeting of 16 Black churches created the **African Methodist Episcopal Church (AME)** with Allen as bishop. For many years, Allen took no salary and supported his religious activity with a series of businesses: blacksmithing, shoemaking and chimneysweeping.

Allen wrote an autobiography, sermons, and pamphlets, organized conventions and meetings, and tried to increase educational opportunities for African-Americans. In 1830, he was one of the convenors of the first national Negro convention, which met at the Mother Bethel Church and formed the American Society for Free People of Color. Under his leadership, the AME Church fought against both slavery and racial discrimination. He sheltered fugitive slaves, opposed the colonization movement, and encouraged self-help and self-reliance.

AMBAR, MALIK (c. 1550-1626). Malik Ambar was a slave who rose to become the ruler of an Indian state. Born a free man in Ethiopia, he was enslaved and sold to the Arabs. He converted to Islam, was given an education in finance and public affairs, and in the 1570s, was sold to the ruler of the Indian state of Ahmadnagar. There, he became a leader of mercenary soldiers who distinguished himself in the service of several Indian kingdoms. He was one of a number of African slave-soldiers who held high office in late medieval India. In 1602, he seized power in Ahmadnagar, imprisoning the king and declaring himself regent. During the generation that followed, he successfully resisted the expanding power of the Mughal Empire. His personal bodyguard was made up of African slaves, but other appointments were distributed among Brahmins, Arabs, and Persians. He reformed tax and land policies, constructed a number of mosques, and was a patron of literature and the arts. *See also* ELITE SLAVES; INDIAN SLAVERY.

AMERICAN ANTI-SLAVERY SOCIETY. Founded in Philadelphia in December 1833, the American Anti-Slavery Society brought together a number of abolitionist organizations. Led by **Arthur and Lewis Tappan**, New York businessmen, and **William Lloyd Garrison**, the editor of the *Liberator,* the society was committed to the immediate end of slavery and to rights for free Blacks. It organized local abolitionist groups, produced a series of publications, and bombarded the United States Congress with petitions. The endorsement of women's rights and militant denunciations of some churches as pro-slavery led to a defection of more moderate abolitionists who formed the American and Foreign Anti-Slavery Society. The breakaway group remained active, but did not develop as extensive a network of local auxiliaries as the American Anti-Slavery Society, which remained the most powerful anti-slavery organization. *See also* ABOLITION, UNITED STATES.

AMERICAN COLONIZATION SOCIETY. The American Society for Colonizing the Free People of Color was founded in 1816. It advocated the resettlement of free blacks from the United States to Africa as a solution to American racial problems. Initially, the society had the support of many free blacks, who despaired of ever achieving equality in the United States, but when it became clear that no African-Americans would hold leadership posts in the organization, most turned against it. Many abolitionists also supported the society, though it carefully avoided taking a position on slavery. After a brief flirtation, however, most of them left. At the same time, many slave holders supported it in the hope of being able to expel free blacks, who they regarded as a threat. The organization's most important success was the creation of **Liberia** in 1821 on land purchased by the society. Though it tried to distance itself from pro-slavery backers, the American Colonization Society was never able to mobilize support from abolitionist or free black groups. In the end, only 15,386 African-Americans migrated to Liberia.

AMERICAN MISSIONARY ASSOCIATION (AMA). In 1839, a group of abolitionists organized a committee to provide legal aid for the slaves freed from the Spanish ship the *Amistad*. After that effort was successful, they joined with several other groups in 1846 to form the American Missionary Association under the leadership of **Arthur Tappan**. The association was hostile not only to slavery, but also to racism. Rare at the time, it had a racially integrated board and the schools it founded were open to both white and black. When the American **Civil War** ended in 1865, **William Lloyd Garrison** dismantled his **American Anti-Slavery Society**, but the AMA entered its most important period.

Even during the war, the AMA sent missionaries and teachers into areas the Union army occupied. They set up schools and churches, helped African-Americans acquire land, and lobbied for public education and the rights of the freed slaves. During the **Reconstruction** years, the AMA expanded its operations and created a series of colleges and universities, among them Fisk University in Nashville, Tennessee (1866), Talladega College in Talledega, Alabama (1867), Hampton Institute in Hampton, Virginia, Dillard University in New Orleans (1869), LeMoyne College in Memphis, Tennessee (1870), and Tillotson College in Austin, Texas (1877). In later years, the AMA worked among Asian immigrants on the West Coast, poor whites in Appalachia, Mexican-Americans in New Mexico, and helped to set up schools in Puerto Rico.

AMERICAN REVOLUTION. The American Revolution provided an opportunity for thousands of slaves to free themselves. It also forced Americans to ask what role slavery would play in the society they were creating. Disputes over the taxation of the **slave trade** were among the many grievances of the colonists.

Both sides used slave soldiers. In 1775, Virginia's governor, the **Earl of Dunmore**, offered to free slaves who joined the British side and organized a regiment of those who responded to his call. His efforts may have convinced many whites to support the rebels, but other British commanders followed similar policies. About 20,000 blacks fought in the war, two-thirds on the British side. Many others sought freedom as civilians behind British lines, working as free artisans or setting up Maroon communities and farming for themselves.

The Continental army also recruited slaves, mostly in the North. Some served instead of their masters and some were freed. In general the war saw a weakening of the control of the masters and, in the North, a strong movement toward abolition. Vermont entered the Union as a free state in 1777. In Massachusetts, a new state constitution passed in 1780 led to the freeing of its slaves. In the same year, Pennsylvania passed a gradual emancipation act, the first such law in the new nation. Connecticut followed after the war. There was also some support for abolition in parts of the Upper South. Enough individual slave holders manumitted slaves that there were about 100,000 free blacks in the South by 1810.

After the war, some blacks were betrayed by the British and were reenslaved, but about 10,000 were evacuated to Nova Scotia and Jamaica. Some eventually settled in **Sierra Leone**. In spite of this, once the war was over, there were more slaves than before, and with the triumph of **cotton**, the South became even more committed to slavery.

See also ABOLITION, UNITED STATES; AMERICAN SLAVERY; BLACK LOYALISTS.

AMERICAN SLAVERY (U.S.). In 1619, about 20 slaves were sold by a Dutch ship at Jamestown, Virginia. At the time, there was very little English law on slavery. Some of these first slaves seem to have been freed after a term of service. Many of them became prosperous farmers. In spite of this, by the end of the century, slaves were found in all of the American colonies and three of them, Virginia, Maryland, and South Carolina, were on the way to becoming **slave societies**. Slaves in New England were a by-product of both trade with the West Indies and wars with Native Americans, but they were numerous only in Rhode Island, which traded a lot with the West Indies. In New York, originally a Dutch colony, slaves were important because of the city's commerce. Most slaves worked in agriculture, but many were domestic servants, artisans, or unskilled workers. Few slave owners had more than one or two slaves.

By contrast, Virginia and Maryland produced **tobacco** for export. During the first part of the 17th century, **indentured labor** was cheaper than slaves, but gradually the price of indentured labor rose and tobacco planters recognized that they could keep slaves indefinitely. In South Carolina, the shift into rice early in the 18th century created a demand for slaves, who were imported largely from rice-growing areas of West Africa. Because of the high mortality in the South Carolina lowlands, few whites lived there year round. South Carolina became the only colony with a Black majority and one where African customs and languages long survived. Georgia, the last of the American colonies, was founded in 1733 by **James Oglethorpe** as a free colony, but almost from the first farmers pressed for a reversal of the prohibition against slavery and in 1750 slavery was authorized.

The context of slavery in what became the United States was very different from the West Indies and Brazil. The number of slaves brought in was much smaller — somewhat over 400,000 compared to almost 4 million to Brazil and over 4 million to the West Indies. That population was also experiencing a natural increase by the middle of the 18th century. By 1860, there were 4 million people of African descent in the United States. In spite of this, most of these African slaves lived in a society where whites formed the majority. Slaves were never much over 20 percent of the American population, though they were much more numerous in parts of the South. This meant that slaves competed in different ways with free white workers and farmers. The opposition of these workers and farmers to the expansion of slavery did as much to destroy slavery as the abolitionists. In 1787, when the **Constitution of the United States** was written some Southerners wanted to end slave imports because they worried about a large African-American population.

The invention of the **cotton** gin in 1793 transformed the situation. Cotton textiles were the most important industry in the first stage of the Industrial Revolution in Great Britain and then, a little later in the Northern U.S. The South contained extensive lands suitable to cotton, a ready source of labor and entrepreneurial skills. It quickly became the most important producer of cotton in the world. Cotton plantations spread from Georgia and the Carolinas into Alabama, Mississippi and Louisiana. When the import of slaves was stopped in 1808, prices rose, but population growth in the older states of Virginia, Maryland and North Carolina provided the slaves the cotton South needed. There were many kinds of slavery in the United States, but in 1860, two out of three American slaves worked in cotton.

Even though slave population grew, so did the hours of work. The Southern slave **plantation** was an efficient operation that forced slaves to work very long hours. Slaves were, however, valuable and planters sought to maintain their health and physical well-being. That did not mean that slave life was easy. The work was hard. Mothers had little time to care for their children, and the children found themselves working from a very young age. Southern states were wary of their own free black populations and moved to limit **manumission**. The internal slave trade was important to the development of new areas. Slave families were often broken up, husbands separated from their wives, mothers from their children. Slave revolts and abolitionist propaganda aroused southern fears and led to a strengthening of slave discipline. Slaves were regularly whipped for a variety of infractions, most notably flight. In some states, it was illegal to teach a black person to read. In spite of the constraints, slaves developed a rich culture, strongly rooted in their African traditions. This was particularly evident in religion and music. *See also* ABOLITION, UNITED STATES; BRAZILIAN SLAVERY; EMANCIPATION, UNITED STATES; SLAVE RELIGION.

AMERINDIAN SLAVERY. Many native American societies took and absorbed captives. Generally, women were taken as wives and children were adopted. Adult male prisoners were often sacrificed or tortured. This was particularly true in Mesoamerica, where large numbers of captives were often sacrificed in ritual ceremonies. There were also in Mesoamerican societies different kinds of servitude. The Aztecs had rural tenants who were like **serfs**. Among the Aztecs, persons could also enslave themselves or dependent members of their families to pay debts or for subsistence needs. Among the Maya, enslavement was largely a result of capture in war.

Slavery was much less developed among most other Amerindian communities. There was, however, a crucial transition in many societies from captive to slave. In these cases, the captives were assigned to menial labor such as gathering wood and seeking water. They were not members of any clan and thus had none of the protections that kinship brought. They could thus be beaten or killed without fear of retaliation. In some cases, however, among the Iroquois and **Cherokee** a captive could be chosen for adoption into a clan and became a full member. When the Iroquois suffered population losses from European diseases, they used adoption to maintain their numbers.

The most elaborate slave system in the Americas was found in the Pacific Northwest. Here, there was a unique civilization based on fishing, and in particular, the annual run of the salmon. They developed a hierarchical social structure, which included war captives who were held as slaves. With the development of the fur trade with Europeans, they also bought slaves from interior peoples. The slaves paddled canoes for raiding and trading expeditions and did menial labor. They also served as important status symbols. Slaves could be killed or traded. They could also, however, marry, accumulate wealth, and purchase their freedom.

European settlement in the Americas led to the transformation and expansion of indigenous slave systems. The Spanish in Mexico abolished human sacrifice, but encouraged native allies to enslave others. These slaves became a major source of labor for the Spanish until the **Catholic Church** began attacking the system. Further north, the development of the fur trade led to an expansion of both warfare and trade. As a by-product of this trade, slaves were traded in small numbers over large areas. In areas where modern slave systems developed, early settlers sought to enslave native peoples or to encourage some of the more warlike to enslave others. In the West Indies, enslavement, harsh treatment, and European diseases led to the decimation of indigenous populations. In Brazil, the decline in population created a situation where local sources were no longer able to meet the needs of the sugar plantations.

In the southeastern part of what is now the United States, demand for slaves at first stimulated warfare among tribes like Cherokee, Choctaw, and Creek. The planters soon, however, found the African **slave trade** a better source of slaves. The local Amerindians sometimes served as slave catchers, returning runaways to coastal plantations. At other times, Amerindians like the **Seminoles** of Florida served as a refuge for runaways. Gradually, many Indians in the southeast began adopting the ways of the settlers, some even using African slave labor. Ironically, this did not save them from the expropriation of their lands. Under Andrew Jackson, the so-called "civilized tribes" were expelled from the southeast and forced to migrate to Oklahoma, which was set aside as Indian territory. Many of the slaveholding Indians brought their slaves with them on what was known as the Trail of Tears. After the conquest of the Seminole, they too were moved to Oklahoma.

AMISTAD. A mutiny by 54 slaves on the *Amistad*, a Cuban slave ship, in July 1839 led to a court case that affirmed human rights in the United States. The slaves had been brought to Havana, sold to landowners in eastern Cuba, and were being transported there when they seized the ship and ordered two slave owners on board to take them back to Africa. Their leader was **Joseph Cinqué**, a Mende from **Sierra Leone**. The slave owners charted a zig-zag course, moving steadily north until after 60 days, the boat was seized by the U.S. Navy off Long Island, New York. The Spanish rulers of Cuba immediately demanded return of their "property," but they were challenged in the courts by a committee of abolitionists led by New York businessman **Lewis Tappan**. Spain had agreed to the abolition of the **slave trade**, though slavery was still legal in Cuba. Spain held that the slaves were property.

Abolitionists wanted to use the case to demonstrate the evils of the slave trade and to establish that slaves were human beings. Their lawyer argued that the *Amistad* mutineers were kidnapped Africans who had been brought to Cuba illegally. The president of the United States, Martin Van Buren, wanted to return the mutineers to Cuba, but they were successful in a district court. Van Buren then insisted that the case go to the Supreme Court, where five of the nine justices were southern slave holders. Here the abolitionist case was argued passionately by the 73-year-old ex-president, **John Quincy Adams**. The Court refused to pass judgment on slavery, but it held that the mutineers were free because they had never been slaves in Cuba. Funds were raised to return 35 of the mutineers to Africa. No one knows what happened to any of them after their return. *See also* ABOLITION, UNITED STATES; CUBAN SLAVERY.

ANCIENT GREEK SLAVERY. As far as is known, ancient Greece was the first **slave society**. Originally most slaves were the result of capture in war or by pirates, but as Greece got involved in trade and colonization between the eighth and sixth centuries BCE,the money economy expanded, and more and more people were enslaved as a result of debt. When an increasing number of Athenians found themselves trapped in servitude and poverty, the city faced civil conflict. In the beginning of the fifth century, **Solon**'s reforms of Athenian law abolished debt slavery and confirmed the citizenship of all Athenians. This was, however, a period in which trade and production were increasing. Those seeking labor or slave dependents could only do so by the acquisition of captives or the purchase of slaves. Slaves from this point on were foreigners or the descendants of foreigners. They could be freed, but could not become citizens. In the centuries after Solon, Athens was marked by a population of free citizens and a large slave population that did most of the real labor. Only the citizens served in the army and navy. Athenian democracy was thus very much based on the labor of slaves.

The Athenian slave was chattel. He or she could be sold, punished, or asked to do whatever the master wished. Any slave, male or female, could be used sexually. Slavery was also permanent. Any child born of a slave mother was a slave, though manumission was possible. Some slaves were able to buy their freedom. Slaves did not form their own kinship groups or participate in public life. Even those born in Athens were totally dependent on their masters. Though slavery was ubiquitous, most slave holdings were relatively small compared to Rome or the Americas. Athenian farms specialized in the production of wine and olive oil, much of which was exported. Most of the labor was done by slaves.

One of the characteristics of Athens, like other slave societies, is that labor was the lot of the slaves, and thus, considered dishonorable. Citizens rarely farmed or did manual labor. Many slaves were also in domestic service. They did the cooking, baking, and made the clothing in most households. Most prostitutes and courtesans were slaves. The many small manufactures in Athens — pottery, weapons, jewelry and clothing, for example — were dependent on slave labor. Slaves were also the carpenters and stoneworkers who produced the temples and other magnificent public building of Athens. The harshest slavery was found in the silver mines, where the mortality was very high. Some historians think that most of the slaves assigned to work there were rebellious or criminal.

Another form of slavery evolved in Sparta and Thessaly. Sparta was a highly militarized and landlocked society. The Spartans were not involved in maritime trade. The people they conquered were kept in place and became helots. The helots were essentially serfs, owned by the state, but assigned with land to Spartan families, for whom they cultivated. Unlike chattel slaves, the helots had the right to marry and raise families. Living in their original communities, they maintained their links with each other, and thus found it easier to organize resistance. Surrounded by a helot majority, the Spartans lived in fear of revolt and were very repressive. By contrast, in Athens, slaves were originally foreigners. They lived and worked in small communities, which made it difficult for a rebellion to coalesce. They also worked in different places, some had a comfortable existence, and many had different interests. Recalcitrant slaves could be sent to the silver mines or marked with tattoos or brands. *See also* HELOTRY; HONOR.

ANCIENT MIDDLE EASTERN SLAVERY. The ancient Middle East was the first area to develop urban civilization, the first known to have grain agriculture, and the area where Judaism, Christianity, and Islam developed.

The first civilization in the Middle East was the Sumerians of lower Mesopotamia from 3500 BCE, who lived in cities and depended primarily on the labor of free peasants and artisans. By 2700 BCE, there is clear evidence of slaves working in the royal households, in the temples, and on the estates of the powerful. All of the great empires that succeeded the Sumerians used slave labor but none were **slave societies,** that is to say, none were dependent primarily on slaves for productive labor. For most of Middle Eastern history, agriculture was largely in the hands of free peasants, often tenants, but not chattel. The most important source of slaves was warfare, but some were purchased from poorer areas on the fringes of the Tigris-Euphrates valley and some were kidnapped. Enslavement for debt also existed in all of the Middle Eastern empires and there were slaves given to temples by poor families. The law codes we have for these societies, including the laws of the ancient Hebrews, sought to regulate slavery and protect the slaves. The Old Testament provided for Hebrew male slaves to be freed after six years of service. It is not clear whether this was done, but the permanent enslavement of fellow Hebrews was clearly seen as immoral. In the early Middle Eastern empires, slaves could marry, have families, and own property.

The Assyrians, who developed in northern Mesopotamia, extended their control beyond the Tigris-Euphrates valley from about 1250 BCE. With the use of iron weapons, chariots, and archers, the Assyrians were more powerful than any earlier empire. As a result, the Assyrians and later the Babylonians took large numbers of prisoners, who were put to work constructing palaces, temples, and irrigation canals. Slaves were important in royal households and temples and worked as domestic servants and artisans. Both Assyrians and Babylonians also forced many conquered peoples to relocate to the central part of the state, where they could be more easily controlled and exploited. They were treated like chattel slaves, but lived in their own separate communities. The Bible tells of the Hebrews being forced to move to Babylon, where they lived until a new conqueror, Persia, allowed them to return to their homeland. By the early centuries of the first millennium BCE, there were slave markets in the major cities and ports of the Middle East and trade routes that extended to the Mediterranean, the Caucasus, and the Persian Gulf.

Persian society was marked by strong patriarchal authority. Though most labor was still provided by free men, slaves were found as servants, artisans, and agricultural labor on royal estates. When Cyrus II began the conquests that established Persian rule from northwest India to the Nile delta and the Aegean Sea, this brought large numbers of captured people into Persia and slave labor built palaces. Trade routes were opened, first to India and the Mediterranean, and eventually to China and Ethiopia. Slaves were an important item of trade on these routes, though slavery never became as important as in Greece and Rome. Both law and custom regarded slaves as persons, protected them from mistreatment, and encouraged manumission. Many of the slaves were skilled artisans or musicians. *See also* ANCIENT GREEK SLAVERY; BIBLE; TEMPLE SLAVERY.

ANCIENT ROMAN SLAVERY. For well over 600 years, Rome was the dominant power at the western end of the Eurasian land mass. The Roman economy, in particular, the economy of the Italian peninsula, was probably more dependent on slavery than any previous society. Slavery clearly existed in Rome from its earliest days, the fourth to sixth centuries BCE, when Rome was a small city-state. As Roman armies spread Rome's control over Italy and then over the Mediterranean, the Middle East, and Western Europe, they took large numbers of prisoners. The Roman word for slave, *servus*, came from the word *servare*, to spare, because the Roman slave was originally a captive whose life had been spared. At the peak of Roman power, at the beginning of the Common Era, there were about two million slaves on the Italian peninsula, about a third of the population. Slaves were common, but not as numerous elsewhere in the empire.

By the third century BCE, the Roman Republic controlled most of the Italian peninsula. In the two centuries that followed, Rome defeated Carthage, absorbed the Hellenistic states of the eastern Mediterranean, and moved into Gaul (France). Many of the slaves taken prisoner in these wars were put to work on farms near Rome. Those who profited from conquest bought land and created estates called *latifundia*, which were worked by slave labor. The rich and powerful accumulated land as a land market emerged. Male peasants were conscripted into the army and often unable to work their lands. Others were pushed off their lands and forced to seek out military careers. Many soldiers were rewarded by the grant of land in distant parts of the empire. There was thus a process in which war captives poured into Italy while Roman peasants headed out to the provinces. During the second century BCE, this process was taking place so rapidly that it was difficult to assimilate all of the slaves. There was a series of major slave revolts, of which the largest was led by **Spartacus**.

The Roman family was strongly patriarchal. The head of the family, the *paterfamilias*, had a control over both slaves and children that included the right to put either to death. Slaves did not marry, but they could enter a *contubernium*, a relationship in which two persons lived together, but had none of the rights that marriage conferred on citizens. The master could sell any slave, even those in *contubernium*. Manumission was widespread, and the freed slave had the right to citizenship. The freed person remained a client of his master until death. Some slaves received a *peculium*, a sum of money that enabled them to conduct a business, and if successful, were able to purchase their freedom. Others were granted it for services to master or state.

Slaves did a wide variety of tasks. On the *latifundia*, slaves did most of the hard labor, but some were farm managers and many worked independently as tenant farmers. Many also lived in the city where rich Romans often had many slave servants, where there were numerous slave artisans, and where slaves were almost all of the workers in industrial establishments like brickworks. Perhaps the harshest form of slavery was in the mines. The movement of slaves into Italy declined towards the end of the first century CE as wars of conquest became more rare. After this, most slaves were born to slavery, though there were always some kidnapped or enslaved as a result of criminal penalties. By the third century, most rural workers were free. The transition from Roman slavery to medieval serfdom had begun. The recovery of Roman law during the late Middle Ages had a great influence on the status of modern slaves, particularly in the Spanish Empire. *See also* HISPANIC AMERICA; LAW OF SLAVERY; MEDIEVAL EUROPE; *SIETE PARTIDAS.*

ANGOSTURA, CONGRESS OF (1819). For much of 1819, nationalist delegates from northern South America debated what kind of government they wanted to create in what had been the Viceroyalty of New Granada (Colombia, Venezuela, and Ecuador). One of the major issues before the Congress was the role of slavery. Slaves were being freed by both the royalist and patriot armies, and even where not formally freed, they were taking advantage of the disorder to free themselves. **Simón Bolívar,** the leader of the patriot forces, advocated total abolition, but slave owners were also a powerful force. Though the population of New Granada was less than 5 percent slave, slave ownership was concentrated in several productive areas and slave owners were wealthy and influential. The result was a compromise. The status of slaves already freed was confirmed. There were to be no further slave imports and the rest were to be freed within a fixed period of time. None of these decisions, however, was binding on the governments that were later established. *See also* CUCUTÁ, CONGRESS OF; EMANCIPATION, HISPANIC AMERICA.

ANTI-SLAVERY INTERNATIONAL (ASI). This is the modern name of an organization which was formed in 1909 as a result of the merger of two of the oldest humanitarian organizations in the world. The Aborigines Protection Society was formed in 1838 to protect aboriginal peoples from exploitation and mistreatment and the **British and Foreign Anti-Slavery Society** was formed in 1839, six years after Great Britain abolished the **slave trade,** to carry on the struggle against slavery and the slave trade wherever it existed. It also sought to protect the rights of slaves who had recently been freed. To achieve its goals, the Anti-Slavery Society held a series of international anti-slavery conventions during the 1840s. It pushed for abolition in India, supported the struggle of American abolitionists, and attacked toleration of slavery in the colonies. Its officials corresponded with missionaries and colonial officials in distant parts of the world and publicized the continued existence of slavery. After the 1909 merger, one of the first issues for the new organization involved a disguised slave trade that supplied Portuguese colonies with labor. After World War I, under the leadership of **John Harris**, the organization was important in persuading the **League of Nations** to investigate the continued existence of slavery in several parts of the world, including colonies of European countries. Since World War II, it has been active in publicizing child labor, bonded labor, child prostitution, and other modern forms of servitude. To this end, it publishes studies, holds meetings, and makes presentations to the **United Nations**. *See also* CONTEMPORARY FORMS OF SLAVERY; STURGE, JOSEPH.

APPRENTICESHIP. This term was used for a transitional status between slavery and freedom in both British and American emancipation legislation. Under the British **Emancipation Act**, apprenticeship was conceived as a period of training for freedom, though it did not work out that way and was abruptly ended in 1838. In the United States, the term was used in **Black Codes** passed by southern states after the **Civil War**. Apprenticeship merely re-created many of the conditions of slavery and was a device to maintain control over the freed slaves. It was quickly prohibited by the **Civil Rights Act of 1866** and then by the **Fourteenth Amendment** to the United States Constitution.

ARISTOTLE (384-322 B.C.). Aristotle was one of the most influential of the founders of modern philosophy. The importance of slavery to ancient Greece forced him to ask a number of basic questions: What was the distinction between slave and free? Was slavery natural? Why were some men slaves? In his *Politics,* he defined slavery as property: "A slave by nature is an individual who, being a man, is by his nature not his own, but belongs to another . . . he is a thing possessed." He thus also assumed that there was something natural in some persons being slaves and others being masters. The master had intelligence, foresight, and the ability to plan and organize. The slave provided only brute force. He argued that slaves and masters needed each other and that some people are naturally suited to be slaves. By giving responsibility to the abler person, slavery was in the interest of both master and slave, was morally justifiable and in the interests of the larger society. He feared only that the slave's servility would influence the master's children and urged masters to teach their slaves virtue. His ideas were later used by many pro-slavery thinkers to defend slavery. *See also* ANCIENT GREEK SLAVERY.

ARO. Slave traders in what is now southern Nigeria. *See also* BIGHT OF BIAFRA.

ASANTE. The Asante kingdom was one of a series of African states that arose after the introduction of sugar plantations to the West Indies increased the demand for slaves in the late 17th century. The Gold Coast (now Ghana) had hitherto been primarily an exporter of gold, and for many years actually imported slaves to work in the gold mines. With the introduction of guns and higher prices for slaves, there was a struggle for control of the hinterland. With its victory over rival Denkyera in 1702, Asante established itself as the dominant power of the Gold Coast.

     Enslavement in southern Ghana was a result of debt, war, or kidnapping, but with Asante's success most came from war or as tribute from conquered states in northern Ghana. Those kept within Asante were better off than those sold into the Atlantic trade. Asante slavery provided for progressive integration into Asante society. The children of the original captives were more integrated, and with the third generation their descendants were free. Such was Asante's power that the core area of the kingdom was one of the safest places in West Africa. Most of the slaves who came to Asante as captives or as tribute were sold into the Atlantic trade. Slaves from southern Ghana were known as Coromantee and seen in the Americas as inclined to be rebellious. *See also* AFRICAN SLAVERY; AFRICAN SLAVE TRADE; ATLANTIC SLAVE TRADE.

ASIENTO. The *asiento* was an exclusive contract to provide slaves for the Spanish colonies. The system originated because Portugal controlled trade with the West African coast, the source of all slave imports in the 16th century. As the Amerindian population declined in the 16th century, Spain granted licenses to foreign merchants to supply the labor no longer available in the Americas. In 1595, Spain set up the *asiento* system, under which a single contractor received an exclusive contract. The contractor then dealt with subcontractors, who provided the slaves. The *asiento* was essential to the development of a **plantation** economy in parts of Spanish America. The Portuguese, then being ruled by the Spanish king, held the *asiento* until 1640. In the subsequent century and a half, with Spain weak and the demand for slave labor in the Spanish colonies increasing, the *asiento* was a major issue in a number of wars. It was held for long periods by the Dutch, Portuguese, French, and

English. Over 900,000 slaves were brought to the Americas by the *asiento* system. In 1789, the Spanish abolished the system. *See also* HISPANIC AMERICA.

ASSYRIA. *See* ANCIENT MIDDLE EASTERN SLAVERY.

ATLANTIC SLAVE TRADE. The Atlantic slave trade was the largest forced movement of people in history. The 15th-century sea captains who sailed south in the service of Portugal were not primarily interested in the slave trade, but for many of them taking captives from coastal communities and selling them was a source of profit for their voyages. There was a market for these slaves in Portugal, in the Mediterranean, and on the Atlantic islands that were colonized during this period. It was justified by the fact that most of the victims during the 15th century were Muslims and therefore assumed to be enemies of Christianity.

Two things led to a dramatic increase in this market. The first was the precipitous drop in population in the Americas as native peoples were exposed to the diseases Europeans brought with them. This meant that European settlers in the Americas faced an increasing shortage of labor. The second factor was the extension of **sugar** cultivation, which demanded a heavy input of unpleasant manual labor not readily provided by free persons. Sugar cultivation was developed on Atlantic islands like Madeira and **São Tomé** and then in Brazil, which was the world's leading sugar producer by the end of the 16th century. In the 17th century, sugar was introduced to the West Indies, sending the demand for slaves shooting up.

Europeans soon found that purchasing slaves was more efficient than trying to capture them. African coastal societies first responded to European demand by making war, but gradually became middlemen as the demand for slaves pushed the slave trade deeper and deeper into the interior. In response to the demand, powerful political systems emerged that were capable of supplying the demand. Europeans also enslaved native Americans. Europeans did not enslave other Europeans, though some of the labor needs of the Americas were met by indentured laborers who contracted for a fixed number of years of labor in exchange for transportation across the Atlantic. This proved inadequate, in part because the labor demanded in the Americas was very onerous, in part because Europeans had a much higher mortality rate than Africans. Also, during the 17th century, rising wages in Europe convinced many poor people that they were better off at home.

The trade was dominated in the earliest centuries by the Portuguese. By the early 17th century, Dutch, British, and French trading companies were taking over the market. Much of the northern European trade was controlled by chartered companies, but from an early date it was attractive to interlopers, who could make large profits. There were, however, great risks. An epidemic, a slave revolt, or calm seas could wipe out profits. Wars exposed slavers to the attacks of privateers and enemy warships. As a result, there was a tendency to spread the risk. In port cities like Bristol, Liverpool, and Nantes that were major centers of the trade, each venture usually involved large numbers of investors. Insurance also provided some protection for the entrepreneurs of the trade. Press gang methods were often used to produce a crew because service in a slave ship involved personal risk and was not popular with sailors.

The increasing demand for slaves led to a steady increase in slave prices. As ship construction improved, the length of the voyage was reduced, which brought down the cost of shipping. At the same time, the organization of slaving and slave trading improved and there was a steady increase in the number of people traded. In the early years of the Atlantic trade, the number of slaves exported from Africa rarely went over a thousand a year. In the 16th century, about 250,000 slaves were carried across the Atlantic. In the 18th century, that number rose to over 6 million. In all, about 12 million slaves were shipped from Africa and almost 10.5 million are known to have landed in the Americas. About 12 percent of the slaves died on the voyage.

Most of the immigrants to the Americas during the period before 1800 were involuntary immigrants who came from Africa in slave ships. Ninety percent of the women who crossed the Atlantic were slaves and 80 percent of the children. *See also* AFRICAN SLAVE TRADE; BRAZILIAN SLAVERY; DUTCH SLAVE TRADE; MIDDLE PASSAGE; PLANTATION; ROYAL AFRICA COMPANY.

ATTUCKS, CRISPUS (c. 1723-1770). Not much is known about Crispus Attucks except that he was the first American to die in the events that led up to the **American Revolution**. He was the slave of a Protestant deacon from Framingham, Massachusetts, but he ran away in 1750 and worked for years on whaling ships. On 5 March 1770, he seems to have been one of the leaders of a group of men who taunted British soldiers guarding the customshouse and pelted them with snow and ice. When the British fired on the demonstrators, five persons were killed. The first to be shot was Attucks.

AZTECS. *See* AMERINDIAN SLAVERY.

-B-

BABYLON. *See* ANCIENT MIDDLE EASTERN SLAVERY.

BAHIAN SLAVE REVOLTS. Bahia was a province in the northeastern part of Brazil which was a major **sugar** producer. From the 1780s to the 1820s, dramatic growth in sugar production led to large imports of slaves, of whom the majority were **Yoruba** from western Nigeria. From 1807 to 1835, there were several slave revolts. This was also a period of political ferment among the free population, a ferment in which slaves participated. Many of the slave revolts seem to have been spontaneous events on single plantations, but many were also large scale. Some were based on *quilombos*, Maroon settlements which proliferated in the hinterland and sometimes in areas quite close to the capital, Salvador. Many of these *quilombos* were centers of African religions like *candomblé*.

A rising was planned during Corpus Christi celebrations in 1807, but a loyal slave betrayed the plot to his master. It was led largely by Muslim Hausa from northern Nigeria and was planned to take place in different parts of the city. The leading plotters were arrested and two were executed. In 1809, 300 residents of a *quilombo* attacked a hinterland town in search of arms, ammunition and food, but were eventually dispersed by troops, who arrested 83 men and 12 women. In 1814, a band of slaves gathered at a *quilombo* and attacked a boat marina. In 1816, slaves in two hinterland towns burned several plantations, killed Whites and loyal slaves, and rampaged for four days before being defeated. Revolts also took place in 1822, 1824, and one or more every year thereafter until 1830. Most of them were rural and many were highly localized, but they led to increasing security precautions in both city and countryside.

The biggest revolt was the **Male revolt** of 1835. Recent slave imports contained numerous Muslims, who were called Males in Bahia. The leaders were mixed Hausa and Yoruba Muslims, some slave and some free. The Muslims knew each other, regularly gathered for prayer, were literate, ran schools, and produced the white garments and skull caps worn during festive occasions. This gave them important organizational skills. They were often respected by other slaves and former slaves. Once again, the revolt was planned for a Catholic feast day, when the Males assumed that the vigilance of the masters would be lax. It was supposed to begin early Sunday morning, but a loyal former slave heard rumors of the plot and informed the authorities. The efforts of the authorities to squelch the revolt led to an early eruption of fighting, which took place in the streets, at the prison, and at one of the barracks. The rebels tried to get out of the city to avoid a siege but were not successful. More than 70 people died in the fighting.

After defeating the rebels, police searched homes of both slave and free blacks throughout Salvador. Whenever they found evidence of Arabic writing or the white robes worn by Muslims, the owner was arrested. They also arrested people who could not adequately explain themselves. Some 231 persons were tried. Only four are known to have been executed, but most of the rest were imprisoned, deported, or flogged. The revolt led to more rigid controls on the slaves. Slaves found outside after 8 P.M. needed a pass from their masters. Another edict made possible the deportation of freed slaves to Africa and facilitated the growth of the **Afro-Brazilian** community there. Other laws tried to repress African street vendors and imposed controls over work. *See also* BRAZILIAN SLAVERY; MAROONS.

BALAIADA REVOLT (1838-1841). Maranhao is a province in northern Brazil that specialized in raising cattle and growing **cotton** during the early 19th century. More than half the population was slaves, concentrated largely in the cotton-growing areas. The revolt began when a group led by Raimundo Gomes attacked the prison in Vila da Manga to free the brother of Gomes. They then marched through the province attracting supporters. It took its name from the fact that one of its leaders was a maker of baskets, *balaio.*

In the disruption, Cosme, a fugitive slave, amassed an army of 3,000 runaway slaves. The slaves became the bulk of the movement. In August 1839, they took Caixas, the second largest city in the state, started to establish an administration, and offered to negotiate an armistice. The government did not negotiate and in 1841 recaptured Caixas. The slaves were returned to their masters, most of the others were given an amnesty, but Cosme was hung. The revolt was one of the longest slave revolts in Brazilian history. *See also* BRAZILIAN SLAVERY.

BALL, CHARLES (1780-?). Charles Ball was born a slave in **tobacco**

country of eastern Maryland. Soon after getting married, he was sold to a **cotton** plantation in South Carolina, and from there was taken to Georgia. The first time he ran away was to return to Maryland, where he married again and worked a small farm. He was eventually recaptured and returned to Georgia. The second time he escaped, he stowed away on ship from Savannah to Philadelphia. There, he was not able to contact his wife and children, who had been sold into slavery. His story was dictated to a white lawyer and published anonymously as *The Life and Adventures of a Fugitive Slave* (1836). A year later, it came out as *Slavery in the United States: The Life and Adventures of Charles Ball.* It was valuable in presenting both a picture of life on a slave plantation and the differences in the styles of slave masters. It also depicts the importance of African culture in slave life. Ball's grandfather was African born and told him a great deal about his origins. While a slave in South Carolina, he witnessed rituals from both Islam and African religions. After publication of his book, he faded into obscurity, perhaps fearing to be enslaved once again. *See also* AMERICAN SLAVERY.

BANAMBA. Banamba was a major slave market town in western Mali, where events began that shattered slave systems in much of French West Africa. Much of the slaving that took place during the late 19th century took place in the southern part of the savannah lands that stretched across the continent. Slaves were moved north to Banamba and traded for horses, weapons, and industrial goods. From Banamba, there were trade routes going down to Senegambia, where peanuts were being grown for export, and to the desert-edge cities, both good markets for slaves. Surrounding Banamba was also a 30-mile-wide belt of slave-worked plantations. Banamba was founded only in the 1840s, so most of the slaves had been recently enslaved and remembered earlier homes. Furthermore, Banamba was in a region where slave-holding was widespread, often over 50 percent of the population.

In 1905, when the slaves began to leave their masters, the masters tried to use force to keep them there. The French arbitrated the differences, but a year later the slaves started to go again. This time the governor, **William Ponty**, told the local authorities to let the slaves go. He was only to insist that they had passes. As they trooped back to earlier homes or moved to places where they could find work, they told other slaves what had happened and slaves began leaving those communities. The French were at this time applying the "Indian formula" for emancipation, in which the state simply withdrew its support of the masters. At the time the Banamba exodus began, there were probably between 3 and 3.5 million slaves in French West Africa. The number who left their masters between 1905 and 1913 was probably over a million. *See also* EMANCIPATION, AFRICA; EMANCIPATION, INDIA.

BANDEIRANTES. The *bandeirantes* were Brazilian frontiersmen based in São Paulo who pushed the Brazilian frontier south and west during the 16th and 17th centuries. During this period, the wealthiest part of Brazil was the northeast, which produced **sugar**. São Paulo developed as a frontier base that provided **Amerindian** slaves for the plantations. *Bandeirante* expeditions involved anywhere from 15 to several thousand men together with their families and dependents. Their horses and guns generally gave them military advantages over the poorly armed Amerindians. They lived off the land and often were away from São Paulo for as long as two years. Eventually, they reached the Jesuit mission settlements among the Guarani of Paraguay. The resulting raids destroyed the settlements and enslaved many of the Guarani. The *bandeirantes* also explored, prospected for precious stones and metals and hunted down runaway slaves for planters who hired their services. They also served as a military force in attacking **Maroon** settlements. *See also* BRAZILIAN SLAVERY; PALMARES; SLAVECATCHING.

BAPTISTS. The Baptists were a small evangelical dissenting Christian sect that expanded dramatically in the 18th and early 19th century. The stress on personal conversion, evangelistic preaching, and a more active worship style were popular in the United States. By 1830, they were the most important religious denomination in the United States. They played a major role in converting slaves and free Blacks to Christianity, and in the process, absorbed into American Christian practice many aspects of African religion: exhorting, giving testimony, singing, and in general, a more accessible and emotional type of religion. Black preachers, many of the slaves, developed an intense, emotional. and eloquent preaching style that shaped African-American religion.

Lacking any central government structure, however, the Baptists were soon deeply divided on the question of slavery. In the Northeast and Midwest, many Baptists were strongly anti-slavery. In 1840, they gathered in the American Baptist Anti-Slavery Convention. The national Baptist leadership tried to maintain a neutral position on slavery, but in 1844 the Board of Foreign Missions decided that it could

no longer appoint slave-holding missionaries. This offended Southerners. The Baptist movement split in 1845 into northern and southern
wings. The Southern Baptist Convention, formed in that year, was a
stronger supporter of slavery and during the **Civil War** identified
strongly with the Confederate cause. This was in spite of the fact that
about a quarter of its congregations were Black. *See also* CHRISTIAN-
ITY.

BARBADOS. Barbados was the island where the West Indian slave-sugar
complex first developed. The first British settlers, who arrived in 1627,
grew **tobacco**, indigo, and **cotton**. Most of their laborers were white
indentured workers from Great Britain. In the 1640s, the Dutch
introduced **sugar**, provided credit, and supplied the technology. The
struggle between the Dutch and Portuguese for control of Brazil led to
high prices during this period. Within a short period of time, Barbados
had shifted into sugar and the small farms of the earlier period were
replaced by large estates, which were more efficient for growing
sugarcane. Tales of the harsh work and the high mortality made it
difficult to recruit indentured labor. By 1670, Barbados was a densely
populated island with 70,000 inhabitants, three-quarters of them
African slaves. It was also a relatively flat island, which made slave
flight and resistance difficult. Though a small island — only 166 square
miles — Barbados was at the time the wealthiest and most important
British colony in the Americas. As the first of the sugar islands, it also
was the first where the population reached a normal balance between
men and women. *See also* CARIBBEAN SLAVERY; DUTCH SLAVE
TRADE; PLANTATION.

BARBARY WARS. The Barbary Wars were efforts by the United States
to force the Muslim states of North Africa to stop seizing American
ships. The background to these wars was centuries of raiding and state-
sanctioned piracy in the Mediterranean, in which Christians seized
Muslims and Muslims seized Christians. If not ransomed, the victims
were enslaved. In 1785, encouraged by Britain, Algiers seized two
American merchant ships, and then again in 1793 a dozen more. In
order to free the crews who were held in captivity, the United States
agreed to pay tribute. In 1801, Tripoli again seized several American
merchant ships. The Americans responded by blockading Tripoli from
1803. In 1805, a treaty ended tribute payments, though the Americans
paid a ransom for the crew of a ship captured after it ran aground.

Finally, during the War of 1812, Algiers took advantage of the absence of the U.S. Navy to seize several merchant ships. A naval squadron under Stephen Decatur seized the Algerian flagship and eventually forced a settlement that included suppression of tribute payments, restoration of American property, and the emancipation of Christian slaves. Tunis and Tripoli soon agreed to similar terms. *See also* REDEMPTIONIST ORDERS.

BARRACOON. The word barracoon refers to buildings in which slaves were held while awaiting sale and export in the **Atlantic slave trade**. The term originally applied to barracks in which slaves were held on Spanish plantations. Barracoons became necessary in the 19th century when the patrols of British Royal Navy **African Squadron** made it necessary to gather slaves in one place so that slavers could transact their business and get back on the high seas quickly. The British navy often burned barracoons. Slaves were also sometimes gathered in fortified locations like the castles of the Gold Coast, but often too they were dispersed in villages near the point of trade so that they could be put to work while awaiting sale. *See also* AFRICAN SLAVE TRADE.

BAXTER, RICHARD (1615-1691). Richard Baxter was a largely self-educated English theologian and an early critic of slavery. He was the author of over 100 books, mostly popular Christian works stressing the importance of faith and piety. Baxter supported Parliament in English Civil War, but opposed the execution of King Charles I. He wrote two books in which he discussed slavery: *A Christian Directory* (1655) and *Chapters from a Christian Directory, or a Summ of Practical Theology and Cases of Conscience* (1673). He accepted the legitimacy of enslavement of war captives or criminals, but he condemned the violence of the slave trade and the cruelty of slave masters in the West Indies. Baxter saw their behavior as unchristian greed and covetousness. He urged slave masters to bring their slaves to Christians and recommended obedience to the slaves.

BEECROFT, JOHN (1790-1854). The first British Consul to the Bights of Benin and **Biafra** (1849-1854), Beecroft was an important figure in the struggles to end slavery and to establish British influence on what had been the **Slave Coast** of West Africa. He first arrived in West Africa as the director of the department of works on the island of Fernando Po, which was then a base for British naval operations. In

1834, he went to work for a **Liverpool** palm oil merchant. In that capacity, he explored the Niger and Cross Rivers, published a number of articles about his explorations, and opened commercial relations with many African chiefs. Because of his influence and his knowledge, he often accompanied navy officers when they tried to negotiate anti-slavery treaties with African rulers. As consul, he pursued an active interventionist policy in trying to persuade African rulers to give up the **slave trade**. He was never reluctant to back up his diplomacy with the guns of the Royal Navy's **African Squadron**. During his short term as Consul, he was the most powerful figure in the Bights. He is best known for the occupation of Lagos in 1851 and for the deposition of Jack Anna Pepple, a powerful slave-trading chief in the Bight of Biafra. *See also* AFRICAN SLAVE TRADE; EMANCIPATION, AFRICA.

BELLA. Freed slave clients of Tuareg of Sahara. *See also* HARATIN.

BELLON DE SAINT-QUENTIN, JEAN (?-1764). Jean Bellon was an influential French theologian and a major opponent of **Enlightenment** ideas on slavery. He was the editor of a four-volume work on the history of superstition and the author of *Dissertation sur la traite et le commerce des nègres* (Dissertation on the Slave Trade) (1764). In this, he argued that slavery was divinely ordained and that while slave and free were one before Jesus, some were destined to serve and others to be served. Bellon claimed that harsh treatment was rare and suggested that without slave laborers Europeans would not be able to survive in the tropics. He also included three letters to a trader who was concerned about the moral legitimacy of buying and selling slaves.

BERBICE SLAVE REVOLT (1763-1764). Berbice was a Dutch sugar-growing colony in what is now Guyana. After an epidemic of yellow fever killed many white settlers, the slaves rose in revolt in 1763 under leaders named Kofi and Akara. The major causes of the revolt were harsh treatment and cruel punishments. Many whites were killed, plantations were sacked, and their houses were set on fire. By late March, the slave rebels controlled most of the colony, but they were not able to take the island's largest fort. Eventually, reinforcements arrived and aided by conflict within rebel ranks were able to reestablish control over the colony. About 60 percent of the whites died during the rebellion and almost 40 percent of the slaves. Of the rebels, 128 were executed in various cruel ways designed to dissuade the slaves from further revolts. *See also* CARIBBEAN SLAVERY; DUTCH SLAVE TRADE.

BERLIN CONFERENCE (1884-1885). At the Berlin Conference, which was convened in November 1884, the major European powers agreed to ground rules for the partition of Africa. The Berlin Act was signed on 26 February 1885. Concerned to justify their presence in Africa, the powers committed themselves to the protection of the "material and moral well-being" of their African subjects "and to help in suppressing slavery, especially the Slave Trade." The act prohibited the **slave trade**, but since it made no provisions for enforcement, it had no effect on the continuation of slaving and raiding. In fact, the decade that followed was one of the bloodiest in African history. Most of Africa was yet to be conquered. Colonial armies were often allied to slave-owning chiefs who they did not want to alienate. In most parts of Africa, serious attempts to end the slave trade and limit slavery came only after the conquest was completed. *See also* BRUSSELS CONFERENCE; EMANCIPATION, AFRICA.

BIAFRA, BIGHT OF. The Bight of Biafra was the stretch of coast from the Niger Delta to the Cameroons. The Biafran hinterland was one of the most densely populated areas of Africa, but it was inhabited by people who lived in very decentralized societies with relatively few slaves. The largest group was the Igbo. There were no centralized slave-raiding kingdoms in the area. The area had high rainfall. The many mouths of the Niger and other rivers that flowed toward the coast facilitated trade, but until well into the 17th century that trade was largely in salt and fish produced by people who lived in the delta and marketed by merchants who worked the creeks in large dugout canoes. The first European traders to reach the area were generally not able to buy many slaves.

That situation began to change in the 17th century, with a group of people called the Aro, who formed around an oracle called Arochukwu. Some slaves were provided by people who brought conflicts to the oracle, but more important the Aro began spreading out and forming colonies throughout the Igbo and Ibibio areas. They allied themselves with village leaders. Previously, people enslaved in local conflicts would either be ransomed or incorporated by the victors. Now, they were exchanged for trade goods which the Aro introduced. Agreements with local communities made it possible for Aro to move these slaves to the coast.

On the coast, slaves supplemented the trade in salt and fish for Ijaw and Efik communities. Coastal traders absorbed many slaves as wives or as canoe men. This enabled them to send trading expeditions into the markets of the interior where they traded with the Aro and other interior peoples. The coastal trade was in the hands of organizations called canoe houses, which sent large armed canoes to trade in the market of the interior. The merging of these two commercial systems led to a dramatic increase in the export of slaves from the Bight of Biafra. In the 16th century, an average of 200 a year were sold to European ship captains. That number increased to 2,500 a year in the late 17th century, to over 6,000 a year in the 1730s, and then to over 22,000 a year in the 1780s. *See also* AFRICAN SLAVERY; ATLANTIC SLAVE TRADE; JA JA.

BIBB, HENRY (1815-1854). The son of a Kentucky white planter and a slave woman, Henry Bibb was a slave who was sold six times before he reached the age of 25. In 1833, he married another slave, Malinda, and had a daughter with her. He first escaped in 1837. He returned to Kentucky a year later to try to get his wife and daughter out, and was captured. He escaped and was captured again when he returned once more to get his wife and daughter. This time, all three of them were then sold down river. He worked for a harsh slave owner in Louisiana and then was sold to two professional gamblers who took him to Oklahoma, where he was sold to a Cherokee. When his Cherokee master died, he escaped once again, crossing the slave state of Missouri, and eventually making it to Ohio, where he became involved with the abolition movement. He once again sought information about his wife, but when he found out that she had become the lover of a white man, he married again, this time to Mary Miles, a black abolitionist. In 1849, he published *A Narrative of Life and Adventures of Henry Bibb, An African Slave*. After passage of the **Fugitive Slave Law** in 1850, Bibb and his wife moved to Canada, where they published a biweekly, *Voice of the Fugitive*. They reported news of Canada, encouraged African-Americans to come there, and also encouraged education and commercial enterprise. They were strong exponents of African-American self-sufficiency. *See also* ABOLITION, UNITED STATES.

BIBLE. Slavery plays a very important part in the biblical version of the history of the Hebrew people. Abraham, the first of the patriarchs, had children by both his wife and a slave concubine. His great-grandson, Joseph, was sold into slavery in Egypt by his brothers. In Egypt, Joseph rose eventually to become one of the pharoah's most powerful officials. When a famine struck, the brothers who sold him took refuge in Egypt, where Joseph helped them. At a later date, the Hebrews were reduced to slavery. Eventually, Moses led them from slavery, and after 40 years of wandering in the desert, they found their promised home in the Land of Canaan. The Exodus from slavery in Egypt is the founding event of the Hebrew people. It is still celebrated every year by Jews in the festival of Passover. Oppressed Christians have also seen in the story of the Exodus the promise of liberation. An example is the moving African-American spiritual, "Go Down, Moses."

The Bible also contained a law code. The laws dealing with slavery are found in different places and can be read in different ways. A Hebrew could only become a slave to another Hebrew as punishment for theft or as a result of self-sale because of poverty. The enslavement of a fellow Hebrew was temporary. They were to be freed after six years' service. Gentiles could be enslaved as a result of capture in war, self-enslavement, or punishment for theft. They were slaves in perpetuity, and their children were slaves, but biblical rules sought to protect them from mistreatment. For example, a slave concubine was to be treated as a wife and a slave injured by his master was to be freed. Biblical law also commanded that a slave fleeing a foreign master be allowed to settle where he wished. The Bible also repeatedly counsels humane treatment of slaves.

If slavery was important to the world of Moses, it was even more so when Jesus lived. There is no evidence that Jesus ever condemned slavery. In the Epistles, Christian slaves are offered equality before the eyes of God, but are urged to be obedient to their masters in this life. In later centuries, this was stressed by defenders of slavery. Abolitionists had difficulty with the Bible. Both Old and New Testaments described slave-owning worlds. They often appealed to the spirit of the Bible rather than the substance. *See also* ANCIENT MIDDLE EASTERN SLAVERY; CHRISTIANITY; JEWS; SAINT PAUL.

BIRNEY, JAMES G. (1792-1857). Born in Kentucky, James Birney was the most important Southern abolitionist. He graduated from the College of New Jersey (Princeton) in 1810 and briefly practiced law in Philadelphia and Lexington, Kentucky. In 1818, he bought a **cotton** plantation in Alabama, but financial problems forced him to sell it and the slaves he owned. In the 1820s, he became active, first, in the temperance movement, and then in the **American Colonization Society**. In 1832, he became a travelling agent of the society seeking funds and recruiting free Blacks interested in resettlement in Liberia. Within a few years, he became convinced that the society was a racist organization and that the result of its activities would be the denial to African-Americans of their place in American life. By the late 1830s, he was advocating the emancipation of all slaves. Attacked by Southerners, he moved to the North, where he worked to recruit supporters to anti-slavery. He edited the *Philanthropist,* an anti-slavery newspaper, and in 1840 and 1844, ran for president as the candidate of the **Liberty Party**. *See also* ABOLITION, UNITED STATES.

BLACKBIRDING. When European ships began exploring the Pacific in the 16th century, they often kidnapped island people to replace lost crewmen on their ships. This was called blackbirding. Even after it became possible to recruit seamen in Tahiti, New Zealand, and Hawaii from the late 18th century, some kidnapping continued to take place to provide crew for the whaling and sealing ships that worked the Pacific, and sometimes women to satisfy the sexual desires of crew men. By the 1840s, a fifth of the crew on American whalers was made up of Hawaiians. The mortality rate among these workers was very high, largely because they had no resistance to European diseases. During the 19th century, European settlement increased the demand for labor, first for the cutting of sandalwood and then for **sugar** and copra plantations. That labor was found by both fair and foul means.

The   worst excesses took place during the years 1862 and 1863, when a shortage of labor in Peru led to Peruvian slave raiders bringing over 3,600 slaves to Peru to work in sugar and **cotton** plantations. Only 148 lived long enough to be returned to their homes. International moral outrage led to the system being suppressed by the Peruvian government less than a year after it began. Other laborers were recruited by indentured labor contracts. From the 1870s, efforts first by Great Britain and Australia and then by other colonial powers led to the reduction of abuses. British ships patrolled the islands and recruiters had to give evidence that recruits had freely agreed to labor contracts. After 1900, labor recruitment was largely from the more densely populated countries of the Asian mainland. *See also* PACIFIC ISLANDS SLAVERY.

BLACK CARIBS. When Columbus arrived in the West Indies in 1492, many islands were inhabited by an **Amerindian** people known as the Caribs. Though some were enslaved and others died from European diseases, the Caribs persisted on many of the less developed islands and vigorously resisted European conquest. From time to time, they raided European plantations, carrying off slaves, who were usually assimilated into their community. Though European regimes often tried to co-opt them into catching runaways, the Caribs also absorbed many of the runaways. The result was a population of mixed African and Carib extraction. In the 1790s, the British deported many of them to an island off the coast of Honduras, from which they spread to the coast of Central America. In the 19th century, there were almost 100 communities strung out along the Atlantic coast of Central America. *See also* CARIBBEAN SLAVERY.

BLACK CODES. After the **Civil War**, Congress moved quickly to pass the **Thirteenth Amendment** which freed those slaves who had not already been freed. Many southern states responded by passing the Black Codes, laws that tried to reassert control over the former slaves and put them back under the control of their former masters. These codes, which varied from state to state, limited the jobs the freed persons could hold, prohibited their owning weapons, and forced them to live in rural areas. Many of them forced freed persons into an "**apprenticeship**" which closely mirrored the conditions of slavery. Freed slaves sentenced for various crimes, often on trumped up charges, were forced to labor for planters. Mississippi even denied them the right to own land.

Disturbed by both the Black Codes and the election of Confederate officers to public office, Congress saw black voters as the basis of a Republican majority in the South. It thus passed first the **Civil Rights Act of 1866**, which guaranteed the rights of the freed persons, then the Reconstruction Acts of 1867, which forced President Andrew Johnson to send federal troops back into the South to organize elections in which freed men would have the right to vote, and finally the **Fourteenth Amendment** in 1868, which defined citizenship and the rights of the freed persons. *See also* RECONSTRUCTION.

BLACK LOYALISTS. During the **American Revolution**, freedom was offered by British commanders to slaves who served the British. They were called the Black Loyalists. There may have been as many as 100,000. Many were workers, but several black regiments were formed. When the war ended, the British evacuated those who wanted to leave. Some were betrayed and returned to slavery, but others went to Great Britain or to Kingston, Jamaica. The largest group went to Nova Scotia in Canada. There, they had to face a cold wet climate and the hostility of many whites, including white Loyalists, who were often slave owners. Inadequate land grants and an unresponsive government magnified their problems. Many were therefore ready to move again, when the opportunity arose to return to Africa and settle in **Sierra Leone**. There too, the first years were harsh and mortality was high. Both in Nova Scotia and Sierra Leone, the Black Loyalists survived and established new and important communities.

BLANCHARD, JONATHAN (1811-1892). Jonathan Blanchard was an evangelical Protestant pastor, an educator, and an abolitionist. Born in Vermont, and a graduate of Middlebury College, he met **Theodore Weld** and left school to become a lecturer for the **American Anti-Slavery Society**. He resumed his studies at Lane Seminary, where he preached in Black churches and continued working for abolition. In 1845, he became president of Knox College in Galesburg, Illinois. In 1850, he attacked the **Fugitive Slave Law** and in 1854, he publicly debated its author, Senator Stephen Douglas. He was known throughout his career for his vehemence and his passionate commitment to abolition. *See also* ABOLITION, UNITED STATES.

BODIN, JEAN (1530-1596). Jean Bodin was a French jurist and political theorist who was one of the first important European thinkers to question the existence of slavery. In Bodin's time, much thinking about slavery reflected **Aristotle**'s notion that some men were meant by nature to be slaves. Bodin argued against this. In his *Six Books of the Commonwealth*, he argued that men of merit were often enslaved by less worthy men. He believed that slavery corrupted a society, that the master-slave relationship inevitably led to cruelty, and that the existence of slavery led to mistrust and social conflict. He also argued that many slavers violated religious law. In spite of his opposition to slavery, he was a practical man and was afraid that freeing the slaves would merely create beggars and criminals. He advocated a gradual emancipation process in which slaves would be freed after being taught a craft.

BOLÍVAR, SIMÓN (1783-1830). Simón Bolívar was the general from Venezuela who led the armies that ended Spanish rule in Colombia, Venezuela, Peru, Ecuador, and Bolivia. In the process he freed many of the area's slaves. Bolívar was born into a wealthy Venezuelan slave-owning family, but he gradually became committed to abolition. He freed his own slaves before the struggle for independence began. In 1816, on a visit to Haiti, he promised Haitian president Alexandre Pétion that in exchange for arms he would free the slaves in areas he liberated. After returning home, he realized that he needed the support of slaves, free Blacks, and mulattoes if he was to defeat the Spaniards. At the Congress of **Angostura** in 1819, Bolívar called for complete abolition. He believed that slavery could not be justified in societies that had freed themselves, but delegates chose a more gradual approach. Everywhere Bolívar's army went from 1819 to 1824, actions were taken against slavery, but the newly independent nations either followed the gradualist approach, or if they chose total abolition, reneged soon afterwards. Slavery was abolished in Colombia and Bolivia, but the abolition was later revoked. In Peru, reform consisted of regulating of slavery to free newborn children of slaves and to restrict abuses like whipping. Measures taken by the nationalist armies were, however, the beginning of the end of slavery in Hispanic America. *See also* HISPANIC AMERICA; PIAR, MANUEL; SAN MARTÍN, JOSÉ DE.

BONDED LABOR. India has since early in its history been marked by the variety of servile statuses. Debt slavery was very important in many areas. When the British East India Company decided to no longer recognize slavery in 1843, landlords increasingly began to use debt to bind landless laborers to them. Drought and crop failure often led to peasants losing their land. Once without land, they often contracted debts. They then had to work for the landlord until the debt was repaid. If not successful, the debt passed to the children of the bonded laborer. Sometimes, families remained in debt to a landlord for generations.

Some writers have suggested that bondage works in the laborer's interest because it guarantees him work, but it also assures his subservience. The landlord's control is facilitated by a lack of alternative sources of credit for the bonded laborer. Bondage has declined where alternative sources of employment exist, where there is a high level of literacy, and where the poor and landless are organized. Such a situation exists in the southern state of Kerala, but bondage persists in much of the rest of India. Since independence, various Indian governments have tried to control or destroy the institution, but only on the local level has there been limited success. In much of India, the landlords control local politics. Thus, bondage has continued into the 21st century. Similar types of debt-enforced servitude exist in other parts of the world. *See also* CONTEMPORARY FORMS OF SLAVERY; INDIAN SLAVERY; PEONAGE.

BONIFACIO DE ANDRADA E SILVA, JOSÉ (1763-1838). Bonifacio was one of the founders of modern Brazil and an early opponent of slavery. José Bonifacio was a member of an elite family who was sent to Portugal to study, and then worked within the royal bureaucracy for many years. He was very much influenced by the European **Enlightenment**. In 1819, he returned to Brazil, where he advised the Portuguese prince Dom Pedro to break away from Portugal and establish a constitutional monarchy. Dom Pedro did this in 1822, becoming Emperor Pedro I.

Bonifacio had already become a critic of slavery, which he regarded as an inefficient and immoral institution. He despised the slaveowners, whom he regarded as a barrier to economic growth. He supported immigration of free labor and used free immigrants on his own estate. In 1825, he published a treatise attacking slavery. He did not believe that human beings could be property. He wanted to replace slave labor with free labor using the latest industrial machinery. However, his attacks on slavery had little effect. Although he remained a central figure in the Brazilian government until 1835, slavery was too important in Brazil for the government to act against it. A later generation committed to abolition admired his work. *See also* ABOLITION, BRAZIL.

BORI. *Bori* is a cult in which female dancers are possessed by spirits. It seems to have originated in northern Nigeria before conversion to Islam and is an important traditional form of healing. It was particularly popular among slave women, though others often attended the dances. Though looked down on by Islam and associated with traditional religion, *bori* dances are an important form of self-expression for low status women and are common in the cities of northern Nigeria. The slave trade took *bori* across the Sahara to the cities of North Africa, where the dances are done primarily by black women of sub-Saharan origin. Here too, the dances are attended by many others. They are also heavily infused by popular forms of Islam. In east and northeast Africa, there are similar cults known as *zar* or *sar*. Slaves took *zar* cults to the Middle East. With *bori* and *zar*, as with African-American slave religion, slaves clung to and reinterpreted earlier religious beliefs, often integrating them with Christian and Muslim beliefs. *See also* SLAVE RELIGION.

BOZAL. Bozal was the Spanish and Portuguese term for recently imported

African slaves who did not yet speak Spanish or Portuguese well. It means "wild" or "savage." The *bozales* were watched carefully because they were more likely to run away or rebel than *criollos*, Creoles born in the Americas, or *ladinos,* who had learned the Spanish and Portuguese language and customs and were, therefore, better integrated into Latin-American society.

BRAZILIAN SLAVERY. After the accidental discovery of Brazil by a Portuguese navigator in 1500, the Portuguese developed a trade in dyewoods. They soon discovered that the land and climate were suitable for **sugar**. The Portuguese had difficulty recruiting local labor, so they resorted to enslaving the local **Amerindian** populations. However, the slaves died in large numbers because they had little resistance to European diseases while others retreated into the interior to escape the Portuguese.

By 1550, a regular **slave trade** from Africa had begun. From 1570, royal law limited enslavement of native people to "just wars," though some enslavement continued. São Paulo in the south became the base for slave raiders who regularly attacked native peoples. By the end of the century, African slaves outnumbered indigenous slaves though both groups worked together for many years. In the subsequent three centuries, between 3 and 4 million slaves were imported from Africa. This was about a third of the slave trade to the Americas. No American nation has been as much influenced by slavery as Brazil. For much of Brazilian history, peoples of African descent outnumbered people of European descent. By 1600, Brazil was the largest producer of sugar in the world.

The work of a slave on a sugar plantation was particularly harsh. The central figure of the Brazilian sugar plantation was the *senhor de engenho*, the "lord of the mill," who controlled a large plantation and a sugar mill. He also processed sugarcane from small farmers who owned land near his mill. The harvest took place over a period of eight or nine months. Once the cane was cut, it had to be brought to the presses as quickly as possible. This was done by men who often worked more than 18 hours a day during the harvest. The greatest danger to a tired slave was getting mangled by the presses. The sugar was then moved into the boiling room. On the plantations, men outnumbered women by three to one. In the early period, male slaves often lived in locked barracks called *senzalas*. This meant a low rate of reproduction, but planters knew they could easily buy more slaves. Slaves were also used on the cattle ranches that developed in the interior, on small food farms, as servants, and as stevedores.

In the cities, wealthy families had many slave servants, and even poor whites and mulattoes often had a slave or two. All kinds of labor was done by slaves. They were skilled workers, prostitutes, street vendors, musicians, and stevedores. In the 1690s, gold was discovered in the interior captaincy of Minas Gerais. The result was the movement of large numbers of slaves to the gold mines. Then, again, in the 19th century, slaves were moved to Rio de Janeiro and São Paulo to work on coffee farms. Newly imported African slaves were often valued for skills they brought with them, for example, animal husbandry, black-smithing, and rice cultivation.

Slave owners had virtually absolute control of their slaves. Owners could be brutal or generous. The only check on them came from the Catholic Church, which insisted on the equality of slaves before God, offered them baptism, allowed them to form their own religious fraternities, and encouraged manumission. Between 1 and 2 percent of the slaves were freed every year. Twice as many women were manumitted as men, many of them the wives, concubines, and lovers of the men who freed them. Men were a majority among both Europeans and Africans, which encouraged a great dealing of mixing. African slaves also often took Amerindian wives. Some slaves were also able to buy their freedom, particularly in the gold-mining areas.

Slaves also responded to harsh conditions of their lives by resisting. The most frequent form of resistance was flight. Some groups of **maroons** formed independent ex-slave communities called *quilombos* or *mocambos*. The most important was **Palmares**, which maintained its independence in the interior for over a century. There were also a number of revolts, particularly in the northeast during the early 19th century. They included the **Balaiada revolt** and a series of slave revolts in **Bahia**. Though most slaves became Catholics, they also preserved their own religions, of which the best known is called *candomblé*. These African religions are still important in Brazil. *See also* ABOLI-TION, BRAZIL; BANDEIRANTES; COLUMBIAN EXCHANGE; SLAVE RELIGION.

BRITISH AND FOREIGN ANTI-SLAVERY SOCIETY. The British and Foreign Anti-Slavery Society was the most important anti-slavery organization for most of the19th century. *See also* ANTI-SLAVERY INTERNATIONAL.

BROWN, HENRY (c. 1816-?). Henry Brown is famous for the way he escaped slavery. Born in Virginia, he lived happily in Richmond with his wife and three children until 1848, when they were sold and moved to North Carolina. Embittered, Brown decided to flee the South. He had a box made large enough to hold him. He then arranged for a white friend to ship it to Philadelphia. He took water with him and made small holes so that air could get into the box. After a 27-hour trip, during part of which the box was upside down, he arrived in Philadelphia. He became known as "Box" Brown and went on the abolitionist circuit talking about the evils of slavery. The white shoemaker who shipped the box north was sent to prison after he was caught shipping two more slaves the same way. His slave helper managed to escape and joined Brown on the circuit. After the **Fugitive Slave Law** was passed, an effort was made to kidnap Brown, but he fled to England, where he lectured for a while. It is not known if he ever returned to the United States. Nothing is known of him after the mid-1850s. *See also* ABOLITION, UNITED STATES.

BROWN, JOHN (1800-1859). One of the most controversial figures in the abolition movement, John Brown helped to polarize the United States in the period leading up to the **Civil War**. Brown was born in Ohio, the son of New England Congregationalists. He was a mature man with 20 children when a failed business enterprise caused him to retire to an African-American community in upstate New York in 1854. Several of his sons had moved to Kansas and were involved in the fighting between pro- and anti-slavery settlers. When his sons pleaded for weapons, Brown came himself. He was responsible for the massacre of five pro-slavery settlers, which led to months of guerilla warfare. When peace was restored to Kansas, he freed a group of 11 slaves and guided them to Canada.

Convinced that slavery was an evil and that its existence corrupted republican institutions, Brown organized a provisional government at a conference in Chatham, Ontario. When a small band under his command attacked Harper's Ferry in northern Virginia, they were speedily defeated by local militias and a band of marines. He was tried and sentenced to hang. His eloquence at his trial and his willingness to die for freedom attracted sympathy among African-Americans and anti-slavery activists. The Harper's Ferry raid helped to bring the war on by arousing southern fears and convincing many to insist on southern rights in the 1860 election. On the other hand, Union troops often marched off to war singing "John Brown's Body." *See also* ABOLITION, UNITED STATES; KANSAS-NEBRASKA ACT.

BROWN, WILLIAM WELLS (c.1814-1884). William Wells Brown was a leading African-American abolitionist, speaker and writer. He was born a slave, the son of a white father and a slave mother. He grew up in St. Louis, Missouri, where he had three different owners. He worked at different times on a farm, on river boats, in a doctor's office and in a tavern.

When his master took him to Cincinnati as his servant, he fled and chanced upon a **Quaker**, Wells Brown, who took him in when sick and nurtured him back to health. To honor his benefactor, he added Brown's name to his own. He then moved to Cleveland and later to Buffalo. His work on Lake Erie steamers enabled him to assist slaves fleeing to Canada. Although self-educated, he lectured on temperance and abolition and eventually became a doctor. In 1847, he published *Narrative of William W. Brown, a Fugitive Slave.* A year later, he represented the American Peace Society at a peace congress in Paris, and then stayed in Europe to lecture. When the **Fugitive Slave Law** was passed, he remained until English abolitionists purchased his freedom. Through all this he kept writing: a travel book, *Three Years in Europe* (1852), a novel, *Clotel* (1853), a play, and four books on African-American history. During the Civil War, he recruited for the Union army. His last book, *My Southern Home* (1880), was about travels through the South after the **Civil War**. *See also* ABOLITION, UNITED STATES.

BRUSSELS CONFERENCE (1889-1890). The Brussels Conference was called by the British to deal with the continued trade in slaves in Africa and the Middle East just as the Catholic antislavery movement led by Cardinal **Lavigerie** was successfully focussing attention of European public opinion on the continued existence of slavery and the slave trade within Africa. The major European powers, the United States, Persia, Turkey and Zanzibar attended. The Brussels Act prohibited the maritime slave trade, though it did not provide the right of search. It committed colonial powers to suppress the overland slave trade, but left each free to pursue that objective in its own way. It provided a sanction for colonial powers to extend their authority by encouraging construction of military stations, establishment of administration and the building of roads and railroads. This was of concern to Leopold, the king of the Belgians, who was interested in using antislavery public opinion to justify the extension of his authority in the Congo. The Act also provided for the limitation of the weapons and alcohol trades. In spite of all of this, the Act was weak. Each of the colonial powers was careful to protect its interests. The Act provided for a central institution to gather information, but no mechanism for enforcement of the Acts's many provisions. It put pressure on colonial regimes to act on slavery, but this they would eventually have done without any Act. They each moved at their own pace, which was often quite slow. Perhaps its most important effect was the notion of international trusteeship, which was expanded under the **League of Nations** and the **United Nations**. *See also* EMANCIPATION, AFRICA.

BUDDHISM. Buddhism was born in India, and developed in Southeast and East Asia. Slavery was a common institution in all of these regions. Buddhism was critical of wealth, inequality and exploitation, but Buddhists believed in withdrawal from a world of suffering rather than efforts to transform it. Siddhartha Gautama, the Buddha, taught his followers to accept their lot in life. Buddhists believe in reincarnation. A person's situation in life was determined by his or her right or wrongs in previous existences. Therefore, a slave was a slave because of sins committed in an earlier existence. It was because of this that the Buddha urged slaves to accept their status and not be jealous of their masters. The Buddha was, however, critical of the behavior of slave owners. He forbade them trading in slaves and urged them to treat their slaves with kindness.

    As Buddhism moved into Southeast Asia, it developed its own form of servitude. Temples acquired slaves, originally by kings giving them war prisoners. Others were donated by private persons or voluntarily submitted as a sign of piety. The slaves did most of the maintenance, washing and cooking in the temple. Others dealt with the dead, kept records, copied manuscripts or maintained the temple library. In Thailand and in China, temple slaves also cleared new lands for rice cultivation. A slave could not become a monk. Though Buddhism recommended withdrawal, many Buddhist temples and monasteries became wealthy institutions controlling land and slaves. *See also* TEMPLE SLAVERY; THAI SLAVERY.

BURACO DO TATU. Meaning the "armadillo's hole," Buraco do Tatu was a typical *quilombo*, a community of about 200 fugitive slaves that survived for many years in a jungle area near Salvador, the capital of Bahia province in Brazil. They survived in large part by raiding plantations and by highway robbery, seizing food and sometimes plantations and by highway robbery, seizing food and sometimes kidnapping women. The fugitives had contacts within the city, which made it possible for them to acquire guns and gun-powder. Their jungle base was also surrounded by pits filled with sharp stakes, which made it very dangerous for attackers. In 1763, it was finally attacked, but only 61 fugitives were taken prisoner. *See also* BRAZILIAN SLAVERY; MAROONS

BURNS, ANTHONY (1834-1862). Born a slave in Virginia, Burns fled in 1854 by stowing away on a boat going to Boston. There, his master had him arrested under the **Fugitive Slave Law**. An abolitionist attorney, Richard Henry Dana, Jr. volunteered to defend Burns, and in a six day trial attracted attention in Boston and around the nation. After the judge ordered him returned to Virginia, mass meetings were held to protest and there were several attempts to free him by force. When Boston's black community raised enough money to buy his freedom, the purchase was blocked by the U.S. attorney. Finally, 15,000 troops were called in to escort Burns to the boat that brought him back to Virginia. There, a slave trader purchased him and sold him to a black church in Boston, which set him free. In his remaining years, he lectured on slavery, got an education and became the pastor of a congregation of runaway slaves in Canada. After the Burns case, there were no further extraditions under the Fugitive Slave Law in Massachusetts. *See also* ABOLITION, UNITED STATES.

BUSSA'S REBELLION. Barbados was the stablest and most secure of the **sugar** islands. It had a mature slave population, which meant relatively equal numbers of men and women and few recent imports. The island was intensively cultivated and there were no hilly or wooded areas where **maroons** could hide. 1815 was a harsh year. The end of the Napoleonic wars led to a slump in sugar prices. Food imports were scarce and slaves were pushed to increase production. Toward the end of 1815, a rumor spread that the slaves were to be freed. When it did not happen, many became convinced that it would happen only if they seized their freedom. An elaborate conspiracy developed. One of the leaders was supposedly named Bussa, though there is no clear evidence who Bussa was. The plan was that on Easter night, when whites were all in town, beacon fires would be lit, and the slaves would seize arms and horses. Everything started well. Within six hours of beacon fires being lit, the revolt had spread to 70 plantations and a third of the island was aflame. No whites were killed, however, and there was no effort to attacked the capital of Bridgetown. Militia and regular army units speedily and brutally then put down the rebellion within two days. Though only one white and one black soldier died in the fighting, at least 50 slaves were killed in combat and 70 were summarily executed in the field. About 300 were brought to Bridgetown for trial. Of them, 144 were put to death and 132 deported. *See also* CARIBBEAN SLAVERY.

BUTLER, BENJAMIN (1818-1894). A lawyer and a Democrat in New England before the war, Benjamin Butler became a general during the **Civil War** and played a key role in developing policy toward slaves. Though he had always supported the notion that slave property should be respected, events forced him to change his position. He was commanding Fortress Monroe in Virginia early in the war when northern generals had to decide what to do about slaves flooding over Union lines. Butler responded by proclaiming them contraband of war and providing them with work. In August 1861, Congress passed the First Confiscation Act, which put this principle into law.

The following year, he set yet another precedent as commander of Union army forces in New Orleans. The Native Guards, an all-black unit organized by the Confederates, was eager to join the Union army. Butler was at first reluctant to use Blacks as soldiers, but he needed manpower. The First Regiment of Native Guards became the first recognized regiment of black soldiers in the Union army. After the war, Butler was elected to Congress as a Republican, where he became one of the most ardent defenders of the rights of African-Americans. He later returned to the Democratic Party and served one term as governor of Massachusetts.

BUXTON, THOMAS FOWELL (1786-1845). Thomas Buxton was the leader of the abolitionist bloc in the British House of Commons. From his **Quaker** mother Buxton developed both a commitment to **Christianity** and an interest in social issues like prison reform and abolition. In 1818, he was elected to the Commons and three years later was asked by an aging **William Wilberforce** to take over leadership of the campaign to abolish slavery. The **slave trade** had been abolished in 1807. Throughout the 1820s abolitionists publicized the evils of slavery. In 1833, he presented a massive petition supporting emancipation and then steered through Parliament a bill to end slavery through-out the British Empire. To do so, he agreed to an amendment requiring a transition period in which the slaves worked as apprentices. He soon regretted making this decision and spent his last years in Parliament trying to get this provision removed. Though Buxton was not returned to Parliament in 1837, the apprenticeship provisions were removed in 1838.

Buxton then turned to slavery in Africa and published *The African Slave Trade and Its Remedy* (1840), in which he argued that slavery kept Africa poor and miserable and prevented the full exploitation of its potential. The remedy which he offered was "Christianity, commerce and civilization." He believed that both the Christian religion and the development of commerce were necessary to open the door to change. Buxton was one of the founders of the British and Foreign Anti-Slavery Society. His ideas dominated the abolitionist movement for much of the 19th century. *See also* ABOLITION, GREAT BRITAIN; ANTI-SLAVERY INTERNATIONAL.

BYZANTIUM (325-1453 CE). Byzantium was originally the eastern part of the Roman Empire. At the time of the split between the eastern and western empires, slaves recruited largely from warfare did much of the productive labor. Slaves came from the shores of the Black Sea: the Balkans, southern Russia and the Caucasus. These areas remained the major source of slaves for Mediterranean Europe and the Arab world. They came both from warfare and trade. This trade was extended in the late medieval period as the **Vikings** developed trade routes that brought slaves and furs down the Russian rivers to Byzantium. From Byzantium, they were sold elsewhere in the Middle East and the Mediterranean world.

The Emperor Justinian (527-565) dealt with the question of slavery in his codification of law. As in earlier Roman law, a slave was property, but Justinian allowed a slave to plead his case in court, limited harsh treatment and treated the killing of slave as murder. Around 726, a revised law code, the *Ecloga*, amended the laws on slavery. In particular, it clarified provisions on manumission and prohibited abusive masters from owning slaves. Amelioration probably resulted from both criticism of slavery within the Orthodox Church and from the declining importance of slave labor.

The spread of Christianity in Eastern Europe posed many questions? Were slaves converting to Christianity freed. The *Ecloga* held that only Christian slaves of non-Christians could claim their freedom. Could a slave become a monk? The law said only with his master's permission. But the most important result was the decline of enslavement in areas that converted to Christianity. It was illegal to enslave another Christian. With time, serfdom replaced slavery as a source of agricultural labor. In later centuries, slaves worked primarily as domestic servants. Slavery did, however, remain important, and the areas bordering the Black Sea remained the major source of slaves for societies bordering the Mediterranean until the fall of the Byzantine capital, Constantinople to the Turks in 1453. *See also* SCANDINAVIA; EAST EUROPEAN SLAVE TRADE.

-C-

CALHOUN, JOHN C. (1782-1850). Successful as a slave owner and planter from South Carolina, John Calhoun served as a Senator, cabinet minister and Vice-President of the United States. He was an important political theorist and for a generation, the most important southern political strategist. He was born in a slave-holding family, educated at Yale University and studied law, but while still young, he displayed a vocation for politics. He was elected to Congress in 1811 and remained in public life until his death. An expansionist, he was particularly concerned to defend the right of slave owners to take slavery into new territories.

An outstanding debater, Calhoun vigorously defended slavery in the halls of Congress. He believed that blacks were racially inferior and argued that slavery was beneficial to both masters and slaves. He is best known, however, for his argument for state's rights. Convinced that the South was in danger of being out-numbered, he argued that important legislation needed a "concurrent majority," that is to say, federal legislation needed the assent of the affected state. He spoke of the right of interposition, that is the right of the state to veto federal legislation and prevent its application within its borders. Calhoun was concerned to protect minorities, but the minority he was trying to protect was not slaves, but slave owners. His ideas were presented in two theoretical treatises, *Discourse on Government* (1852) and *Discourse on the Constitution and Government of the United States* (1852).

CAMBODIAN SLAVERY. During the period from the Ninth to the 15th century, a powerful Cambodian empire ruled a large part of Southeast Asia. During this period slaves formed the majority of its labor force. They were either war captives or prisoners taken in raids on upland areas, or their descendants. Chinese sources tells us that slaves were scorned, that only the poor lacked slaves and that the rich had many. The temples had particularly large work forces, many of them gifts from the state or from wealthy people. Some of the slaves labored in the fields, while others performed ritual functions or produced the beautiful art for which the period is known. Slaves were often treated harshly and could be punished at will by their masters.

In later centuries, commerce became more important. Debt slaves became common as did the enslavement of criminals. Many of the slaves still were non-Khmer, either purchased from Thailand or Laos or the product of raids in mountainous border areas. They were divided between state slaves and private slaves. The state slaves were war captives, criminals or their descendants and were settled in villages scattered around the country. They owed goods, agricultural produce or corvée labor to the state. Many of them were directly controlled by the king. Slavery was only abolished in 1897 after occupation by the French. *See also* EMANCIPATION, SOUTHEAST ASIA; THAI SLAVERY.

CANDOMBLÉ. *Candomblé* is a religion of African background followed largely in Bahia in northeast Brazil. Bahia, with its overwhelming slave majority, was marked by a mixture of religions — Yoruba, Dahomeyan, Angolan, Muslim and Catholic. *Candomblé* lived underground during the period of slavery and the *babalawos* used elements from many different sources, both traditional and Christian. Most of them were women. *Candomblé* uses African music to call up the spirits and involves divination and the worship of different kinds of spirits. It was used by slaves to deal religiously with the power of their white masters, but it also provided its believers the security of contact with the divine. *See also* SLAVE RELIGION.

CAPE COLOUREDS. Descended from both slaves and the indigenous Khoisan peoples of South Africa, the Cape Coloureds came to be seen as a separate racial group. When the Dutch settled at Capetown in 1652, the only inhabitants were the Khoi-Khoi, herders who were once known as Hottentots, and the San, hunter-gatherers once known as Bushmen. None of the Khoisan were interested in providing supplies the Dutch wanted. Slaves were imported to work on European farms and in the town. Most came from Mozambique and East Africa, but a large number also came from Asia. Particularly important among them were the Cape Malays, who have maintained their commitment to Islam and much of their Asian culture. Islam, in fact, proved more attractive than Christianity to the urban slave population. At the same time, the Khoisan were decimated by disease and either pushed out of their best lands or reduced to slaves or servants on the farms of Dutch settlers. Most of these people joined the Dutch Reformed Church.

In an effort to implement a social system based on racial separation and called *apartheid* or separateness, the descendants of the Dutch, now called Afrikaners, tried to classify South Africa's diverse peoples. Those persons who were neither white nor black or a mixture of the two were classified as Coloured. This included not only the Cape Coloured, but also the products of marriage and sexual relations between different groups on the frontier. Physically, the Coloureds include a range of physical types. The effort to classify them as a single group demonstrates the illogical nature of such a racial classification system. *See also* DUTCH SLAVE TRADE; SOUTH AFRICAN SLAVERY.

CAPITALISM.   Slavery has existed in many different social and economic systems. The nature of the system usually shapes the form slavery takes. Capitalism is an economic system in which the means of production are in private hands and are operated for profit in a market system. In many societies, planters have been concerned to make a profit, but with the modern capitalist slavery of the 17th and 18th centuries, slaves were purely a factor of production. Slaves were used because they were the most efficient way for the planter to use his capital. The **sugar, tobacco,** and **cotton** plantations of the New World operated within a world market system. The slave-sugar complex was the forerunner of other capitalist **plantation** systems. The planter took his own and borrowed money and invested it in land, labor and equipment. His largest investment was in his slaves. He also had to buy food and clothing. The slaves produced not for the planter's use, but for the market. The planter had to sell at a profit in order to be able to buy more slaves and feed them.

The slave trader was also a capitalist. He bought and sold slaves for profit. If the captain spent too much to buy the slaves, or if there was a ship-board rebellion or a high mortality rate from disease, the ship lost money. At the core of the system was the broker in Europe, who provided credit to the trader and planter, arranged the sale of the slaves in the Americas, and handled the sale of the sugar produced. Every actor in the system except the slave was concerned with the maximization of profit. The rise of the slave plantation was symbolic of changes in the nature of European enterprise abroad. Early colonial enterprises in the 15th and 16th centuries were dominated by the interests of the royal houses of Spain and Portugal. The expanded colonialism of the 17th century was built on joint-stock companies, capitalist plantations and international markets for capital, labor and commodities. *See also* GENOVESE, EUGENE; SLAVE TRADE.

CAPOEIRA. The *capoiera* was a very elaborate dance done by slaves on Brazilian plantations, in which two dancers engage in a simulated combat to the beat of music. Each encounter can take from several minutes up to two hours. When the encounter is finished, the dancers join the musicians and two more dancers come forward. It combines both west and central African musical traditions. Both the songs and many of the stylized dance steps recall slavery. For example, the dancers often move as if in chains. Planters and urban police tried for centuries to suppress the *capoiera*, but it remained popular and is still performed. *See also* SLAVE MUSIC.

CARIBBEAN SLAVERY. No part of the world has been as marked by African slavery as the Caribbean. At the peak of slave period in 1790, two-thirds of the population of the region was African slaves. Only in some parts of West Africa was the ratio of slave to free as high. This reliance on slave labor was a product of the Spanish conquest. After **Christopher Columbus** landed on Hispaniola in 1492, Spain tried to enslave local **Amerindian** populations and force them to work. The Spanish also brought with them diseases for which the Amerindians had no resistance. They had a very high mortality rate. Already, in the early 16th century, African slaves were being brought in to meet the demand for labor.

After Spanish *conquistadors* invaded Mexico in 1519, the Spanish became more interested in the mainland. The result was that during the early17th century, the Caribbean contained a series of fertile underpopulated tropical islands. They were colonies waiting to happen. With Spain weak, the British and French moved in, followed by the Dutch and the Danes. **Barbados**, settled in 1627, was the first to develop a slave-based economy. Most of the early settlers were small-holders, who cultivated tobacco, indigo and cotton with the aid of indentured labor from Europe. In the 1640s, settlers began shifting into **sugar**. Investment in a mill, an efficient labor force and the ability to get newly-cut cane processed all required some capital and encouraged the emergence of large plantations. Land prices rose and small-holders were forced out. At the same time, the demand for labor increased, but Europeans were increasingly reluctant to sign indenture contracts. It was unpleasant labor and in a climate where Europeans had a higher mortality than Africans. Furthermore, the African slave was a life-long dependent. Thus, Barbados soon was getting all of its labor from Africa.

The shift into sugar was aided by the Dutch, who had briefly ruled Northeast Brazil and knew how to grow sugar. The Dutch introduced the latest technology, taught Brazilian methods, and supplied slaves and credit the planters needed. The high profits led to rapid expansion. Soon, the French, Dutch, Swedes, and Danes all had colonies and the Spanish developed the islands they retained, most notably Cuba. Other crops were also developed — indigo, cacao, coffee, cotton — but sugar was the major source of profit. The Caribbean sugar-slave complex also stimulated growth elsewhere.

By 1800, a quarter of Great Britain's overseas trade was with the Caribbean. Seventy per cent of France's overseas trade involved the import and re-export of Caribbean produce. North American colonies exported fish, grain and lumber to the Caribbean. All of this was at a very high price. Sugar planters preferred men and imported twice as many men as women because they were not concerned with creating communities that could reproduce themselves. It was cheaper to import more slaves and replace them if they died. Sugar involved long hours of back-breaking labor and living conditions were harsh. In all of the sugar colonies, the death rate exceeded the birth rate until the end of slavery. In the 17th and 18th centuries, about 3,700,000 slaves were brought to the Caribbean, but at the end of the 18th century, there were little more than 1,600,000 people of African descent in the Caribbean.

Reliance on slavery meant that slaves were trained to do all kinds of work. Skilled artisans and domestic workers were slaves. About a third of male slaves did skilled labor. The climate meant that there was a shortage of European women. Furthermore, successful planters often moved back to England and appointed managers to run their farms. Planters, managers, foremen, and merchants often lived with slave women. Manumission was possible in most colonies, but most of those manumitted were the lovers or offspring of Europeans. There were a number of **slave revolts**, but the most common form of resistance was flight. On islands like Jamaica where there were forested or mountainous refuges, **maroon** communities emerged. Fear of revolt led to the creation of harsh **slave codes**. Slaves could only leave their plantations with signed passes. They were not allowed to drum because drum-beats could be used to send messages. Punishments were very harsh for escape, for burning sugar cane, or for any other act of resistance. A slave could be executed for striking a white person. *See also* DEMOGRAPHY OF SLAVERY; DUTCH SLAVE TRADE; PLANTATION.

CASTE. See HINDUISM; INDIAN SLAVERY.

CATHOLIC CHURCH. From its earliest dates, the Catholic Church has had to face the problem of balancing the view that all human beings were equal in the eyes of God with acceptance of a social order in which slavery was common. **Saint Paul** stressed the unity of all believers, but also recommended that slaves remain obedient to their masters. Augustine argued that slavery was based on original sin and therefore a legitimate institution. Other Medieval Catholics protested enslavement of children, urged manumission and tried to impose limits on the exploitation of slaves, for example the sanctity of marriage. The tendency in Catholic thought was impose moral controls on slavery, never to do away with it.

Canon law even imposed enslavement as a penalty for certain crimes. The Council of Pavia in 1012 decreed the enslavement of the children of priests who violated their vows of celibacy. Some medieval thinkers held that slaves had a right to disobey a master who tried to prevent them from procreating, who worked them too hard or denied them adequate sustenance. The slave was justified in fleeing if the master tried to force him to commit a sin. One 13th century theologian, John Duns Scotus, accepted the enslavement of felons, but felt that hereditary servitude was unjust, and by the late Middle Ages, there was a widespread belief that enslavement was only morally acceptable in a just war. The problem with this was that any Muslim was considered to be at war with Christendom and thus enslavable.

With the discovery of the Americas and the increasing use of slave labor, the Church faced several dilemmas. First, Catholic missionaries who saw the native peoples of the Americas as potential Christians were horrified by enslavement and its effects. In the early 15th century, the Dominican, **Bartolomé de Las Casas**, attacked the enslavement of Indians in Mexico, and though driven from his bishopric in Chiapas, persuaded the Spanish King Charles V to prohibit the enslavement of Indians. Though Las Casas at first favored substituting African slaves for Indians, within a generation, Seville theologian **Tomás de Mercado** contended that most African slaves were enslaved through violence and deceit and were thus unjustly enslaved. Mexican law professor **Bartolomé de Albornoz** argued that under natural law, even Africans had the right to liberty. In Brazil, a century after de las Casas, **Antonio Vieira** fought against the enslavement of Indians, was driven from his position in the Amazon, but persuaded King John of Portugal to protect Indians.

The second dilemma was whether Indians and Africans were equal before God, and if Catholic, had the right to the sacraments. Throughout Latin America, many Catholic priests insisted that slaves be baptized, given religious instruction, allowed time for worship and have the right to marry. For masters, if slave marriage was sacred, then it was a sin either to have sexual relations with slave women or to sell a slave separate from his or her spouse. Most slave masters were unwilling to yield either of these rights. Missionaries also had to cope with the fact that both Africans and Indians had their own religions and even when they became Catholic, incorporated elements of their own religions in their Catholicism or in many cases, practiced both religions.

In the 19th century, the Catholic Church faced another dilemma. It had been attacked during the **French Revolution**, saw the **Enlightenment** and the Revolution as hostile forces and it associated abolition with these forces. In Great Britain and the United States, Protestant Churches were the backbone of the abolition movement, but the Catholic Church remained hostile until the late 19th century. Several Popes criticized the **slave trade**, but in 1888, pushed by missionaries from Africa like **Alexandre Le Roy** and **Cardinal Charles Lavigerie** of Algiers, Pope Leo XIII authorized a Catholic anti-slavery movement and in 1890, attacked slavery itself in the encyclical *Catholicae Ecclesiae. See also* BIBLE; CHRISTIANITY; SLAVE RELIGION.

CEDDO. The *ceddo* were slave soldiers among Wolof, Sereer, and Fulbe kingdoms of Senegambia during the period of the **Atlantic slave trade**. They were known for their colorful clothes, their hard-drinking hedonistic life style and their loyalty to the rulers they served. They rode horses, raided for slaves, and lived by a code that placed great emphasis on generosity and courage. Boys taken prisoner often served as grooms and porters, and if they served well, could become *ceddo*. They received booty from their raids and generally had their lands worked by slave wives taken prisoner in those raids. Loyal service gave them access to military commands. The slave chiefs were usually the most influential and the most trusted office-holders. *See also* MILITARY SLAVES; WEST AFRICA.

CENTRAL AFRICA. Soon after the Portuguese arrived at the mouth of the Congo river in 1482, Central Africa became a major source of slaves. The largest state in the area, the **Kongo** kingdom, was interested in Christianity and eager to learn from the Portuguese. The slave trade rose within a generation to about 7,000 a year, but turned out to be disastrous for Kongo. Portuguese traders, many of the based on the island of **São Tomé** encouraged warfare and the autonomy of provincial chiefs. In 1526, **Afonso**, the able Catholic King of Kongo complained in a letter to the Portuguese king that the Portuguese were destroying his kingdom, but he was unable to stop the trade. In 1576, the Portuguese founded Luanda, which grew into the colony of Angola

By the middle of the 17th century, there were a series of European bases along the coast. The Dutch and English dominated the trade north of the Congo River, from which trade routes by-passed the cataracts on the Congo River and went overland to Malebo Pool. At the Pool, they tapped into riverine routes that drained slaves from the much of the Congo basin. Further south, Luanda was the center of a small colony and the terminus for routes into the interior. Outside the Portuguese lands were a series of warlord-dominated states, which slaved and provided commercial outlets for slaves coming from deeper in the interior. Another set of routes went through the Ovimbundu kingdoms of central Angola to Benguela. By the late 18th century, routes based in Luanda intersected in the far interior with routes based in Mozambique.

When the British abolished the **slave trade** in 1807, the Portuguese sought to continue it. The Brazilian **sugar** industry was expanding to meet the demand caused by the decline of sugar production in the British West Indies. But in 1850, Brazil stopped importing slaves. Changes were already underway in Central Africa. The demand for ivory was increasing and the demand for slaves persisted, but now, the slaves were being used within Africa. Newer and more efficient weapons made it easier both to hunt elephants and to enslave. Swahili, Arab, and Nyamwezi traders from the East Coast penetrated Central Africa. From the West coast, a new competitor emerged, Cokwe, who started as elephant hunters, but gradually found slave-raiding and trade more profitable. From the north, traders based on the Nile and on Saharan trade routes penetrated into Central Africa.

All of the new invaders were using efficient late-model rifles. The result was the destruction of old kingdoms and the ravaging of communities which were unable to defend themselves against the well armed intruders. Central African peoples had no time to learn how to defend themselves from the new predatory structures. The process only ended with the conquest of Central Africa between 1885 and 1914 by European powers. These powers brought in new forms of exploitation, but they ended the slave trade. *See also* EAST AFRICAN SLAVE TRADE; TIPPU TIP.

CERVANTES, MIGUEL DE (1547-1614). Cervantes is Spain's most famous literary figure. Early in his life, after serving in wars against the Ottoman Empire, Cervantes was on a ship that was seized by Algerian pirates. He spent five years in slavery in Algiers while his captors tried to extort a generous ransom from his family. Well-born captives taken by North African pirates were often held for a ransom. In this case, his master was a convert to Islam born in Venice. He was almost shipped to Istanbul before his family finally provided the ransom. His most famous novel, *Don Quixote*, contains a fictionalized account of his captivity. Other writings present a very critical picture of slavery in Spain, where there was an important slave population. *See also* REDEMPTIONIST ORDERS.

CHAVANNE, JEAN-BAPTISTE (?- 1791). Chavanne was one of the leaders of the revolt that began the Haitian revolution. He was a landowner and had served in French forces that aided the **American Revolution,** but he was also one of the free *gens de couleur* **(people of color).** In 1790, the French National Assembly decided that in the colonies all men who owned property and paid taxes could vote, but it left to the colonial assemblies the right to apply this decision. The all-white assembly in Saint-Domingue ignored the claims of the people of color. **Jacques Vincent Ogé** and Chavanne gathered a force of 200 men and seized a town in northern Haiti. Their revolt was suppressed. Both Ogé and Chavanne were executed and their heads were publicly displayed. The act shocked the French, and in May 1791 the National Assembly granted citizenship to people of color born of free parents. Three months later, a massive **slave revolt** broke out. In 1792, the assembly extended citizenship to all people of color and in 1793 it abolished slavery. *See also* FRENCH REVOLUTION; HAITIAN REVOLUTION.

CHAVIS, JOHN (1763-1838). John Chavis was a free Black preacher and a conservative who was opposed to the freeing of the slaves. He somehow managed to get a very good education, attending Washington Academy (later Washington and Lee University), and by some accounts, the College of New Jersey (now Princeton University). These same accounts suggest that he was sent to school to see if Blacks could learn as well as Whites. He excelled in classics and rhetoric. In 1801, he was licensed to preach by the Presbyterian Church. After marrying, he settled in Raleigh, North Carolina, where he opened an integrated school. He was eventually forced to separate White and Black students, teaching the Whites by day and the Blacks in the evening. Though he seems to have been a genuine conservative, his opposition to abolition was probably a case of self-interest. In the 1830s, after the **Nat Turner** rebellion, there was a movement to expel free Blacks from the South and they were in 1835 deprived of the vote. He was clearly anxious to reassure White society, which saw free blacks as a threat.

CHENG HO (1371-1433). Cheng Ho's career shows how much power some slaves could exercise when they were the agents of a powerful king or emperor. Cheng Ho was a **eunuch** who served the Ming Emperor of China, Zhu Di. Between 1405 and 1433, while Portuguese navigators were cautiously beginning the exploration of the West African coast, Cheng Ho led seven fleets in a series of expeditions to Southeast Asia, India, the Persian Gulf, and East Africa. The purpose of Cheng Ho's voyages was to open up commercial and political ties with nations on the shores of the Indian Ocean. After 1433, the Ming dynasty ended the voyages and turned inward, discouraging international trade and ending efforts to reach out to other societies. One result was that Europeans discovered China rather than Chinese discovering Europe. *See also* CHINESE SLAVERY; ELITE SLAVES.

CHEROKEE. The Cherokee originally inhabited an area that stretched from North Carolina to Alabama. Before the arrival of Europeans, they often took prisoners, but those prisoners were eventually absorbed into Cherokee families. With the coming of British settlers, Cherokees began selling those prisoners to the settlers. Gradually, however, some Cherokee became Christians, intermarried with settlers and began to farm in the European manner. Some even used African slaves and became successful planters. In 1828, they organized a republic centered at New Echota, Georgia. Their constitution was modelled after the United States Constitution. They also had a code regulating slavery, which prohibited marriage with slaves or the sale of liquor to them. The Republic was run by slave-holding Cherokee who also controlled most of the businesses and the plantations. Though most of the Cherokee had accepted Southern culture, when gold was discovered on their lands, the state government asked that they be removed to the Indian Territory, now Oklahoma. The long trip to Oklahoma, on which many died, is called the Trail of Tears. Most Cherokee slave owners took their slaves with them. *See also* AMERINDIAN SLAVERY.

CHESNUT, MARY (1823-1886). The daughter of a Southern planter and the wife of another, Mary Chesnut was critical of slavery and sympathized with abolition. She was well educated and widely read, but she spent most of her life in South Carolina. Her attitudes were recorded in a diary she kept during the **Civil War**. Her distaste for slavery seems to have originated with her friendship with two slave servants and with a mulatto who was the ward of the headmistress of the school in Charleston where she was educated. "God forgive us," she wrote, "but ours is a monstrous institution." She also remarked sardonically that on most plantations, the mulattos resemble the white children, "and every lady tells you who is the father of all the mulatto children in everybody's household, but those in her own she seems to think drop from the clouds." (Woodward, *Mary Chesnut's Diary*) She kept her views to herself, and the diary was not published until the 20th century.

CHILD, LYDIA MARIA (1802-1880). Lydia Child was an important abolitionist author. Born in Massachusetts, she first established herself as a writer with a novel about miscegenation entitled *Hobomok* (1824). She also wrote several domestic self-help books for women, which did well financially and established her reputation. Along with her husband, David Lee Child, she became active in the New England Anti-Slavery Society led by **William Lloyd Garrison**. In 1833, she published *An Appeal in Favor of That Class of Americans Called Africans.* In it, she set American slavery within an international perspective and argued against the notion that emancipation would lead to economic collapse. Child edited the *National Anti-Slavery Standard* from 1841 to 1843 and remained an active abolitionist writer. In 1859, her offer to be a nurse for **John Brown** led to an exchange of letters with Margaretta Mason, the wife of the senator from Virginia. This exchange was printed in many newspapers and reproduced as a pamphlet by the **American Anti-Slavery Society**. *See also* ABOLITION, UNITED STATES.

CHINESE SLAVERY. Slavery existed in China since well before China was unified in 221 BCE. Many slaves originated as war captives.

Others were sold into slavery by families or enslaved as a a punishment for crimes. Chinese slavery is striking in that slaves were almost never used for productive labor. This was because China was marked from an early date by a high population density. When free land was not available, people who did not have enough land had to go work for other people, usually as share-croppers. In these conditions, land was for the wealthy a more secure investment than persons. A person who owned land could always buy labor, and that labor was usually more efficient than slave labor. Necessity created a culture of hard work in China.

Slaves were used in two sectors of the economy. State slaves were convicts, the relatives of criminals and prisoners of war. Many were also offspring of such people because the status was hereditary. They were used in constructing public works like irrigation canals. Sometimes, because state slavery was a form of punishment, they were sent to live in harsh and poorly populated regions. Most dynasties did not make systematic use of state slaves. In addition, many were freed when there was a change of dynasty. As a result, the institution declined over the years.

There were also private slaves. Some originated from self-sale or the sale of a wife or children, usually because of debt or natural calamity. There was also some kidnapping or raiding, particularly during periods of social disintegration, and occasionally the gift to a meritorious individual of state slaves. Private slaves lived and worked almost exclusively in wealthy households. The best treated were concubines, but slaves also served as personal servants, doorkeepers, commercial assistants, private soldiers and entertainers. It was also possible for a man who had no offspring to buy a young boy, who then was adopted as his heir. This could only be done with agreement of the man's family and the boy ceased to be a slave the minute he was adopted. Wealthy families often had large numbers of slaves, but because the institution was limited to the very wealthy, the percentage of Chinese in slavery was small. Slavery was hereditary and the master had almost absolute control over the slave. The slave owed his or her master total obedience. The killing of a slave or excessive violence was prohibited, but slaves could be sold or given away. The slave could not testify in court except in cases where the master was plotting treason against the state. Some slaves were able to pursue an education, accumulate wealth and purchase their liberty.

The Chinese state generally discouraged the institution of slavery because slaves were not productive. It also feared **slave revolt**. In 1685, the Emperor Kangxi freed all slaves belonging to families of the ruling Manchus. There was, however, one very privileged group of slaves, the **eunuchs**, who played an important role at court and in the government. In 1909, three years before the fall of the Qing dynasty, all slaves were freed and given the status of commoners. *See also* CONCUBINES AND CONCUBINAGE; CONFUCIANISM; EMANCIPATION, EAST ASIA.

CHIRINO, JOSE LEONARDO (?- 1796). José Leonardo Chirino was the leader of the Coro revolt in Venezuela. Coro is a small city on the coast of Venezuela. The son of a male slave and an Indian woman, Chirino worked for a trader in the city of Coro, and in that capacity visited **Saint-Domingue** with his employer. He seems to have been impressed with the Haitian situation. In May 1795, he led a band of slaves and free blacks, who marched through the countryside, killing plantation owners, burning plantations and trying to gather support. He called for a republic based on French law and social equality. His forces were, however, speedily defeated by a local Spanish force. He was hung and quartered and many of his followers were decapitated. *See also* HISPANIC AMERICA.

CHRISTIANA SLAVE CASE. In September 1851, some **slave catchers** commanded by Edward Gorsuch, a Maryland slave-owner, and a deputy U.S. Marshal crossed into Pennsylvania to re-claim a runaway slave named William Parker. They were acting under the **Fugitive Slave Law** which had been passed only a year earlier. A group of African-Americans gathered at Parker's home in Christiana to prevent his seizure. They soon received the support of some local whites. The whites refused the Marshal's effort to deputize them. In the ensuing struggle, Gorsuch was killed and several members of his party were wounded. Parker fled to Canada, but four Whites and 36 Blacks were charged with treason. At this time, U.S. President Millard Fillmore was anxious to curry favor with the South. After a two week trial, the Judge instructed the jury to hold the defendants not guilty because a refusal to aid the authorities under the Fugitive Slave Act could not be considered treason. Other charges were then dropped. This was one of many incidents indicating both the increased militance of African-Americans and the hostility of many Whites in the North to the return of runaway slaves.

CHRISTIANITY. Christianity was created in the Roman Empire where slavery was common. It stressed from the first the belief that all human beings were one in the eyes of God. At the same time, survival in the Roman world involved acceptance of the established order. Slavery was thus a problem for Christians throughout their history. Many of the early Christians were slaves, but Church Fathers like **Saint Paul** counselled obedience while at the same time recommending that masters be humane. Paul and later, Augustine, suggested that the social order was divinely ordained. For the obedient slave, the reward would come only in the afterlife. And yet, some Christian groups used common funds to purchase the freedom of fellow Christians and some protested aspects of slavery like the kidnapping of children.

Over 2,000 years, Christianity has given birth to a large number of different churches, each of which has dealt with slavery in its own way. What they have in common is a conflict between ideas of obedience, of universal moral truths, and individual moral responsibility. One result of this is while most Christians have accepted the legitimacy of slavery, there have always been critics. Christians believe that masters and slaves share the same human nature and are subject to the same moral laws. From the early Middle Ages, Christian bishops and theologians have encouraged manumission and recommended that slaves be treated kindly. The Church Fathers insisted and the Church has continued to insist on the sanctity of marriage between slaves. This meant that extramarital intercourse with a slave woman, common in most societies, was considered morally wrong. Finally, there was also a belief that a person could be legitimately enslaved only in a just war.

Most slaves in medieval Europe were domestic slaves and there was a high rate of manumission. With the European voyages of discovery, the beginning of the African slave trade and the expansion of plantation systems, harsher and more exploitative forms of slavery emerged. There were two major Christian reactions to these harsher forms. First, Catholic missionaries protested against the enslavement of **Amerindians** and the treatment of slaves. Only a few actually opposed slavery, but many criticized the immorality of enslavement, the brutality of the slave trade, and the ways slaves were treated. They also insisted on Christian education and the right to marry.

A more intensive attack came from some British and American Protestants. Though influenced by ideas from the French **Enlightenment**, the British and American abolition movements were rooted in the Protestant Churches and in a re-thinking of Christianity, which stressed the spirit more than the letter of the Bible. Anti-slavery Protestants objected to any institution that kept persons from living a Christian life. They believed not only in moral responsibility, but in the necessity of each person being free to make his or her own moral choices. They came from this to believe that any institution that subordinates one individual to the absolute authority of another was immoral. *See also* ABOLITION, GREAT BRITAIN; ABOLITION, UNITED STATES; BAPTISTS; CATHOLIC CHURCH; QUAKERS.

CHRISTOPHE, HENRI (1767-1820). Henri Christophe was a military leader in the **Haitian revolution** who became the head of a northern Haitian state. He was born a slave on Granada and went to sea as a cabin boy at age nine. He served with French forces during the **American Revolution** and seems at some point to have been freed. He was manager of an inn when the Haitian Revolution began, but speedily became an officer in forces commanded by **Toussaint-Louverture**. When Toussaint was killed, command of the army went to **Jean-Jacques Dessalines**, who proceeded to proclaim independence and declare himself emperor. Fearing a new despotism, Christophe allied himself to the mulatto general Alexandre Pétion in the assassination of Dessalines, but their alliance soon broke down. Christophe commanded the north and Pétion the south. Christophe proclaimed himself king and tried to set up a constitutional monarchy. Fearing a French invasion, Christophe sought international recognition, a reopening of commerce, and the assistance of abolitionists in creating an education system. He tried to improve living conditions but the need for money led to restoration of the plantation system. He established order, but the harsh work and discipline were resented by former slaves. In 1820, when southern forces were threatening, Christophe had a stroke. Knowing that the end was near, he committed suicide.

CHURCH MISSIONARY SOCIETY (CMS). The Church Missionary Society was founded in 1799 and rapidly became the most important Anglican mission society. From the first, the CMS sought to combine religious conversion and economic development to end the **slave trade**. In 1804, it established a mission in Freetown, **Sierra Leone**. With the abolition of the slave trade, the CMS created a network of institutions to help free slaves establish themselves. More than any other mission, CMS created from the ragged ex-captives a Christian elite. CMS and this allied elite gradually spread through Great Britain's West African colonies. Part of its success was the confidence that CMS leaders had in African converts. Under Henry Venn, secretary from 1834 to 1873, the CMS preached its gospel of "Christianity, Civilization, and Commerce." Venn's program involved education, industry, conversion, and self-improvement. To create a self-sustaining church, Venn encouraged African ministers like **Samuel Ajayi Crowther** and the creation of a middle class of entrepreneurs, who would provide lay leaders for the church. The economic program of the CMS involved the introduction of new crops that could replace incomes lost with the end of the slave trade. It was often referred to as an alliance between "the Bible and the plow." The CMS also worked in other parts of the British Empire. *See also* KRIO; RECAPTIVES.

CIMARRON. Cimarron is the Spanish word for runaway, which became *maroon* in English and *marron* in French. Originally an Arawak Indian word, it first referred to feral cattle that ran wild in the hills of Hispaniola. It then was used for runaway Indian slaves and came to have a connotation of wild or fierce, which is how colonial society saw the runaway slave communities that developed in many parts of the Americas.

CINQUÉ, JOSEPH (c. 1811-?). Joseph Cinqué was a Mende slave from **Sierra Leone** who led a revolt on the slave ship *Amistad*, and tried to sail back to Africa, but instead found himself in the middle of a famous American legal case. Cinqué was seized by slavers in 1837 or 1838. He was taken to a Portuguese slaving station on the coast, leaving behind a wife and three small children. The slaves were taken to Havana, Cuba, and sold. The *Amistad* was taking them to slave plantations further east on the island when Cinqué used a rusty nail to pry open the locks that bound the chains of the slaves to the hull of the boat. The slaves then broke into the hold and armed themselves with knives, with which they attacked the crew, killing all but two seamen, who were spared so they could sail the boat back to Africa. They sailed instead northeast by day and due north at night until they were intercepted by the Coast Guard off the coast of Long Island, New York.

The Spanish government sought the return of the slaves. The United States government supported the Spanish claim, but Cinqué and his fellow slaves were supported by the abolition movement. After two years of court cases, they were freed. While the case was being heard, Cinqué was out on bail and went on the abolitionist lecture circuit. His speeches were given in Mende and translated into English. In 1842, he returned to Sierra Leone. Little is known about his life after that. *See also* AFRICAN SLAVE TRADE.

CIVIL RIGHTS ACT OF 1866 (U.S.). The Civil Rights Act of 1866 was an attempt to force the defeated states of the Confederacy to obey the will of the United States Congress. After the **Thirteenth Amendment** to the U. S. Constitution abolished slavery, most states of the former Confederacy responded by passing **Black Codes** which sought to perpetuate the legal inferiority of the former slaves. These acts sought to regulate where freed persons could live, what kind of jobs they could hold, whether they could own property, their right to own weapons, and the terms of **apprenticeship**. Apprenticeship was used to re-create the conditions of slavery. Congress responded with "An Act to Protect All Persons in the United States in Their Civil Rights and Furnish Means of Their Vindication." This act conferred citizenship on the freed persons, guaranteed the equal rights of African-Americans in legal proceedings and the right to make contracts, to sue, to testify in court, and to buy and sell property. It also gave federal commissioners the authority and the power to enforce the act. When President Andrew Johnson vetoed the act, Congress overrode the veto. It then passed the **Fourteenth Amendment** defining citizenship and the **Fifteenth Amendment** guaranteeing African-Americans the right to vote. *See also* RECONSTRUCTION.

CIVIL WAR, U.S. In the American Civil War, the South fought to protect slavery, the North to protect the Union. In the end, the slavery issue shaped the progress of the war and the abolition of slavery was its most important result. The war resulted from the election of **Abraham Lincoln** as president. Lincoln and his supporters did not oppose slavery where it already existed. They were simply opposed to its extension. For many Northerners, the issue was not the immorality of slavery but competition between slave labor and free labor. The South, however, was not concerned with such distinctions. It was fighting to protect slavery and southern sovereignty. In the wake of **John Brown**'s raid on Harper's Ferry and massive northern resistance to the **Fugitive Slave Act**, the South felt its way of life threatened.

The North was more populous than the South, but there were an equal number of slave states and free states. An equal number of senators for each state meant that Southerners could block any legislation they opposed. Thus, when Lincoln's election threatened that majority, seven of the slave states seceded. Lincoln tried to reassure them and to keep the other slave states in the Union, and throughout the first part of the war did nothing that would make return to the fold more difficult. He refused to free slaves and he refused to recruit Black troops. He also offered federal funds to assist the emigration of free Blacks. He was particularly concerned to protect the interests of slave holders in border states which remained within the Union. When General John Fremont abolished slavery in Missouri, Lincoln objected and Fremont's order was overruled.

Events, however, moved too fast for Lincoln. From the earliest days of the war, and in spite of Union defeats, slaves began fleeing across Union lines. At first, the responses of Union commanders varied. Some returned runaway slaves to their masters. General **Benjamin Butler**, a lawyer in civilian life, proclaimed runaway slaves contraband and in August 1861 Congress passed the First Confiscation Act, which provided for the seizure of all property, including slaves used in aid of the rebellion. At the same time, Union commanders were finding uses for the former slaves. Men were put to work digging ditches and building fortifications, women as cooks and washerwomen. Some Union generals began asking for the right to enlist African-American troops. In April 1862, Congress abolished slavery in the District of Columbia. Three months later, the Second Confiscation Act provided that all captured or runaway slaves were "forever free." Finally on 1 January 1863, Lincoln issued the **Emancipation Proclamation** freeing all slaves in those areas that were in rebellion. By late 1862, a number of Union generals had started using Black troops recruited in the South, and in January 1863 the War Department began authorizing northern states to raise black regiments. Some 186,000 African-Americans served in the Union armies, about half of them former slaves from the Confederacy, and most with great distinction.

By 1862, many slave men had fled the plantations. Most of the slaves left on plantations were women and children. In other areas, whites fled. In many lowland areas, slaves began reorganizing their lives. In others, rebellious slaves refused to do what their masters wanted. By 1864, many Confederate generals were convinced that the Confederacy could only survive if it agreed to gradual emancipation and used African-American troops. Other Confederate leaders rejected their plans. The South fought on until their greatest general, Robert E. Lee, was forced to surrender to Union General Ulysses Grant at

Appomattox Court House, Virginia, on 9 April 1865.

To deal with the problems of the freed slaves, Congress created in the last months of the war a Bureau of Refugees, Freedmen, and Abandoned Lands, better known as the **Freedmen's Bureau**. This agency played a major role in the years after the war. By the time the war ended, slavery was shattered. The **Thirteenth**, **Fourteenth**, and **Fifteenth Amendments** to the **Constitution** provided the legal basis for a new, more egalitarian social order. *See also* CONFEDERATE STATES OF AMERICA; RECONSTRUCTION.

CLARKSON, THOMAS (1760-1846). Clarkson was one of the major figures in the British campaign to abolish first the **slave trade**, then slavery. In 1779, he entered Cambridge University intending to become a clergyman. His career changed when he won an essay contest on whether it was right to enslave others against their will. It was published in 1786 as *An Essay on Slavery and the Commerce of the Human Species, particularly the African.* Much of it was based on information he gathered by going to the docks at Liverpool and Bristol, England's major slave ports, and talking to men who worked in the trade. It won him the attention of other abolitionists and when the **Society for the Abolition of the Slave Trade** was organized a year later, he became a key figure. As an Anglican, he helped to broaden the movement from its **Quaker** base. He was indefatigable as both a researcher and organizer. He travelled widely, covering 35,000 miles between 1787 and 1794, organizing local committees, establishing links with abolitionists in other countries, and researching the slave trade. He described the campaign in the two-volume *History of the Abolition of the British Slave Trade* (1808). After abolition, he worked with the **African Institution** to ensure that the law was enforced. In 1823, he became vice president of the Anti-Slavery Society. Though now over 60, he played an active role in the struggle to abolish slavery itself. *See also* ABOLITION, GREAT BRITAIN; SHARP, GRANVILLE; WILBERFORCE, WILLIAM.

CLAVER, PEDRO (1580-1654). Pedro Claver was a Jesuit missionary who worked to ease the suffering of slaves. Born the son of peasants in northern Spain, he arrived in America in 1610 and became a priest in 1616. He was sent to Cartagena, then the only port in Spanish America allowed to import slaves. He first worked among Amerindians, but early was assigned to give religious instruction to newly arrived slaves.

When slave ships arrived, Claver would meet them with water, oranges, lemons, brandy, and tobacco. He baptized the dying and started religious instruction for the others. To do so, he learned several Angolan languages. He also used interpreters chosen from among slaves owned by the Jesuits. Claver often toured the hinterland, observing conditions and staying in slave cabins. Though supported by some members of the elite, he attacked slave owners for opposing slave marriages and tried to protect slave morality. To that end, he opposed African drumming and dancing, which he regarded as idolatrous. He did not oppose slavery, and on occasion, whipped slaves, but he struggled all of his life to improve the treatment of slaves. In 1888, he was canonized by Pope Leo XIII. *See also* CATHOLIC CHURCH.

COARTACIÓN. Under Spanish colonial law in Cuba, if a master refused to permit a slave to purchase his freedom, the slave could initiate a legal process called a *coartación*. The slave and the master each appointed an assessor, who estimated the value of the slave. If the two assessments were far apart, the court sometimes appointed a third assessor. Once the price was set, the master's rights were limited. The slave could work independently and make installment payments on his self-purchase. Once the slave had made the required payments, he or she received a notarized document of emancipation. Similar processes existed in many other Hispanic areas. *See also* HISPANIC AMERICA; *SIETE PARTIDAS.*

CODE NOIR. The Code Noir or Black Code was promulgated in 1685 by the French naval minister, Jean-Baptiste Colbert, for use in all of France's slave colonies. It had a number of protections for the slave. It prohibited the separation of families, required minimum standards of food and clothing, guaranteed the care of the elderly, and gave the slaves the right to a trial in criminal cases. It also, however, defined slaves as property. Slaves could be mortgaged and seized for debt. They could not own property, had no right to assemble or to testify in court. The code also provided for harsh treatment for a whole range of crimes, particularly for running away, theft, or striking the master or any other free person. Masters could whip or chain slaves or have the authorities brand, mutilate, or execute them. Many of the protections were often ignored. The harsher provisions were used to intimidate the slaves. The Code Noir differed from most other slave codes primarily in its concern to guarantee the practice of the Catholic religion. Similar, but often harsher legislation, was passed in most of the other slave colonies. *See also* SLAVE CODES.

COFFIN, LEVI (1789-1877). Though born and raised in North Carolina, Levi Coffin was a **Quaker**, an abolitionist, and one of the organizers of the **Underground Railroad**. In 1821, Coffin and his cousin organized a school for African-Americans, but slave holders forced them to close it. In 1826, he and his wife moved to Newport, Indiana, where he became a prosperous businessman. Learning that many fugitive slaves came through Newport, he let it be known that he could provide shelter, food, and transportation to other anti-slavery homes farther north. He also helped organize a school for African-American children in the Newport area. In 1844, he visited former slaves he had assisted in Canada and organized assistance for newly arrived former slaves who needed help.

In 1847, he moved to Cincinnati to take charge of a depository for goods made by free labor. As part of the project to encourage the use of cotton goods made by free labor, he moved a cotton gin purchased by abolitionists to Mississippi and made contact with planters who used free labor. The result was a successful business producing cotton goods. With the passage of the **Fugitive Slave Act** in 1850, he created in Cincinnati the same kind of network for runaway slaves he had in Indiana. During the **Civil War**, he worked among freed slaves and after the war was involved in efforts to assist the former slaves. In 1876, he published his autobiography, *Reminiscences of Levi Coffin, Reputed President of the Underground Railroad.*

COLES, EDWARD (1786-1868). Born a member of an influential slave-owning family, Coles was convinced as a student at the College of William and Mary that slavery was immoral. He served briefly as the private secretary to President James Madison, who was married to his cousin. Virginia law required any freed slave to leave the state within a year of manumission. Coles knew that if he was to free the 20 slaves he had inherited, he had to find land and establish them elsewhere. He found land in southern Illinois and brought his slaves there by wagon and boat. Only after they started down the Ohio River did he tell them that they were free to do what they wanted and could leave him if they wished. None of them did so. In Illinois, both Coles and his slaves faced harassment and lawsuits that questioned both the manumission of his slaves and their title to the lands he provided. Coles entered politics in order to defeat efforts to rescind Illinois's anti-slavery constitution.

The move was defeated and Coles became the state's second governor in 1823. The hostility slaves faced convinced him that freed slaves would be better off back in Africa, but none of those he freed chose to go. He remained active in the anti-slavery cause the rest of his life. *See also* ABOLITION, UNITED STATES.

COLUMBIAN EXCHANGE. An important effect of European voyages of discovery, perhaps the most important, was the exchange of people, plants, animals, and diseases between the New World and the Old. For example, maize, tomatoes, and cassava were introduced to Africa. Domesticated animals like horses, pigs, and cattle were introduced to the Americas. For the history of slavery, two elements of the Columbian exchange were particularly important. First, Europeans brought to Africa new crops suitable for the tropics, which could be efficiently raised on plantations. **Sugar** was the most important, but **tobacco** and indigo were also grown and in the 19th century **cotton** became important. These slave-grown crops all became profitable exports from the new economies of the Americas.

The second element was demography. The most disastrous effect of the exchange was the introduction of new diseases like smallpox, measles, whooping cough, bubonic plague, and malaria, to which local people had no resistance The resultant loss of life was drastic. The population of central Mexico is estimated to have dropped in less than two centuries from about 25 million to less than a million. In Peru, the drop is estimated at about nine million to about 600,000. Population losses meant that Europeans were unable to staff their plantations with local workers. Africans were linked geographically to Europe and as a result, Africans had been exposed to most European diseases and vice versa. Africans also had greater resistance to tropical diseases, like malaria, that killed large numbers of Europeans. This meant that the mortality rate for Africans in the Americas was lower than both the rate for Europeans and for Amerindians. *See also* DEMOGRAPHY OF SLAVERY.

COLUMBUS, CHRISTOPHER (1451-1506). The arrival of Christopher Columbus in America in 1492 was the beginning of European exploitation of slave labor. Columbus had earlier experience of slavery in Portugal, in Africa, and on the Atlantic islands. The enslavement of **Amerindians** speedily became part of his vision for the development of the lands he discovered. In 1493, on his second voyage, Columbus made the island of Hispaniola his base and started to conquer it. He distinguished between those who accepted Spanish rule and those who were subject to enslavement because they resisted it. Though the Spanish monarchs, Ferdinand and Isabella, ordered a moratorium on enslavement of Amerindians, Columbus shipped to Spain 500 persons enslaved because they rebelled against Spanish authority and suggested an export of Amerindian slaves to Spain. No large-scale export trade developed, partly because there was a shortage of labor on Hispaniola and it rapidly got worse as European diseases and harsh labor obligations decimated the Amerindian populations. Columbus also introduced the first African slaves into the New World. He was eventually removed from his position in 1500, in part because he disobeyed royal instructions on enslavement. He made one more voyage in 1502. *See also* COLUMBIAN EXCHANGE; HISPANIC AMERICA; SAINT-DOMINGUE.

COMFORT WOMEN. The term comfort women has been used for sexual slaves who served the Japanese army during World War II. About 80 percent were Korean and 10 percent were Japanese. Others included Chinese, Dutch, Indonesians, Burmese, Russian, Eurasians, and Filipinos. Korea was at this time a colony of Japan. The Dutch women came from prisoner of war camps in Indonesia. The Japanese women were mostly prostitutes. The others were recruited by force or by fraud and were beaten if they did not cooperate. Most were between 14 and 18 years old when enslaved. The Japanese army was concerned to control the spread of sexually transmitted diseases. They also believed that men who were sexually satisfied would be better fighters. Those in brothels for common soldiers were expected to service 30 to 40 men a night, with heavier demands when troops were in transit. They received a small sum for each sexual act, but were often cheated out of their money. *See also* SEXUAL SLAVERY.

COMPENSATED EMANCIPATION. In the majority of societies that debated emancipation, a major conflict was between the slave's human rights and the master's property rights. Few societies have been willing to ignore the wealth invested in slaves. This issue has often slowed emancipation. The debate was often over when and how to compensate the slave owner. The reluctance of some societies to appropriate the necessary funds was often a reason for postponing emancipation or using **free womb laws**, a gradual method that involved freeing children at birth. Sometimes, costs could be stretched out by issuing bonds redeemable at a later date.

Massachusetts freed its slaves in 1780 by adopting an anti-slavery constitution, but in other states of the northern United States, compensation was provided for slave owners. Many states like New York and New Jersey opted for gradual programs and some asked the freed slaves to pay some of the costs of their own emancipation. British emancipation in 1833 involved a program under which the British government set compensation levels in the West Indies, South Africa, and other British colonies. This policy was also adopted by France and Denmark in 1848 and the Netherlands in 1863. Most Latin American states compensated owners when they freed their slaves during the 1850s and 1860s, but Cuba and Brazil opted for gradual emancipation.

In the United States, early in the **Civil War**, **Abraham Lincoln** proposed a program of compensated emancipation in the hope of conciliating the South, but the South had already opted for war. By fighting to protect slavery, southern slave owners ended up losing any possibility of compensation. The **Emancipation Proclamation** freed all slaves in areas under rebellion without compensation and the **Thirteenth Amendment** extended emancipation elsewhere. Later in their African and Asian colonial domains, European powers were not willing to pay the money necessary for compensation. The pressures of humanitarian public opinion at home meant that most of them felt obliged to act in some way against slavery. The usual solution to the problem was the "Indian formula," in which the state simply withdrew its support for slavery. Without the coercive power of the state and its courts behind them, masters had difficulty maintaining control over their slaves. No compensation was paid and large amounts of wealth were simply wiped out. *See also* EMANCIPATION ACT; EMANCIPATION, AFRICA; EMANCIPATION, HISPANIC AMERICA; EMANCIPATION, INDIA; EMANCIPATION, UNITED STATES.

COMPROMISE OF 1850. Until 1848, the United States maintained a balance between slave states and free states. This was essential because Southerners believed that the Senate, where each state had two senators, was the only protection it had against anti-slavery legislation. In 1848, the end of the Mexican-American War added a huge area to the United States. The South saw these lands as potential slave states. A year later, California applied to enter the Union as a free state, threatening the balance. A compromise suggested by Henry Clay involved eight components, of which the most important were admission of California as a free state, the right of New Mexico and Utah to choose their own status, settlement of a boundary dispute between Texas and New Mexico, and a **Fugitive Slave Law**.

The measures were passed as separate pieces of legislation. Only a few supporters of the compromise supported all of them, but through deft manipulation by congressional leaders, they all passed. For a time, the compromise reduced tensions, but the Fugitive Slave Law offended Northerners who found themselves required to protect slavery by returning runaways to the South. Then, the idea of popular sovereignty, introduced for New Mexico and Utah, was offered to older territories with the **Kansas-Nebraska Act** of 1854. This opened up an issue that was once resolved, the lands acquired in the Louisiana Purchase, and led to a virtual civil war in "bleeding Kansas."

CONCUBINES AND CONCUBINAGE. In most slave-using societies, the highest prices are paid for beautiful young women. Some became high-priced prostitutes or companions, but most became concubines. In much of Asia, rulers and powerful figures maintained many concubines in large **harems**. Elsewhere, men with enough money to purchase a concubine often maintained just one instead of or in addition to a wife. In one form or another, concubinage existed in most parts of the world and always involved a relationship of a man with a socially inferior woman. In the Middle East, concubinage can be traced as far back as the Assyrian Empire. Under Islam, men were limited to four wives, but could own an indefinite number of slave concubines as long as they had the ability to support them. Sultans and emirs usually had large harems.

When a Muslim concubine gave birth to her master's child, she was treated virtually as a wife, could no longer be sold, and was freed when the master died. Furthermore, her offspring had equal right of inheritance with the children of wives. In many Asian and African kingdoms, it was not unusual for the son of a concubine to inherit. In Muslim areas and in China, a concubine could achieve great power if she were the royal favorite or if her son inherited power. In China, many concubines were essentially servants, but a few became powerful empresses. By contrast, in Rome, where monogamy was the legal norm, rich men often kept a concubine in addition to a wife, but many men lived monogamously with a concubine. In contrast to Islam, Roman men sometimes preferred a concubine because her offspring did not inherit and therefore did not infringe on the rights of their legitimate children. In China and the Muslim world, only the father's status determined legitimacy.

Not all concubines were slaves, but most were. In most societies, the attraction of a slave concubine was that she was totally dependent. She had no family, could be sold, dismissed from the patriarchal bed, or punished. That meant, of course, that her tenure depended on her ability to satisfy. She was insecure. On the American slave plantation, masters sometimes engaged in promiscuous relations with their female slaves. This was even true of many married men. Others, including some married men, maintained a long-term relationship with a single slave woman. These relationships could be tender and caring. Often in such cases, the man arranged for the liberation of the concubine and the offspring he had with her. This was more common in the Caribbean where many men did not have wives with them. Young men were often hired by absentee owners to work as managers and overseers. They often kept slave concubines and sometimes maintained these relations over long periods of time. In urban Latin America, the **Catholic Church** fought against concubinage, but the institution was widespread. *See also* SEXUAL EXPLOITATION.

CONDORCET, MARIE-JEAN-ANTOINE-NICOLA, MARQUIS DE (1741-1794). Condorcet was a mathematician, a political theorist, and a leading figure in the French **Enlightenment**. Secretary to the French Royal Academy of Science, Condorcet was a firm believer in the rights of all human beings to freedom. He defended women, slaves, Jews, and other oppressed groups. In 1781, he wrote *Réflexions sur l'esclavage des nègres*, a pamphlet which attacked slavery and advocated an immediate end to the **slave trade** and a gradual emancipation of all slaves. He argued that slavery was morally wrong and economically unproductive. He believed, like Adam Smith, that free labor was more productive than slave labor. He became a good friend of **Benjamin Franklin** when Franklin represented the American colonists in Paris, and may have influenced Franklin's views. In 1788, Condorcet was one of the founders of the *Société des amis des Noirs* (**Society of the Friends of Blacks**). During the French Revolution, he pushed his views with passion, but was also an opponent of Robespierre's Reign of Terror. He was in hiding when slavery was abolished by the National Assembly in 1794. He was arrested a month later and died in prison. *See also* ABOLITION, FRANCE; FRENCH REVOLUTION.

CONFEDERATE STATES OF AMERICA. After the election of **Abraham Lincoln** in 1860, seven slaveholding states voted to secede from the United States, fearing that Lincoln's election meant an end to the expansion of slavery, and thus, eventually an end to slavery. In February 1861, they met and voted to form the Confederate States of America. Jefferson Davis was elected president. Though Davis did not want war, he moved immediately to take control of forts and military installations on southern soil. On 12 April, Confederate guns fired on Fort Sumter in Charleston harbor and Lincoln called for volunteers to suppress the rebellion. The war was on. Four more slaveholding states joined the Confederacy, but the border states of Maryland, Delaware, Kentucky, and Missouri remained with the Union.

The Confederate constitution was based on the American Constitution, but it affirmed the rights of the states and the institution of slavery. It prohibited any measure restricting the property rights of the master or the master's right to take their slaves anywhere in the Confederacy. The leaders proclaimed their belief in black racial inferiority. Slavery was the cement of the Confederacy even though only a quarter of white Southerners actually owned slaves. In spite of this, the Confederacy eventually found itself dependent on its slaves. The Confederacy did well in the early stages of the war, largely because its military leadership was more experienced, but the Union was wealthier and more populous. Confederate slaves built fortifications, were the workers in industry and the nurses in military hospitals. Some free blacks were armed, but many more slaves fled across Union lines.

In the summer of 1863, the Confederate invasion of the North failed at Gettysburg and Union armies seized Vicksburg, Mississippi. In desperation, as Union armies seized Atlanta and moved through the South, Jefferson Davis asked the Confederate Congress to approve the arming of black troops, who would be offered their freedom in exchange for military service. The Confederate Congress approved the recruitment of black troops, but rejected the offer of emancipation. On April 9, 1865, Robert E. Lee surrendered to Union General Ulysses Grant at Appomattox, Virginia, and the Confederacy was ended. *See also* CIVIL WAR.

CONFRATERNITIES. Confraternities were communal organizations of laymen within the **Catholic Church**. They were important in medieval Europe. When large numbers of African slaves began arriving in Spain and Portugal in the 15th century, confraternities integrated them into Catholic religious life. In Africa and Latin America, missionaries organized confraternities in their effort to evangelize local populations. There were separate confraternities for whites and blacks, for men and women, and sometimes, for people from different regions of Africa. For slaves, they provided mutual aid, a role in religious festivals, and a dignified funeral. They were particularly important in Brazil, where the African population was very large. The confraternities were often devoted to black saints and helped preserve African religious customs and even African religious beliefs. They were probably most important in providing a religious life and meaningful social bonds for slaves. They played an important role in breaking slaves' isolation and in helping to integrate them into Portuguese culture. They also helped slaves to maintain African traditions within a Catholic context. They tended to be most important in the cities. *See also* SLAVE RELIGION.

CONFUCIANISM. Confucianism was more an ideology of social relations than a religion. It was not concerned with God or with understanding the spiritual world. Central to Confucianism was a concern with hierarchical relationships such as ruler and subject, father and son, and master and slave. In the abstract, the position of the slave under Chinese law was quite limited. Punishments for crimes by slaves were harsher than those committed by free persons. Masters could beat slaves, who were considered lifelong children, and they could take female slaves as sexual partners. A slave could not wear fine clothes and could be punished for making accusations against his master. The great power that the master held over the slave was checked only by the humane values of Confucianism, which stressed the moral obligations that superior and inferior had toward each other. The slave owed the master obedience. The master owed the slave kindness and consideration. The superior was obligated not only to the slave but to the ethical standards of Confucianism. Slaves were property, but were also human beings. During the last years of the Chinese Empire, Chinese reformers favorable to abolition based their critique of slavery on Confucian ethical ideas. *See also* CHINESE SLAVERY.

CONSTITUTION OF THE UNITED STATES. In the debates at the convention that produced the U.S. Constitution in 1787, slavery was not a major issue. Though the use of slaves was becoming an important divide between North and South, the abolition movement was only in its early stages. Though slavery was coming under attack in northern states, it still existed there and some Southerners also had reservations about the morality of slavery. The Constitutional Convention met before the introduction of the **cotton** gin increased the demand for slave labor and at a time when a lot of Virginians were worried about their large slave surplus. Slaves were a major source of labor in the South, but were less important in the North.

The question of slavery came up in a number of contexts. The first was the debate over representation. When the decision was made that Congress be chosen by population, the question was whether slaves would count in calculating how many representatives a state got. The compromise was that three fifths of the slave population would count. This increased southern representation in Congress, but not as much as they wanted. The second question was over the continuation of the **slave trade**. Many delegates, including several Southerners, wanted to end it. The compromise protected it until 1808. Congress would then have the authority to ban the slave trade. This gave Southerners 20 years to accumulate slaves. By 1808, most southern states had already ended the import of slaves. Third, the Constitution denied the federal government the authority to interfere with slavery where it existed.

North-South relations were also influenced by two issues pushed by small states. One was the formula for amending the Constitution. It was decided that an amendment could only be approved when it had the accord of three-quarters of the states. This essentially made amendment difficult and meant the South could block changes prejudicial to its interests. The convention also decided against direct election of the president. Instead, he was to be chosen by an electoral college, whose numbers were based on a state's representation in the Senate and the House of Representatives. Since the Senate involved equal representation of each state, this increased the electoral importance of the less populous southern states. Finally, the equal division of the Senate between pro- and anti-slavery states meant that as the slavery issue became more divisive, the South could block legislation that threatened slavery or its extension.

The constitutional protection of the slave system extended into many institutions. Many clauses of the Constitution were litigated over the years. The Supreme Court tended to be a conservative body with strong southern representation. Where questions involving slavery were taken to it, the Court generally insisted that slaves were property. The most important decision was the **Dred Scott case** (1857), in which the Court insisted that a slave owner had the right to take his slaves with him into federal territories. The Constitution limited President **Abraham Lincoln** during the American **Civil War**. He was able to act against slavery in those states that had rebelled against the Union, but had no right to do so in the border states, which remained in the Union. The question of slavery was thus not definitively decided until the passage of three amendments to the Constitution after the Civil War. The **Thirteenth Amendment** abolished slavery. The **Fourteenth Amendment** made African-Americans citizens. The **Fifteenth Amendment** banned racial discrimination in voting rights. *See also* AMERICAN SLAVERY (U.S.).

CONTEMPORARY FORMS OF SLAVERY. Since 1970, slavery has no longer been legal anywhere in the world. In spite of this, millions of people are controlled by others, forced to do work they do not wish to do, and do not have the freedom to leave these onerous situations. **Anti-Slavery International** estimates that approximately five million people are held in conditions approximating slavery. The number could be higher. It depends on how one assesses different kinds of people whose freedom is restrained.

The largest part of this group is children. In some cases they are kidnapped, but usually they were provided by parents who live in oppressive poverty. Sometimes, those parents think their children were taking jobs that would give them opportunities. In most cases, the parents involved probably have little knowledge of the fate they are consigning their children to. Often they think their children can send money home, and some do. In yet other cases, the children involved are runaways who are trapped into relationships they do not choose. Many of these children, mostly girls, but some boys, work in the sex industry as prostitutes, catering to the tastes of men who like their partners young. Others work in industries like rugmaking where they are valued because their small fingers are more dexterous than those of adults.

Adults also find themselves in servile relationships. Chattel slavery still exists in Mauritania, though slavery is illegal there. It has returned during the 1990s in the Sudan as the result of a civil war, in which militias raided rebellious areas and took prisoners who were either sold or given to members of the militia. There is also adult prostitution. Most prostitutes choose their profession, but there are criminal networks that recruit women from poor countries in Eastern Europe, Africa, or Latin America, who once away from the protection of their homes, find themselves being sold into brothels, where they are kept confined and forced to work as prostitutes for low salaries. There are also peasants locked by debt into conditions of bondage in India and Nepal. There are workers in the Brazilian Amazon and the Dominican Republic who are forced to work in abusive conditions.

Most of these people, in particular the sex workers and the child laborers, will be discarded when they no longer serve anyone's interest. Others like the bonded laborers are legally free, but lack the ability to make that freedom effective. Since 1975, the **United Nations** Working Group of experts on Contemporary Forms of Slavery has met every year to take evidence on different forms of slavery-like institutions. *See also* BONDED LABOR; INDIAN SLAVERY; SEXUAL SLAVERY.

CONTUBERNIUM. Under Roman law, a *contubernium* was a form of marriage between slaves in which the two partners had none of the rights of marriage. Everything they had was owned by their masters, their children were owned by their masters, and any commitment each had to the other could be overruled by the master. *See also* ANCIENT ROMAN SLAVERY.

CORO REVOLT, VENEZUELA. The coastal lowlands of Venezuela experienced from about 1530 large slave importations to work in mines and on plantations. With a large, poorly populated hinterland, the area also experienced regular flight and many **slave revolts**. The first slave revolt was led by a slave known as King Miguel in the 1550s. The best known revolt took place at Coro, a small Venezuelan port in a predominantly black province. The two leaders were **José Leonardo Chirino**, who worked for a Coro merchant, and José Caridad Gonzalez, a free black who was believed to have magical powers. The stimulus was a visit by Chirino to Saint-Domingue, then in the first flush of the **Haitian Revolution**. In May 1795, Chirino proclaimed a French-style republic and set off with a small band, killing about a dozen planters and burning their *haciendas*. The rebels quickly gathered a force of slaves, Indians, and free blacks, and besieged a number of whites in a church. The second day of the siege, the local militia arrived and quickly dispersed Chirino's force. Within a month, 171 persons were executed and over 50 imprisoned. *See also* HISPANIC AMERICA.

COTTON. Until the end of the 18th century, most slaves in the Americas worked in **sugar** production. Brazil and the West Indies had populations that were largely slave, on some West Indian islands, as much as 90 percent slave. In the United States, only in South Carolina was there a slave majority. Slaves in the United States were used to cultivate diverse products, **tobacco** more than anything else. More than two-fifths of the slaves in the United States in 1790 lived in Virginia. The biggest problem with cotton was the expense of removing the seeds from cotton by hand. Then, in 1793, Eli Whitney invented the cotton gin, which could clean 50 pounds of cotton a day. This was at a time when Great Britain was hungry for cotton for its rapidly expanding textile industry. Cotton exports went from 200,000 pounds a year before Whitney's invention to over 18 million in 1800. Cotton continued to grow and rapidly spread across Georgia, Alabama, and Mississippi and then later to Texas after it was annexed by the United States. These lands could be exploited only if labor could be found. It was found on the declining tobacco fields of the Chesapeake region.

The United States is one of the few places in the world where slave populations have grown by natural reproduction. Demographic growth was particularly rapid in the old slave states of Maryland and Virginia. With the end of slave imports in 1808, slave prices rose sharply and there was a massive movement of slaves from Virginia and Maryland to the new cotton areas, sometimes taken by owners who wanted to be part of the cotton boom, often sold off by tobacco **plantations** that were no longer productive. In 1800, about one of 10 United States slaves worked on a cotton plantation. By 1860, that number had risen to two of three. Cotton, like sugar, was well suited to slave labor. The slaves could be used most of the year, and gang labor, if well organized, was very productive.

The major result of the cotton revolution was the polarization of the United States. The rising price of slaves meant that most southern planters had their capital tied up in their slaves. At a time when slavery was gradually being eliminated in the North, the South was becoming more dependent on it. Before the cotton gin, many Southerners were worried about the South's large slave populations and some, like Thomas Jefferson and George Washington, had reservations about slavery. After the cotton gin, the South was even more dependent on slave labor than before — and Southerners were very conscious of the fact. *See also* DEMOGRAPHY OF SLAVERY.

CRAFT, WILLIAM (1827-1900) AND ELLEN (1826-1890). The Crafts were slaves in Macon, Georgia, who became well-known because of the way they escaped the South. William was a cabinetmaker, who was able to earn enough money to pay their travel expenses. Ellen was the daughter of a white man. She dressed with glasses and a muffler to cover her face and pretended to be an elderly master, while William claimed to be her servant. After a number of adventures, they made it to Philadelphia and then to Boston, accompanied on the last part of the trip by **William Wells Brown**, another former slave. In Boston, they married again and became active in the abolition movement. After passage of the **Fugitive Slave Law** in 1850, agents for their masters appeared with warrants for their arrest, but they fled to England, where they were active in the abolition movement. After the **Civil War**, they returned to Georgia and founded an industrial school. Their first school was burned by the Ku Klux Klan. They told the story of their adventures in *Running a Thousand Miles for Freedom* (1860).

CREOLE **INCIDENT (1841).** The *Creole* was a vessel engaged in the interstate **slave trade**. In 1841, it was carrying 135 slaves from Virginia to Louisiana when 19 slaves mutinied, seized the boat, and took it to Nassau in the Bahamas. The Bahamas were a British colony where slavery was illegal. The attorney-general of the Bahamas freed both the mutineers and the rest of the slave cargo. Though there was no extradition treaty between the two countries, President John Tyler asked for the return of the slaves. The British refused, but the disagreement led to a decision to negotiate a series of major differences. The Webster-Ashburton Treaty of 1842 settled some of these differences. It protected United States ships stopping in British ports and included an extradition treaty. Because of abolitionist pressure, the British did not accept mutiny as grounds for extradition. In 1853, a claims commission provided compensation to southern slaveowners who owned the slaves on the *Creole*.

CROWTHER, SAMUEL AJAYI (c. 1806-1891). Born as a **Yoruba** in western Nigeria, Samuel Crowther was taken prisoner in 1821 in the wars that troubled the Yoruba during the early 19th century and sold to Brazilian slavers. When the ship was stopped by the British navy's anti-slave trade patrol, the ship and the slaves were taken to Freetown, **Sierra Leone**. He was educated by the **Church Missionary Society (CMS)** and baptized in 1825. Two years later, Crowther became the first student at newly founded Fourah Bay College, and in 1843 was ordained an Anglican minister. Starting with the Niger expedition of 1841, he served as an interpreter on a number of expeditions up the Niger River. He was also the principal translator of the Bible into Yoruba. Crowther was appointed head of the Niger Mission in 1857 and opened mission stations at a number of points in the Niger Delta and along the Niger River. The Niger Mission was staffed exclusively by Africans, most of them, like Crowther, former slaves educated by the CMS.

By 1850, Crowther had become the recognized leader of the new Christian educated elite in Great Britain's African colonies. He faced the hostility of some white missionaries and imperialist interests. The Yoruba missions were never placed under his authority. In 1864, he became an Anglican bishop. In keeping with the CMS program, he worked for evangelization, for economic development and for the suppression of slavery and the slave trade. In 1890, he was forced to resign by a group of young European missionaries. Today, Crowther is regarded as the most important African Christian leader of his time. See also AFRICA SQUADRON; AFRICAN SLAVE TRADE; RECAPTIVES

CRUMMELL, ALEXANDER (1819-1898). Alexander Crummell was the leading African-American exponent of repatriation to Africa. The son of a Sierra Leonean, he was born in New York and studied at Cambridge University. Like **Martin Delany**, he confronted racism and despaired of African-Americans ever winning equality in the United States. In 1853, he emigrated to **Liberia**, where he worked as a minister, taught school, was a professor at Liberia College, and farmed. He wrote numerous articles in *African Repository*, the journal of the **American Colonization Society**, and in 1862 published *The Future of Africa*. In Liberia, he fought with white missionaries about the organization of a black diocese and he fought for the indigenous Africans in their conflicts with the elite of Americo-Liberian settlers. In 1872, he returned to the United States.

CUBAN SLAVERY. Cuba was first settled by the Spanish in 1511. By mid-century, African slaves were being used to mine gold. Cuba soon became the major base for the Spanish in the Caribbean. **Sugar plantations** were not as important as on the British and French islands until the late 18th century. Slaves worked in farming, ranching, petty trade, and domestic service. Then, from the 1760s, growth was rapid. When the **Haitian Revolution** shattered Saint-Domingue's sugar and coffee economy in the 1790s and Great Britain abolished the slave trade in 1807, the Spanish expanded sugar, **tobacco**, and coffee production even more rapidly until by 1840 Cuba was the world's largest sugar producer. Coffee production was stimulated by the arrival of refugee planters from Saint-Domingue. Between 1774 and 1841, the slave population grew from a little over 40,000 to over 400,000. Slave imports continued until almost 1870.

Cuba differed from other sugar-producing islands in that it always had more whites than blacks. This was partly because the island had a long history before it focussed on sugar and partly because it had a more diversified economy. It also had a large population of free Blacks, up to 40 percent of the Afro-Cuban population in the 1860 s, many of them skilled workers in the cities. Spanish law encouraged manumission. Of particular importance was *coartación*, a procedure by which a slave could pay for his freedom in installments.

In spite of this, conditions on sugar plantations got worse as sugar grew in importance. At its peak, they were as harsh as elsewhere: gang labor, 14- to 16-hour days during the five-month harvest season, brutal punishments, and poor nutrition. There is a Cuban saying that "sugar is made with blood." During the 19th century the mechanization of mills and the introduction of light rail systems to move the cane to the mills made Cuban plantations more efficient, but this increased rather than reduced the pressure on workers. The system was very productive. Three years of a slave's labor could pay for his or her purchase price. In the cities, the **Catholic Church** supported **confraternities** called *cabildos*, which were often rooted in African ethnic or regional consciousness and combined free and slave blacks. *Cabildos* raised money for manumissions, organized recreational activities, and dealt with white institutions.

Cuba had a long history of slave resistance, marked by revolt and by flight. There were at any time a number of small **Maroon** communities in the mountains, some with more than 100 members. There were professional slave hunters who went searching for Maroons, but they were often frustrated by fortifications around the runaways' communities called *palenques.* Between 1825 and 1845, there was a series of **slave revolts**, many of them involving primarily Yoruba slaves from Nigeria. Plantations were burned and repression was brutal. This led to the importation of Chinese workers. Between 1847 and 1874, 124,813 were imported, only 80 of them female.

Eventually, slave resistance merged with the struggle for freedom from Spain during the Ten Years' War (1868-1878). Rebel leader Carlos Manuel de Cespedes began his call to arms by freeing his own slaves. Many of the leaders supported gradual emancipation, but before long former slaves and free blacks formed a majority of the liberation army. Faced with both domestic opposition and foreign sympathy with the rebels, Spain responded with the **Moret Law** of 187o, which freed all slaves born after 1868 and all over 60 years of age. In 1880, another law set up a system under which slaves were called *patrocinados* and worked for payments to be used for self-purchase. If this law had worked as projected, all of the slaves would have been freed by 1888, but slaves increasingly took matters in their own hands. An 1886 law recognized this by freeing all of the *patrocinados*. *See also* HISPANIC AMERICA; MACEO, ANTONIO.

CUCUTÁ, CONGRESS OF (1821). The Congress of Cucutá followed an earlier **Congress of Angostura** (1819). It produced a constitution for the Republic of Gran Colombia, which included what is now Colombia, Venezuela, and Ecuador. Slavery was a major subject of debate. The Congress confirmed the abolition of the **slave trade** and the freedom of those slaves emancipated during the liberation struggle. Many, however, remained in slavery in **mining** areas and on **plantations** in coastal Colombia and Venezuela. Their owners fought against a general emancipation. The resulting compromise was a **free womb law**, which freed all children born subsequently, but only after reaching the age of 18 and subject to a review of the slave's personal conduct. Very few slaves were freed under this law. The president of Gran Colombia, **Simón Bolívar**, tried to strengthen it, but failed, and when Gran Colombia collapsed in 1830, the formal emancipation of the slaves was deferred for more than a generation. *See also* EMANCIPATION, HISPANIC AMERICA.

CUGOANO, OTTOBAH. Though Ottobah Cuguano was the author of one of the first books about slavery written by a former slave, very little is known about him. He was born about 1757 in southern Ghana and shipped to Grenada, where he worked on a plantation for a year. Then, his master took him to England as a servant in 1772. It is not known how he was freed, but that very year, Lord Mansfield held in the **Somerset case** that one could not be a slave in England. In 1773, he was baptized. During the following years, he wrote letters on the slavery issue and seems to have been involved with abolitionist groups. In 1786, he informed **Granville Sharp** that another former slave, Henry Demane, had been kidnapped and was being returned to the West Indies. Sharp got a writ of habeas corpus and rescued Demane as the ship was about to leave.. In 1787, he published *Thoughts and Sentiments on the Evil and Wicked Trade of Slavery and the Commerce of the Human Species*, which tried to refute arguments for slavery and argued for the slave's duty to resist. In 1791, he published an abridged version, in which he said he intended to open a school. Nothing is

known of him after that date. *See also* ABOLITION, GREAT BRIT-
AIN.

CUJO (c.1680-1744). Cujo was a common name among Akan of southern
Ghana. Many Cujos found their way to the Americas in the **slave trade**,
but the most famous was the leader of a **Maroon** state in the interior of
Jamaica that successfully fought off the British. Cujo's father, Naquan,
was enslaved in the 1640s and shipped to Jamaica. Soon after his arrival in Spanish Jamaica, he led a group of rebel slaves into the mountainous interior. When Jamaica was conquered by the British in 1655,
many slaves took advantage of the disorder to join the Maroons in the
interior. When Naquan died, Cujo succeeded him. He organized his
community into five towns, all set in rugged mountainous terrain. The
Maroons often raided plantations and freed runaway slaves. When the
British invaded during the First Maroon War in 1730, command of the
Maroons was divided between Cujo in the west and his sister, Nanny,
in the east. The Maroons proved adept at guerilla warfare, using camou-
flage, ambushes, and a communication system that involved drums and
horns. After a series of defeats, the British asked for negotiations.
Eventually, a treaty was agreed upon in 1739 that confirmed the inde-
pendence of the Maroons in exchange for a promise to return runaway
slaves. Cujo died five years later. He was succeeded by his brother,
Accompong. The Jamaican Maroons remained free. *See also* SLAVE
REVOLTS.

CURAÇAO SLAVE REVOLT (1795). Curaçao was primarily a base for
Dutch trade in the West Indies. The revolt began in the small plantation
sector. It was stimulated by the successful **slave revolt** on Saint-Domingue several years earlier and the defeat of the Dutch by the French
in Europe. It began when slaves on two plantations stopped work, and
spread quickly as free blacks and runaways joined in. The slaves were
unhappy about Sunday work and punishments given to all of the slaves
for the actions of one. They were armed and seem to have carefully
prepared their action. Troops were called in and suppressed the revolt
within a month. Most of the slaves were returned to their plantations,
but leaders were hung after being tortured on the rack. Free persons
involved in the revolt were expelled from the island. It led, however, to
a new body of regulations, which clarified the rights and obligations of
the slaves. It guaranteed Sunday as a day of rest and required adequate
food and clothing. It also limited punishment to those accused of actual
wrongdoing. *See also* DUTCH SLAVE TRADE.

-D-

DAHOMEY. Dahomey was one of the most efficient producers of slavers in West Africa was the kingdom of Dahomey in what is today the Republic of Benin. It first developed somewhat inland from the coast early in the 17th century. In the second half of the 17th century, it developed a very effective army and gradually extended its control. Under King Agaja (1708-1740), it achieved its opening to the sea with the conquest of the coastal states of Allada (1724) and **Whydah** (1727). For much of the rest of the 18th century, Whydah was the most important slaving port in West Africa, exports rising often to 20,000 a year.

In the early years, most of the slaves came from an annual campaign waged by Dahomey's army, but with time, Abomey developed as a slave market and slaves were brought there by traders from further north. In Whydah, a representative of the king, the *yevogan,* maintained a very tight control over the trade. European merchants were restricted to the coast and traded with licensed merchants who brought the slaves from Abomey. In spite of its success, Dahomey was a tributary of its larger and more powerful neighbor, the **Yoruba** kingdom of **Oyo**. In the early years of the 19th century, that relationship was reversed when Oyo collapsed during the Yoruba civil wars and Dahomey preyed on Yoruba areas.

Dahomey was also a large user of slave labor. Both the king and the powerful merchants had **plantations** worked by slave labor. Many slaves were also **concubines** and servants and some were sacrificed in annual festivals. In the 19th century, Dahomey continued to export slaves. Like other parts of the Bight of Benin, it was the center of commercial activity by **Afro-Brazilian** traders. As the British navy gradually limited Dahomean exports, slaves were gradually shifted into producing palm oil within Dahomey. In 1892, Dahomey was conquered by the French. *See also* AFRICAN SLAVE TRADE.

DE BOW, JAMES D. B. (1820-1867). James De Bow was one of the most influential pro-slavery political theorists in the southern United States. A graduate of the College of Charleston, James De Bow studied law, but did not enjoy working as a lawyer. In 1846, he founded *De Bow's Review* in New Orleans. He was also a professor of political economy at the University of Louisiana. *De Bow's Review* quickly became one of the most influential defenders of slavery, southern nationalism, and doctrines of racial superiority. De Bow wrote exten-

sively himself. He served as superintendent of the 1850 census and was
effective in his use of census data. De Bow also believed that reliance
on a single crop was unwise, but was convinced that slave labor could
be the basis for the industrial development of the South. He believed
that slaves were well suited for both agricultural and industrial work. In
1860, he advocated secession, but during the war he was forced to
suspend publication of the *Review*. He resumed publication in 1865,
unrepentant in his views, but died two years later.

DEBT SLAVERY. In many slave systems there were various provisions
for a person to be enslaved or to put a member of his family into slavery
in payment of debts. Often this was voluntary, though on other occasions enslavement was a judicial response to debt. Debt slavery existed
in the ancient Middle East, where a man could be condemned to slavery
for debt. The law of Hammurabi in Babylon (1700 BCE) limited debt
slavery to a three-year term, but the same law code permitted a man to
use his wife as security for a loan or to sell himself or a child.

The **Bible** sought to regulate enslavement for debt. A Hebrew debt
slave had to be freed at the end of his seventh year of servitude or
during the jubilee year. Throughout the Indian subcontinent and southeast Asia, it was possible for a man to enslave himself or a member of
his family either because of extreme poverty or debt. In some cases,
men were enslaved because of lost wagers. The Hindu lawgiver,
Narada, listed a number of other causes of debt slavery: famine, debt,
and the need for maintenance. The only restriction was that a member
of the Brahman caste could not be enslaved. In most cases, debt slavery
was reversible. That is to say, if the debt were repaid, the debtor could
be freed. Most forms of debt slavery were also not hereditary.

In Africa, debt slavery is called **pawnship**. Generally, a borrower
or a debtor enslaved a member of his family, usually a girl child. It was
often done as surety for a loan or because of famine. The child's labor
functioned as if it were the interest on the debt. When the debt was repaid, the child was returned. Africans generally did not see the pawn as
a slave because she remained a member of her family which could
redeem her. Some writers think that when such a pawn was not
redeemed, she could often became a full slave. By contrast, in ancient
Greece, debt often led to the enslavement of adults. During the sixth
century BCE, as Athens began shifting into the production of wine and
olive oil for market, debt slavery was a major source of labor. When a
social crisis emerged, **Solon**'s legal reforms abolished debt slavery and
guaranteed the citizenship of all Athenians. That forced entrepreneurial

farmers to seek slaves outside Athens and led to Athens becoming a **slave society**.

There are modern forms of debt servitude. In colonial America, a person could be sold into servitude for failing to pay taxes or fines. In India, there is a system called **bonded labor**, under which debts keep many people in a permanent dependent relationship. In the Americas, debt has been used to keep landless laborers dependent and force them to work for a landlord at low wages. This is often referred to **peonage**. *See also* ANCIENT GREEK SLAVERY; INDIAN SLAVERY; INDONESIAN SLAVERY; THAI SLAVERY.

DECLARATION OF THE RIGHTS OF MAN. The Declaration of the Rights of Man is one of the most important and most enduring documents of the **French Revolution**. It was approved on August 26, 1789, as the preamble to a new constitution. The constitution in question has long since disappeared, but the Declaration of the Rights of Man remains one of the most important statements of human rights. It began with the words "Men are born and remain free and equal in rights." It listed those rights as "liberty, property, security and resistance to oppression." It claimed that sovereignty lay not with the king but with the people and guaranteed the people the right to take part through their representatives in the writing of laws.

Once approved, the question became who the men were to whom the declaration applied. The constitution distinguished between active and passive citizens. Only the active citizens could vote. They were men over the age of 25, who paid a tax equal to three days pay. A small group within the National Assembly gathered in the **Society of the Friends of Blacks** believed that slaves also had the rights enumerated in the Declaration. Pro-slavery elements rallied to oppose them and a delegation of white planters from Saint-Domingue asked for seats in the National Assembly. A delegation of mulatto planters, led by **Vincent Ogé**, also asked for representation. When the matter was referred back to the governor of Saint-Domingue, Ogé returned to Saint-Domingue, where in October 1790 he led a rising of mulattoes. Though his forces were defeated and he was killed, a rising of slaves began 10 months later. The divisions in the planter community and the debates about human rights had opened the door to one of the few successful slave revolutions. *See also* ENLIGHTENMENT; HAITIAN REVOLUTION.

DELANY, MARTIN R. (1812-1885). Martin Delany was an important mid-19th century African-American thinker. He was born the son of a free mother and slave father in Charleston, Virginia, but his family early moved to Chambersburg, Pennsylvania. He had a very varied career: doctor, journalist, ethnologist, editor, judge, scientist, orator, politician, and novelist. From 1843 to 1847, he edited *Mystery*, an African-American newspaper in Pittsburgh. Then, he worked for two years with **Frederick Douglass** on his newspaper, *Northern Star*. In 1852, he brought out his most important book, *The Condition, Elevation, Emigration, and Destiny of the Coloured People of the United States, Politically Considered*. Up to this point, most black intellectuals assumed that if they got an education and earned the respect of their white peers, slavery would be ended and they would be accepted as citizens. Delany was angry about the failure of northern states to grant citizenship to African-Americans. This anger was exacerbated when Harvard admitted him and two black colleagues to its medical school on condition that they practice outside the United States, and then, when racist white students protested, withdrew that admission.

Delany was now convinced that African-Americans would only get justice in a state of their own making. He attacked the **American Colonization Society**, but advocated emigration. Delany was the father of a tradition of black nationalism that did not so much look to White society to do right as to African-American society to take care of itself. In 1856, he moved to Chatham, Ontario, and in 1859 he led an expedition to Africa. In 1859, the novel *Blake; or the Huts of America* began to appear serially. It involved a black revolutionary hero. During the Civil War, Delany recruited for black regiments, and after the war he worked for the **Freedmen's Bureau**. *See also* ABOLITION, UNITED STATES.

DEMERARA SLAVE REVOLT (1823). One of the largest **slave revolts** in American history, the Demerara slave revolt began on a **sugar** plantation in Guyana called Success, which was owned by John Gladstone, the father of future British prime minister, William Ewart Gladstone. Eventually it involved over 10,000 slaves on more than 60 plantations. The revolt was influenced by Methodist missionaries of the London Missionary Society, who had been working in Demerara since 1803. The leaders were elite slaves who gathered at a chapel the missionaries had created. The missionaries also communicated their own disapproval of slavery.

A number of factors made Demerara vulnerable to revolt. First, as in **Saint-Domingue**, the whites were a small minority. Slaves numbered

75,000 of 80,000 in the district. Second, it changed hands six times between 1780 and 1803 before being incorporated into the British Empire. There had been an earlier revolt in 1795. Though Demerara was originally Dutch, most of the planters were British. Finally, the planters were heavily in debt. When sugar prices dropped, they tried to drive their slaves harder, producing considerable discontent. The direct stimulus was a rumor that slavery had been abolished, but the planters had withheld the information. The planters blamed the missionaries. One of them, John Smith, was convicted of fomenting treason and died in prison while appealing his conviction to Parliament.

DEMOGRAPHY OF SLAVERY. It is often difficult to do an accurate demography of a slave community. This is because there were always newcomers entering it and there was always a flow-through, a number of slaves who were being manumitted, or slave women who were producing free children. Nevertheless, some generalizations can be made about slave demography. The first is that there was almost always a high mortality. Mortality was highest in the **slave trade**. Those being moved were sometimes sick to start with; they were taken from one climatic zone to another, being introduced to new diseases, and the maintenance of discipline often lead to harsh treatment. They were also often held in tightly packed small enclosures: slave ships, **barracoons**, or the dungeons of slave castles. Finally, they often lost the will to live and committed suicide or "pined away."

Even after they arrived in a new environment, the **seasoning** period was still a period of high mortality because they had to adapt to a new climate, to new diseases, and to a new social environment. Even after they were settled in a new community, they often still had a higher mortality than free persons. They were less well fed and clothed, and during periods of hardship, were often the first to suffer. In parts of West Africa, during droughts, slaves who could not be fed were simply turned out to fend for themselves.

Slaves also tended to have a lower rate of reproduction. In many areas, this was because of a skewed male-female distribution. Where slave women were numerous, as in the Arab world, many women were isolated in **harems**, where only one male had access to them. Many slave women were servants, who rarely had sexual relations. Even the favorites tended to have few children. In the West Indies, Brazil, and the Dutch East Indies, there was the reverse problem, a male majority, many with no female partners. Even when slaves did marry, many chose to have few children. In the African communities, where they lived in families, the slave menage bore the cost of raising the child, but could never be sure the child would be around to support them in old age. The economics of the slave family forced them to restrict reproduction. Slaves were also in most situations less well fed, housed, and clothed. In almost all slave societies, the rate of infant mortality was higher for slaves than for free persons.

There are very few areas where slave populations increased. This is most striking for the United States and for the Captaincy of Minas Gerais in Brazil. Both were areas that early had gender parity, where the climate and disease environment were attractive, where slaves were well fed and given good medical treatment. The importation of slaves to the United States ended in 1808. From 1810 to 1860, the slave population multiplied almost four times. Slaves in the United States lived in family units. The rise in slave prices after the end of slave imports provided an incentive for slave masters to provide adequate food, shelter, and medical care for their slaves. The rate of infant mortality was still high, but the health of older children and adults was as good as other working populations.

DE SOUZA, FELIX FRANCISCO (c. 1760-1849). Felix Francisco De Souza was a Brazilian merchant who first established himself on the Bight of Benin as a small merchant in 1788. He dealt mostly in slaves. When the wars of the **French Revolution** forced some European slave trading operations to close down, De Souza and other Brazilians like Domingo Martins filled the void. De Souza's trading posts extended along the lagoon from Grand Popo to Lagos. He also was careful to make influential friends. In 1818, he helped one of those friends, Ghezo, seize the throne of Dahomey. As his reward, Ghezo created a new office, that of *chacha,* and gave it to De Souza, superseding the power of the *yevogan*. His role was to represent the king, selling the king's slaves and collecting customs. This made him the most powerful slave trader in the region, but he also recognized that the **slave trade** was threatened and encouraged Ghezo to develop royal palm oil **plantations**, which would use slave labor within Africa. The Brazilian community increased when Brazil deported many free blacks after the **Male revolt** in Bahia in 1835. The De Souza family has remained very influential in Benin. *See also* AFRO-BRAZILIANS; BAHIAN SLAVE REVOLTS; DAHOMEY.

DESSALINES, JEAN-JACQUES (c. 1758-1806). Dessalines was one of the generals in the army of former slaves who won Haitian independence and was briefly emperor of Haiti. He was born a slave, probably in a coffee-growing area that was one of the centers of the Saint-Domingue revolt. In later life, he often displayed his scarred back to explain his hatred of his former French masters. He got involved early in slave resistance and was by 1794 a battalion commander in the army of **Toussaint-Louverture**. By 1799, he was a general and the commander of an expedition to bring the mulatto controlled southern province under Toussaint's control. He established a reputation for brutality by executing hundreds of prisoners.

Dessalines was then given responsability for bringing the **plantation** economy under control. Slavery had been abolished, but the new regime needed money and **sugar** was the only way to get it. The army reestablished the plantation system and made labor compulsory. In the process, many officers acquired estates. Dessalines controlled 33. Then, in 1802, Napoléon Bonaparte invaded and attempted to reestablish the French slave system. When Toussaint surrendered, Dessalines also submitted and briefly became an ally of the French, but in October 1803 all of the black generals turned against the French, who were quickly defeated. Toussaint had died in a French prison earlier that year.

On January 1, 1804, Dessalines proclaimed the independence of the former French colony under the name Haiti, an Amerindian name for the island. He became emperor. Whites were denied the right to own land and all French residents were ordered executed. Slavery was definitively ended. His most controversial policy, however, was his effort to maintain the plantation system, which increasingly fell under the control of the new black and mulatto elites. In October 1806, he was killed by a plot within his army, and two other generals took power, Alexandre Pétion in the south and **Henri Christophe** in the north. *See also* HAITIAN REVOLUTION.

DEVSHIRME. In the Ottoman Empire, the *devshirme* was a levy on boys in the Christian provinces of the empire. It originated in the 14th and 15th centuries, when the expansion of the state created a need for both civilian and military personnel. The boys taken from Christian families were converted to Islam and were trained for either bureaucratic or military service. The soldiers recruited in this way were the **janissaries**, the most prestigious military units in the Ottoman army. Those who entered the civil service also held many of the highest offices in the empire. The *devshirme* remained important in the Ottoman Empire until the middle of the 17th century. *See also* MILITARY SLAVES; OTTOMAN SLAVERY.

DEW, THOMAS RODERICK (1802-1846). Thomas Dew was one of the leading pro-slavery theorists in the South. He was born in Virginia in a **plantation** family, was educated at the College of William and Mary, and in 1827 became professor of political economy there. In 1831, in a reaction to the **Nat Turner** revolt, the Virginia state legislature debated a proposal that slaves be gradually emancipated and deported from the state. As part of the debate, Dew wrote *Review of the Debate in the Virginia Legislature of 1831 and 1832*, which laid out many arguments against the proposal and for slavery. Resettlement, he argued, would be too expensive. He went on to argue that Virginia's slaves would work only under compulsion and would be worse off if freed. He argued that the slaves were happy and well off. He then marshalled biblical and historical examples in support of his argument. Dew's essay was widely distributed and influenced other southern theorists. He became president of William and Mary in 1836.

DIALLO, AYUBA BEN SULEIMAN (c. 1701-1773). A Muslim trader from the kingdom on Bundu in the upper Senegal valley, Ayuba ben Suleiman was captured by slavers in 1730, while trading on the Gambia River and was shipped to Maryland. He was first put to work on **tobacco**, but when it became clear that he was not suited to such labor, he was shifted to tending cattle. His ethnic group, the Fulbe, were by tradition cattle herders, though Diallo was a merchant. He attracted attention by going into the woods every day to pray in seclusion. When he ran away because of conflict with a white youth, he was caught. He could not speak English, but tried to communicate by writing in Arabic. Surprised that he was literate, his master called him to the attention of well-known English intellectuals, who arranged for him to be freed and brought to England.

In 1734, Ayuba was brought back to **West Africa** accompanied by a British representative. He seems to have worked for a while as a representative of the Royal African Company, a British company that was competing with the French for the trade in slaves, gold, and gum from the upper Senegal-upper Gambia region. He is mentioned in company correspondence until the early 1740s. Little is known of him after that date. He was one of many educated Muslims taken in the **slave trade**, but fortunate that his existence came to the attention of English intellectuals interested in his knowledge and a company that wanted to use him as an agent.

DORT, SYNOD OF. As European states developed slave **plantations,**

European Christian churches had to deal with a number of religious questions. One was whether slaves should be baptized, and if baptized, whether they could then still be held as slaves. The Synod of Dort was a meeting of Calvinist theologians that met in 1618 and 1619 to deal with a series of theological questions. On the slavery issue, it held that slaves should have the same right to liberty as other Christians and should never be sold to non-Christians. It did not, however, require that slaves be converted. That was up to the conscience of the individual slaveholder. One result was that most Calvinist slave owners, largely in the Dutch colonies, refused to give their slaves a religious education or to baptize them for fear that this would require manumission.

DOUGLASS, FREDERICK (1818-1895). The most influential African-American abolitionist and one of the most eloquent black voices of the 19th century, Douglass was born a slave on Maryland's eastern shore. He had harsh memories of his early childhood. He never knew his father, who was white, and he had little contact with his mother, who worked a distance away and died when he was a child. Douglass was raised by his grandmother. He remembers being poorly clothed and cold and hungry during the winter. He was early assigned to his master's house and then sent to Baltimore to serve as a companion for his new master's son. His master's wife taught him to read, and though her husband stopped the lessons, Douglass continued to read whenever he could.

Douglass was working as a caulker in the Baltimore shipyard, when in 1838 he escaped to New York. By chance, he met abolitionists on the streets of New York, who sent him to New Bedford, Massachusetts, an abolitionist stronghold. Ironically, he could not get a job as a caulker in New Bedford because of racism. He soon, however, proved himself to be a powerful orator, and became one of the movement's most effective speakers. His effectiveness was the best possible antidote to pro-slavery racism. Douglass soon left New Bedford to establish himself in Rochester, New York, where he published an anti-slavery newspaper, begun as the *North Star* (1847) and renamed *Frederick Douglass' Paper* in 1850. He also published three versions of his autobiography. The first, *Narrative of the Life of Frederick Douglass* (1845), was the most popular slave narrative of the prewar period. Such narratives gave free people a sense of what life was like under slavery.

Douglass was originally a follower of **William Lloyd Garrison**, but he broke with Garrison because Garrison believed in moral suasion rather than politics. Douglass felt that the movement had to try to influence politics. During the **Civil War**, he was a strong advocate of using black troops, and when the 54th Massachusetts Regiment was organized, he recruited for it and two of his sons served in it. When it became clear that black troops would not be treated as well or paid as much as white troops, he attacked the War Department. Though he was often unhappy with the way Lincoln pursued the war, Douglass was an active Republican after the war. In 1881, he was appointed recorder of deeds for Washington, D.C., and in 1889 minister to Haiti. Until the end of his life, he fought against racism and discrimination. *See also* ABO-LITION, UNITED STATES.

DRED SCOTT CASE (1857). The Dred Scott case was a major victory for pro-slavery forces in the United States, but it brought closer the **Civil War** and the end of slavery. Dred Scott was a slave who was the personal servant of John Emerson, a U.S. Army surgeon from St. Louis, Missouri. Emerson had taken Scott with him to postings in Iowa and Wisconsin territories, where slavery was prohibited by the **Missouri Compromise**. In 1843, Emerson died, leaving Scott to his wife. The executor of the will was her brother, John Sanford. Scott sued for his freedom on grounds that setting foot on free territories made him free. Scott lost in the trial court, won on appeal, and then lost in the Missouri Supreme Court. He did not appeal to the U.S. Supreme Court at the time because his lawyers believed that the court did not have jurisdiction.

Then, however, ownership of Scott was transferred to Sanford and Sanford moved to New York. The case now involved residents of two separate states. When Scott lost again, he appealed to the U.S. Supreme Court. Chief Justice **Roger Taney** gave a sweeping response. First, he argued that because of their race, blacks were not citizens of the United States and could not sue in a federal court. Second, he argued that visiting a free territory did not make a slave free because the Constitution guaranteed the right of a person to his property, including the right of the slave owner to his slave. He therefore argued that the Missouri Compromise, which prohibited slavery in territories acquired as part of the Louisiana Purchase, was invalid because the federal government could not limit the slave owner's rights over his slaves.

The case delighted Southerners, but it offended many Northerners. Hostility to the Dred Scott decision and fear that the Court might restrict the right of free states to prohibit slavery helped the Republican Party, which was opposed to the extension of slavery. It contributed to the election of **Abraham Lincoln** in 1860. Soon after the case was decided, Dred Scott was sold to a man who set him free.

DRIVERS. In most **plantation** systems, there was a class of privileged slaves that directed the labor of the others. In **West Africa**, slaves were often settled in separate villages under slave chiefs. Any collective labor was usually directed by these chiefs. In the Americas, work gangs were often led by drivers, who woke the slaves before dawn, assigned tasks, directed labor in the fields, and arranged the feeding of slaves and animals at midday. They also often kept accounts, mediated conflicts, and were responsible for policing the slave quarters at night. As a reward, they received extra rations, better clothing, better housing, a more secure family life and bonuses of cash, liquor, or tobacco. They were also freer of restraint in their movements. Drivers often had to punish their fellow slaves, and were sometimes resented as the master's agent. On larger plantations, they often worked under the direction of and overseer.

Caught in the middle, they often found themselves forced to mediate conflicts. Nevertheless, the drivers were clearly very useful to slave owners. They often understood agriculture better than their white superiors and they could interpret the mood of the slaves to the slave owner. It is estimated that about two-thirds of the slaves in the United States worked under Black drivers. *See also* ELITE SLAVES.

DU BOIS, WILLIAM EDWARD BURGHARDT (1869-1963). W. E. B. Du Bois was the most influential African-American historian of the early 20th century and the first to examine the history of slavery. Born in western Massachusetts, he studied at Fisk University in Nashville and the University of Berlin. In 1896, he completed a thesis at Harvard University entitled *The Suppression of the African Slave Trade to the United States of America, 1638-1870*. Though most recent scholars disagree with his estimate of 250,000 slaves illegally imported into the U.S. after the 1808 abolition of the trade, his use of primary sources made the study a model for later research.

Du Bois was interested in Africa throughout his life. In 1903, his *Souls of Black Folk* probed the rich African tradition of music and religion and the way they were forged by African-Americans into powerful consolations for their sufferings. In *The Negro* (1915), he celebrated the African heritage and chronicled the accomplishments of African-Americans. He was a key figure in a number of Pan-African conferences and in the development of Pan-African ideology. From 1910 to 1934, he was also the editor of *Crisis*, the publication of the National Association for the Advancement of Colored People (NAACP). In 1935, he published *Black Reconstruction in America,*

1860-1880, which began a reconsideration of the **Reconstruction** period. The themes he identified and the methods he developed had a great influence on other historians. Throughout his long life, his works focussed not only on the immorality of slavery, but also on the way its heritage continued to deny African-Americans the fruits of freedom. He spent his last years in Ghana, where he died at age 95.

DUNMORE, JOHN MURRAY, EARL OF (1730-1809). In 1775, as the **American Revolution** was beginning, the earl of Dunmore, the governor of Virginia, sought to undercut the rebels by offering freedom to slaves and indentured servants willing to desert their masters and support the king's cause. From the hundreds who responded to his call, he organized a unit called the Ethiopian regiment. Dunmore, however, was defeated in his first major engagement and his black troops were decimated by smallpox. Eventually, he withdrew them to New York. Dunmore's actions, taken on his own initiative, pushed many white Southerners into supporting the rebel cause, but his approach was later used by other British commanders who saw slave flight as a way to undercut white planters. Over 10,000 slaves fled to British-controlled areas. Most worked as laborers. Many were evacuated to Nova Scotia after the British defeat. After the surrender of the British General Cornwallis at Yorktown in 1781, Dunmore wanted to raise an army of 10,000 former slaves, but the British government was ready to concede independence. *See also* BLACK LOYALISTS.

DUTCH SLAVE TRADE. The Dutch were important in the exploitation of slave labor, were very large slave traders, and played a major role in developing the West Indian **plantation** economy. The wealthiest part of the Hapsburg Empire, the Dutch declared their independence from Spain in 1569. When the Spanish and Portuguese crowns were united in 1580, the Dutch saw the far-flung Portuguese Empire as the weak point in the armor of Europe's most powerful state. They turned first to the East, challenging Portuguese hegemony from 1596. In 1602, the Dutch East India Company was chartered and began building an empire in Indonesia and India.

The slave trade was a small part of the business of the Dutch East India Company, but it had a regular trade from East Africa to its Asian colonies and from the Asian colonies to its supply post at Capetown. Slave labor was used in Dutch enterprises in India and Java, and the households of Dutch officials contained large numbers of slave **concu-**

bines and servants. The original population of Batavia, the capital of the Dutch East Indies, was mostly slaves. By contrast, the Dutch West India Company was primarily a slave-trading operation, though it aspired to be more. Founded in 1621, it captured many of Portugal's trading posts on the West African coast and the colony of Angola. In 1630, the Dutch began the conquest of Brazil when they seized Pernambuco. Brazil became briefly the major outlet for the slaves Dutch ships carried from Africa. The Brazilians, however, rallied, drove the Dutch from Brazil and in 1648 recaptured Angola. By 1654, the Dutch had been pushed out of both Brazil and Angola. During their brief tenure in Brazil, the Dutch had, however, learned a lot about **sugar** and the management of slaves.

The Dutch were well placed to develop an industrial sugar complex in the West Indies. They had the technology, capital, and commercial system to do so. They developed sugar plantations in Surinam and had a small **plantation** sector on several of the islands they controlled, but none of these islands was an important sugar producer. They were primarily trade entrepôts. More important, the Dutch introduced sugar technology and provided credit for English planters on **Barbados** and the French on Martinique. They also helped English and French planters organize their plantations and provided them with slaves. The Dutch also controlled the *asiento*, the contract to supply slaves to the Spanish, from 1662 to the 1690s. The Dutch supplemented the *asiento* trade with an illegal trade into the Spanish colonies. After the loss of Angola, most of the Dutch slaves came from the Gold Coast, where the Dutch West India Company maintained about a dozen forts. With the loss of the *asiento*, the British and French replaced the Dutch as the world's biggest slave traders. In all, Dutch ships carried about 540,000 slaves to the Americas. The Dutch West India company was dissolved in 1791. *See also* BRAZILIAN SLAVERY; INDONESIAN SLAVERY; SOUTH AFRICAN SLAVERY.

- E -

EAST AFRICAN SLAVE TRADE. The coast of East Africa was from an early date involved in the trade of the **Indian Ocean**. A series of Swahili-speaking commercial towns and cities developed along the coast, which traded regularly with Arabia, India, and the Middle East. Slaves were a significant element in the towns, where they did manual labor and were domestics. Some slaves were exported to the Middle East and to India, and African slaves were found in more distant parts of Asia, but until about 1800 the number was very small. Trade with the interior was limited and focussed on areas that could provide gold. Interior peoples tended to live in dispersed settlements without fortifications, which suggests that enslavement was not a problem.

The Dutch East India Company began buying slaves in East Africa for their settlements at the Cape and in Asia in the 17th century, but the rapid growth of the trade began in the late 18th century, when French planters began developing **sugar plantations** on the islands of the Indian Ocean. The demand for ivory was also increasing. Traders began penetrating deeper into the interior. Then, **Said ibn Sultan**, the sultan of Muscat, Oman, and **Zanzibar**, supported the development of clove plantations on Zanzibar and Pemba. To provide labor for the plantations, he also encouraged Arab and Swahili slave traders to penetrate the interior and to develop bases for the trade there. Indian financiers were given tax contracts to encourage them to settle on the coast, where they were able to provide finance for the caravans. There was also in the 19th century a **slave trade** from Mozambique to Brazil, which had a high death rate because of the length of the voyage.

The result was a rapid expansion of the slave trade, the encouragement of slaving, and the destruction or transformation of many interior societies. Coastal traders either settled at the courts of powerful chiefs, whom they supplied with arms, or in towns like Tabora and Ujiji, which they created in western Tanzania. These new settlements were often surrounded by plantations worked largely by slaves. The Swahili traders alternatively competed with and complemented trade routes organized by interior peoples like the Nyamwezi of central Tanzania and the Yao of Malawi and Mozambique. In the 1860s, Swahili traders like **Tippu Tip** began developing settlements in the Congo basin. Others formed settlements in Malawi, Zanzibar, and Uganda. Most of the peoples of East and **Central Africa** were poorly equipped to deal with the threat of raiders armed with the latest European rifles. The 19th century was without a doubt the bloodiest period in the region's history

The 19th-century slave trade through Zanzibar has been estimated at from 750,000 to a million. Others were exported from Kilwa and the ports of Mozambique, or in the latter part of the century, moved overland up the coast. About half of the slaves that passed through Zanzibar were kept there, mostly to work on the clove plantations. Others were sold in the Middle East or along the coast, where the availability of slaves encouraged the development of plantations to provide grain for

Zanzibar and copra and sesame for export. Slave use had also increased around the various commercial centers in the interior.

By 1840, when Said moved permanently to Zanzibar, the island was wealthier and more important than Oman. It had become a major trade entrepôt, the world's largest producer of cloves, and a **slave society**. It also commanded a loosely organized commercial empire that extended into the Great Lakes region of eastern Africa and the Congo River basin. The British put pressure on Zanzibar to stop slave exports across the Indian Ocean, and then, in 1873, to abolish the slave trade. There was a significant illicit slave trade under British occupation in 1890. In 1897, slavery itself was abolished, and in 1907 it was abolished in British East Africa (now Kenya). *See also* MAURITIUS AND RÉUNION.

EAST EUROPEAN SLAVE TRADE. From rise of ancient Athens on, eastern Europe was a major source of slaves for the Mediterranean and the Middle East. The Greeks imported slaves from the Balkans and the Black Sea areas. The Black Sea remained a source of slaves for almost 2,500 years. Roman conquests also took slaves from the Balkans. During the eighth and ninth centuries, as Christianity was pushing into eastern Europe, warfare along the German-Slavic frontier, now Poland and the Czech Republic, was a major source of slaves, who were moved across Europe to Muslim Spain and the cities of the Mediterranean. During the same period, **Viking** traders developed trade routes that moved through what is now Russia on the Dnieper and Don Rivers. They bought slaves and brought them to **Byzantium**, which sold them to the Arabs and to the western Mediterranean.

Eastern Europe remained the major source of slaves for the Mediterranean until the 15th century, when Portuguese voyages to **West Africa** opened up the **African slave trade**. The land-based trade across western Europe was ended with the conversion of Poland, Lithuania, and Kievan Russia to Christianity at the end of the first millennium. Dubrovnik was for a while a source of slaves from the southern Balkans to Venice. The Turks, however, continued to take slaves from this region. From their Christian provinces, they took a levy of male children called the *devshirme*, and from the shores of the Black Sea and Caucasus, they took slaves that originated in warfare, raiding, and trade. The slave trade on the southern steppes of what is now the Ukraine ended only with the conquest of this area by Russia during the 18th century. *See also* RUSSIAN SLAVERY; SCANDINAVIA; SLAVS.

ELITE SLAVES. In different societies, some slaves could become wealthy and powerful. There were a number of important categories. Thus, **eunuchs** in Asian societies and in parts of Africa were originally castrated in order to serve as guards for **harems**, but many rulers learned to use them as administrators and policy makers. Such a person was **Cheng Ho**, the Chinese admiral who sailed to south Asia and East Africa in the 15th century.

Soldiers were also often slaves, particularly in the Muslim world. In Africa, many of the slave raiders were themselves slaves. Some of these soldiers became generals or powerful chiefs. In **West Africa**, slave chiefs were often those closest to the ruler. Egypt was ruled for centuries by slaves called **mamlukes**. In Rome, a group of state-owned slaves emerged from the second century BCE. Their role increased with the elaboration of administrative structures under the empire. In Rome, too, slaves often tutored the children of the powerful and worked as farm managers or land agents. A slave could also be given a sum called a *peculium* to manage and could become wealthy as a merchant. In West Africa, too, a slave could trade on his own account and become wealthy.

Some scholars have asked whether such privileged persons should be considered slaves, but in fact, their power was dependent. The "slaves of Caesar" could not wear the toga, which was a symbol of citizenship. In the West African kingdom of Kano, in 1926, a slave official who had become too powerful was humiliated by being stripped down to his loincloth, the common garb of the simple farm slave. The elite slave was valuable because he was dependent. The slave who was given administrative responsibility could not became a king. He could only enjoy power in the name of others. There were exceptions, like **Malik Ambar**, an African slave general, who became the ruler of Ahmednagar in late-16th-century India or slave soldiers in different places who deposed a king or imposed their candidate for royal power. *See also* CHINESE SLAVERY; ISLAM; MILITARY SLAVES.

ELKINS, STANLEY (1925-). Stanley Elkins was born in Massachusetts and earned his Ph.D. at Columbia University. In 1959, he published *Slavery: A Problem in American Institutional and Intellectual Life*. In this book, he argued that the slave system in the United States was harsher than those in Latin America and the Caribbean. He attributed the difference to the role of the **Catholic Church**. The most controversial part of the book was an effort to describe a slave psychology. He compared the impact of slavery on slaves to the effect of Nazi concen-

tration camps on their inmates and argued that the authoritarian paternalism produced a "**Sambo**," who was docile, lazy, jovial, loyal, and
often a liar and thief. He argued that slavery infantilized the slave.

The questions Elkins asked revolutionized slave studies as a number
of scholars struggled to attack his analysis. Most scholars today would
argue that the differences in slave systems were more a result of the
political and economic system than of the national culture, and that the
crops produced often dictated the labor regime. American slavery was
harsh but the conditions of life and the rate of reproduction were better
than Brazil and the **sugar** islands of the West Indies. Efforts to disprove
the infantilization thesis produced a body of work on slave culture, for
example, John Blassingame's *The Slave Community* (1972) and Sterling
Stuckey's *Slave Culture* (1987). *See also* BRAZILIAN SLAVERY;
HISPANIC AMERICA.

ELLISON, WILLIAM (1790-1861). Born as a slave in South Carolina,
William Ellison became a slave owner himself as result of his successful **cotton** gin business. His mother was a slave and his father was a
white man, probably his owner, Robert Ellison or Ellison's son, William. As sometimes happened with the slave children of planters, he was
taught a skill. He was apprenticed to a white cotton gin maker. He also
learned to read and write. He bought his own freedom in 1816 with
money he had earned and opened his own cotton gin business. He took
the name William after being freed. By 1820, he had purchased his wife
and daughter and had begun to accumulate slaves, at first to help him in
his business, later to work land he bought. His business prospered and
he gradually expanded his holdings of land and slaves until, by 1860, he
owned 900 acres and 63 slaves, more than the vast majority of white
slave owners. Respected by his white neighbors, he and his family were
allowed to sit at the back of the main floor of their church, and not in the
gallery with the slaves and free blacks. He was probably the richest
former slave in the South. He never freed any of his own slaves. *See
also* MANUMISSION.

ELMINA. The Portuguese first arrived on the Gold Coast, now Ghana, in
1471. In 1482, they began construction of the castle of *São Jorge da
Mina*, which became the most powerful fortress on the West African
coast. For.years, it was primarily concerned with the gold trade. The
Portuguese actually sold slaves in exchange for gold. Slave labor was
also important in and around the castle and other European posts. In
1637, Elmina was taken by the Dutch, who improved its fortifications

and built areas where slaves could be held. Increasingly, trade shifted from gold to slaves, and other European nations followed with fortified castles and trading posts along the coast. Elmina remained an important base for the slave trade. The Dutch also recruited freed slaves there for service in the Dutch East Indies. In 1871, Elmina was ceded to the British and the Dutch withdrew from the Gold Coast. *See also* AFRICAN SLAVE TRADE; DUTCH SLAVE TRADE.

EMANCIPATION ACT (1833). The British Emancipation Act freed all of the slaves in the British Empire. It was the culmination of a half century of struggle by abolitionists. In order to get the act passed, abolitionists had to make two important concessions to the intransigent slave owner lobby. First they had to agree to compensation. Over 800,000 slaves were freed, 700,000 in the West Indies, the rest in South Africa and Mauritius. Small numbers were also freed in British posts elsewhere. A sum equivalent to one-third of the British budget was given to the slave owners as compensation for the loss of their property.

Second, abolitionists accepted the idea of a transition period, during which slaves would be called apprentices. The transition proved difficult to enforce. Even magistrates appointed to enforce the act did not understand what the apprentices were supposed to be. For many of the slave owners, it was a continuation of slavery. The abolitionists received stories of the worst cases and began criticizing the **apprenticeship** system almost from the first, and slaves began asserting their independence. Eventually, it was West Indian assemblies that ended apprenticeship on 1 August 1838.

Though there were fears of indiscipline and disorder, the transition was peaceful and slaves speedily became self-sufficient. The most significant disruption came not from slaves, but from Afrikaner farmers in South Africa, who resented interference with their social order. About 10,000 to 12,000 migrated into the interior, where they founded two new republics. Most of the trekkers were actually not big slave owners. In the West Indies, the process differed from island to island. Wherever possible, former slaves sought their autonomy. On islands like **Barbados** and Antigua, where almost all of the land was being cultivated, former slaves had nowhere to go. There was no free land and no alternative employment. Most of the freed slaves continued to work for the planters. On those islands with mountainous areas not suited to **sugar**, slaves withdrew from the **plantations** and started farming for themselves. In many cases, the men continued to work for wages, but the women withdrew to private plots. On Jamaica, sugar production dropped by a third. The increasing demand for sugar was largely filled by Cuba and Brazil, where planters were still using slave labor. British planters responded by seeking contract labor from India. *See also* ABOLITION, GREAT BRITAIN; BUXTON, THOMAS FOWELL; COMPENSATED EMANCIPATION; SOUTH AFRICAN SLAVERY.

EMANCIPATION, AFRICA. When slavery was abolished in the British Empire in 1833 and in the French Empire in 1848, the number of areas under European sovereignty were very limited. One such area, **Sierra Leone**, was created free and colonized as a settlement for free Blacks and freed slaves. Elsewhere, slaves were freed when slavery was abolished, but colonial governors generally recognized that their relations with nearby African states depended on toleration of slavery. They usually acted quickly to prevent their colonies from becoming places of refuge for runaway slaves. Some mission stations did receive runaways, but the nascent colonial state often tried to keep the doors closed and even returned slaves to their masters.

As colonial officials began expanding European rule, they not only compromised with slave owners, but actually exploited slavery. Africa was largely conquered for European states by African armies made up largely of slaves. The French freed slaves who served in their army, but it often bought men in the slave markets. When the Germans moved into Cameroon in 1885, they bought slaves in **Dahomey** and trained them as soldiers. Equally important, as Europeans established their control over much of Africa, they carefully avoided applying European laws on slavery. They sometimes used legal fictions like that of a protectorate to avoid applying European law. A protectorate was ruled indirectly by European officials, but using an adapted version of the conquered state's law code.

The first colony to abolish slavery in part of the hinterland was the Gold Coast in 1874, but the law was only enforced in areas close to the coast. In most areas, slave raiding was ended within a few years of conquest, and often the **slave trade** too, but colonial regimes were cautious about ending slavery. They feared disruption and depended on slave-owning elites to administer their colonies. Slavery was abolished in **Zanzibar** in 1897, but only in 1916 in western Nigeria. The abolition of slavery by the Portuguese in Angola in 1910 was not completely effective. By the first years of the 20th century, Great Britain and France had more slaves living under their flags in Africa than they did when they first abolished slavery. In many areas, slaves freed themselves in the period after conquest. Some went home. Some found free land, and in collaboration with other former slaves, started to work it. Others gathered at mission stations eager to learn. Slaves who freed themselves were a large part of the early colonial working class and the educated elite.

The most massive exodus was in French **West Africa**, where events at a market town named **Banamba** started an exodus soon after France abolished transactions in persons in 1905. The exodus may have involved as many as a million former slaves. In other areas, colonial regimes feared disruption. In Nigeria, **Frederick Lugard** moved quickly to end slave raiding and the slave trade. Lugard also used an Islamic procedure called *murgu* by which slaves could purchase their own freedom. Otherwise, slaves were expected to continue working for their masters. Slaves were freed only in cases of maltreatment. Slavery was only abolished in Sierra Leone in 1927 and Nigeria in 1936. In the Sudan, the vestiges of the slave trade continued almost to World War II. In many areas, slavery declined as much through slave initiative and social change as through colonial legislation. Wage labor, military service, and migration aided slaves to establish their autonomy. In some areas, memories of slavery still affect social relations, but only in the Sahara and in a few areas where masters controlled access to land did slaves remain under control of their masters toward the end of the 20th century. *See also* AFRICAN SLAVERY; CONTEMPORARY FORMS OF SLAVERY.

EMANCIPATION, EAST ASIA. East Asian societies had very hierarchical social systems, but in modern times none of them depended on slave labor. In China, several forms of slavery existed, but the state had always discouraged a large-scale development of slavery. Slaves were more likely to be servants, entertainers, or prostitutes than agricultural workers. In 1909 China abolished slavery, but the Ch'ing Dynasty was in its last days. The period after the end of the dynasty in 1912 saw disunity, natural disasters, poverty, and misery. Poor families often sold their daughters, who became servants and prostitutes, and sometimes their sons. Only with the triumph of the Chinese Communists in 1949 was slavery effectively destroyed.

Korea moved away from slave labor before coming in contact with the West. Korea had a highly developed slave system, but in 1775 Korea established a policy of gradual emancipation. From 1806, slave status could no longer be passed to the next generation. In 1895, it was abolished altogether. In Japan, slavery had never been important. Under the Tokugawa Shogunate (1603-1868), there was a rigid system of hierarchical obligation, but no slavery. In Viet Nam, slavery was not important and was ended by the French colonial regimes. *See also* CHINESE SLAVERY.

EMANCIPATION, HISPANIC AMERICA. The process of emancipation in Hispanic America took a half century. The speed with which the former Spanish colonies embraced emancipation depended on the importance of slave-based production and the development of **capitalism**. Slave resistance and flight were also important. Slaves were less numerous than in Brazil or the West Indies. Only in a few areas, such as the coasts of Venezuela and Peru, did slaves number more than 10 percent of the population. Furthermore, there were traditions of **manumission**, which had created large free black and mulatto populations.

The wars of independence started the process. Leaders like **Simón Bolívar** in Venezuela and José Artigas in Uruguay believed that Spain's colonies could not struggle for liberation while leaving large populations in chains. In 1816, in exchange for arms aid, Bolívar promised Haiti's President Alexandre Pétion that he would free all of the slaves in lands that he liberated. The early stages of the struggle for independence were usually led by white elites, who owned both land and slaves. The Royalists appealed to slaves of the rebels and to landless groups. Increasingly, as the war progressed, both sides offered freedom to slaves who enlisted in their armies. Bolívar and **José San Martín** often freed slaves in contested areas and different kinds of anti-slavery legislation were passed in different countries.

The **slave trade** was abolished in Chile and Venezuela in 1811, then in Argentina in 1812 and Mexico in 1821. In many areas, **"free womb"** laws were passed, which granted freedom to children born of slave mothers, though in some cases only on reaching maturity. Such laws were passed in Chile in 1811, Argentina in 1813, Peru and Gran Colombia in 1821. Promises made during the war aroused the expectations of slaves. Many left their masters, particularly during periods of disorder. Some fled to rural refuges, but many sought anonymity and new lives in the cities

Slave owners were, however, almost everywhere able to block total emancipation. Only in four of the new states was slavery completely abolished: Chile in 1823, the Central American Federation in 1824, Mexico in 1829, and Uruguay om 1830/ These were all areas with few slaves. Bolivar's plea for emancipation at the **Congress of Angostura** (1819) was rejected. The congress was only willing to confirm the emancipation of those freed by rebel commanders and to approve the end of the slave trade and a gradual process of emancipation. Two years later, at the **Congress of Cucutá**, it was decided that children of slave mothers would be freed, but would receive that freedom only at age 18 and then only if a local committee thought they were able to cope with freedom. In Bolivia, slavery was prohibited by the constitution in 1826, but a form of **peonage** was established. Wherever plantations existed, once the struggle was over, planters tried to restore their controls over slaves or former slaves. Peru and Argentina even reestablished the slave trade for a while. In most of the new states, landowners were powerful enough to influence the ways laws were interpreted.

The independence struggles had reduced the number of slaves. Few new slaves were being imported and many were purchasing their freedom. The contraction of slave numbers often made slavery uneconomic. Slaves also resisted **plantation** discipline and sometimes they fled or revolted. Free labor was used in the development of coffee lands, partly because slaves were no longer available. Where industrial development took place, it involved free labor. The end of slavery was attractive to industrial capital because it created a more mobile labor force. In addition, many educated Latin Americans, influenced by European liberal ideals, were convinced that slavery was inefficient and some thought it immoral. By mid-century, many nations were abolishing. Bolivia and Colombia abolished slavery in 1851, Ecuador in 1852, Argentina in 1853, Venezuela in 1854, Peru in 1855, Paraguay in 1862. By this time slavery existed only in Cuba and Puerto Rico, which were still Spanish colonies, and in Brazil. In these areas, **sugar** had created a powerful interest in the perpetuation of slavery. Emancipation was to take another generation there. *See also* ABOLITION, BRAZIL; CUBAN SLAVERY; HISPANIC AMERICA.

EMANCIPATION, INDIA. Slavery was a recognized institution in most Asian countries. The patterns of emancipation varied. Emancipation came first in India. The British Emancipation Act of 1833 did not affect India because India was ruled by the British East India Company rather than by the British Crown. The British Parliament, however, pressured the East India Company, and in 1843, Act V abolished slavery in India by withdrawing support of the state and guaranteeing the rights of slaves. A master could no longer go to court to enforce his control and could be punished for violence against the slave. No government official could sell slaves to collect taxes. No person could be deprived of property on the grounds that he was a slave. The company did little to publicize the act and the officials responsible for enforcing it had little interest in doing so. Many of them profited from the labor of slaves.

In 1858, the Government of India Act gave Great Britain control of India. The Indian Penal code of 1860 made slave trading, keeping slaves, and abduction for the purpose of slave trading criminal offenses punishable by up to 10 years of imprisonment. It is not clear how much effect these laws have had. Landowners continued to exercise power locally. The problem in India is also that there was a variety of servile statuses and relationships. They differed from one part of India to another. Traditional forms of servitude had faded, but masters often found other ways to maintain control over their dependents. Caste rules often helped them do it, but the most important institution is **bonded labor** in which debt is used to keep rural labor under the control of landlords. In the transformation of forms of labor control, masters have often benefited from the sympathy of local officials. Freed slaves were a major source of indentured labor as various parts of the British Empire turned to India to meet the needs of **plantation** economies. Indian indentured laborers went to Fiji, Mauritius, South Africa, and the West Indies, often to replace freed slaves no longer willing to work on plantations. *See also* INDIAN SLAVERY.

EMANCIPATION, MIDDLE EAST. The relations of the Muslim Middle East with Europe faced many challenges during the 19th century. Some Muslims prospered in trade with Europe and often invested some of their profits in the purchase of slaves, mostly from Africa. At the same time, Muslim states faced pressure from Great Britain to end the **slave trade**. In 1846, both Tunisia and Persia prohibited further imports of slaves. In Ottoman Turkey, the Istanbul slave market was closed in 1846 and slave imports were ended in 1857 after the Crimean War. In 1877, Egypt agreed to suppress the slave trade, and after the establishment of British hegemony, slavery itself was gradually phased out. By 1900, there were almost no slaves left.

Conservative forces in the Muslim world resisted these pressures to abolish slavery. Though Islamic law contains more restrictions on slavery and slaving than Christian law, many Muslims resented the imposition of abolition by Christians. These groups were particularly important on the Arabian peninsula. Elsewhere, change was affecting the very groups who once held slaves. Elites found themselves going to Europe and investing more in consumer goods than in the service of slaves. In the early 20th century, new modernizing groups of intellectuals, bureaucrats, and army officers were coming to power in many

Muslim countries. They were often hostile to slavery as an institution that slowed economic and social change. Before the First World War, the Young Turks ended the slave trade within the Ottoman Empire, and after the war, in 1924, Kemal Ataturk's sweeping reforms ended the caliphate, imposed European law codes, and abolished slavery. The Persians did the same in 1927.

In 1962, Saudi Arabia abolished slavery and in 1970 Yemen did so. The last country to abolish slavery was Mauritania, where the French tolerated the continued existence of slavery throughout the colonial period and in spite of French law. Mauritania abolished slavery in 1980. *See also* ISLAM; OTTOMAN SLAVERY.

EMANCIPATION PROCLAMATION. When the American **Civil War** began, **Abraham Lincoln** was reluctant to emancipate the slaves because he still hoped to negotiate the return of the rebel states to the Union. He also wanted to keep the slave-owning border states in the Union. It eventually became clear that these hopes were futile. In 1862, under pressure from abolitionist and African-American leaders, he began to move on the issue. In April, Congress approved emancipation in the District of Columbia with limited compensation. Two months later, he signed bills freeing slaves who came over to the Union side and slaves in the territories. By this time, slaves in various war zones were voting with their feet and crossing Union lines. In September, after a Union victory in the battle of Antietam, Lincoln issued a Preliminary Emancipation Proclamation in which he warned southern states that on 1 January 1863, he intended to free slaves in areas still in rebellion. Finally, on that date, he issued a proclamation that "all persons held as slaves within any state or designated part of a state, the people whereof shall be in rebellion against the United States, shall be, then, thenceforward, and forever free."

The Emancipation Proclamation was greeted by African-Americans with thanksgiving services and other kinds of celebration. It helped to further undermine the Confederate economy as slaves continued to leave southern plantations in large numbers and offer their services to Union forces. It did not affect more than 800,000 slaves in the border states, which had remained within the Union or areas already occupied by the Union army. They had to wait for state action or for the **Thirteenth Amendment** to the U.S. Constitution. *See also* EMANCIPATION, UNITED STATES; RECONSTRUCTION.

EMANCIPATION, SOUTHEAST ASIA. Slavery was important over most of Southeast Asia, but the paths chosen for emancipation were very different. With most Southeast Asian states, emancipation came with colonization, but in Thailand it was part of a policy of modernization designed to fend off the European powers. Thailand always had a large slave population. Nineteenth-century estimates ran as high as one-third of the population. In the 19th century, economic life in Thailand was changing. Chinese were immigrating in large numbers. Rice exports were growing, as was wage labor. Hiring wage labor increasingly became more attractive than purchasing slaves. At the same time, Thailand was interested in avoiding colonization. Two modernizing monarchs, Mongkut (r.1851-1868) and Chulalongkorn (r.1868-1910), moved first to limit slavery and then to gradually abolish it. In 1868, it was forbidden for a man to sell his wife or children without the wife's consent. Six years later, Chulalongkorn set up a schedule under which the price of liberty for any person born after 1868 would be reduced year by year. Thus, when slavery was abolished in 1905, it was no longer a major source of labor.

Indonesia included many very different cultures and had a number of forms of servitude. The exploitation of slave labor was intensified under the Dutch from the early 17th century. Dutch officials often ran large households staffed with slaves. They also rented slaves to the Dutch East India Company. The agricultural economy in many areas also depended on slave labor, though in some areas slavery had evolved into a kind of serfdom. Elsewhere, particularly on Java, the importance of slavery declined as the growth of population and the increased impoverishment of the peasantry made cheap labor readily available. In addition, tributary states grew in power to the point where they could get labor without reliance on slaves. The Netherlands abolished the slave trade in 1807. This was repeated in 1818 by the restored monarchy, but trading in slaves continued as did raiding by pirates. Only in 1860 did the Netherlands prohibit the ownership of slaves, but this was applied only to Europeans and Chinese in areas under direct Dutch control. From 1874, the colonial government required local administrators to propose measures for freeing slaves under their jurisdiction. From 1878, they pushed emancipation more vigorously, but some forms of bondage persisted until World War II. In the long run, only population growth, impoverishment, an increase in wage labor, and an increased concern for liberty have eroded traditional forms of bondage.

Elsewhere, emancipation came with colonization. The French signed treaties with Cambodia in 1877 and 1884 that had anti-slavery clauses, but they did not act decisively until after occupation in 1897. In **Ma-**

laya, the British moved in piecemeal fashion, state by state, against slavery and debt bondage. Anti-slavery legislation was not firmly in place in all states until 1915. In Burma, the British acted with similar caution, acting in eastern Burma only in 1926. *See also* CAMBODIAN SLAVERY; INDONESIAN SLAVERY; SULU SULTANATE; THAI SLAVERY.

EMANCIPATION, UNITED STATES. In the United States, there were three patterns of emancipation. In the North, emancipation was freely voted by state legislatures and usually gradual. In the South, it was sudden and cataclysmic because it was produced by war. West of the Appalachians and north of the Ohio River, states entered the Union free.

Slaves in the North were engaged in many different kinds of work and in some states were quite numerous, particularly in New York and New Jersey. Slavery was not, however, crucial to the functioning of the economy, nor were there powerful groups that depended on slavery for their wealth and well-being. Still, slavery was abolished first in areas with few slaves. Vermont, scheduled to become the 14th state, prohibited slavery in its first constitution in 1777. Many states used **free womb laws** to minimize the cost to the state and the losses to slave owners. In 1780, Pennsylvania approved a law under which all children born after that date were freed. In Massachusetts, efforts to pass an abolition law failed, but the courts held that slavery was incompatible with the Bill of Rights, which was part of the state's 1780 constitution. By 1790, there were no slaves left. Connecticut ended the import of slaves in 1774, freed slaves who served in the colonial army, and after the Revolution passed a gradual emancipation law that all slaves born after 1784 should be free on reaching the age of 25. Rhode Island passed a similar law. New York in 1799 and New Jersey in 1804 passed weaker laws that made possible some payment to the masters. Slavery was not definitively ended until 1827 in New York, 1846 in New Jersey.

In the border states, slavery was not abolished, but **manumission** was more frequent than in the **cotton** states of the Deep South. With escape to free states very easy, slave owners in the border states were more anxious to keep their slaves satisfied. By 1860, most African-Americans in Delaware and about half of those in Maryland were free. Manumission was less common in Kentucky, which was almost a quarter slave in 1860, and Missouri, which was only about 10 percent slave.

The South was another matter. After his election victory, **Abraham**

Lincoln tried to convince the South that he did not intend to do anything about slavery where it already existed. He was even willing to support a constitutional amendment to protect slavery in the South. Once the war began, however, slaves took the issue into their own hands by fleeing into areas controlled by Union troops. Some Union generals returned slaves to their masters, but others like **Benjamin Butler** treated slaves as contraband, preferring to have them working for the Union army rather than constructing fortifications for the rebel armies. Congress supported this policy with the Confiscation Acts of 1861 and 1862. Lincoln remained reluctant, but as Union armies advanced, slave owners fled and many slaves, while not yet legally freed, began organizing their lives and work. In 1862, Congress freed slaves in the District of Columbia and in all of the slave territories.

Then, on 1 January 1863, Lincoln issued the **Emancipation Proclamation**, which freed all slaves in areas in rebellion. From that point, the war became a war to end slavery. African-American soldiers, most of them former slaves, were recruited and Union armies freed slaves wherever they went. Lincoln asked the border states to approve gradual **compensated emancipation**, but they resisted. Nevertheless, slavery collapsed in Maryland and Missouri. Elsewhere it ended when Congress passed the **Thirteenth Amendment** in 1865 and it was ratified by the states before the end of the year.

The period after the war saw radical differences over what freedom meant. Congress created the **Freedmen's Bureau**, which for four years played a major role in assisting the former slaves. Missionaries and teachers went into the South to help the former slaves. The southern states tried to reestablish their control over the free slaves with **Black Codes**, which severely restricted the freedom of slaves. Congress responded with the **Fourteenth Amendment**, which defined the rights of the freed slaves and limited the ability of the states to restrict those rights. The **Fifteenth Amendment** guaranteed the freed slaves the right to vote. The freed slaves, however, wanted land, which few of them got. Lacking land and capital, most freed slaves became sharecroppers and slipped back into a dependent position after the end of **Reconstruction** returned control of the southern states to white elites.

ENCOMIENDA. The *encomienda* served as an alternative to slave labor in Spanish America. During the 16th century, conquered people were often "commended" to one of the Spanish *conquistadors*. The *encomendero* was to teach Indians in his charge basic tenets of the Catholic faith and how to live in a "civilized" manner. In exchange for this, they owed him tribute and labor. In theory, the Indians could not be sold or rented out. In practice, there were many violations of the system. The system became a massive tribute collection system. From an early date, Spanish priests like **Bartolomé de Las Casas** and **Antonio de Montesinos** criticized the abuses and called for an end to the system and protection of the rights of native people. The New Laws issued by King Charles V in 1542 prohibited the commandeering of labor by the *encomendero*, but the system was eventually replaced by the *repartimiento*, in which royal officials controlled allocation of labor. *See also* CATHOLIC CHURCH; HISPANIC AMERICA.

ENCYCLOPÉDIE. The *Encyclopédie* (Encyclopedia) was the most famous reference book of its time. Begun as a translation of an early British encyclopedia, it eventually had 17 volumes of text and articles by many of the leading thinkers of the French **Enlightenment**. It came out between 1750 and 1772 and several times was banned because its ideas were considered subversive. A number of the articles dealt with slavery, for example articles on "Slavery," "Slave Trade," "Natural Liberty," and "Maroons." They summed up the thought of Enlightenment abolitionists. They argued that freedom is an inalienable natural right, that people cannot dispose of their freedom and that slavery is a crime against nature because it denies a basic human right. They criticized Europeans and European institutions such as the state and church for condoning and participating in slavery and the slave trade. Finally, they argued that free labor was more productive than slave labor and would create greater prosperity.

ENLIGHTENMENT. The Enlightenment was a body of thought in the 18th century which was based on a belief in progress and in the ability of reason to make a better life for humanity. Most Enlightenment thinkers were not abolitionists, but they were the first to collectively question slavery. They did so by questioning the traditional justifications of slavery: its existence in biblical times, Aristotelian philosophy, and the belief that enslavement in a just war was morally acceptable. Baron de **Montesquieu**'s *Spirit of the Laws* (1748) argued that slavery was immoral and that all humans had certain natural rights. Voltaire's *Candide* (1759) mocked the cruelty of slavery and **Jean-Jacques Rousseau** in *The Social Contract* (1762) argued that humans are born free and endowed with certain natural human rights. Many of these ideas were incorporated in the *Encyclopédie*.

If the French thought in terms of natural rights, the Scotch philosopher, **Adam Smith**, argued in *The Wealth of Nations* (1776) that slavery was inefficient. Smith believed that labor was more efficient where free and motivated by self-interest. Smith, **Benjamin Franklin**, David Hume, Mirabeau, Dupont de Nemours, and Turgot criticized slavery not on humanitarian grounds, but because they saw it as a barrier to social and economic progress. If a lot of Enlightenment thought remained abstract, it was partly that many Enlightenment thinkers believed that Africans were inferior and some even had money invested in the **slave trade**. A number, however, did move to a more activist position. The *Reflections on Slavery* (1781) by the Marquis de **Condorcet** proposed a plan for gradual emancipation. Condorcet was one of the founders of the **Société des Amis des Noirs** (Society of the Friends of Blacks), the first French abolitionist organization. The main contribution of the Enlightenment, however, was not action, but its attack on the justifications of slavery and its argument that all human beings have certain natural rights. Enlightenment thinkers undercut most justifications for slavery. *See also* ARISTOTLE; NATURAL LAW.

ENSLAVEMENT. There were many ways for people to became slaves. The largest number were born into slavery and had no choice, particularly if both parents were slaves. Of the others, the largest group was probably prisoners of war. These could be either enemy soldiers, camp followers, or members of a conquered society. Victorious armies in many parts of the world ravaged their enemies. Slaves were a form of booty. In Christian thought, there was a notion that a person taken prisoner in a just war was subject to enslavement. Islamic law was even stricter in authorizing enslavement only of prisoners in a religious war. **Orlando Patterson** has suggested that for those taken captive, enslavement was an alternative to death.

Where slaving had become a business, slave raiding and kidnapping became a major source of slaves and there was little effort to justify enslavement. Bands of warriors raided neighboring societies and in some cases kidnappers operated within their own community. Persons had become commodities. Some like the Phoenicians, **Vikings,** or the sea raiders of the **Sulu** Archipelago ranged far from home. In addition to raiding and kidnapping, a number of other sources became important. Criminal penalties were converted into enslavement. Conviction for theft, witchcraft, or sexual crimes could lead to enslavement. So too, debt was a major source of enslavement. Where money had became important, but land had little value, a person's only source of credit was himself or members of his family. In much of Asia, the debtor and/or his family could be enslaved if a debt was not paid. Finally, there were levies on conquered peoples. The Ottoman *devshirme* was a tax in which a certain number of boys were taken from Christian communities to become soldiers or bureaucrats. *See also* SCANDINAVIA.

EQUIANO, OLAUDAH (1745-1797). According to his autobiography, Olaudah Equiano was kidnapped as an 11-year-old boy along with his sister from the Igbo village (Nigeria) where he was born. He was sold to slavers and shipped to America, where he was fortunate not to be sent to a **plantation**. Instead, he was sold to a British navy officer. After serving with his master in the Seven Years' war, he expected to be freed, but was instead returned to the Americas, where he worked for a merchant. Serving on sailing ships, he was able to make enough money from petty trading to buy his freedom at the age of 21. He spent most of the rest of his life in England, where he became a Christian, a leader in the African community, and an active abolitionist. He was involved briefly in the effort to resettle free blacks in Freetown, **Sierra Leone**, but had a falling-out with the organizers of the project. In 1788, he published *Interesting Narrative of the Life of Olaudah Equiano*, which described his childhood in Nigeria, the horrors of the **Middle Passage**, and the racism that slavery brought in its wake. An eloquent book, it was translated into a number of other languages. Equiano spent his last years lecturing on the evils of slavery.

EUNUCHS. Eunuchs are men who have been castrated. They have almost always been slaves. There is evidence of eunuchs as far back in antiquity as the ancient Near East and ancient China. Eunuchs have been associated in most societies with **harems**. As men deprived of their sexuality, eunuchs were used to guard and administrate harems. Often, they were the only men with access to the harem beside the king himself. This, however, put them in the heart of many royal courts. Both the king and his potential heirs lived in close proximity to eunuchs. They were men who had been removed from their families and unable to create families of their own. This made them very dependent and usually loyal. They were thus entrusted with important positions in the palace and from that, often moved into key administrative positions in the state. This was true in China, in the Roman Empire and many Muslim states like the Ottoman empire. Some served as military leaders. The Chinese eunuch, **Cheng Ho**, led a series of great voyages to South Asia and **East**

Africa. The Prophet Mohammed criticized the use eunuchs, but many later Muslim states used them.

- **F** -

FAMILIA CAESARIS. The "family of Caesar" consisted of those slaves and ex-slaves of the Roman Empire who served in either the administration of the palace or of the state. They were a very powerful group. The origin of their power was their proximity to the emperor and the rivalry between the emperor and the Senate. The emperor could trust slaves, who were totally dependent on him. Slaves handled most of the finances, petitions to the emperor, and correspondence with provincial governors and foreign states. Many members of the *familia caesaris* were **eunuchs**. Most slaves in the administrative services were freed about the age of 30, so senior positions tended to be held by freedmen. Even before they were freed, the emperor's slaves had more rights than other slaves, for example, the right to marry free women. Many of them also grew wealthy. They had the right to dispose of their wealth. *See also* ANCIENT ROMAN SLAVERY; ELITE SLAVES.

FÉDON'S REBELLION. Grenada was a West Indian island that had been ceded to Great Britain by the French in 1763 after their defeat in the Seven Years' War. Both French whites and the free **people of color** resented restrictions on their language, religion, and right to hold office. It was, however, the **Haitian** and **French Revolutions** that stimulated the Grenadans. The leader, a free colored planter named Julien Fédon, took action under the French revolutionary slogan of "liberty, equality and fraternity." When the revolt began on 1 March 1795, Fédon freed the slaves and armed them. With the aid of a small force from Guadeloupe, Fédon seized most of the island and confined the British to the capital, St. George. In March 1795, a British force of 5,000 men landed. Fédon tried to wage a guerilla campaign, but within four months his forces were destroyed. His fate is not known. The British used summary executions, show trials of free colored leaders, and deportation of many participants. The revolt was the most important challenge to British authority during its wars with the French. It came close to replicating events on **Saint-Domingue**. One effect of the damage caused by the revolt was that the British gave up trying to convert Grenada into a major **sugar** producer. Many of the remaining planters turned to the less demanding cultivation of spices, which produced a more mild kind of slavery. *See also* SLAVE REVOLTS.

FIFTEENTH AMENDMENT. The Fifteenth Amendment was the last of three amendments to the United States **Constitution** passed after the American Civil War to guarantee that every male citizen had the right to vote. The **Thirteenth Amendment** freed the slaves. The **Fourteenth** defined U.S. citizenship, established that the freed slaves were citizens, and gave adult men the vote. In 1868, when when the votes of former slaves were crucial in the election of Republican Ulysses S. Grant as president, Republicans realized that their majority was dependent on Black votes. The Fifteenth Amendment guaranteed that right to vote and limited states's rights by prohibiting disenfranchisement on the basis of "race, color, or previous condition of servitude." The wording of the amendment seemed so decisive that many abolitionists like **William Lloyd Garrison** thought that their work was over. In spite of this, former Confederates gradually regained control of most of the southern states during the 1870s. They used measures that were not specifically prohibited by the Fifteenth Amendment such as poll taxes, property qualifications, and literacy tests to deny African-Americans the right to vote. This right was not definitively established until the civil rights struggles of the 1960s. *See also* RECONSTRUCTION.

FINLEY, MOSES (1912-1986). Moses Finley was the most important student of slavery in classical antiquity and has influenced scholars writing on slavery elsewhere. Born and raised in New York, he taught at City College of New York and Rutgers University. When he declined to answer questions about his alleged membership in the Communist Party before a U.S. Senate committee in 1952, he was fired by Rutgers. He immediately received an offer from Cambridge University in England and spent the rest of his career there.

Though influenced by both Karl Marx and Max Weber, Finley was a consistent critic of communist historical thought, in particular, the use by communist scholars of the concept of a **slave mode of production**. He developed instead the concept of a **slave society**, which was based on slave labor. He underlined the differences between slave societies which were relatively rare and societies in which slavery existed, was often important, but was not basic to the operation of the economy. He described the emergence of a slave society in ancient Greece with the replacement of debt slavery by chattel slavery and of local slaves by those purchased or taken prisoner elsewhere. He argued that slavery was only one of a series of dependent statuses that existed on a continuum and that the history of slavery and freedom in antiquity was closely linked. For Finley, the lack of kinship ties was as important as the property relationship in defining slavery. He argued that any slave system had to be understood in the context of its time and place. Finley's views were presented in *The Ancient Economy* (1973), *Ancient Slavery and Modern Ideology* (1980), and in numerous other books and articles. *See also* ANCIENT GREEK SLAVERY; MARXISM.

FITZHUGH, GEORGE (1806-1881). George Fitzhugh was a lawyer in Port Royal, Virginia, who became one of the most articulate defenders of slavery. He wrote extensively in *De Bow's Review* and wrote two books, *Sociology of the South; or the Failure of Free Society* (1854) and *Cannibals All! or Slaves without Masters* (1857). He vigorously attacked the idea of equality, arguing that free laborers were "wage slaves" who would be better off in slavery and that slaves on Southern **plantations** were happy and well taken care of. He attacked liberal thinkers like John Locke, **Adam Smith** and **Thomas Jefferson**. He defended patriarchy and argued that the southern slave plantation was a harmonious society in which both slaves and masters had obligations to each other. By contrast, he believed that only the existence of free land prevented industrial labor from being more intensely exploited, an argument that anticipated the later work of Frederick Jackson Turner. His analysis of industrial labor has echoes of Karl Marx, though he turned his analysis in a very different direction, arguing not for revolution but for patriarchal slavery. After the **Civil War**, he disappeared from view and died a poor man.

FOGEL, ROBERT WILLIAM(1926-) AND ENGERMAN, STAN LEY (1936-). Fogel and Engerman are economic historians, who tried in *Time on the Cross: the Economics of American Negro Slavery* (1974) to use modern statistical methods to understand American slavery. They were both trained at Johns Hopkins University. Engerman got his Ph.D. in 1962, Fogel in 1963.

In *Time on the Cross*, Fogel and Engerman argued that **American slavery** was destroyed not because it failed economically, but because of ideological opposition. They presented evidence that American slavery was linked to a very flexible form of **capitalism** that was returning large profits and stimulating economic growth in the South. They argued that in material terms, slaves were often better off than many industrial workers in the North, and that they actually worked fewer hours than their free counterparts in Northern factories. Fogel and Engerman insisted that slave labor was highly productive and that most slaves lived in normal families. They argued that rewards were more important than whipping and other forms of brutality in getting slaves to work hard. The book produced bitter attacks. Herbert Gutman, Paul David, Richard Sutch and Gavin Wright argued that Fogel and Engerman used the wrong statistics or misinterpreted them. Most historians question the argument that slavery was relatively mild, but most would concur with its most important argument, that slavery was economically productive. Most historians today would argue instead about why it was productive.

Fogel and Engermen have remained major figures in the economic history of slavery. Fogel won the Nobel Prize for Economics in 1993. He is particularly well known for *Without Consent and Contract: The Rise and Fall of American Slavery* (1989), which picked up some of the themes not resolved by *Time on the Cross*. Engerman has continued to do research on slavery, much of his best work appearing in articles. With Joseph Inikori, he edited *The African Slave Trade: Effects on Economies, Societies and Peoples in Africa, the Americas, and Europe* (1992).

FORTEN, CHARLOTTE (1837-1914). Charlotte Forten was a free black woman, who was active in the movements for abolition and womens' rights. Born into a well-to-do African-American family in Philadelphia, she was sent to a girls school in Massachusetts because her father was dissatisfied with the segregated schools in Philadelphia. At age 17, she joined the Salem Anti-Slavery Society and began publishing poetry in **Wlliam Lloyd Garrison's** *Liberator*. She taught at the Salem Normal School and in 1862, during the **Civil War**, went to the recently conquered Sea Islands to teach freed children. Her memoirs of this period were published in *The Atlantic Monthly*. In 1878, she married Francis Grimke the son of a slave-owner and a slave woman. Grimke was also the nephew of abolitionists **Angelina** and **Sarah Grimke**.

FOSTER, ABIGAIL KELLY (1811-1873). Abby Kelly was an abolition ist, a feminist and a provocative figure in radical movements. A supporter of **William Lloyd Garrison**, she began lecturing in 1838. At the 1840 conference of the **American Anti-Slavery Society**, she was elected to an important committee. Her insistence on speaking led to a split in the abolition movement when it provoked a group led by Lewis Tappan to leave the organization over the question of the role of women. The fight brought her to prominence and influenced younger women like **Lucy Stone** and Susan B. Anthony. Kelly believed that the end of slavery and racial prejudice had to come first, but she was also a passionate supporter of women's rights. She was an effective organizer and fund-raiser. She lectured, organized campaigns, and raised money throughout the Northeast and the Middle Atlantic states. She was also one of the more radical figures in the movement. In 1859, Garrison attacked her fund-raising methods, leading her to withdraw from organizations he controlled, but she remained a radical figure. Throughout the **Civil War**, she was sceptical of the commitment of Lincoln and the Republican Party to emancipation and to the rights of the freed slaves. In the last years of her life, she turned her considerable organizational skills to women's rights and temperance.

FOURTEENTH AMENDMENT. Right after the American **Civil War**, Congress passed the **Thirteenth Amendment** to the **Constitution**, which freed all remaining slaves. Many of the southern states then passed "**Black Codes**," which restricted the former slaves, denied them many rights guaranteed by the Bill of Rights, and forced them to work for former masters. Congress, which was dominated by Republicans, then moved to protect the freed persons. The Fourteenth Amendment defined United States citizenship, affirmed that the freed slaves were citizens, and reduced the representation of states that denied blacks the right to vote. It also restricted the rights of the states by making the Black Codes illegal and barring any legislation that would "deprive any person of life, liberty and property without due process of law." Finally, it barred from office politicians who had served the Confederacy and it repudiated the Confederate debt. Congress sought to guarantee the rights of the freed slaves, but Southerners still managed to restrict the right to vote. As a result, Congress presented the states with the **Fifteenth Amendment**, which guaranteed adult black males the right to vote. It was ratified in 1870. The Fourteenth Amendment became the basis of much litigation in the century that followed as African-Americans used it in the quest for equality. It still took a century before the Civil Rights Act of 1965 guaranteed them the rights the Fourteenth Amendment sought to protect. See *also* RECONSTRUCTION.

FRANKLIN, BENJAMIN (1706-1790). Benjamin Franklin was a late but effective convert to the abolitionist cause. As a young businessman, he owned slaves and even sold them as part of his retail business. In the 1750's, he became involved with a program to set up schools for

African-American children. In the process, he became convinced of the abilities of black children. During the **American Revolution**, when he represented the American cause in Paris, he became a popular figure in France. He had warm relations with French scientists, with **Enlightenment** thinkers, and particularly with the founders of the French abolition movement. Even after returning home, he corresponded with French scientist and abolitionist **Condorcet**. He remained silent, however, because he felt that while he was representing his country abroad during a war, he could not afford to alienate southern slave owners. After his return to Philadelphia in 1785, Franklin spoke out on slavery and became president of the Pennsylvania Abolition Society. In the debates at the Constitutional Convention, he was concerned to compromise issues that divided North and South, but after the **Constitution** was adopted, he advocated an end to slavery and suggested a plan for freeing slaves and integrating them into American life. One of his last political acts before his death was a debate with a southern congressman, in which he parried a hostile attack with the wit and sense of humor for which he was known.

FREEDMEN. In almost all known slave societies, some **manumission** was allowed. Manumission made it possible for masters to reward those who served them well and also provided an outlet for the energies of people of talent. In societies where slavery was highly developed, freed slaves had a status somewhere between slaves and those born free. They also often remained attached to the families of their former owners as clients. In Africa the slave remained dependent because he or she had no family. In a society where kinship relations were important, the slave often had no choice but to maintain links with the former master's family. In some ethnic groups this might involve gifts to the former master, but the freedman also had the right to seek help when in need. Former slaves also played a role in family festivities, for example, doing the cooking at a wedding or a naming ceremony.

In Rome, freed slaves became citizens, but continued work for the patron was often part of the manumission agreement. Slaves also had an obligation to "respect." They could not join the army and rarely became senators. Some freedmen became wealthy or were successful in other spheres. In the Americas, such a clientship relationship was rare. The problem freedmen faced in the Americas was rooted in racial difference. Both those who were freed individually over the years and those freed when slavery was abolished faced racial discrimination and legal disabilities because they were black. Many of the free blacks in the Americas were the light-skinned offspring of white fathers and slave women. In some cases, their fathers arranged for them to learn a skill and a few became quite wealthy. They tended to gather in the cities where they intermarried and formed self-sufficient communities. Nevertheless, free **people of color** often faced great difficulty. The Spanish and Portuguese were more generous, the English and Dutch less so, but no society in the Americas accepted freed slaves or their offspring as the social equal of whites. In the United States, they could not vote, were regarded with suspicion by whites, and were often in danger of being reenslaved. In spite of this, there was a small number of freed persons who became wealthy and even came to own slaves, such as **William Ellison** and **Simon Gray**.

FREEDMEN'S BUREAU. In March 1865, five weeks before the **Civil War** ended, Congress set up the Bureau of Refugees, Freedmen, and Abandoned Land, better known as the Freedmen's Bureau, to administer the process of emancipation. It was given the right to distribute confiscated lands in plots of not over 40 acres, to adjudicate disputes, to investigate violence, and to distribute food and clothing. It was headed by General O. O. Howard and many of its agents were former Union officers. The Freedmen's Bureau helped mission societies build and establish schools for the children of freed slaves. It also helped to feed and cloth refugees during the hectic period after the war, it monitored state courts, investigated violence against freed persons and reported on their conditions. It was particularly concerned that freed persons were treated fairly.

It faced the hostility of Andrew Johnson, who had become president of the United States after **Abraham Lincoln**'s assassination. Its original mandate was for one year. When Congress voted to extend it, Johnson vetoed the bill, but Congress overrode his veto. Johnson also gave an amnesty to former Confederates and ordered land restored to its former owners. This meant that the former slaves received nothing but their freedom. When the Bureau closed operations in 1869, most former slaves were poor landless rural peasants. *See also* RECONSTRUCTION.

FREE SOIL PARTY. The Free Soil Party did not support abolition of slavery. Organized in 1848 to oppose the extension of slavery into territories taken over in the Mexican-American War, its slogan was "No more slave states and no more slave territories." Free Soilers believed in the superiority of small farmers to slaves and preferred family farms to large **plantations**. The Free Soilers replaced the **Liberty Party** as the major anti-slavery political party. Where the Liberty Party was not successful, the Free Soilers received 14 percent of the northern presidential vote. They also elected seven congressmen and two senators. When the Republican Party was formed in 1854 with a commitment to a Free Soil policy, most Free Soilers joined it. In 1860, **Abraham Lincoln**'s platform was a Free Soil program, opposed to extension of slavery, but careful not to threaten slavery where it already existed.

FREE WOMB LAWS. Under free womb laws, children born after the date the law was passed were freed. This was a low-cost approach to emancipation because no person in slavery was freed and emancipation was gradual. Since the nominally free children were raised under the master's control, these laws also gave the masters a generation to find some way to control the labor of former slaves or find a new source. Free womb laws usually required the slave to work for the master until age 21, and sometimes 25. They were used in some of the states of the northern United States. For example, the New York law passed in 1799 freed all slaves born after that date, but women after 21 years and men after 25. They were equally important in many parts of Latin America. Free womb laws were passed in Chile in 1811, Argentina in 1813, Gran Colombia in 1821, Cuba in 1870, and Brazil in 1871. *See also* ABOLITION, BRAZIL; EMANCIPATION, HISPANIC AMERICA; EMANCIPATION, UNITED STATES; MORET LAW.

FRENCH REVOLUTION. When the French Estates General gathered in May 1789, slavery was not one of its major concerns. For the bankrupt King Louis XVI, the major issue was raising money. For most of the delegates gathered in Paris, the issues were their own grievances. They carried with them petitions of grievance, *cahiers de doléances*, from people of all classes in France and in the colonies. Most of their grievances were local. Within seven weeks, the Third Estate had proclaimed itself the National Assembly and unleashed a 26-year struggle that divided Europe and transformed the political life of Europe and much of the rest of the world.

Underlying many of the issues debated by the revolutionaries was a belief in natural law and universal human rights. This found its first expression in the **Declaration of the Rights of Man**, which proclaimed that "Men are born and remain free and equal in rights." Though the declaration, like most documents of the Revolution, spoke in universal terms, its authors were still divided over exactly who were entitled to these rights. Only a small group gathered in the **Society of the Friends of Blacks** believed that such rights extended to black slaves, but they argued passionately for the rights of slaves.

In the short run, the most important effect of these debates is that they led to the **Haitian Revolution.** The island of **Saint-Domingue**, which was then the world's largest **sugar** producer, contained a sizeable mulatto population, some of whom were free planters and merchants. They sent a delegation to Paris headed by **Vincent Ogé** to ask for the extension of citizenship to free **persons of color** and for their representation in the National Assembly. When the National Assembly turned Ogé down and referred the issue back to the governor of Saint-Domingue, Ogé returned home and led a brief unsuccessful revolt. Ten months later, taking advantage of the disorder, a rising of slaves began. The Haitian Revolution took 13 years and became the most successful slave revolution in history. It created fear among slave owners in largely slave societies and inspired slaves in societies all over the Americas.

In the long run, the most important result of the French Revolution was that it entrenched two ideas in popular discourse. The first was that sovereignty lay with the people, that all people, including slaves, had the right to have a say in how they were governed. The second was that all human beings are endowed with the right to personal liberty. The French Revolution led to rule by Napoléon Bonaparte and after Bonaparte's defeat, to the restoration of the monarchy in 1815. This was, however, only a temporary setback. In 1848, when another revolution took place in France, there was even less discussion of slavery. The abolition of slavery throughout the French Empire was approved quickly and with little debate. Anti-slavery had become part of the republican agenda. By the time the Third Republic was created in 1871, the superiority of free labor and a belief in human rights had been accepted all over Europe. Among European societies, slavery existed only in Cuba and Brazil and was on the defensive there. *See also* ABOLITION, BRAZIL; ABOLITION, FRANCE; CONDORCET; ENLIGHTENMENT; NATURAL LAW.

FUGITIVE SLAVE LAWS, UNITED STATES. Slave societies generally take measures to prevent the flight of slaves. At an early point in their history, United States and Brazilian colonists made arrangements with Amerindian tribes to return runaway slaves. In Jamaica, there was even a treaty with the **Maroons**, themselves originally runaways, to return all new runaways. The first fugitive slave law in the United States was part of the act prohibiting slavery in the Northwest Territory (1787). In the same year, a fugitive slave clause was added to the U.S. **Constitution**. It provided that any person fleeing labor obligations should be returned to his owner. A 1793 law set up procedures for returning runaway slaves to their owners and . The fugitive slave clause of the Constitution assumed that states would enforce the law, but many northern states responded with **personal liberty laws**, which guaranteed the fugitive a jury trial and required that state officials supervise the process to make sure that free blacks were not kidnapped. The Supreme Court held that these acts were unconstitutional, but some of the states responded with even stronger laws, which forbade state officials enforcing the federal law and denied the use of state prisons and courtrooms in fugitive slave cases. Throughout, the issue remained a basic issue for the South.

The **Compromise of 1850** included an amendment to the 1793 act, which created local officials to enforce the law in every county in the United States and established fines and prison sentences for anyone helping a slave escape from custody. Many African-Americans who were former slaves fled the United States, taking refuge in Canada or Great Britain. This included leaders like **Frederick Douglass** and **William Wells Brown** , who had been free for many years, but feared a claim from their former masters. In carrying out the law, federal officials were empowered to use the army and federal marshals. The law was bitterly resented in the North. Between 1850 and 1864, when it was repealed, fewer than 400 slaves were returned. Often the arrest and return was physically contested by abolitionists and free blacks. The Fugitive Slave Act increased sectional polarization in the decade before the **Civil War**. *See also* KANSAS-NEBRASKA ACT; NORTHWEST ORDNANCE.

- G -

GABRIEL'S REBELLION (1800). Gabriel's rebellion was an effort to overthrow slavery in Virginia. Gabriel was a literate slave blacksmith, 24 years old, physically large and respected for his intelligence. As a blacksmith, he was frequently rented out by his owner. He was thus able to move around and make contact with slaves over a large area. The immediate stimulus to the revolt was an incident in which he was caught trying to steal a pig and got into a fight with its owner. He escaped the gallows only because he was able to recite a verse from the Bible, but his treatment angered him. The plan of the rebellion was for three columns of slaves to march on the state capital, Richmond, to seize guns stored there and to take Governor James Madison and a number of city leaders hostage. The plan failed when a thunderstorm on the day set for the rising prevented many slaves from arriving at the meeting place. Of the 500 to 600 who were aware of the plot, only 12 showed up. Recognizing that it had failed, two slaves informed their master. The militia was called out. Gabriel was arrested fleeing on a boat. Twenty-six slaves, including Gabriel, were hanged. Eight others were sold to New Orleans. Unsuccessful as it was, the plot scared Virginia slave owners. Laws were passed prohibiting slaves from congregating on Sunday for religious services and requiring that any manumitted slave leave the state within 12 months of **manumission**. *See also* SLAVE REVOLTS.

GALLEY SLAVES. Galleys were boats that were powered primarily by oars, using sails only when winds were favorable. They were important in the Mediterranean for at least two thousand years, particularly in war. The Greeks and Romans relied primarily on poor citizens to row their galleys, though slaves may have been used in some crises. In the Middle Ages too, the oarsmen were mostly free, but from the 16th to the 18th centuries, galleys were rowed primarily by slaves and convicts. The slaves tended to be better oarsmen. In Christian ships, they were mostly Muslim prisoners or Orthodox Christians from Greece and eastern Europe. The Turks used galley slaves from Russia and Italy. Most were under 35 years of age. Poorly fed and harshly treated, they had a high mortality rate. When not on the water, they were often used for heavy work around the port. Galleys stopped being used about the middle of the 18th century.

GARNET, HENRY HIGHLAND (1815-1882). Henry Highland Garnet was a distinguished African-American minister and abolitionist. He was born a slave on a Maryland **tobacco** farm, but his family escaped in 1824. He left school to go to sea at age 13, but on his first voyage was crippled. Unable to do physical labor, he undertook theological studies. After receiving honors, he was ordained in 1842 and became the minister of a Presbyterian church in Troy, New York. He also became a leading abolitionist orator, founded the *Clarion,* a black weekly, and was one of the organizers of the National Convention of Colored Citizens and their Friends. In 1843, he gave a speech to the annual conference of the National Convention calling for a slave insurrection.

Its advocacy of violence very much divided abolitionists. He remained a militant voice for abolition, African culture, voluntary emigration, and aid to fugitive slaves. During the **Civil War**, Garnet recruited for several black regiments and served as a chaplain. In 1866, he became the first African-American to address the U.S. Congress at a ceremony celebrating passage of the **Thirteenth Amendment**. In 1882, he died of malaria in Monrovia while serving as the U.S. minister to **Liberia**.

GARRETT, THOMAS (1789-1871). Born into an anti-slavery **Quaker** family, Thomas Garrett early became involved in the problems of runaway slaves when kidnappers tried to sell a servant from his family home into slavery. He allied himself to **William Lloyd Garrison**, unlike most of his fellow Quakers who found Garrison's style too confrontational. He lived most of his life in Delaware, where he was a successful businessman. Delaware was a slave state where there was strong abolitionist sentiment. Collaborating with **William Still** in Philadelphia, he and a group of accomplices provided food, shelter, and transportation to runaway slaves. He later claimed that he aided over 2,700 runaways. This contributed to the legend of the **Underground Railroad**. On several occasions, **Harriet Tubman** led slaves to his home. Garrett was open about his activities. He was sued several times and on one occasion was almost thrown from a train while trying to keep a woman from being sold into slavery. After the **Civil War**, he worked for civil rights, women's suffrage, and temperance.

GARRISON, WILLIAM LLOYD (1805-1879). Garrison was the most important and most controversial abolitionist of his time. Born in a poor family with an alcoholic father and a deeply religious mother, Garrison was largely self-educated. He was apprenticed first to a shoemaker and then to a printer. In the 1820's, he became a protégé of **Benjamin Lundy**, one of the leaders of the **American Colonization Society**, but he soon moved to more radical positions. In 1831, he began publishing the *Liberator*. Though it generally lost money, Garrison brought the *Liberator* out every week for 35 years. Most of its readers were African-Americans. His penchant for controversy and his radical positions often divided abolitionists and frequently aroused the ire of northern mobs. A deeply religious man with a strong belief in his own righteousness, Garrison denounced colonization and gradualism and repeatedly attacked slavery as a sin and slave holders as sinners. He also denounced the United States **Constitution** because it sanctioned slavery, and advocated secession by the North. He favored "moral suasion" over political action, and he supported an active role for women in the movement. During the early years of the **Civil War**, he regularly attacked **Abraham Lincoln** for moving slowly on abolition, but after the **Emancipation Proclamation**, he changed, supporting Lincoln's 1864 election campaign. *See also* ABOLITION, UNITED STATES.

GENOVESE, EUGENE (1930-). Eugene Genovese has been controversial for his questioning of many accepted ideas and for his application of Marxist theory to the history of slavery. After studying at Brooklyn College and Columbia University, Genovese made his mark with two books. In *The Political Economy of Slavery* (1961), he argued that slavery created a powerful slaveholding elite who needed **capitalism** and used capitalism, but were hostile to many of its fundamental values. He developed these ideas in *The World the Slaveholders Made* (1969).

Genovese's most important book was *Roll Jordan Roll: The World the Slaves Made.* In it, he argued that slavery was shaped by the balance between paternalism and coercion on the master's side and accommodation and resistance on the slave's side. In Genovese's hands, **Marxism** was freed from economic determinism and transformed into a powerful tool for analysis. He saw class struggle, not in physical resistance, but in the give-and-take of the **plantation**. Genovese used this approach to discuss religion, sexual relations, family life, and work. He argued that the slaves successfully maintained a measure of human dignity and created a distinct African-American culture, but he also argued the importance of planter's paternalism in preventing revolt and encouraging a psychology of dependence. Genovese argued that American slavery differed from the West Indian variant because the planter usually lived on the plantation and maintained a personal relationship with his slaves. Genovese's later work is marked by a continuing fascination with the slave masters and the way of life they created.

GERMAN COAST REVOLT. The German coast was a stretch of the Mississippi River north of New Orleans. In January 1811, a group of slaves attacked a planter named Manuel Andry and killed his son. They then marched off downriver, burning plantation buildings and recruiting other slaves as they went. Many whites fled to New Orleans or hid in the woods. A militia force was quickly gathered and with the aid of regular army troops cornered the slaves three days later. Most of the slaves were only armed with knives and axes. They were no match for the well-armed troops. At least 60 were killed and many were arrested. After a trial, 21 were sentenced to death and executed. To serve as example to others, their heads were cut off and placed on posts along the river. It is not known what caused the revolt, but many observers thought that the resettlement of refugees from **Saint-Domingue** in the area was a factor.

GHULAMS. The term *ghulam* refers to **elite slaves** of a type common in the Muslim world. The term originally meant youth. The term developed its meaning of elite slaves under the Abbasid Empire, which ruled the Middle East from 750 to 1258. The ghulams were generally purchased as boys from non-Muslim areas. The Abbasids generally got them from Central Asia. They were converted to Islam, trained for the army or bureaucracy, and eventually manumitted. Lacking family ties, they were usually loyal to the rulers they served and held many of the highest offices of the state. Many became wealthy and some were important benefactors of the arts and of religion Ghulams were also important among the Seljuk Turks, who gradually took over Abbasid areas from the 11th century. Ghulams are similar to the **Mamlukes** and **Janissaries**.

GLADIATORS. Most gladiators in ancient Rome were slaves who fought each other in the bloody spectacles. The original gladiatorial games were part of a religious ritual to appease the dead, but with time they just became a form of bloody entertainment. Most were war prisoners or convicts who were trained at special gladiator schools. They usually fought to the death. The most famous **slave revolt** in Roman times began with the revolt of a series of gladiators led by **Spartacus**. Though there were attempts to abolish the games, they did not end until the fifth century. *See also* ANCIENT ROMAN SLAVERY.

GOLD COAST. When the first Portuguese navigators cruised along the **West African** coast in the late 15th century, they were particularly interested in tapping into the sources of gold they knew were there. They were successful only when they reached what is now Ghana. This became known as the Gold Coast. While Europeans increasingly bought slaves elsewhere, gold was the most important item traded on the Gold Coast until the end of the 17th century. Slaves were actually bought elsewhere for sale on the Gold Coast, where they could be used to mine gold. One effect of the gold trade was that different European powers built trading posts and castles in the area, among which were the most formidable structures built by Europeans in Africa.

Toward the end of the 17th century, however, the demand for slaves was rising, as was the possibility of profit. The Dutch started selling guns and buying slaves. Soon, other European traders increased their purchases of slaves. In 1702, **Asante** defeated its major rival Denkyera to become the major state in the area. The ability of Asante to control the **slave trade** over the whole of what is now Ghana made the Gold Coast a major source of slaves in the 18th century. The production of gold declined, though Asante was able to supplement the slave trade with a continuing trade in gold and a growing trade in kola nuts. About 600,000 slaves were exported from the Gold Coast during the 18th century.

When the British established control over the area, their colony was called the Gold Coast. In 1874, slavery and the slave trade were abolished, but the abolition of slavery was not effective far from the coast until the early years of the 20th century. The Gold Coast was renamed Ghana after independence. *See also* AFRICAN SLAVE TRADE; DUTCH SLAVE TRADE; ELMINA.

GOLDEN LAW. The Golden Law of 13 May 1888 abolished slavery in Brazil. The first article stated simply: "From this date slavery is declared extinct in Brazil." The second article repealed all earlier laws that contradicted this statement. This simple statement ended a struggle that began when Brazil ended the **slave trade** in 1850. Brazil moved toward abolition in small steps, beginning with the **free womb law** of 1871, which freed all children born of slave mothers when they reached the age of 21. After 1880, a number of states began to take action, and in 1887 slaves began to leave their plantations.

On 3 May 1888, when the legislature opened, Princess Isabel, the daughter of Emperor Dom Pedro II, urged it to abolish slavery. Ten days later, the law passed. The debate was short because many planters recognized that slavery was doomed, and some, particularly coffee planters in the south, were convinced that slavery was a barrier to the adoption of a free labor system using immigrant labor, which was then becoming available. The Golden Law provided the slaves with freedom, but it did little to meet their need for land and education. *See also* ABOLITION, BRAZIL.

GORÉE ISLAND. Gorée is today a small 65-acre tourist attraction in the harbor of Dakar, Senegal's capital. When the Portuguese ship captain, Dinis Diaz sighted it in 1444, it was uninhabited because it was not suitable for agriculture. It speedily became useful for trade with the opposite coast and then with areas farther south. In 1617, the Dutch built two forts on the island. It changed hands several times before the French took it in 1677. It remained French thereafter except for several brief periods of British occupation. The population was small, a little over 1,800 in 1780, rising to about 4,000 in the mid-19th century. About two-thirds of the population was slaves who worked for French and *métis* traders. In particular, they manned the small boats that worked the rivers and beaches of the Senegambia coast and amassed goods for trade. There was also a small free black population and an even smaller French population. Even in 1835, there were only 22 white French persons on the island. Particularly important among the *métis* were the *signares,* elegantly dressed women who were the partners of French men. Many of them profitted from these relationships and became the owners of ships and houses. Gorée was a port where traders could put on goods, supplies, and extra slaves before attempting the **Middle Passage**. *See also* AFRICAN SLAVE TRADE; WEST AFRICA.

GRAY, SIMON (c. 1810-1870). Simon Gray was a slave who ran his own business. Originally hired as a laborer by Andrew Brown and Company, a Natchez, Mississippi, lumber firm, he became a raft crew chief in 1838 and then chief boatman for the company in 1845. As raft chief, he placed orders and collected debts. As chief boatman, he supervised white workers, paid their wages, and kept records. He was never formally manumitted. That required an act of the legislature, but he seems to have been effectively free from 1853. He may have had a private arrangement with his owner. Though he continued to work for Brown and Company until 1862 and his family was owned by the company, he also owned flatboats and was hauling sand to New Orleans. In 1863, after Vicksburg fell to the Union army, Gray and his family family were freed.

GREEK SLAVERY. *See* **ANCIENT GREEK SLAVERY.**

GRÉGOIRE, BISHOP HENRI (1750-1831). The Bishop of Blois, Henri Grégoire, was the leading abolitionist during the French Revolution. He had earlier supported legal equality for French Jews. In 1787, he joined the leading French abolitionist organization, **Société des Amis des Noirs** (Society of Friends of Blacks). During the early months of the French Revolution in 1789, a key issue was whether mulatto populations should be given the vote. A strong supporter of political rights for mulattoes, Grégoire published a pamphlet, *Lettre aux Citoyens de couleur* (Letter to Citizens of Color), which pro-slavery elements accused of fomenting the **Haitian Revolution**. He corresponded with the Haitian leader, **Toussaint-Louverture**, and became a regular spokesman for the Haitians in France. He criticized the reenslavement of Haitian blacks by Napoléon in 1802.

When the revolutionaries tried to reorganize the **Catholic Church**, Grégoire was one of the few Catholic priests to accept the reform. This made him a controversial figure within the church and probably hurt the abolition movement because it made it difficult for him to ever seek church support. In 1808, he published *De la Littérature des negres*, which argued for the equality of blacks. He believed that all men were equal in the eyes of God and saw slavery as an immoral and debilitating institution. *See also* ABOLITION, FRANCE.

GRIMKÉ, ANGELINA AND SARAH. The Grimké sisters, Sarah (1792-1873) and Angelina (1805-1879), were born into a wealthy Charleston slave-owning family. When Sarah Grimké visited Philadelphia in 1819, she was attracted by the **Quaker** religion, to which she converted, rejecting the Episcopalian faith in which she had been raised. Her sister joined her ten years later and went through a similar conversion. In 1836, with the support of **William Lloyd Garrison**, Angelina published *An Appeal to the Christian Women of the Southern States*, which based an argument for emancipation on a belief in natural rights. The same year, Sarah published *Epistle to the Clergy of the Southern States*, in which she denied the biblical arguments for slavery. Southern postmasters destroyed copies of Grimké writings. The two sisters were no longer welcome in Charleston, but they became key figures in both abolitionism and a nascent feminist movement. Both became active as public speakers, originally addressing primarily women's groups. The question of the role of women was a factor in a split in the **American Anti-Slavery Society**. The challenge to their position led the Grimkés to argue strongly for the right of women to participate in political life. In 1838, Angelina married **Theodore Dwight Weld**, another abolitionist leader. Sarah lived with the Welds for the rest of her life. *See also* ABOLITION, UNITED STATES.

GRINNELL, JOSIAH B. (1821-1891). A key abolitionist and one of the founders of the Republican Party, Josiah Grinnell was born in Vermont. After being ordained a minister in 1846, he accepted a pulpit in Washington, D.C. When he gave an abolitionist sermon, he was forced to resign and to leave Washington. In 1854, he moved to Iowa, where, with two business associates, he bought 5,000 acres of land and founded the town of Grinnell. Two years later, the college that was eventually to bear his name moved there. A founding member of the Iowa Republican Party, he served in the state senate from 1856 to 1860. He also became Iowa's leading abolitionist. In 1859, he hosted **John Brown** when Brown was escorting a group of fugitive slaves to Canada. He served two terms in the United States Congress, where he strongly supported **Abraham Lincoln** and advocated the use of black troops. *See also* ABOLITION, UNITED STATES.

GUERRERO, VICENTE (1783?-1831). A *mestizo* mule driver born in southern Mexico,Vicente Guerrero became the second president of Mexico and the liberator of its slaves. Known as "el Negro" because of his dark skin, Guerrero enlisted in the army of José Maria Morelos, who was fighting for independence from Spain. He rose quickly and, when Morelos was killed by the Royalists in 1815, became the leader of the independence forces in southern Mexico. He held a number of important positions during the 1820s. In 1829, he lost the presidential election, but was installed in office by a military coup.

On 15 September 1829, Guerrero abolished slavery, promising that slave owners would be compensated when funds were available. Mexico did not have a large number of slaves. The strongest opposition to Guerrero's act came from American settlers who were moving into Texas at that time and regarded abolition as an infringement of their property rights. As a result, Guerrero excluded Texas from the law. In December 1829, the military men who put him in office removed him. He was later shot, but remains a much admired figure. One of the Mexican states bears his name. *See also* EMANCIPATION, HISPANIC AMERICA.

GUINEA. The term Guinea originally referred to the coast of **West Africa**. Slave traders were often called Guinea Men. Upper Guinea was the area from Senegambia to the Ivory Coast. It was the first area where the **slave trade** developed, but it was eventually replaced by Lower Guinea, which consisted primarily of the **Gold Coast** and the **Slave Coast**.

GULLAH. Gullah is an African dialect spoken on the **Sea Islands** of South Carolina and Georgia. African languages and African culture persisted on the Sea Islands for several reasons. First, many of the slaves came from the rice-growing areas of **Sierra Leone** and **Guinea**, and in fact were brought in because of their skill in cultivating rice. Second, the malarial climate meant that few whites wanted to live there year-round. Thus, the slaves were free to preserve much of the culture and folklore they brought with them. *See also* PORT ROYAL.

-H-

HAITIAN REVOLUTION. By the late 18th century, the French colony of **Saint-Domingue** had become the most populous and most productive of the **sugar plantation** colonies in the West Indies. From 1791 to 1803, it experienced the biggest and most effective anti-slavery revolution in history, one that inspired other **slave revolts** and spread fear in slave-owning societies throughout the Americas. Saint-Domingue was vulnerable because its half million slaves outnumbered whites by over 12 to 1. There were also over 30,000 free coloreds. The **French Revolution** created the opportunity by weakening the colonial government and creating divisions within the free community.

In 1791, both slaves and free **people of color** revolted. The leaders of the slave revolt were mostly drivers and skilled slaves born on the island. Within a month, over a thousand plantations were burned. When a French army was sent to put down the revolt, it was weakened by tropical diseases and ineffective against rebel guerilla methods. Hoping to prevent an alliance between free colored and slaves, the French government granted the free people of color equality. In spite of this, by 1793 the rebels controlled part of the north. The plantation system remained in most of the rest of the colony. Then, war broke out with Great Britain and Spain. When the Spanish, who shared the island with the French, began recruiting rebel slaves, the French state abolished slavery throughout the empire. British troops occupied Martinique before the slaves could be emancipated, but revolutionary regimes established themselves on Guadeloupe and Saint-Domingue.

On Saint-Domingue, a former slave named **Toussaint-Louverture** established his ascendancy and drove out the Spanish invaders. To finance his armies, he established a forced labor regime that frustrated the desire of most slaves to farm for themselves. On Guadeloupe, the revolutionaries were led by Victor Hugues, a French radical. In 1802, Napoléon Bonaparte reestablished slavery and invaded both Saint-Domingue and Guadeloupe. French troops were successful in Guadeloupe, but were defeated in Saint-Domingue. Toussaint was captured and taken to France, where he died in prison, but in 1803, the French were driven out by a new regime under another slave general, **Jean-Jacques Dessalines**. To underline its break with colonial rule, the new state took an Amerindian name, Haiti.

The Haitian Revolution had several effects. It forced revolutionary regimes in France to consider questions of slavery and racial equality. It created a free black society in the Americas, awakened the hopes of slaves and free blacks throughout the Americas, and it created fear among slave owners, who tightened discipline in all slave-owning societies. *See also* CARIBBEAN SLAVERY; OGÉ, VINCENT.

HALE, EDWARD EVERETT (1822-1901). Edward Hale was a minister in the Congregationalist Church and an active abolitionist. Born to a wealthy and distinguished family in Boston, he graduated from Harvard University in 1839, and became first a teacher and then a minister. As a minister, he worked for the freeing of the slaves and then, after the **Civil War**, for the economic betterment of freed persons. In 1862, he was one of the founders of the New England Freedmen's Aid Society, which raised funds to provide an education for newly freed African-Americans. During his last years, he was chaplain of the United States Senate.

HAM. Ham was the son of Noah. According to the **Bible**, Ham saw his father drunk and naked and did not cover him. When Ham called attention to their father's state, his brothers, Shem and Japheth, covered Noah. When Noah awoke, he cursed Ham's son, Canaan, and his descendants to remain forever the servants of Shem and Japheth and their descendants. The myth developed that Ham was the ancestor of black people and that their enslavement was a result of this curse. The Curse of Ham was a myth used in later centuries to justify enslavement of Africans. There is neither scientific nor biblical justification for it.

HAMMOND, JAMES HENRY (1807-1864). James Henry Hammond was one of the South's most important leaders in the generation before the **Civil War**. Born and raised in South Carolina, he graduated from South Carolina College in 1825 and became a lawyer in 1828. In 1831, he married a wealthy Charleston heiress, whose dowry included a **cotton plantation** with 147 slaves. Hammond knew nothing about farming, but he learned quickly. By 1860, he owned 14,000 acres and over 300 slaves.

He served briefly in the U.S. House of Representatives during 1836.

He claimed in one of his first speeches that slavery was "the greatest of all the great blessings which a kind Providence has bestowed upon our favored region." In 1842, he was elected governor of South Carolina, where he served two terms. In 1857, he was elected to the Senate. He was a passionate defender of the South and its slave system and an early proponent of the idea of southern secession. He is perhaps best known for a speech given on the floor of the Senate in 1858 in which he proclaimed: "No, you dare not make war on cotton. No power dares make war on cotton. No power on earth dares to make war on it. Cotton is King." He resigned from the Senate after the election of **Abraham Lincoln** and retired to his plantation, where he died near the end of the war.

HAMMURABI. Hammurabi was a ruler of ancient Babylonia who tried in about 1750 BCE to codify legal practice. This compilation is known as Hammurabi's Code. It is one of the fullest expositions of early Mesopotamian law. Many of the laws refer to slaves, who were the lowest of three categories of person. In the code, the harshest penalties were reserved for slaves, who had to wear a distinctive haircut. Habitual runaways were permanently marked and persons who harbored runaways were severely punished. The punishment of runaways was not discussed in the code, which suggests that they were simply returned to their owners. The code provided for a free person to be sold into slavery if he could not pay his debts. Slaves were also less protected than free persons. For example, if a man struck a slave, the compensation was half what would be paid to a free person. See also ANCIENT MIDDLE EASTERN SLAVERY; LAW OF SLAVERY.

HARATIN. In the western **Sahara**, *haratin* were intermediaries between slave and free. The exact origin of the term is not clear, but most were freed slaves or the descendants of freed slaves, who remained in a client relationship to the warrior and clerical tribes. They cultivated palm groves, worked as herdsmen, gardeners, and water carriers, but they were also free to work for themselves. During and since the period of French colonial rule, some of them have been able to profit from their willingness to do different kinds of work. In the central Sahara, among the Tuareg, there is a similar group called the **Bella**.

HAREM. In much of Asia and Africa, the harem was the women's quarter of the houses of the wealthy and powerful. The term can refer to either the physical space or the women who lived in it. Most of these residents were slaves, though legal wives and children also resided there. Harems could be very large, with as many as 1,000 women in many imperial harems. Wealthy men, leading aristocrats, and powerful officials also had harems, but very much smaller. Access to the harem was generally restricted to the master of the house and to **eunuchs**. The harem was generally managed by the senior wife or, in the case of the Ottoman sultan, by the sultan's mother, who was called the *valide*. She was herself usually a concubine, though as the mother of the sultan often very powerful. Harem politics often centered on the struggle of women to get their sons placed so as to succeed. In any harem, many of the women were servants rather than sexual companions of the master. The Ottoman *valide* was in charge of the kitchen, hospital, school, and garden. She was also in charge of the training of **concubines**. Slave women prepared and served meals, washed and prepared clothing, and kept the area clean. Children usually remained with their mothers until sexual maturity. Then, the boys were taken elsewhere for training and the girls were married.

HARPER, ROBERT GOODLOE (1765-1825). Robert Harper was from backcountry South Carolina. He had been educated at Princeton University and was influenced by the egalitarianism of the **American Revolution**. In the 1790s, he became an advocate of racial equality and an opponent of the extension of slavery to the western territories at a time when the **Haitian Revolution** was awakening fears of **slave revolt**. He served as a congressman from South Carolina from 1794 to 1801, and then moved his law practice to Maryland. There, he became active in the **American Colonization Society**. It was he who suggested the names of **Liberia** for the nation and Monrovia for its capital.

HARPER'S FERRY. *See* JOHN BROWN.

HARRIS, JOHN (1874-1940). John Harris was a former missionary who served as secretary of the Anti-Slavery and Aborigines Protection Society from 1910 to his death in 1940. Though the society was no longer as important as it had been, slavery and the **slave trade** persisted in many parts of the world. Harris was very adept at organizing press campaigns and mobilizing public opinion to put pressure on political leaders. In 1920, after five weeks spent lobbying the newly founded **League of Nations** on slavery issues, he realized that the league could be used to raise humanitarian issues. The opportunity to act came with news stories on slavery and the slave trade in Ethiopia. Harris persuaded a representative from New Zealand to raise the issue at the League. The result was an inquiry into slavery by the league. This involvement persisted, and regularly prodded by Harris the league put pressure on colonial governments to act on slavery. Harris also wrote a number of books, including, *Dawn in Darkest Africa* and *A Century of Emancipation*. He served briefly in Parliament, but he was probably more influential outside Parliament. *See also* ANTI-SLAVERY INTERNATIONAL.

HAYNES, LEMUEL (1753-1833). Born a slave in Connecticut, Haynes was freed at the age of 21. In 1775, he joined George Washington's army and served in the fighting around Boston and at Fort Ticonderoga. He wrote a patriotic balled entitled "The Battle of Lexington," and in 1776 was the author of an esssay, "Liberty Further Extended," which argued that the principles of freedom and liberty proclaimed in the Declaration of Independence should be extended to all people. The essay concluded that slavery was sinful and a corrupting institution and called for slave owners to free their slaves. After the Revolution, he became a minister. He was ordained in 1785 and spent the rest of his life as a pastor in Congregationalist churches in New England and New York.

HELOTRY. Helotry was a form of state-controlled captivity in ancient Sparta. The helots were people living in areas that had been conquered by Sparta. They remained where they were and were owned by the state, but they were controlled by landowners. They differed from slaves in that they were bound to the land, much like serfs. The helots also maintained their own family and religious life and were almost all agricultural workers. The helots outnumbered the free Spartans and were occasionally armed when Sparta was threatened. *See also* ANCIENT GREEK SLAVERY.

HELPER, HINTON ROWAN (1829-1909). Born to a non-slaveholding family in western North Carolina, Helper briefly became the leading southern white abolitionist. A self-educated man, he travelled widely in the United States and became a writer in the 1850s. His travels convinced him that the North was more prosperous than the South because slavery limited southern economic development by exhausting the soil and degrading the value of work. In 1857, he published *The Impending Crisis of the South and How to Meet It*, which called for immediate abolition of slavery. Though Helper had a difficult time finding a

publisher even in the North, the book was actively promoted by Republicans, who hoped to find some support in the non-slaveholding whites
of the South, who outnumbered slave owners. His book was very hostile
to the planter elites of the South, but also to slaves, who Helper wanted
to resettle in Africa or Latin America. After the **Civil War**, Helper
wrote a number of racist tracts, but never again played an important
public role.

HEMINGS, SALLY (1773-1835). Sally Hemings was the mulatto slave
owned by and perhaps the daughter of **Thomas Jefferson's** father-in-
law, John Wayles. When Wayles died in 1773, Jefferson inherited the
Hemings and moved them to his estate of Monticello. Sally was widely
believed to have been Jefferson's mistress for many years. Jefferson's
wife died young and he never remarried. In 1787, five years after his
wife's death, when Jefferson was sent as minister to the court of French
King Louis XVI, Sally Hemings was a 14-year-old servant and companion to Jefferson's daughter, Mary. She lived the rest of her life at Jefferson's estate, Monticello, where most of the staff were members of her
family. Over two decades, she bore six children, four of whom grew to
adulthood. Several of them supposedly resembled Jefferson. Two of her
sons, Madison and Eston, were freed by Jefferson's will. Both of them
claimed to be Jefferson's sons. Eston changed his name to Jefferson
after moving to Wisconsin. A DNA study published in 1998 is not
absolutely conclusive, but suggests the probability that they were right.
Jefferson never admitted to the relationship. *See also* SEXUAL EX-
PLOITATION

HENSON, JOSIAH (1789-1883). Josiah Henson was born as a slave in
Maryland, but escaped to become a minister and educator in Canada. As
a young man, he was an overseer on his master's plantation. In 1825 he
escorted a group of slaves to his master's brother's plantation in Kentucky. Though he had to pass through free territory in Ohio, he refused
to let the slaves escape. Five years later, he and his wife fled to Canada.
There he became a minister, served in the Essex Company of Coloured
Volunteers, and founded a manual training school for former slaves who
fled to Canada. In the 1840s, he went back to Kentucky to help other
slaves to escape. In 1849, he published his autobiography, *The Life of
Josiah Henson, Formerly a Slave, now an Inhabitant of Canada as
narrated by himself*. Henson claimed to be the model for Uncle Tom in
Harriet Beecher Stowe's *Uncle Tom's Cabin*. In the novel, however,
Tom is sold to the Deep South, where he is beaten to death by a cruel

overseer. Henson escaped slavery and went on to help others.

HEPBURN, JOHN (c. 1667-c.1773). John Hepburn was the author of an early abolitionist tract. He originally came to the colony of New Jersey in 1684 as an indentured servant. He became a tailor, owned some land, and was a **Quaker**. Otherwise, little is known about him except his book, *The American Defence of the Christian Golden Rule* (1715). This was one of the first abolitionist works published in the Americas. In it, he deplored the growth of slavery in New Jersey, criticizing the way slaves were clothed and housed, the beatings, and the separation of families as a violation of Christian principle. He attributed to slavery the laziness and vanity of slave owners. He included his fellow Quakers in his criticism and may have influenced the Quakers in that area to use their wills to free their slaves.

***HERMOSA* CASE.** The *Hermosa* was a vessel which was carrying slaves from Richmond, Virginia, to New Orleans and ran aground in the Bahamas in October 1840. When the ship was taken into Nassau harbor, the captain refused to allow the slaves to leave the ship or have contact with anyone on the dock. British troops, however, removed the slaves, who were then freed over the protests of the captain and the United States Consul. The *Hermosa* case was one of several in which the British freed slaves removed from U.S. ships. The Americans contended that the ship had done nothing wrong and was only seeking help. The British contended that under British law, the slaves became free when they entered British territory. The two countries argued about this and several similar cases until 1854, when they finally agreed to put the case before an umpire. He decided in favor of the Americans, but awarded them only $16,000, a fraction of the market value of the slaves.

HIGGINSON, THOMAS WENTWORTH (1823-1911). A Unitarian minister and an abolitionist, Thomas Higginson was the commander of black troops during the American **Civil War**. After graduating from Harvard College (1841) and Harvard Divinity School (1847), Higginson served as a minister in Newburyport and then Worcester, Massachusetts. During the 1850s, he became an increasingly radical abolitionist, even favoring northern secession. He was active in efforts to protect fugitive slaves like **Anthony Burns** and after passage of the **Kansas-Nebraska Act**, in supporting free state emigrants to Kansas. He was one of a group of abolitionists who funded **John Brown's** efforts in "bleeding Kansas" and later, his raid on Harper's Ferry. After Brown's arrest, he raised money for the defense.

Higginson welcomed the coming of the Civil War. In November 1861, he was authorized by the governor of Massachusetts to raise a regiment, which he did. A year later, he accepted a commission as colonel of the first all-black regiment in the Union, the first South Carolina Volunteers, which was composed completely of freed slaves. He trained his recruits and sought action so that they could prove themselves in combat. In 1864, a leg wound and the effects of malaria forced him to resign. His account of these years was later published as *Army Life in a Black Regiment* (1870). After the war, he became involved in women's issues, serving as coeditor of the *Women's Journal* from 1870 to 1884.

HINDUISM. The institution of slavery was widespread in ancient India. The classics of Hindu literature contain numerous references to slavery, for example, laws regulating gifts of slaves or the ability of slaves to enter into contracts. One document refers to 15 different kinds of slave. They include persons born into slavery, those captured in war, and those enslaved as payment of a debt. Some slaves were temporary and some permanent. The treatment of slaves was regulated in these early law codes. Slaves could be beaten, for example, but only on the back and only with a rope or a thin piece of bamboo. These law codes would suggest that slavery was not particularly harsh.

The operation of slavery was influenced by the importance of caste. Caste involves a structured system of inequality in which different strata are ranked, separated socially and tied to certain occupations. Status was inherited and not based on wealth or power, though the restrictions of caste status made it almost impossible for many people to achieve wealth or power. Caste often influenced slavery because it shaped who could do what and with whom. It involved prohibitions on sexual relations and physical contact. Most slaves came from the lower castes. Many writers have suggested that a Brahman could not be enslaved. Caste also influenced who could own who and what kind of relations people of different castes could have. A slave could also not perform certain important rites. A slave could, however, marry a free person, but a free woman who married a male slave became a slave, while a free man who married a female slave became her owner and could therefore free her. The difference between caste and slavery was that caste was permanent. *See also* INDIAN SLAVERY.

HISPANIC AMERICA. Spain was the first European power to enslave **Amerindians** and the first to import African slaves to the Americas, but with the exception of a few areas like Cuba and coastal regions of the Caribbean basin, slave labor never became as important in Hispanic America as in Brazil, the West Indies, and the United States. The desire for slaves was rooted in the low population of large areas and the eradication of these populations by European diseases.

Slavery existed in 15th-century Spain and there was a law code, the *Siete Partidas*, that regulated it. Thus, it was natural for **Christopher Columbus** to think first of selling Amerindian slaves and then of importing slaves to Hispaniola, his base in the Americas. In 1518, long after Columbus was gone, King Charles V approved the importation of African slaves. On the mainland, the Spanish did not at first need slaves. The two major centers of *conquistador* activity, central Mexico and Peru, were the most densely populated areas of the Americas. There, Spain used the *encomienda* and other forms of forced labor. Soon, however, European diseases severely decimated Amerindian populations. Spain purchased African slaves from the Portuguese under the *asiento* system to be used in **sugar plantations** in the Caribbbean and in coastal lowlands, but also in gold and silver mines and as urban workers. Eventually 1.6 million slaves were imported. The vast majority went to the Caribbean islands and the lowland areas of the mainland.

From the first, the **Catholic Church** made an effort to check the harsh excesses of slavery. **Bartolomé de Las Casas** and other Catholic missionaries described the horrors of the enslavement of Indians and agitated against it. In 1542, King Charles V outlawed Indian slavery as part of the New Laws, though some enslavement continued on the periphery of the empire. By the end of the 16th century, Spanish sugar production was in decline as Brazil was producing cheaper sugar. Still, slaves remained important in areas like the lowlands of Peru, and New Granada (Colombia and Venezuela). Slaves were also present in most cities, where they were servants and did most of the heavy labor and a lot of the artisanal labor. The dispersed nature of slave populations contributed to the high degree of racial mixing among both European and Indian populations. In some areas, like Mexico and the Rio de la Plata, where slaves were briefly important, there are almost no visible African populations, largely because the descendants of slaves have been absorbed within other populations. Hispanic America was also marked by a high degree of **manumission** due to laws that made manumission relatively easy and procedures like *coartación*, which made it possible for a slave to ask a court to set a price for his or her manumission.

From the wars of independence to the middle of the 19th century, most states of Hispanic America freed their slaves. Only in Cuba and Puerto Rico, which still remained in Spanish hands, did slavery remain important. A true **slave society** emerged on Cuba as it became more intensively involved in sugar production. This fueled the last major slave imports from Africa. *See also* BRAZILIAN SLAVERY; CUBAN SLAVERY; EMANCIPATION, HISPANIC AMERICA.

HISPANIOLA. See SAINT-DOMINGUE.

HISPANIOLA REVOLT (1521). On Christmas Day 1521, a group of about 20 Wolof slaves revolted in what was probably the first revolt by African slaves in the Americas. The slaves were the property of Governor Diego Colón, the son of **Christopher Columbus**. In what seems to have been a well-planned revolt, they waited until Christmas Day, when the Spaniards were celebrating and not paying careful attention. They marched toward Azua, the center of Hispaniola's **sugar** industry, ransacking several **plantations**, accumulating supplies, and gathering supporters on the way. Several Spaniards were killed, many buildings were burned and about a dozen hostages were taken. Colón gathered a troop of soldiers and pursued the rebels. The lightly armed slaves were no match for the horses and swords of the Spaniards. After a week's fighting, most of them were captured or killed. The captured rebels were hung and their bodies were displayed along the road as an example to other slaves. *See also* SLAVE REVOLTS.

HONOR. In most societies where slavery was important, honor was an important differentiating feature between the slaves and the free. These were societies where honor was important. Slaves were seen as lacking honor because they were dependent and submissive and because they were subject to the commands of others. **Orlando Patterson** has suggested that enslavement was usually an alternative to death and that slavery was thus often seen as a form of "social death" and the slave was thus not honorable. In addition, slave women were often sexually accessible. Slave women often had license to behave in ways that were considered dishonorable for the free-born. For example, in the ancient Middle East, slave women did not have to wear veils, and in parts of Asia and Africa slave women often were asked to do dances that were considered licentious. By being submissive or deferential or by not wearing a veil, a slave underlined the difference in status.

At the same time, the service of slaves tended to enhance the status of their owners. In slave-owning societies, the noble was often marked by his entourage. Slaves enhanced the noble's status by serving, but also by begging from and obeying nobles. People served the noble. In some societies, slaves could achieve wealth and power, but they lacked honorable status and could be humiliated if they pretended to be noble. The noble ideal often involved courage, generosity, and the ability to command. The slave could only achieve honor in war. While there are numerous sagas of slave courage, these were always unique individuals and they often demonstrated the ultimate characteristic of the good slave: loyalty.

HOUSEHOLD SLAVES. In those societies with large slaveholdings, the households of the rich and powerful were generously staffed with slaves. For the wealthy slave owner, one of the rewards of wealth was to be served. This was true in societies where most labor was done by free peasants. In China, for example, most slaves were **concubines** or servants. The wealthy and powerful had people to serve them. It is also true of **slave societies** and the European colonial cities of Asia and Africa. Even where slaves were valued for their labor and where slave work was subject to the rigorous accounting of capitalist rationality, many slaves worked in the household. This was true in towns, in the planter's house, and in the cities of various colonial empires. Officials and merchants maintained large households staffed with slave labor. In both the urban household and the plantation, slaves did the cooking, cleaning, sewing, and laundering; they took care of the master's children, ran messages, and were coachmen and butlers. The master's wife was usually freed from labor, though she often managed the house. Her babies were suckled by a wet nurse and the cooking was done by slave cooks. In societies as diverse as Rome and the U.S. South, the master's child often had a slave companion.

The most favored slaves often had a privileged relationship with the master's family. The slave "mammy" of the U.S. South, the slave tutor in Rome, and the personal servant were close to the master's family and often cherished. House slaves were generally fed and clothed better than the field slaves. Where **manumission** was common, a favored household retainer was most likely to be freed. On the other hand, household slaves worked longer hours and had less independence. They often had to be available at all hours of the day and night. *See also* URBAN SLAVERY.

-I-

IGBO. See BIGHT OF BIAFRA.

INDENTURED LABOR. In the 17th century, indentured labor was the major alternative to slave labor in the West Indies and the English colonies of North America. The indentured laborer was a person who agreed to a fixed term of service in exchange for transportation. The persons seeking indentures were generally poor persons who felt that they had few prospects of betterment at home. They would contract with either an employer in the New World or a merchant, who would sell the indenture contracts after the worker arrived in America. The employer or the merchant would pay the worker's transportation and he would then be committed to anywhere from three to 10 years of labor for the American employer. During the term of the indenture, the employer was obligated to feed, house, and clothe him. In many cases, he was also committed to help the indentured laborer to establish his independence at the end of the indenture. In the early 17th century, indentured labor was actually cheaper than slave labor.

By the end of the 17th century, slaves were preferred to indentured servants. There were several reasons for this. First, slaves became more readily available and as slave law developed, so too did the farmer's control over his slaves. The proprietor buying a slave was getting a person for life, and the slave's offspring too. Second, wages were rising in Great Britain and Europe during the latter part of the century and conditions were improving for the poor. Third, both prospective indentures and prospective employers became aware of harsh conditions and high mortality, particularly on the **sugar plantations** of the West Indies, where the mortality rate for white indentured servants was two to three times as high as for slaves. On the **tobacco** farms of the Chesapeake, the movement to slavery was a little slower. In a sense, indentured servants provided a school for slavery as planters learned to control a labor force. By the early 18th century, planters in both the southern United States and the West Indies looked primarily to slaves for the labor they needed.

INDIAN, NATIVE AMERICAN. *See* AMERINDIAN SLAVERY.

INDIAN OCEAN. The Indian ocean was the site of an ancient **slave trade**. It was never as large as the **Atlantic trade** but it was older. The Indian

Ocean is easier to navigate than the Atlantic. The monsoon winds blow in toward central Asia half of the year and outward half of the year. This meant that there was an important trade across the Indian Ocean at least as far back as the beginning of the common era. Slaves were only one item traded. Most of the slaves moving north into the Middle East and the Mediterranean came from the Horn of Africa. There was, nevertheless, a small slave trade from the coast of East Africa. Some slaves went to the Middle East, where they were called **Zanj**. Others were shipped to India. A few were then sold farther east to Indonesia and China.

The slave trade moved both ways. In the 17th century, the Dutch settled at the Cape of Good Hope, which became a market for slaves from Madagascar, East Africa, India, and Indonesia. During the 18th century, the French began to cultivate plantation crops on the islands of Ile de Bourbon (now Réunion) and Ile de France (now Mauritius). Like the West Indies, these islands had a low population. Slaves were brought in from Africa, India, and Indonesia. As **sugar plantations** grew, the French developed contracts with the African coastal port of Kilwa and then with the Portuguese in Mozambique to provide the needed slaves. The development of clove plantations on the island of **Zanzibar** created a second market for slaves. On Madagascar, the expansion of the Merina kingdom and the development of agricultural exports created yet another market. These new markets for slaves stimulated the penetration of the interior of East Africa by slave traders and an increase of slavetrading on Madagascar. One of the by-products of these developments was the increased availability of cheap slaves. The plantation economy was expanded on the coast and slaves were moved toward the Middle East.

From the 1820s on, the British tried to restrict this trade. An 1820 treaty with the Merina briefly ended slave exports and the Moresby treaty of 1822 with Zanzibar banned the sales of slaves to Christian powers and the Merina. The French abolished slavery in 1848. One by one, various markets were closed off. Zanzibar abolished the export of slaves in 1873. The trade continued, however, to the last years of the century. Slavery was abolished on Madagascar in 1896 and a year later, on Zanzibar. *See also* EMANCIPATION, AFRICA; MAURITIUS AND RÉUNION; MIDDLE EASTERN SLAVERY..

INDIAN, NATIVE AMERICAN. See AMERINDIAN SLAVERY.

INDIAN SLAVERY. Slavery has existed for a long time in India, though generally embedded in a very complex system of hierarchical relationships. Early Sanskrit texts describe the different ways a person could become a slave: capture in war, penalty for a criminal act, purchase or birth to a slave. Later texts refer to enslavement resulting from debt or cohabitation with a slave. During the period from 700 to 1100, when warfare was common, capture in war was the most important source of slaves. In more recent centuries, when warfare was less common, capture gave way to enslavement for criminal acts and particularly to debt slavery. Slaves were also imported from other parts of Asia and Africa. During the period of European penetration from the 16th century, slaves were regularly traded within India and were for sale in the port cities where European merchants lived. Slaves did agricultural labor and served in the households of the wealthy and were important in the households of Europeans.

British data on slavery is not reliable because the British were often confused about different kinds of servile status. India is a large continent with a wide range of different kinds of social arrangements, which differed by region and by time period. Voluntary forms of bondage and caste provided labor and services for elites. Caste was linked to occupation and involved prohibitions against social and sexual mixing. As the Mughal Empire and then the British East India Company increased taxation in areas under their control, members of the poorer castes were often forced into dependence on richer and more privileged groups. The British saw these castes as slave castes because they labored for others. By making large groups dependent, caste may have made slaves unnecessary, but slavery continued to exist. In theory, caste rules should have limited the operation of slave systems. For example, it should have prevented lower caste persons being taken into the houses of high caste persons and conversely, the enslavement of high persons to those of lower caste. It should also have limited **sexual exploitation**. In fact, these prohibitions seem to have often been violated over the years.

India was not included in the British abolition of slavery in 1833 because the East India Company was sovereign there. Nevertheless, pressure was placed on the company by parliament. Act V of 1843 did not abolish slavery , but it denied slave owners the use of the state and its courts to enforce their rights. This meant that a master could not use the law to get back a runaway slave. The act was deliberately not well publicized. As a result, forms of servitude continued to exist for many years. In 1858, Great Britain took control over India. The penal code of 1860 clearly prohibited slavery and provided penalties for sale or ownership of slaves. The Indian approach to emancipation was copied by colonial regimes elsewhere in Asia and in Africa. See also AMBAR, MALIK; EMANCIPATION, INDIA; HINDUISM; INDIAN OCEAN.

INDONESIAN SLAVERY. The many islands of what is now Indonesia were never united before the Dutch brought the archipelago under colonial control in the 17th century. There was thus a variety of social and economic systems. In Indonesia, as elsewhere in Southeast Asia, population densities were low, though the land was fertile. Land, therefore, had little value. There was always a surplus. Kings and powerful men, therefore, sought not to conquer new lands but to acquire dependents to work land they already controlled. Slavery was therefore widespread throughout the islands. In the more developed areas of Java and Sumatra, slaves existed within hierarchical social orders marked by patron-client relationships and a range of what Anthony Reid calls relations of obligation.

Different variants of slavery are noted in inscriptions from the first millennium. Many slaves served in the palaces and temples of medieval kingdoms. Evidence also suggests that even commoners often owned slaves. Some resulted from capture in war or punishment for crimes, but Indonesia is also marked by the importance of debt slavery. In 15th-century Melaka, most laborers and **concubines** were slaves. Some merchants had hundreds of slaves. Early observers usually saw slavery as mild, though slaves could be sold and beaten. The sources do not, however, indicate a clear differentiation between forms of obligation.

The nature of slavery was transformed by **Islam**, by the development of a commercial economy, and by European colonization. Conversion to Islam influenced patterns of enslavement. Islam prohibited the enslavement or sale of Muslims. Thus, with Islamization, trade, and the raiding of non-Muslim areas became the major source of slaves. With commercialization from the 16th century, more rigid concepts of slaves as property developed. Pirates from the Sulu archipelago became experts at slave raiding.

The Dutch used slaves as agricultural laborers and as a source of servants and concubines for their officials. Batavia, the capital of the Dutch East Indies, became a major slave market. Within the Indies, there were radical differences in population density. In fertile, but less densely populated areas, particularly on the Spice Islands, slaves were brought in because it was difficult to get free peasants to work for others. In many areas, within a generation or two, relationships were transformed from slavery to a form of **serfdom**. Slaves also worked as miners, artisans, soldiers, prostitutes, and entertainers. *See also* DUTCH SLAVE TRADE; SULU SULTANATE.

INTERNATIONAL LABOR ORGANIZATION (ILO). Created in 1919

as part of the **League of Nations**, the purpose of the International Labor Organization was to protect the rights and well-being of working people. One of its major concerns has been the elimination of different forms of forced labor and relationships resembling slavery. It collaborated with the Temporary Slavery Commission to produce the Slavery Convention of 1926. It also produced conventions that sought to abolish forced labor in 1930 and 1961. Over the years, the organization has produced a large number of agreements which regulate conditions of labor and seek to protect the rights of working people to freely contract for their labor. The ILO has also publicized violations of its conventions and has assisted countries interested in developing a modern system of free labor movement.

IRANUN. The Iranun were a seagoing people from the **Sulu Sultanate**, an island state north of Indonesia. During the 18th century, the Iranun turned to piracy. They lived in small colonies scattered throughout the many islands and ranged widely, sometimes going south to Borneo, Sumatra, Celebes, and the Moluccas, sometimes north into the Philippines. They operated in fleets of well-armed boats, about 90 to 100 feet long, taking advantage of the isolation of many coastal communities. Sometimes, fleets contained as many as 40 boats. They assimilated some of their young male prisoners, but sold others to members of the Sulu elite, to Dutch officials, and to Chinese merchants. Almost all of the Dutch and most of the Chinese came to Southeast Asia without women. There was, therefore, a market for **concubines** and servants. Other slaves were put to work gathering marine products for the China market, producing food, or working as servants, artisans, and officials in Jolo, the Sulu capital. *See also* INDONESIAN SLAVERY.

ISLAM. Slave systems varied radically from one end of the Muslim world to the other. Islam, however, offered slaves protection, limited the kind of people subject to enslavement, and established a law code to regulate enslavement and the treatment of slaves. Islam was founded by the prophet Muhammed in the seventh century CE. Slavery was at this time a well-established institution in the Arabian peninsula and in the Middle East. Muhammed prohibited the enslavement of Muslims. He also insisted that good Muslims had the obligation to feed, clothe, and care for their slaves and to guarantee them the right to marriage and to the protection of Muslim law. There are many traditions of the Prophet's kindness to his slaves. Muslims also had the obligation to educate their slaves.

The conversion of a slave to Islam did not guarantee freedom, but **manumission** was recommended and regarded as a pious act. Manumission of slaves was also an act of penance for certain crimes. A high rate of manumission was thus characteristic of many Muslim societies. Finally, Muhammed limited men to four wives. Men were allowed extra **concubines**, but Islamic law gave all children equal rights of inheritance (though daughters received half the share given to sons). This meant not only that the children of a slave concubine were free, but also that they shared in the father's wealth and had equal rights to titles he bore. Islamic history is full of the children of concubines who inherited royal office. The concubine who bore her master a son was freed on the master's death, and if her son achieved power, she could become well-off and influential.

Muhammed differed from other great religious prophets in that he was a ruler in the last years of his life. When he died in 632 CE, he ruled the Arabian peninsula. In the century that followed, Arab armies swept over the Middle East and then west to North Africa and Spain and east to Persia. Arabs thus achieved within a century a wealth and power probably not imagined by Muhammed. In the process, Muslims elaborated the law of slavery and adopted institutions that eroded some of the principles of Muhammed's teaching. Large **harems** became the marks of power and **eunuchs** were procured to protect them. Slave soldiers and slave administrators became common in much of the Muslim world. On the other hand, within the core area of the Middle East and North Africa, the prohibition on the enslavement of Muslims meant that slaves could not be recruited there. The result was that Islam moderated the treatment of slaves but contributed to the development of a long-distance slave trade. Turkish slaves from Central Asia included the soldiers who eventually came to rule the Middle East. Warfare and a regular slave trade brought slaves from the Balkans, Russia, and the Caucasus. Black slaves also crossed the **Sahara** or came by sea from Ethiopia and East Africa. Enslavement thus became common on the fringes of the Islamic world.

Islam limited enslavement to persons taken prisoner in a *jihad* (holy war), but the conditions of *jihad* were severely limited. The would-be warrior had to purify himself and he had to try to convert the object of his attentions by persuasion. Instead, Muslim slave raiders used the prohibition on enslaving Muslims as a justification for enslavement of non-Muslims — and in some cases, even attacked other Muslims. Slaves imported into the core area were largely used as concubines, soldiers, and servants. Agricultural slavery was rare, though slaves were used for specialty crops like **sugar** and dates.

The situation was different on the fringes. Thus, all manual labor in Saharan oases was done by slaves while **slave societies** based on the exploitation of agricultural slave labor emerged on the Swahili coast and among societies like the Hausa that bordered the Sahara. In India too, Muslim law was interpreted so as to allow the enslavement of peasants unable to pay their taxes. In the Mediterranean and the Middle East, there was a low rate of reproduction and a high rate of manumission. Most of the slaves did not reproduce slaves — if they reproduced at all. Where a society based on slave labor emerged, the rate of manumission was lower, exploitation was more systematic, and slaves reproduced slaves. *See also* GHULAMS; HAREM; JANISSARIES; MAMLUKES; ANCIENT MIDDLE EASTERN SLAVERY; SAHARA; ZANZIBAR.

-J-

JACOBS, HARRIET (1813-1897). Harriet Jacobs was born a slave in North Carolina. Her mother died when she was a child. Her mistress treated her well and taught her to read and write. When her mistress died, she was inherited by a local doctor, who wanted her to have sexual relations with him. She refused, but she did have a relationship with a white lawyer, with whom she had two children. Her master was persistent, however, and she fled his house in 1825. For seven years, she lived hidden in a tiny attic in the home of her grandmother, who was free. She could watch the world go by but not be part of it. Finally, she was smuggled aboard a ship and escaped to the North. After the passage of the **Fugitive Slave Law** in 1850, she had to move several times to avoid agents of her master. With the help of her abolitionist friends, Jacobs was eventually able to free herself and her children. In 1861, using the pseudonym, Linda Brent, she published *Incidents in the Life of a Slave Girl: Written by Herself.* The book highlighted the harassment to which slave women were exposed. During and after the **Civil War**, she did relief work among former slaves. *See also* SEXUAL EXPLOITATION.

JA JA. Ja Ja was a slave who rose to became the ruler of a small kingdom in the Niger Delta. Born in an Igbo village, he was enslaved at about 12 years old. Bought and sold several times, he ended up the property of the Anna Pepple canoe house in Bonny, a small city-state in the Niger Delta. The trading settlements were dominated by canoe houses, trading firms that competed first for slaves and then for palm oil in the markets of the hinterland. The trade was very competitive. As a result, a slave who proved himself in military conflicts and as a trader could advance very quickly. Ja Ja was entrusted with the command of one of the large trading canoes that dominated trade with interior markets. By 1861, though still a slave, Ja Ja had become one of the wealthiest traders in Bonny. When the head of the Anna Pepple house died, Ja Ja was chosen to succeed him. In 1869, faced by opposition in Bonny, he withdrew with all of his followers to form a new settlement called Opobo. Within a few years, Bonny was ruined and Opobo dominated the delta's palm oil trade. Though at first recognized by Great Britain, he refused many British demands. In 1887, the British consul, Sir Harry Johnston, invited him to a conference on board Johnston's boat. Johnston refused to let him off and sent him to exile in the West Indies. *See also* BIAFRA, BIGHT OF; WEST AFRICA.

JAMAICAN SLAVE REVOLT (1831-1832). After 1823, restlessness increased on the slave islands of the British Caribbean, a restlessness probably linked both to the intensification of labor regimes and the radical expectations engendered by the British abolition movement. Incidents took place on many islands, but the most important was the Jamaican slave revolt. By 1831, rumors of freedom were widespread, but slaves were also afraid that the planters would intervene to prevent it. The provocation seems to have come when an unpopular slave owner struck a female slave for stealing cane. When her husband, a driver, refused to whip her, the planter was chased away and two constables sent to make arrests were manhandled and disarmed. By the time the militia arrived, the slaves had disappeared. Ten days later, a plantation near Montego Bay was set afire. A group of elite slaves had been plotting a rising since April of the previous year.

The leaders included a carpenter, a wagoner, and most important, an eloquent Baptist deacon named **Sam Sharpe**. Sharpe's plan was a strike in which the slaves refused to work until concessions were made to them. Some did patiently refuse to work, but almost from the first, slaves began plundering **plantations** and burning down hated **sugar** works. Other leaders expected to fight and organized slave regiments, but when the fighting began, they were no match for British troops. It still took more than a month to restore order. More than 200 plantations had been burned and plundered. Over 200 slaves were killed in the fighting and at least 340 were executed. Among them was Sam Sharpe. A disproportionate number were members of the slave elite: masons, carpenters, **drivers**, blacksmiths. A large number were also Baptists, though the missionaries seem to have been ignorant of the conspiracy. Many of the missionaries were jailed, several chapels were burned by white mobs, and one missionary was tarred and feathered. Forced to return to England, some played a role in persuading Parliament to abolish slavery two years later. *See also* ABOLITION, GREAT BRITAIN; SLAVE REVOLTS.

JANISSARIES. The Janissaries were the elite slave troops in the Ottoman Empire. Originally, they were recruited from prisoners of war, but a system called *devshirme* or "roundup" evolved early in the history of the empire. Christian communities in the Balkans were required to provide boys — one for every 40 families — between the ages of 12 and 18. These levies took place every seven years. The conscripts were converted to **Islam** and were trained in special schools. The best students, about 5 to 10 percent of the group, entered the palace or the Ottoman administration. Some of them eventually held high office. The rest became soldiers. There were at the end of the 17th century about 80,000 Janissaries. They were known for their discipline and camaraderie. They served all over the empire. They were the crack infantry on military campaigns, they repressed rebellions, protected the frontiers, and guarded cities. They were legally slaves, but as the sultan's best troops, they were well rewarded. The *devshirme* system lapsed by the middle of the 17th century. By that time, the Janissaries were accepting as recruits the sons of Janissaries and free Muslims. *See also* GHULAMS; MAMLUKES; MILITARY SLAVES; OTTOMAN SLAVERY.

JAPAN. Slavery existed in early Japan, but does not seem to have been important at any time. Instead, the tendency in Japan was to tie peasants to the land in a kind of **serfdom**. Serfs, however, have their own family life and are not slaves. By the latter part of the first millennium, there were two groups at the bottom of Japanese social order. There were slaves, probably mostly prisoners of war, who could be bought and sold and could not marry. There were also outcasts — butchers, leather workers, and those who handled the dead. The slaves were never a major source of labor and the outcasts, who did labor that was "polluted," were not owned. By 1200, slavery had disappeared. The Tokugawa Shogunate (1603-1867) provided a long period of peace, which meant no prisoners. The Tokugawa system involved a rigid hierarchy with peasants, who paid most of the taxes, tied to the land. The feudal nobility were served by retainers who sought service.

JEFFERSON, ISAAC (1775-c.1850). Isaac Jefferson was a son of slaves purchased by **Thomas Jefferson,** who eventually took Jefferson's family name. He was a blacksmith and tinsmith. From 1797, he worked for Thomas Jefferson's son-in-law, Thomas Randolph. Later in life, he had his own blacksmith shop in Petersburg, Virginia. Author Charles Campbell heard that Isaac Jefferson liked to tell stories of life at Monticello and interviewed him in 1847. Though prepared for publication in 1871, Jefferson's tales were only finally published in 1951 as *Memoirs of a Monticello Slave.* Though the account does not touch on the harsher aspects of slavery and leaves many questions about the narrator's life unanswered, it is a valuable source for life at Monticello.

JEFFERSON, THOMAS (1743-1826). The third president of the United States, Thomas Jefferson's life embodies many of the contradictions of early American history. He was an intellectual, very much influenced by **Enlightenment** thought. He was the primary author of the Declaration of Independence, which proclaimed that "all men are created equal," but he was also the second largest slave owner in his Virginia county. His opposition to slavery was articulated in his *Notes on the State of Virginia* (1787), but over the course of a long life, he freed only eight of the several hundred he owned. At the Constitutional Convention of 1787, Jefferson strongly supported an end to slave imports, but he sold many of his slaves into the internal trade and gave others to members of his family. He proposed restrictions on the extension of slavery to the new territories west of the Appalachians. He is widely believed to have had a long relationship with a beautiful slave woman, **Sally Hemings** and to have had a number of children with her.

There are two explanations for these contradictions. The first is that he was in debt much of his life. Some were debts he inherited from his father-in-law. His career in the public service took him away from his estate, but did not bring him enough income to enable him to pay those debts. He was wealthy, but much of his wealth was in the form of human chattel. He was also concerned with creating the base for a republican society. The form of government created in the United States was new and unproven. Jefferson believed that a republic had to be based on independent farmers and artisans. He believed in innate racial differences and did not believe that the slaves, if freed, could be easily integrated into American society. He believed that black people were intellectually inferior and that freeing them would create great problems for the Republic.

JEWS. The ancient Hebrews were a slave-owning society, but since the conquest of ancient Israel by Rome, Jews have been dispersed around the world, living from trade, moneylending, and artisanship. The vast majority of Jews have lived in societies where they were governed by others and were a minority, often a small minority. In societies without slaves, Jews did not have them. In slave-owning societies, Jews were often limited by laws preventing them from owning members of the majority religious community. There were, however, periods when their international connections enabled them to be brokers in commerce between different parts of the world. Thus, in the ninth and 10th centuries, Jewish merchants were active in the trade between the Slavic frontier in eastern Europe and the Mediterranean.

A second period when Jewish merchants were important was during the rise of the Netherlands. Dutch religious tolerance contributed to the rapid growth of a Jewish community of Iberian origin. Some Jewish merchants got involved in the **slave trade** and in running slave **plantations**, but the only significant community of Jewish planters was in Surinam, where by 1700, Jews owned 40 plantations and about 9,000 slaves. In the United States, Jews owned fewer slaves than Christians, though Jews were found on both sides of the ideological divide. Judah Benjamin was an influential Confederate cabinet minister during the **Civil War**. On the other hand, August Bondi was a member of the free state faction in Kansas and a supporter of **John Brown**. Rabbis in Baltimore, Philadelphia, and Chicago were active abolitionists. Rabbi David Einhorn was chased out of Baltimore by an angry mob because of an anti-slavery sermon.

Jewish law carefully regulated slavery. Slaves were to be converted to Judaism and could not be asked to work on the Sabbath or important holidays. If a slave were manumitted, the slave became a full member of the community. A slave was freed if punishment caused serious injury. Jewish teaching, like the teachings of other major faiths, insisted that slaves be treated humanely, fed well, and not excessively punished. *See also* ANCIENT MIDDLE EASTERN SLAVERY; BIBLE; DUTCH SLAVE TRADE; MANUMISSION.

JOHNSON, ANTHONY (c. 1621-1669). Anthony Johnson was a slave brought by a Dutch ship to Virginia in 1621. He was one of the first slaves in Virginia. At the time, however, there was no slave statutes and Johnson, like many other early slaves, was treated as an **indentured laborer**. After about 20 years of service, Johnson, his wife, and four children were freed. It was at that time that he took the name Johnson.

By 1650, he owned 250 acres of land, some cattle, and black indentured servants. As Virginia moved to created slave law in the 1660s, life became more difficult for Johnson. He moved at that time to the eastern shore of Maryland. When he died, his son Richard inherited 50 acres in Virginia, but the will was challenged under a Virginia statute that made it illegal for African-Americans to own land. A window of opportunity in the early labor system had been closed. The Johnson family disappears from the public record early in the next century.

JONES, ABSALOM (1746-1818). Born a slave in Delaware, Absalom Jones was the first African-American to be ordained a priest in the Episcopal Church of North America. Brought to Philadelphia to work in his master's retail business, he worked nights to earn money to purchase his freedom and that of his wife. In 1787, he joined with **Richard Allen** in forming the Free African Society. Later that year, when their church, the St. George Methodist Church, insisted that African-Americans sit in a segregated gallery, Jones and Allen led a walkout. Where Allen created the **African Methodist Episcopal Church**, Jones founded St. Thomas Church, which affiliated with the Episcopalians in 1794. He was ordained a deacon in 1794 and as a priest in 1804. Jones was active in creating African community organizations such as an insurance company, a Masonic lodge, and an anti-slavery society and was active in anti-slavery work, organizing petitions to the state and national legislatures.

JONKONNU. Jonkonnu was one of several varieties of slave carnival that developed in the slave societies of the West Indies. The slaves were generally freed from work for the week between Christmas and New Year's Day. This was the occasion for a weeklong festival that involved masked and costumed stilt-walkers, singers, dancers, rattles, drums and other musical instruments, and much singing and dancing. The *Jonkonnu* dances often involved a ritual inversion of the power relations of slavery. Wearing masks and elaborate costumes, the dancers would move from one planter's house to another, dancing until the proprietor sent them off with a small gift. The dances often involved miming and mockery of European music and social institutions. Its roots lay in West African masquerades and the mummery of the British Isles.

-K-

KANSAS-NEBRASKA ACT (1854). The **Missouri Compromise** of 1820 prohibited slavery in all territory in the Louisiana Purchase north of latitude 36°30′. For years, the issue was not important, but by 1850, there was an interest in organizing the area that is now Kansas and Nebraska to encourage settlement and facilitate the construction of a transcontinental railroad. Southerners did not want to create more free states. To win their support, Senator Stephen Douglas suggested that the prohibition on slavery in the territories be repealed and that "popular sovereignty" be used to resolve the issue. This meant that the settlers would decide. Passage of the Kansas-Nebraska Act, however, merely opened Kansas up to civil war. Slave owners from Missouri moved into Kansas to make sure that it became a slave state. This brought a response from Free Staters like **John Brown** and his sons. "Bleeding Kansas" was marked by raids and counterraids for two years. For a while, there were two separate legislatures, but Kansas was not land suited to slave labor. In 1858, the voters rejected a pro-slavery constitution and in 1861, Kansas was admitted to the Union as a free state. At the height of the conflict, there were 500 slaves in Kansas, but the 1860 census recorded only two slaves. The major effect of the conflict in Kansas was the emergence of the Republican Party opposed to the extension of slavery. *See also* COMPROMISE OF 1850.

KEMBLE, FANNY (1809-1893). Fanny Kemble was a British actress who met Pierce Butler, a wealthy Georgia slave owner while, touring in the United States. In spite of her opposition to slavery, she married him and they had two children. For years, she kept her opinions quiet, but a winter spent on one of the Butler **plantations** gave her firsthand experience with slavery and intensified her hostility to it. It also led to the end of her marriage to Butler. The diary she kept there circulated among northern abolitionists, but she refused to publish it for years, even after she returned to England. After the **Civil War** broke out, however, she was alarmed by British sympathies with the Confederacy. In 1863, it was published as *Journal of a Residence on a Georgia Plantation*. It was a major anti-slavery document.

KIRK, JOHN (1832-1922). John Kirk was the son of a Scottish minister, who became a naturalist, explorer, and diplomat. After graduating from the University of Edinburgh in 1854 with an M.D., he was appointed to accompany **David Livingstone** on an exploration of **Central Africa** that lasted from 1857 to 1863. He brought botanical collections back to England, but also saw firsthand the ravages of the **East African slave trade**. In 1866, he was appointed British vice-consul in **Zanzibar**. In 21 years as consul and as consul-general, he was for long periods the second most powerful figure in East Africa, second only to Sultan Barghash of Zanzibar. He used the British navy and his diplomatic influence in the struggle to suppress the **slave trade** on the **Indian Ocean** and to limit the trade in both slaves and weapons on the mainland. In 1873, he persuaded Barghash to sign a treaty abolishing the slave trade, and several years later, to close the slave market in Zanzibar. He retired in 1887, but two years later served as a British representative to the **Brussels Conference**.

KONGO. When the Portuguese cruised down the western coast of Africa during the 15th century, they found few large kingdoms. One of the most impressive was Kongo, on the south shore of the Congo River. From the first, the Portuguese found Kongo an eager trading partner. Kongo was impressed with Portuguese skills and wanted European goods. For many years, it was the most important source of slaves for the Portuguese trade. The Portuguese sent missionaries, craftsmen, and soldiers and educated some members of the elite in Europe. In 1506, **Afonso I**, a Christian, became king of the Kongo. Much of the elite was Christian and literate. Afonso wanted development, but from early on, Portuguese at the court of São Salvador conspired to increase conflict. The worst were traders from **São Tomé**, who traded with provincial chiefs and dissident factions. Slaves from the Kongo were the basis of a **sugar** boom on São Tomé. Afonso complained bitterly to the Portuguese king that his subjects were being taken captive, and then tried to stop the **slave trade**, but it was too late. In 1576, the Portuguese shifted their base in **Central Africa** farther south when they founded Luanda. The much-weakened Kongo remained a presence in the lower Congo River, but never exercised the power of earlier years. *See also* AFRICAN SLAVE TRADE.

KOREA. Slavery has existed in Korea at least as far back as the beginning of the common era. The people enslaved were generally conquered people and criminals, but the status was hereditary. Slaves do not seem, however, to have been a large part of the population until Korea was conquered by the Mongols in the 13th century. During this period, large estates were created, which were owned by absentee landlords and worked by servile labor. It is not clear whether these people should be seen as slaves or serfs. When the Mongols were replaced by the indigenous Yi dynasty, slavery remained important. Under the Yi dynasty, Koreans were divided into classes, whose obligations to the state were rigidly defined. The slaves were divided between public slaves, essentially owned by the state and attached to offices, and private slaves, owned by persons. By the 15th century, wage labor was increasing, which made it possible for slaves to flee their masters. Increased population densities meant that there was less and less logic for the wealthy to own slaves. They could hire labor and services. In 1775, a gradual emancipation policy was approved. In 1806, servitude was limited to a single generation and in 1895, it was abolished. *See also* EMANCIPATION, EAST ASIA.

KRIO. The Krio, or as they are also called, Creoles, of **West Africa**, are a community formed from ex-slaves on the **Sierra Leone** peninsula. The Sierra Leone colony was established by abolitionists in 1787. Three groups were settled there: blacks from England; **Black Loyalists** who had sided with the British during the **American Revolution** and were dissatisfied with their situation in Nova Scotia; and **Maroons** from Jamaica. The largest part of the population was made up of slaves on ships stopped by the British navy's **African Squadron** and taken to Freetown, the location of the only prize pourt in West Africa. Under international law, a ship seized at sea had to be brought before a prize court before it and its cargo could be freed. About 74,000 slaves were freed in this way. Christian missions often gave these people assistance and taught them English. These people, often called **recaptives**, had no common culture and no common language. They had also gone through the traumatic experience of enslavement and shipment on a slave ship. Many of them eagerly learned English and accepted Christianity.

The only African language that persisted in the Krio community was **Yoruba**, but the Krio usually communicated with each other in English and Krio, a pidgin dialect. The community had a very high educational level and came to be of great assistance to the British. During the 19th century, Europeans still had a high mortality in West Africa. As a result, the British used the Krio agents extensively. Krios settled in Bathurst, Lagos, Calabar, Cape Coast, and Accra. They were crucial to the operation of the mission societies. Bishop **Samuel Ajayi Crowther** was the outstanding Christian leader in West Africa. They worked in commerce and some went into business for themselves. They also served as judges, administrators, and clerks in the nascent colonial administrations. The Krio community produced the first African doctors trained in European medical schools and the first African lawyers trained in British law. The largest Krio community was in Freetown.

-L-

LAS CASAS, BARTOLOMÉ DE (1474-1566). Bartolomé de Las Casas was a Spanish priest who arrived in Santo Domingo in 1502. Like many Spaniards, he was given an *encomienda,* which entitled him to tribute in the form of labor from a number of Amerindian communities. Las Casas was early horrified by the harshness of Spanish rule and the destruction of Amerindian populations on **Hispaniola** and Cuba. In 1514, he renounced his *encomienda* and dedicated himself to the protection of Amerindians. He worked briefly in Venezuela where he was unable to stop Spanish slavers who were providing Amerindian slaves for Santo Domingo. In 1524, Las Casas joined the Dominican order. In the years that followed he produced a number of books that documented the mistreatment of Amerindians: *History of the Indies*, *The Apologetic History of the Indies*, and *A Brief Relation of the Destruction of the Indies*. His works influenced Pope Paul III to issue his *Bulla Sublimis Deus* (1537), which accepted that the Amerindians were rational and could become Christians. This undercut the argument that they were by nature slaves. In 1540, he returned to Spain, where he persuaded the King to issue his New Laws, which prohibited the enslavement of Amerindians and weakened the *encomienda* system. At one time, Las Casas had suggested substituting African slaves for Amerindian slaves, but with time he rejected that option.

In 1543, Las Casas became Bishop of the largely Indian province of Chiapas, but was driven out by the local Spanish community. In 1547, he returned to Spain, where three years later, he had a famous public debate with the historian, Juan Ginés de Sepulveda. Sepulveda defended the position of **Aristotle** that some people were by nature slaves. *See also* CATHOLIC CHURCH; HISPANIC AMERICAN SLAVERY.

LATIFUNDIA. The latifundia were large slave-worked agricultural estates in ancient Rome. They originated in the second century BCE, when

Roman conquests began bringing large numbers of slaves back to Rome. Many farms were empty because farmers had gone off to war and not returned. It was thus easy for members of the Roman elite to accumulate land which was worked by slave labor. The growth of a large urban population provided a market for the grain, wine and olive oil the estates produced. The latifundia reached their peak during the first and second centuries, CE, when Roman armies were bringing large numbers of captives back to Italy. *See also* ANCIENT ROMAN SLAVERY.

LATINO, JUAN (1516-1599). Enslaved in West Africa, Juan was taken to Europe at age 12. A noblewoman purchased him to work in her house. When she saw that he was interested in books, she allowed him to attend the Cathedral school, where he excelled at Greek and Latin. He was so enamored of Latin that he changed his name from de Sessa to Latino. He studied at the University of Granada and in 1557 was appointed a professor there. In 1565, he became professor of grammar.

Latino was a man of many talents and a leading figure in Spanish intellectual life. He translated the Latin poet Horace into Spanish and was known for his Latin orations. His ability as a singer of madrigals gave him access to the homes of the rich and powerful. He was perhaps best known for his poetry, particularly for a long Latin poem, the *Asturiad*, honoring his friend, Don Juan, son of Emperor Charles V. His orations and his poetry were marked by wit and learning. Though he praised his powerful acquaintances, he also felt deeply and referred in his poetry to European racial attitudes.

LAVIGERIE, CHARLES (1825-1892). A leading figure in the **Catholic Church**, Cardinal Lavigerie was the founder of the modern Catholic anti-slavery movement. The son of a civil servant from southwestern France, Lavigerie became a priest in 1849. In 1863, he was appointed bishop of Nancy. The Catholic Church had been hostile to progressive forces, including supporters of abolition because of links these forces had with efforts to create a state-controlled church during the French Revolution. As bishop, Lavigerie tried to disengage the church from reactionary forces in Nancy. In 1867, Lavigerie was appointed archbishop of Algiers. A year later, he formed the Society of Missionaries to Africa, better known from the color of their robes as the White Fathers. The White Fathers were originally interested primarily in the Muslim world, but they had little success there. From 1878, they concentrated on sub-Saharan Africa, where they immediately confronted the ravages of the **slave trade**. In 1884, Lavigerie became a cardinal. In 1888, with the approval of Pope Leo XIII, he launched a crusade against the slave trade within Africa. He made a tour of Europe, leaving behind anti-slavery committees in every Catholic country he visited and forging links with British abolitionists. Lavigerie was influential in the convening of the **Brussels Conference** of 1889-1890. The Société Antiesclavagiste de France (Anti-slavery Society of France), was an important force in French colonial politics until 1968, when it became Aide aux missions d'Afrique (Aid to African Missions). It remained, however, a Catholic organization and did not collaborate with the anti-clericals of the earlier anti-slavery movement. *See also* ABOLITION, FRANCE; EAST AFRICAN SLAVE TRADE.

LAW OF SLAVERY. The existence of slavery necessitated a slave law. This law had several functions. The first was to reinforce the authority of both master and state over the slave. The second was to reinforce the social distance between the two. There are many things that were common to all slave laws. Thus, slave law was always concerned to maintain the person as property, which meant the right of the slave's owner to sell, trade, give, or bequeath the slave. It also meant the right to punish. In the sale of slaves, the law often also protected the right of the purchaser. Under Islamic law, the purchaser could see only the slave's face, but if he found the slave defective, either because of disease or bad habits like drunkenness or incontinence, he had the right to ask for return of the purchase price. In Rome, the master could even kill his slaves. Others prohibited killing, for example, **Islam** and the Anglo-American common law, though in few societies was a master ever punished when a slave died from whipping or from abuse.

The mechanisms by which social distance between slave and free was maintained varied from society to society. In the Americas, slaves tended to be physically distinct, but elsewhere, there were often physical markers: a distinctive haircut or tattoo in Mesopotamia, a pierced ear among the Hebrews, the prohibition of certain kinds of clothing in China or parts of Africa. There were also limits in what slaves could do or where they could go. In ancient Greece, they could not attend political assemblies. The law also often enforced subservience. Slaves could be punished for talking back, and in the southern United States, did not even have the right to defend themselves against whites. In the South, too, slaves could not be witnesses except against other slaves. In many ways, law codes treated slaves as the instruments of their masters. Thus, where a slave was injured, the slave had no legal recourse, but the master could ask damages. Conversely, the master was often responsible when the slave committed a wrong.

A few slave systems prohibited sexual intercourse with slave women. Most did not discuss it, but the property relationship implied the master's right to use a female slave as he wished and this right was widely exercised in almost all slave-owning societies. Societies differed, however, in the ways they dealt with marriage and offspring. Some prohibited marriage with slaves. Islamic and Germanic law allowed it only if the slave were freed first. They differed even more in treatment of offspring. In most **slave societies**, the child belonged to the mother's owner. The basis for this was often livestock law. Islamic law, however, freed a woman who bore her master a child, though only on the death of the master. The children, however, inherited the father's status, were free, and had equal rights of inheritance.

Some law codes recognized a right to **manumission** and some even encouraged it. Deathbed manumissions were common under Islam because Islam offered the master who freed his slaves the promise of paradise. Roman and Germanic law encouraged manumission and Spanish law set up a procedure called *coartación* by which the slave could ask a court to set a price and a payment schedule. On the other hand, southern law either prohibited manumission or made it difficult. The same split is present on education. Mediterranean and Middle Eastern societies encouraged it because slaves were used in government, but many American states made it illegal to teach a slave to read. The major universal religions insisted on humane treatment of slaves. They treated the slave as a person, equal in the eyes of God, and their law codes sometimes were explicit on the master's obligation to feed, clothe, and not abuse his slaves. In societies with massive slave populations, there was often a fear of slave revolt. These societies, particularly in the Americas, had detailed **slave codes**, which were often detailed in what slaves could and could not do and were brutal in the punishments for acts of rebellion. *See also* SEXUAL EXPLOITATION; *SIETE PARTIDAS*.

LAY, BENJAMIN (1681-1759). Benjamin and Sarah Lay were **Quakers** who moved to **Barbados** in 1718. Though they went there for business and not as missionaries, they quickly got involved in the conditions of slaves. Their efforts to introduce their Quaker religion to slaves and their efforts to improve the conditions of slave life so alienated their neighbors that they were forced to leave in 1731. They then moved to Pennsylvania, where they devoted themselves to convincing the large Quaker community there that slavery was incompatible with Christian morality. At the time, many Quakers owned slaves. On one occasion, Benjamin fasted for 40 days. On another, he stood with one foot in the snow to demonstrate the condition of ill-clad slaves. He also wrote a number of pamphlets, among which was *All Slave-Keepers, That Keep the Innocent in Bondage, Apostates Pretending to Lay Claim to the Pure and Holy Christian Religion* (1737). The Lays were not immediately successful, but in 1754 the Philadelphia meeting of the Quakers voted to deny membership to slave owners.

LEAGUE OF NATIONS. After World War I, the major world powers were so convinced that the issue of slavery had been resolved that they abrogated the Brussels Convention, though the Treaty of St. Germain committed them to "the complete suppression of slavery in all its forms" and to the suppression of the **slave trade**. The Covenant of the League of Nations did not mention slavery. In 1922, however, press reports of slaving in Ethiopia and Arabia led to discussion of the issue and eventually to creation in 1924 of the Temporary Slave Commission to study the question. The commission report discussed the continuation of slavery, slavetrading, and slave raiding and suggested an international convention.

The result was the Slavery Convention of 1926. The convention called for the immediate suppression of the slave trade and the submission of annual reports by member nations. It contained no enforcement provisions, but its very existence put pressure on **Liberia** and Ethiopia to end slavetrading and raiding and on colonial powers to abolish slavery. It is only after 1927 that slavery was abolished in British colonies like **Sierra Leone,** Nigeria, and Sudan. In 1932, the Advisory Committee of Experts on Slavery was formed to receive the national reports and compile regular reports of its own. In spite of efforts to keep it weak, the committee made public information on slavery and other kinds of coercive labor in different parts of the world. It provided an arena that organizations like the **British and Foreign Anti-Slavery Society** could use to publicize servile institutions. In the long run, this was the most important result of the league's involvement in questions of slavery. The league's work was eventually continued by the **United Nations.** *See also* ANTI-SLAVERY INTERNATIONAL; BRUSSELS CONFERENCE; CONTEMPORARY FORMS OF SLAVERY.

LE CLERC, CHARLES VICTOR EMMANUEL (1772-1802). Charles Le Clerc was the general sent by Napoleon Bonaparte to win **Saint-Domingue** back from the rebel armies of **Toussaint-Louverture.** He was also married to Napoleon's sister, Pauline. Though Napoleon had pledged not to restore slavery, Le Clerc had secret instructions that he was to disarm Toussaint's black armies, restore slavery, and return the island to its slave **plantation** economy. His initial efforts were successful. He won a series of victories, persuaded some of Toussaint's generals to join his side, and captured Toussaint, who was sent to France and died there. Opposition to the French, however, stiffened when news arrived that slavery had been reestablished on Guadeloupe. Le Clerc's black allies went back into opposition, **Maroon** communities waged effective guerilla action, and yellow fever decimated his forces. Finally, in November 1802, he died of yellow fever. The French were soon forced to admit failure. Saint-Domingue became independent under **Jean-Jacques Desssalines**, who renamed the island Haiti. *See also* HAITIAN REVOLUTION.

LE ROY, ALEXANDRE (1854-1938). Born in Normandy, Alexandre Le Roy joined the Holy Ghost Fathers in 1877. His first assignments as a missionary were in Pondichery in India and the island of Réunion. In 1881, he was sent to **Zanzibar**, where he confronted the horrors of the **East African slave trade** and made his mark as an explorer and as a very vigorous missionary. He wrote two books on his years in East Africa: *A Travers le Zanguebar* (1884) and *Au Kilima-Ndjaro* (1893). In 1889, he published a pamphlet, *L'esclavage africain*, which was an appeal to the great powers then convening in Brussels to take action against the African trade. After serving briefly as a bishop in Gabon, he became the superior-general of the Holy Ghost Fathers in 1896. Le Roy was twice reelected, remaining in that post until 1926. He also served a number of times as president of the Anti-Slavery Society of France. He oriented the work of his order and of the society toward questions of the status of women, opposing polygamy and arranged marriages. During these years, however, the society was active in Africa, pressuring the colonial administration to end pawning in West Africa, which usually involved young girls. *See also* ABOLITION, FRANCE; CATHOLIC CHURCH; PAWNSHIP.

LIBERIA. Liberia was founded in 1822 by the **American Colonization Society** for former slaves who wanted to resettle in Africa. The U.S. navy lieutenant who escorted the first settlers to Liberia had difficulty finding land for them, but he finally was able to buy a strip 130 miles long where Monrovia now is. Until 1847, the settlement was run by white governors. The increasing opposition of African-Americans to colonization meant that relatively few former slaves actually re-settled – a little over 12,000 between 1822 and 1867. In addition, 5,700 slaves taken from ships stopped by the U.S. Navy were settled there.

The constitution of the new republic stated clearly that "there shall be no slavery within the Republic. Nor shall any ... person resident therein deal in slaves either within or without this Republic, directly or indirectly." Slavery and the **slave trade** had long existed in the area. Over the years, about 300,000 people from what is now Liberia were sold into the **Atlantic slave trade**. As the Americo-Liberians spread their influence, they made their compromises with the existing social order. Many Liberians owned slaves, and toward the end of the 19th century, they used coercive methods to recruit labor for the construction of the Panama canal, for Spanish cocoa **plantations** on Fernando Po and for German companies working in Cameroon. Forced labor was also used within Liberia.

Though the American Colonization Society wanted the settlers to introduce Christianity and end the slave trade in the interior, Americo-Liberians were not numerous enough to have much influence over the interior until the 20th century. The Americo-Liberians continued to speak English, to wear European clothes and to keep themselves separate from other Liberians. Most of them continued to live near the coast, but gradually they established their control over interior peoples. Though not formally a colony of the United States, they used the U.S. dollar and depended on U.S. diplomatic support in their efforts to fend off covetous French and British neighbors. The Americo-Liberian hegemony was ended only in 1980 when a coup d'état brought an African sergeant, Samuel Doe, to power.

LIBERTY PARTY. The Liberty Party was founded as an abolitionist party in 1839. It ran **James G. Birney** as its candidate in the presidential elections of 1840 and 1844, but it attracted few voters away from the major parties. Even in 1844, when both major candidates were pro-slavery, Birney attracted only 60,000 votes. This only convinced members of the **Garrison** wing of the abolition movement that politics would not be successful. Nevertheless, members of the Liberty Party decided that if they had more limited goals, they might do better. In 1848, the joined with disgruntled members of the Whig and Democratic parties to form the **Free Soil Party**, which opposed the extension of slavery to new territories in the West. The Free Soilers got 14 percent of the vote and in 1854, many Free Soilers joined the newly formed Republican Party.

LIBREVILLE. Just as Freetown was developed to serve as a reception center for slaves freed by the British, Libreville, which means "free town," was founded for slaves freed by the French navy. It was built on land in the Gabon estuary ceded to the French by a local ruler, King Denis, in 1839. Missions were established there in 1842 and a French navy post in 1843. After the abolition of slavery in the French Empire in 1848, it was decided to make Libreville a settlement for freed slaves. A group of 261 freed slaves were settled there in 1849. Some later groups were brought there, but the French navy never developed the zeal the British displayed for stopping slave ships and Libreville was far from **West Africa** where much of the French navy operated. The **slave trade** continued to function for many years on the other side of the estuary. The freed slaves were never numerous enough to develop into the kind of self-conscious community that emerged in **Sierra Leone** and **Liberia**. Most of the freed slaves were eventually absorbed into the Mpongwe population around the estuary. Libreville is today the capital of Gabon. *See also* ABOLITION, FRANCE; AFRICAN SQUADRON.

LINCOLN, ABRAHAM (1809-1865). Abraham Lincoln is known as the Great Emancipator. He was the American president who fought the **Civil War** and freed the slaves. He did not at first want to do either. Born in Illinois on what was then the frontier, Lincoln became a lawyer and a politician. Neither as a state legislator nor as a U.S. congressman was he involved in anti-slavery issues. By 1856, when he joined the recently founded Republican Party, he seemed to have been convinced that slavery should be gradually ended. He allied himself with moderate **Free Soiler** elements opposed to the extension of slavery to the new territories of the West. Lincoln believed that if slavery could not expand, it would begin to die. Many Southerners shared this belief and thus, when Lincoln was elected president, there was an immediate move to secession and Lincoln had to act to protect the Union.

From the moment of his election and well into the second year of the war, Lincoln tried to reassure, first the South, and then the slave-owning border states, that he had no intention of abolishing slavery. He insisted that he only wanted to save the Union and suppressed decrees by his military commanders that might arouse southern fears. The slaves themselves forced the issue by fleeing in large numbers across Union lines. After major Confederate victories in the early part of the war,

Lincoln became convinced both that a voluntary return of the Confederates was impossible and that the North needed the larger sense of
purpose that abolition would provide. The result was the **Emancipation
Proclamation** of 1 January 1863 which declared free slaves in areas still
in rebellion against the Union. The rest were freed only after Lincoln's
death when the **Thirteenth Amendment** to the **Constitution** was
passed. The importance of the proclamation was that it changed the
nature of the war and undermined the authority of slave owners. Lincoln
also resisted the recruitment of black troops, but once it became clear
that the Union had no choice but to destroy slavery, he agreed to recruitment of black soldiers. Almost 200,000 joined up and served with
distinction.

On 14 April 1865, five days after the surrender of the Confederate
General Robert E. Lee, Lincoln was assassinated at Ford's Theater in
Washington, D.C. He died the next day.

LIVERPOOL. During the second half of the 18th century, Liverpool was
the world's most important slaving port. Originally, a small fishing port
at the mouth of the Mersey River, it became a wealthy city. The first ship
from Liverpool to the West African coast sailed in 1700. By 1730, there
were 15 a year, and in the 1770s, over a hundred. Liverpool ships carried
about half of the three million slaves Great Britain shipped to the
Americas. Liverpool ships traded in other products, but slaves made up
between a third and a half of the Liverpool trade.

A major factor in Liverpool's success was its access via canals to
many of the trade goods sought in **West Africa**: textiles from Lanca-
shire, guns from Birmingham, and metal goods from Staffordshire and
Cheshire. The last British slaver sailed from Liverpool in July 1807.
With the end of the **slave trade**, Liverpool merchants played a major
role in the import of palm oil from West Africa and **cotton** from the
southern United States. Liverpool's ties with the South meant that there
was substantial sympathy with the southern cause during the American
Civil War. Much of the Confederate navy was built in Liverpool. *See
also* ATLANTIC SLAVE TRADE.

LIVINGSTONE, DAVID (1813-1873). David Livingstone was a doctor,
a missionary, an explorer, and a crusader against slavery in Africa. His
career was marked by a deep concern and a respect for the African
people, among whom he spent his adult life. Born to a Scottish working-
class family, he was first sent to Africa by the London Missionary

Society in 1841 and worked among the Tswana people of South Africa. In 1849, he left on a series of great explorations that covered large areas of East and **Central Africa**. Here he confronted the horrors perpetrated by slavers based in **East Africa**. His books described the burned villages and the long lines of manacled slaves being moved to the coast. They contributed to a renewal of the abolition movement. Among them are *Missionary Travels and Researches in South Africa* (1857) and *Narrative of of an Expedition to the Zambesi and Its Tributaries and of the Discovery of Lakes Sherwa and Nyasa* (1865).

In 1856, on a visit back to Great Britain, he made an impassioned plea in a lecture at Westminister Abbey for the introduction of a program of "Christianity, commerce and civilisation" to Central Africa. It led to the creation of the Universities Mission to Central Africa and the foundation of a number of missions dispersed across East and Central Africa, especially in the ravaged Lake Malawi area. He inspired many Christians to dedicate themselves to the struggle against slavery. He then returned to his explorations. After many years, when he was not heard from, a New York newspaper sent Henry Morton Stanley to find him. Livingstone was not lost and refused to be rescued, but two years later he died and his body was carried to the east coast by his porters. He was buried in Westminister Abbey along with many of Great Britain's greatest heroes.

LOCKE, JOHN (1632-1704). John Locke was a British philosopher who had a great influence on many of the Founding Fathers of the United States. In his *Second Treatise on Government*, he argued that people were born with the right to life, liberty, and property, and that people united to form a government in order to protect these rights. Slavery was for Locke nothing but a continuation of the state of war. The slave had no moral obligation to obey.

In spite of this, he argued that it was legitimate to enslave a person under two conditions. The first was as punishment for a criminal act. The second was as a result of defeat in a just war. The ultimate contradiction in his thought was his defense of chattel slavery. He justified it because he believed that Africa was a continent marked by misery and suffering, and therefore Africans were better off as slaves. In 1669, he wrote the Fundamental Constitutions of Carolina, which gave the master absolute authority over his slave. His idea that people had a natural right to liberty lived longer than the constitution he wrote. *See also* ENLIGHTENMENT.

LONG, EDWARD (1734-1813). A planter in Jamaica, Long was also a historian and a defender of slavery. Born in England and trained as a lawyer, he moved to Jamaica in 1757 to take over management of his family's estates after his father died. He became a judge, but was forced to return to England in 1769 because of ill health. His first published work, *Candid Reflections* (1772), was an attack on Judge Mansfield's decision freeing the slave James Somerset. In *History of Jamaica* (1774), he polished up his arguments. His defense of slavery was based in part on historical precedent and a belief in social hierarchy, but he bolstered his case with racist arguments. He argued that Africans and their slave descendants were savages. He also described mulattoes as inferior beings and Africa as a continent marked by brutal despotism. By contrast, he defended Jamaican plantation slavery as a benign patriarchal system. Long had a lot of influence on later defenders of slavery. *See also* SOMERSET v. STEWART.

LOVEJOY, ELIJAH (1802-1837). Elijah Lovejoy was an abolitionist who was murdered for his principles. He was born in Maine the son of a Congregationalist minister. After graduating from a college in Waterville, Maine (now Colby College), he moved to St. Louis where he taught school and was a partner in a newspaper. After studying for the ministry, he returned to St. Louis in 1833 to open a Protestant newspaper, the *Saint Louis Observer*. By 1835, he was regularly attacking slavery and had become an advocate of gradual emancipation. In 1837, he attacked the lynching of a black man. When the judge attacked him instead of indicting the lynchers, he criticized the judge in print. The next day, a mob attacked and destroyed his office and the presses. Lovejoy relocated his publishing enterprise to Alton, Illinois, but on November 1837, a mob made up mostly of men from Missouri attacked his office. He was killed while trying to defend his presses. He became a martyr to the abolitionist movement. His death was often cited as evidence that denial of the rights of slaves affected the rights of free white men.

LUGARD, FREDERICK JOHN DEALTRY (1858-1945). Frederick Lugard was one of the dominant figures of the 20th-century British colonial administration and had a great impact on slavery policy. Born in India to missionary parents, he served in the British army in India from 1879 to 1886 and then led several expeditions to East Africa. In 1900, he became the high commissioner to Northern Nigeria, and during the next three years conquered the powerful **Sokoto Caliphate**, which contained at least a million and perhaps as many as 2.5 million slaves. With only 1,200 soldiers, he opted for a program of indirect rule through the existing rulers. This necessitated respect for local institutions and recognition of the large slaveholdings of the elites. Immediately after the conquest, Lugard abolished the **slave trade**, prohibited slave raiding and closed slave markets. At the same time, at least 200,000 slaves fled their masters.

Though Lugard saw the end to slavery as his objective, he feared disorder and the creation of a rootless population of ex-slaves. He immediately moved to stop slave flight. Slaves were not allowed to leave their masters, but *murgu*, an Islamic legal procedure, allowed them to purchase their freedom. Lugard wrapped a program of gradual change in abolitionist rhetoric. Slavery was not definitively abolished in Northern Nigeria until 1936. After World War I, Lugard was the British representative and the strongest figure on various **League of Nations** committees dealing with slavery. He influenced the Slavery Convention of 1926 and supported a more activist role for the league than the colonial powers wanted. His ideas influenced British policy in other African colonies. *See also* EMANCIPATION, AFRICA.

LUNDY, BENJAMIN (1789-1839). An early abolitionist and a newspaper editor, Benjamin Lundy was born in New Jersey. Repelled by the treatment of slaves he saw while working as a saddle-maker's apprentice in West Virginia, he founded the Union Humane Society in 1816 to oppose racial discrimination. In 1821, he began publishing an abolitionist newspaper, the *Genius of Universal Emancipation*. In 1828, Lundy recruited **William Lloyd Garrison** to work with him on the newspaper. He and Garrison soon split. Garrison became a critic of colonization, which Lundy supported. Lundy tried unsuccessfully to set up colonies of free blacks in Haiti, Canada, and Mexico. He also strongly attacked the admission of Texas to the Union as a slave state, fearing that it would strengthen slavery. He continued to edit anti-slavery newspapers until his death in 1839.

-M-

MACEO, ANTONIO (1845-1896). Antonio Maceo was one of the most successful generals in the Cuban struggle for liberation from Spain. Born the son of a Venezuelan mulatto and a free black woman, he enlisted in the rebel army in 1868 at the beginning of the Ten Years' War. He speedily displayed a genius for guerilla warfare, frequently out-maneuvering Spanish generals. Though he rose in rank, he did not avoid combat and was wounded 26 times in his career. A determined opponent of slavery, he often raided **plantations** and freed slaves. In 1878, most rebel leaders were convinced that they could not win and accepted a Spanish peace offer. Maceo opposed the settlement, insisting that he could only accept total independence and complete abolition of slavery. He had to leave Cuba, but he returned at the invitation of nationalist leader José Marti for the 1895-1898 war and led a spectacular invasion of western Cuba, which covered a thousand miles in 92 days and captured 2,000 rifles. At the time, he was second in command of the rebel forces. Then, at the peak of his success, he was killed in a minor skirmish. Throughout his career he strongly supported an end to slavery and insisted on racial equality. *See also* CUBAN SLAVERY.

MALAYA. Slavery was common in precolonial Malaya. Little is known about slavery in Malaya before the 14th century. When **Islam** moved into Malaya in the 14th century, the prohibition of enslavement of other Muslims limited enslavement among the Malays, but raiding parties often attacked the aboriginal communities of the hill areas. Generally, men and older women were killed, but young women and children were brought back to serve as slaves. There were three other sources of slaves. One was raiders who operated in the waters of Indonesia and the Philippine islands and who sold slaves. Second, many pilgrims brought slaves back from Mecca. Finally, criminals could choose enslavement instead of corporal punishment. There were also people who were enslaved because they could not pay debts. They were not considered true slaves because they were Malays and they could be redeemed if they or their families had the money to pay the debts. It seems, however, to have been rare for debt slaves to redeem themselves.

Slaves were considered property. A master could do what he wished to a slave. Some were well treated, but the slave had no guarantee. Slaves could be sold or given away and their children were automati-cally slaves. Many slaves, probably the largest group, worked as ser-vants. The household of the wealthy and powerful sometimes had hundreds of slaves. Other were artisans or worked in commerce. Some were allowed to trade on their own and became quite wealthy, even owning their own slaves. Some slave couples also worked in agriculture.

The importance of slavery was linked to the low population density. It was not easy to find labor. When the British extended their control over Malaya, they brought labor in from China, India and Indonesia. Wage labor became cheaper than slave labor. Malayan Sultans were thus often willing to abolish slavery. Many household slaves in powerful families remained with their masters, but others left. *See also* EMANCIPATION, SOUTHEAST ASIA.

MALE REVOLT. *See* BAHIAN SLAVE REVOLTS.

MAMLUKES. The Mamlukes were originally **slave soldiers** who served various Arab regimes from the ninth century on. Most of them were Turks, but some were African, Slavic, or Greek. The term Mamluke, which comes from an Arabic word for slave, referred particularly to slave soldiers in Egypt. Generally, they were captured or enslaved as children, converted to **Islam**, and raised in barracks. They were trained both for war and administration. They were freed on becoming adults, but generally continued to live in a closed community.

Like other military slaves, the Mamlukes were considered very loyal to their royal masters. In 1250, however, a Mamluke took power in Egypt with the support of other Mamlukes. Though power passed several times from one group of Mamlukes to another, the Mamlukes remained in power in Egypt until 1798. The most famous of the Mamluke Sultans, Baybars, stopped the Mongol advance into the Middle East in 1260. The early Mamluke Sultans, tried to pass power to their sons, but eventually, succession was limited to those recruited as youths. In 1517, Egypt was conquered by the Ottomans. Though the Ottoman Sultan, Selim, executed 800 Mamlukes, he soon found it desirable to operate through the Mamlukes. Thenceforth, the Ottomans appointed a governor, who was chosen from another part of the Ottoman empire, and he ruled through a Mamluke administrative class. *See also* ELITE SLAVES; OTTOMAN SLAVERY; SLAVE SOLDIERS.

MANUMISSION. Manumission was the act of freeing an individual slave. Almost all slave systems have some provision for manumission. Some slaves were manumitted for service, some paid for their freedom, and some were given it by their masters. The possibility of manumission was important in motivating slaves to work hard, obey their masters, and save their money. Slaves were sometimes freed for bravery in war. Most slaves were not freed, but the hope was important to the functioning of the system. Those freed were usually **household slaves** who worked closely with their masters or slaves who were able to accumulate money because of the nature of their work.

In ancient Rome, the freedman became a client of his former master. A woman could be freed for bearing numerous children, but she was still dependent on her master. The prophet Muhammed encouraged manumission and treated it as a pious act. Thus, slaves were often freed by Muslims facing death. Usually those freed were trusted retainers, but in Arab countries, the rate of manumission was very high. Freeing a slave was often an act of penance for a criminal act. Also, a slave **concubine** who bore a child was freed upon the death of her master. If the slave paid for his or her freedom, manumission could be profitable. In parts of **West Africa**, the convention was that the slave paid for two replacement slaves. One result was that many slaves chose to purchase a slave rather than their freedom.

In the Americas, many freed slaves were the offspring or lovers of their masters. Some were also trusted servants or slaves who had grown wealthy in business. In the early years in the British colonies, manumission was widespread, involving between a fifth and a quarter of the black population. In Maryland and Delaware, the number of free blacks came to outnumber the slaves, but in the Deep South, the free black population was regarded as a potential threat. Most states insisted that manumission have public approval, and some made it virtually impossible. In South Carolina, slaves could be freed only by legislative act, and in Mississippi, only by bequest.

In Latin America too, many of those freed were lovers or children of their masters. Iberian law was generally very open to manumission. Most Latin American cities had large free black populations. In some Spanish colonies, there were procedures like the Cuban *coartación*, under which a price for manumission was agreed on and the slave gradually paid for his or her manumission. *See also* HISPANIC AMERICA; LAW OF SLAVERY; SELF-PURCHASE.

MAROONS. For slaves, the most common form of resistance was flight. Sometimes, the fleeing slaves were able to form autonomous and independent communities capable of defending themselves against the slaveholder's state. These slaves were called Maroons. They were most successful in areas where they could flee into wooded or mountainous areas and could defend themselves. There were different kinds of *marronage.* Some writers speak of *petit marronage*, in which slaves fled individually or in small groups and eventually returned to the **plantation**. Sometimes they hid out in the cities, sometimes in rural retreats. The majority of maroon communities were short-lived.

Grand marronage involved large independent communities. These communities threatened the plantation system because they raided the plantations for women, supplies, and weapons. Many of the original Maroon settlements were created by men who remembered Africa and created states modelled on those they knew in Africa. The most successful were also skillful at guerilla warfare and masters of warfare in the forests. Maroon raids and the attraction of the Maroons threatened the authority of the planters. The Maroons were also often effective fighters. In a number of cases, Europeans were forced to seek an accommodation. Usually, they offered security if the Maroons would stop raiding and return runaways.

One of the most successful was in Jamaica, where the British sued for peace in 1739 after a long period of warfare. Though the peace settlement broke down in 1795, the Jamaican Maroons were never conquered. In Surinam, there were a number of Maroon communities. In 1760, the Dutch signed a treaty with some of these communities that involved the regular payment of tribute to the Maroons. This treaty, however, did not stop the raiding. There were many Maroon communities in Brazil, where they were called *mocambos* or *quilombos*, most of them short-lived. Many of these communities were also centers of African religious observances. The most powerful Maroon community in Brazil, **Palmares**, survived for almost a century before it was finally conquered. In Hispanic America, they were often called *palenques*.

Even in the United States, some Maroons survived for years, but the only large Maroon community was among the **Seminole** Indians of Florida. The Seminoles provided a refuge for runaway slaves, who often formed distinct communities that accepted Seminole authority. The result was two wars, 1817-1818 and 1835-1842. The second was particularly bitter and hard fought because the Americans were determined to destroy the refuge and the slaves were fighting to protect their freedom. There were also maroon communities in Hispaniola, Colombia, Ecuador, Mexico, and Cuba. Maroons were also found in other parts of the world, for example in Mauritius and several parts of Africa. *See also* CUJO; JAMAICAN SLAVE REVOLT; SLAVE RELIGION.

MARRIAGE. In most slave-owning societies, slaves did not marry. They did cohabit, often in long-term recognized relationships, but they did not have the rights in relationships that spouses have. This flowed from the notion that slaves were things, that they were property. Marital rights could infringe the master's property rights. As property, for example, slaves could be sold. Husbands could be separated from their wives, children from their parents. Slaves could also not usually bequeath or inherit. They, therefore, had no rights in each other.

In spite of this, slaves developed deep attachments to each other, related to each other as man and wife, and raised children. Society often recognized the bond with ceremonies. The heavy work obligations often made it necessary for people to share obligations to children and created a kind of extended family. In West Africa, for example, slaves were rarely allowed to farm for themselves before they formed a stable relationship. In the Americas, slave masters usually discovered that slaves who lived with their spouses and children in two-parent households were the most effective workers. They generally lived in separate cabins. Among skilled slaves, parents often trained their sons and daughters, trying to provide them with a minimum of security.

MARXISM. Karl Marx and Friedrich Engels both saw slavery in their own times as inhumane, but saw it as a necessary stage in the evolution of human society. For Marx, the motor of history was the struggle between classes, but in the beginning, primitive society was egalitarian. When human society reached a certain level of productivity, private property emerged, and some men established their control of others by converting captives into slaves. Slaves thus became the most important form of property, and the state became necessary to preserve the property rights of the masters. This was thus the beginning of history.

Marxists distinguish between systems called modes of production largely according to the means by which the dominant social classes extracted wealth from the producers. Within the **slave mode of production**, this was direct. The master owned the slave and the product of his or her labor. Marx himself was primarily concerned to analyse **capitalism** and its contradictions. Marxist ideas on slavery were spelled out by his collaborator Friedrich Engels in a short book entitled *The Origin of the Family, Private Property and the State* (1891), which developed the idea of a series of stages. He proposed five stages: primitive communism, slave, feudal, capitalist, and communist. With the development of communism after the Bolshevik Revolution of 1918, these stages became a part of communist orthodoxy. Communist scholars working on different parts of the world tried to determine when the slave, feudal, and capitalist periods began. This proved to be a straitjacket for historical research. Many of the societies being studied followed a course of historical development very different from Europe.

In the 1960s, following the discovery of Marx's early writings, many scholars went back to Marxist ideology, but in a more supple way, using it to understand processes of historical change rather than imposing a rigid framework on the study of the past. The new Marxists saw not a single slave mode of production, but different modes. Some scholars have even said that each society has its own unique configuration of forces and relations of production. Slavery must, therefore, be analyzed in terms of the ways slaves are recruited and exploited. **Claude Meillassoux**, in his *Anthropologie de l'Esclavage* (1986), describes a tension between warriors and merchants that regulated the way slaves were traded and exploited in **West Africa**. **Eugene Genovese** was concerned with a society where land-owners profited from the convergence of slave and capitalist modes of production and from their position in each. In *Roll Jordan Roll: The World the Slaves Made* (1974), he asked how social classes made themselves, that is to say, how slaves acted.

MAURITIUS AND RÉUNION. Mauritius and Réunion are part of the Mascarene islands of the southwestern **Indian Ocean**. They were uninhabited when first discovered by the Portuguese in the 16th century. Mauritius was occupied by the Dutch in 1638, and Réunion (then called Ile de Bourbon), by the French in 1670. In 1710, the Dutch abandoned Mauritius, and it was occupied by the French in 1721 and called Ile de France. The French used it as a base to threaten British shipping, but during the second half of the 18th century, both islands developed as important producers of tropical crops. Slaves were imported from all over the Indian Ocean, 160,000 slaves in all, about half of them between 1769 and 1783. They came from all sides of the Indian Ocean: **East Africa**, Madagascar, **India**, **Malaya**, and **Indonesia**.

The Mascarenes very much resembled Caribbean islands. They were dominated by a small planter elite, many of whom were **people of color**. After experimenting with other crops, they became primarily **sugar** producers. With no other source of labor, slaves did everything. They were sailors, artisans, fisherman, and servants, as well as field workers. Tales of slavery days suggest that Mascarene slavery was particularly harsh. During the 1820s, death rates on Mauritius were almost twice the birth rates. The **manumission** rate most years was only about 0.2% of the slave population, and these were mostly women and children, probably the lovers or offspring of French colonists. Slaves regularly fled into the mountainous interior, though no permanent **maroon** communities were ever formed.

The British occupied Mauritius in 1810 and restored its Dutch name. British efforts to end the slave trade led to a period of illegal slave trading, but by the mid-1820s that had ended. Ile de Bourbon also had a large, illegal slave trade that persisted until the French abolished slavery in 1848. When Great Britain abolished slavery in 1833, there was a massive flight from the **plantations** as freed slaves chose to become peasant farmers in the mountainous interior. During the 1840s, the former slaves were totally replaced on the sugar plantations by indentured labor from India.

MEDIEVAL EUROPE. Medieval Europe was an area in which slavery declined. In large parts of Europe, it disappeared completely. The decline began in the late years of the Roman empire. As Roman armies ceased bringing prisoners from frontier areas and the money economy declined, gang labor disappeared and slavery gave way to other forms of tenure in which farmers were bound to land and paid dues to their lords. Enslavement revived briefly every time new conquerors made their appearance, first the Germans, then the Hungarians and the **Vikings**. Slaves were also found along various warlike frontiers, for example, that of German expansion into eastern Europe, or the boundaries between Anglo-Saxon and Celtic peoples in the British isles. In none of these areas, however, did **plantation** systems emerge. The long-range pattern of change was for slavery to give way to **serfdom** in which serfs were bound to the land and owed rent and services to a feudal lord.

In Western Europe, slavery coexisted with serfdom, but slaves were more likely to be found in the households of the powerful and on church-owned estates. Slaves were thus usually closer to power than serfs and more likely to share in its rewards. Some slaves were also purchased by artisans. The major source of agricultural production was serfs. The medieval state was often too weak to prevent slaves from fleeing. The ninth and 10th centuries were periods of agricultural innovation and expansion into hitherto uncultivated areas. Increasingly, there was competition for labor and more favorable terms for those who grew the crops. Where slavery still existed, it yielded to serfdom. By the 12th century, slavery had disappeared in most areas north of the Alps and Pyrenees. Even serfdom was undermined after the bubonic plague killed a quarter to a third of the European population in the mid-14th century. Efforts were made to force workers and peasants to work on the same terms as before, but the competition for labor was such that terms for peasants and workers improved dramatically. This development was further encouraged by increasingly powerful royal courts, which preferred free, tax-paying peasants to serfs or slaves. Slavery persisted much longer in the Mediterranean. Christian and Muslim corsairs fought each other and raided each other's shores.

The price of defeat or capture was enslavement. There was a constant flow of slaves from eastern Europe, so much that the Roman word for slave, *servus,* gave way in most European languages to words based on the root 'Slav': *esclave* in French, *esclavo* in Spanish, *escravo* in Portugese, *schiavo* in Italian, *Sklave* in German. *Servus* came to mean serf. The presence of slaves never, however, led to the creation of a **slave society**. Slaves were mostly urban. They lived and worked within households. There was a high rate of **manumission**. Some were owned by artisans and some worked in specialized areas like vineyards, but agriculture remained a peasant responsibility. The number of slaves from Africa was small until the 15th century, when the activity of Portuguese ships in West Africa made increasing numbers of Africans available. Most of the African slaves, however, were directed to the Atlantic islands and then, in the 16th century, to the Americas, where **plantation** systems developed. Domestic slavery continued to exist in Spain and Italy into the 18th century.

The pattern of change was very different in eastern Europe. During the first millennium of the common era, population concentrations were low. Slavic peasants were free, but gave part of their crops to local rulers. During the ninth and 10th centuries, there were two parallel developments. First, there was increased enslavement for markets in the Mediterranean and the Muslim world. This declined only when various eastern European rulers converted to Christianity. Second, there was an expansion into the area of German speakers from both north and west. The development of a market economy contributed to the growth of both an indigenous nobility in some areas and a class of German planters in others. Thus, when slavery was disappearing and serfdom was easing in the West, serfdom was increasing in eastern Europe. This serfdom involved heavier obligations and tighter controls than any experienced in western Europe and has often been compared to slavery. *See also* ANCIENT ROMAN SLAVERY; EAST EUROPEAN SLAVE TRADE; SCANDINAVIA; SLAVS.

MEILLASSOUX, CLAUDE (1925-). Claude Meillassoux is a French anthropologist who has done important research on the evolution of social forms in **West Africa**. Slavery is important in two aspects of his thought. First, he has been interested in the transformation of small-scale decentralized societies into more differentiated and more centralized states. He has described a process that began with conflict between older and younger males over the control of women and wealth. In this process, trade and the accumulation of slaves played a major role.

His best-known work deals with slavery in the highly differentiated societies of the West African savannah, which are marked by some of the largest slave concentrations in the world. He sees the basis of slavery as violence and, in fact, treats as slaves only those enslaved by violence. His *Anthropology of Slavery: The Womb of Iron and Gold* (1986) looks at relationships between two kinds of social formation, the warriors and the merchants, and the way each society produced a different kind of slavery. He has been the most supple exponent of a revival of Marxist thought, that took place in the 1960s when Marxist scholars went back to Marx's early thought to develop a more flexible analysis of social change than was being provided by communist thinkers. *See also* MARXISM; SLAVE MODE OF PRODUCTION.

MERCADO, TOMÁS DE. Tomás de Mercado was a Dominican friar, a theologian, and an early critic of Spanish slavery in the Americas. He was born in Seville, Spain, but emigrated to Mexico. His most important work was the *Suma de Tratos y Contratos*, first published in 1569. In it, he examined the Atlantic economy of his time. One chapter discussed slavery and the **slave trade**. Mercado accepted the traditional Christian legal teaching that people could be enslaved as war captives or as punishment for crimes. They also could sell themselves into slavery and fathers could sell their children. He was critical, however, of the way the **Atlantic slave trade** was conducted. He criticized conditions in slave ships and argued that the profits from the trade stimulated warfare, raiding, kidnapping, and the abuse of their power by judges and fathers. He therefore argued that the trade was immoral and that participation in the slave trade was a sin. *See also* HISPANIC AMERICA.

MEXICAN-AMERICAN WAR (1846-1848). By adding a huge area to the United States, the American victory in the Mexican-American War made possible the extension of slavery. Southern leaders were interested in areas where slavery could expand and saw the war as an opportunity for just that reason, but it also strengthened the resolve of anti-slavery and free soil forces in the North to resist that expansion. The war came after Texas became the last slave state admitted to the Union in 1845, a decision opposed by many northern congressmen and by Mexico. The issue was joined in 1846, when a Pennsylvania congressman named David Wilmot proposed an amendment to a military appropriations bill barring slavery in any territories acquired in the war. It was passed in the House of Representatives after a bitter debate but was defeated in the Senate. This was known as the **Wilmot Proviso**. Once the war was over, the question became the organization of the new territories. The bitter conflicts were resolved temporarily by the **Compromise of 1850**, but were definitively settled only by the **Civil War**. *See also* FREE SOIL PARTY.

MIDDLE PASSAGE. The Middle Passage was the maritime voyage of slave ships from ports in Africa to ports in America. It could take anywhere from three weeks to three months, depending on the ports involved and the wind conditions. It was called the Middle Passage because it was often the middle part of a triangular voyage from Europe to Africa to the Americas and back to Europe. The experience was the most horrible in the slave's journey. Men were usually kept chained except during brief periods when they were brought on deck for exercise or feeding. Women or children were usually allowed a certain amount of freedom of movement, but women were also often sexually abused by the crew. During stormy weather, all slaves were kept below deck.

The worst ships were the so-called "tight-packers," in which slaves had little room to move, but even loose-packers gave slaves less room than any other kind of transport ship. One ship much publicized by abolitionists, the *Brookes*, gave slaves 2.5 feet of headroom and a space 16 inches wide for each person to lie in. The number of human beings chained below deck meant that it was almost impossible to clean up the vomit and the human waste. The few accounts we have of the trip describe the stench as the most offensive part. **Olaudah Equiano** describes being hit by the odor as soon as he was brought onto the ship. Passing ships could generally identify a slaver by its smell. The close confinement of slaves, who were often weak, undernourished, and sometimes ill before they boarded the ship also meant that there was a danger of epidemic disease. Smallpox or dysentery could wipe out a large part of the cargo. With profits dependent on delivering most slaves alive, owners and captains did their best to keep them healthy. Ships often carried a surgeon and efforts were made to ensure that slaves ate regular meals. Slavers did manage to reduce the mortality rate from over 20 percent in the 16th century to about 5 percent in the 19th. The psychological trauma was also so great that one of the problems the slavers faced was melancholy in which slaves lost the will to live and often tried to starve themselves to death. Forced feeding was common, as were harsh punishments.

Sailors did not like working on a slaver and often had to be pressed into service. The mortality rate for European sailors both in Africa and on the seas was often high. Epidemic disease was not the only problem.

Calm seas and poor winds could result in the ship using up its food supplies or water before reaching its destination. Sometimes, some of the weaker slaves were thrown overboard to preserve supplies, but slaves still died of hunger or dehydration. There was also a constant fear of slave rebellion. For that reason, slavers generally carried twice as many crew as other ships the same size. Though slaves did not know how to sail large ships, many of them preferred death to the horrors they were experiencing and others they anticipated. Slaves often feared that they were going to be eaten.

Conditions were similar on other long sea voyages. Though waters of the **Indian Ocean** were usually calmer and the voyage shorter, conditions for slaves were poor on voyages to **Mauritius and Réunion** and mortality was high. *See also* ATLANTIC SLAVE TRADE.

MILITARY SLAVES. Slaves were frequently used as soldiers in Asia and Africa as they had been in ancient Rome. They were either recruited from boys given as tribute or from young men taken in slave raids. They were often privileged troops that were well rewarded. They were particularly valuable in societies where it was difficult to maintain a large army or where most soldiers were loyal either to their local communities or to military leaders. Military slaves were owned by the king or sultan, rewarded for service to him, and loyal to him. Most slave soldiers remained legally slaves, the exception being the **Mamlukes** of Egypt, who were freed on completion of their military service. Many of these groups became hereditary slave elites, though others depended on constant recruitment of new blood. They often had a very strong esprit de corps.

During the ninth century, the Abbasid Caliphate began recruiting slave units from outside the Arab world, probably because their conquests had outrun their manpower resources. Their slave soldiers, called *Ghulams,* were mostly Turks from Central Asia. The use of slave soldiers was important to most subsequent Middle Eastern states into the 19th century. The Ottoman Turks, who replaced the Abbasids, recruited an elite corps called the **Janissaries** taken from young boys given in the Caucasus and Balkans as tribute. In North Africa, particularly in Morocco, young male slaves were often imported from south of the Sahara to serve as soldiers. In 1820, the Egyptian ruler, Mohamed Ali, invaded the Sudan to get a source of African soldiers.

Slave soldiers were also important in other parts of the world. In Africa, slaves provided a loyal fighting force for many kingdoms. The *Ceddo* of the Senegambian kingdoms became a hereditary slave fighting force. Captured boys were often used as grooms or porters and if they proved able, became ceddo themselves. The *Tonjon* of Bambara Segou (Mali) were owned by a hunting society that became the nucleus of a state. The **Yoruba** rulers also used slaves as soldiers, bodyguards, and messengers. In the upper Nile valley, the Funj recruited slave soldiers among boys taken prisoner in areas farther south.

Slave soldiers often got first access to improved weapons. These slave units were housed separately, treated generously, and their leaders often became influential chiefs. In India, slave soldiers were recruited either from Central Asia or East Africa. Though valued because of their loyalty, slave soldiers often developed a sense of corporate identity, particularly where they became a hereditary group. They could then interfere to impose a ruler of their choice, influence the policies of the state, or even impose one of their leaders as a ruler. One late medieval slave general, **Malik Ambar**, became an important ruler in western India.

Many European armies in 19th-century Africa were recruited largely from slaves, sometimes purchased in slave markets for military service, in other cases, freed as a reward for enlistment. In many cases, they were nominally freed, but their slave origins often shaped their identities. German armies in Cameroun and East Africa were purchased as slaves. The French used an army of slaves to conquer French **West Africa** and much of the British West African Frontier Force was of slave origin. Slave soldiers were often rewarded for loyal service with booty, of which the most important kind was female captives.

In Asia and Africa, slaves were the most privileged soldiers, the palace guard. Slaves also served in militias and regular military forces in the Americas, but here they were usually adjuncts to citizen armies. Slave troops were more common in Latin America, even being used to track runaways and fight **Maroons**. They were often freed as a reward for service. In the English, French, and Dutch colonies, the arming of slaves was much more rare. There were black units, but mostly free blacks and mulattoes. Slaves were sometimes armed during military conflicts and often played subaltern roles, for example, as scouts, trackers, artisans, or messengers and servants. Some slaves were, however, used on both sides during the **American Revolution** and the British created a slave regiment during the wars of the French Revolution. *See also* OTTOMAN SLAVERY.

MINING. Many of the harshest forms of slavery were found in mining. In fourth century BCE Greece, anywhere from 10,000 to 40,000 slaves worked in silver mines. Slaves were also used to mine gold, silver, copper and precious stones in the Roman empire. Often those selected for mining were convicts or recent prisoners of war, who worked in shackles. In the **Sahara**, slaves were used to mine salt and elsewhere in Africa, some were used to work for gold. In the United States, they mined for coal, gold and lead. Though often rented from planters, many of them became valuable skilled miners. In Spanish America, slaves were used to mine silver in Mexico and Central America and gold in Colombia. When gold and diamonds were discovered in the interior of **Brazil** during 18th century, many slaves were brought to the mining areas.

Working conditions were particularly harsh in underground mines. The Greek silver mines often had galleries only two to three feet high. Workers spent long hours underground, working on their backs, with poor ventilation. Many died from overwork, unhealthy conditions or cave-ins, but some of those who survived became skilled miners and were able to eventually purchase their freedom. In the United States, planters were often reluctant to rent slaves to mining operations. Working conditions were somewhat better where there were surface mines.

Some frontier areas like the Brazilian Minas Gerais or the Colombian Chocó were more open to slave initiative and had opportunities for slaves to advance themselves and purchase their freedom. Such areas were marked by a high rate of **manumission** and miscegenation. In Brazil, slaves were allowed some time to pan gold for themselves and some were able to purchase their own freedom. Frontier conditions also made escape possible. The mining province of Minas Gerais in Brazil had many small **maroon** communities. Violent resistance was also a problem in ancient Greece, Rome and the United States. In the United States, while mining disasters caused much loss of life, the value of skilled slaves brought them some rewards. Cash incentives were often offered for performance.

MISSOURI COMPROMISE. In 1803, the Louisiana Purchase added to the United States the whole western part of the Mississippi basin. It also posed the question of the balance between slave and free. In 1812, Louisiana was admitted to the Union as a slave state. Seven years later, northern Congressmen opposed the admission of Missouri as a slave state because they feared the spread of slavery throughout the purchase area. At the time of its application for statehood, Missouri`s population was almost a sixth slave. A compromise was reached under which Missouri's admission was balanced by the admission of Maine as a free state. In the rest of the Louisiana Purchase area slavery was prohibited north of 36°30′, which was the southern border of Missouri. Though hotly debated, this compromise regulated the extension of slavery until victory in the **Mexican-American War** raised the question of what to do with territories acquired from Mexico. *See also* COMPROMISE OF 1850; KANSAS-NEBRASKA ACT.

MOCAMBO. A *mocambo*, like a *quilombo,* was a **maroon** settlement in **Brazil**.

MONTEJO, ESTEBÁN (1860-1973). Born as a slave in Cuba, Esteban Montejo was at different times a runaway, a day laborer and a soldier in the struggle for independence from Spain. When he was 103 years old, he told the story of the first 40 years of his life to the Cuban writer, Miguel Barnet, who published it as *Biography of a Runaway Slave.* Blessed with an exceptional memory, Montejo provided details on the life of a slave and a poor freedman in the late 19th century. He described the harsh life of the **plantation**, slave culture and pastimes, and Afro-Cuban religious practices. He also described his life as a runaway in the mountains and the experience of combat under the black general, **Antonio Maceo**. Barnet's book is one of the first to make available an account of the life of slaves in their own words. After independence, Montejo was active in the Partido Independiente de Color, which struggled for equality with whites and was suppressed by the Cuban government. *See also* CUBAN SLAVERY.

MONTESINOS, ANTONIO DE. Antonio de Montesinos was a Dominican missionary who criticized the brutal treatment of native peoples during the first years of Spanish settlement on the island of Hispaniola. The *encomienda* granted to Spanish colonists gave them both tribute and labor. The system was harsh, and for many natives, it amounted to slavery. In 1511, Montesinos gave the first of several sermons denouncing the enslavement of Indians. When these sermons were criticized by settlers, he was called back to Spain, where his self-defense led to the promulgation of the Laws of Burgos (1512), which attempted to protect Indians from abuses common within the system. Five years later, he was one of 23 missionaries to write the royal government to protest the harsh treatment of native people. *See also* COLUMBUS, CHRISTOPHER; HISPANIC AMERICAN SLAVERY.

MONTESQUIEU, CHARLES-LOUIS DE (1689-1755). Montesquieu was a leading **Enlightenment** thinker who had a great influence on the leaders of the **American** and **French Revolutions**. Though he was from Bordeaux, a major slave-trading port, he was the founder of the Enlightenment critique of slavery. In *De l'esprit des lois* (1748), he argued that slavery corrupted both master and slave and called into question previous justifications of slavery. He saw slavery as a violation of natural law and believed that a man was no more justified in selling himself than in committing suicide. He rejected the enslavement of prisoners of war and the idea that slavery was justified by the conversion of the slave to Christianity. In spite of this, there were ambiguities in his beliefs. Montesquieu may have been influenced by the pro-slavery environment in Bordeaux. In his satirical *Lettres persanes* (1721), he was critical of treatment of slaves by Iberians in America, but said nothing about French **plantations** in the West Indies, with which Bordeaux did a profitable trade. His critique of slavery in *L'esprit des lois* was linked to climatic determinism which contrasted the inertia and passions of tropical societies with the hard-working and dynamic temperate societies. Thus, though he condemned slavery in the abstract and influenced abolitionist thought, he also justified slavery as a response to sloth in tropical societies.

MORET LAW (1870). The Moret law provided for the gradual abolition of slavery in Cuba. It was proposed by Segismundo Moret, a Spanish abolitionist, who was minister of colonies in the liberal government that came to power in Spain in 1868. It was a response to the promise by rebels in Cuba to freed all slaves who fought on their side. The law began with a **"free womb"** clause, which emancipated at birth children born of slave mothers. Slaves born after September 1868 were to be freed once the insurrection in Cuba stopped. The law also freed slaves who fought on the Spanish side and reimbursed for their losses slave owners who supported the Spanish cause. Slaves over 60 were also freed, but without compensation to their owners. Planters in Cuba were able to delay the implementation of the law for two years and engaged in effective stalling tactics after that. Efforts to apply the law ended with a coup d'état in 1874, but in 1880, the more cautious Law of the Patronato proclaimed a more gradual abolition over an eight-year period. This was shortened in 1886 when slave flight and the threat of slave insurrection forced Spain to approve total emancipation. By this time, there were only 25,000 slaves left in Cuba. *See also* CUBAN SLAVERY.

MOROCCAN SLAVERY. Sijilmassa in southern Morocco was for long the northern terminus of a major trade route that brought gold and slaves across the Sahara. Moroccans thus early became major slave users and providers of slaves for other Mediterranean societies. This trade was the source of power of a number of dynasties that ruled Morocco. Thus, the Almoravids, who originated in Saharan Mauritania in the llth century, had a force of 2,000 slave cavalry men. The Almohads, who succeeded them in the 12th century, also used slave troops as did Mulay Ismail (1672-1727), who was himself born of a slave mother. There were also military units raised from among Christian slaves, for example, much of the army that destroyed the Songhay Empire in 1591.

Slaves filled a number of other functions. At the court, they were **concubines**, wet nurses, **eunuchs**, and domestic servants. Male slaves worked in the stables and cultivated food for the court. Slaves were important in the households of the rich and powerful, worked some of the larger estates, and were often artisans. Slavery was particularly important in the desert-side areas of southern Morocco, where there were numerous villages of slaves and of *haratin*, freed slaves who maintained a dependent relationship with their former owners. They farmed and they tended the date plantations on desert oases. In the late 19th century, over 4,000 slaves a year were being imported into Morocco. In the 1890s, the French conquest of the western Sudan (Mali) finally closed off the most important sources of slaves. The French conquest of Morocco after 1912 led to the end of the **slave trade**, though children were still being kidnapped in the south into the 1930s. Eventually, economic change opened up opportunities for former slaves to earn money and led to the breakdown of the slave system. *See also* ELITE SLAVES; MILITARY SLAVES; SAHARA.

MORTALITY. It is probable that in all times and all places, slave trading has involved a high death rate. Slaves were never easy to move. It is unlikely that any group of slaves ever accepted their status willingly. Slaves being moved, whether by caravan or by boat, were often interested in revolting or running away. Because of this, they were often kept in chains, watched carefully, and treated harshly. They were usually poorly fed. In slave caravans, those who resisted or claimed to be sick were often killed to prevent others from feigning illness. In addition, slaves were frequently being moved into new disease environments. Even with caravans, the movement from one climate zone to another was often disastrous for weak, tired, and disheartened slaves. On slave ships, crowded conditions facilitated the communication of disease.

Smallpox, dysentery, and other diseases could sweep through a ship very quickly. There is little data on mortality except in the Atlantic world. Ship captains generally wanted to keep slaves alive because they were valuable property. In spite of this, the mortality rate was about 12 percent. The most important variable was the length of the voyage. For voyages from Mozambique to Brazil, the rate was over 18 percent.

In ongoing slave systems, slaves often had a higher mortality than free persons. In some cases, the environment was poor. **Miners** or **galley slaves** often had a high mortality because the work was harsh. So too did **sugar** plantations. Though Africans survived better in tropical lowlands than other people, they were subject to a range of tropical diseases like malaria, yellow fever, and dysentery. The biggest problem with sugar was the work itself. During the harvest, which lasted anywhere from five to eight months, slaves were often pushed to the limits of human endurance. The sooner sugar was in the presses after being cut, the greater the amount of liquid that could be extracted from the cane. There was rarely enough labor and slaves sometimes worked 18- and 24-hour shifts. Men who were tired were often killed or injured by industrial accidents. In other societies, nutrition was a factor. Slaves were not always well fed, and during famines, they were the ones most likely to suffer most. During droughts in Africa, slaves were sometimes turned lose to fend for themselves. Sometimes, too, slaves died as a result of resistance or harsh punishments. Other times, there were psychological variables like despair, which probably influenced health. *See also* DEMOGRAPHY OF SLAVERY; MIDDLE PASSAGE.

MOTT, LUCRETIA COFFIN (1793-1880). Lucretia Mott was a leading abolitionist and feminist. Born to a **Quaker** family in Philadelphia, she became a Quaker minister in 1821. She and her husband, James Mott, were supporters of the free produce movement, which encouraged people to buy only products made by free labor. After **William Lloyd Garrison** persuaded them to support immediate abolition, the Mott household became the Philadelphia center of the Garrison movement.

In 1833, Mott was the founder of the Philadelphia Female Anti-Slavery Society, and in 1837 she was the principal organizer of the First Anti-Slavery Convention of American Women. When the Second Convention was convened a year later, a mob hostile to female political activity disrupted the convention and burned down the hall in which it was being held. The meeting was reconvened elsewhere. Opposition to women in abolition politics led Mott and Elizabeth Cady Stanton to convoke the Seneca Falls convention in 1848, which played a major role in the women's rights movement. Mott was active throughout the 1840s and 1850s as a lecturer and organizer. She was also involved with the African-American community and with the fight against racial discrimination. After the **Civil War**, she became president of the American Equal Rights Association, which fought for universal suffrage.

MUI TSAI. The *mui tsai* were young girls sold into slavery in China. They were sold by poor families, particularly during difficult years, and became household servants in rich families. They were often harshly treated. As they matured, some became concubines and some were put to work as prostitutes, but most were servants. The institution was investigated by the **League of Nations** slavery committees during the 1930s. On the mainland, it was suppressed by the Communist regime after 1950. In Hong Kong, it persisted until the late 1950s, but probably disappeared with economic growth in the latter half of the 20th century. *See also* CHINESE SLAVERY.

MURGU. In precolonial Hausa society in Northern Nigeria, *murgu* was a contractual arrangement under which the slave worked independently and made fixed payments to his master. It was always instituted by the master. Under the British colonial regime of Lord **Frederick Lugard**, it became a system under which a slave could request that a price be set for his or her freedom. The slave paid it off as he or she was able to earn the money. For the colonial administration, it provided an orderly path out of slavery, but it was a path that placed most of the costs on the slave. *See also* SOKOTO CALIPHATE.

-N-

NABUCO DE ARAUJO, JOAQUIM (1849-1910). Nabuco was one of the leaders of the Brazilian abolition movement. His father, a landowner and senator from northeastern Brazil with the same name, was one of the sponsors of the Rio Branco Law of 1871, which freed all children born after that date. After 10 years of travel and education in Europe, the younger Nabuco decided to devote himself to abolition. In 1879, he was elected to parliament and immediately proposed legislation that would totally end slavery within 10 years. Defeated two years later as a result of his outspoken views, he retreated briefly to Great Britain, where he wrote *O abolicionismo* in 1883. His book argued that slavery had a negative effect on the social and economic development of Brazil. A good orator, he spoke widely within Brazil, wrote newspaper articles and was one of the founders of the Brazilian Anti-Slavery Society. He played a crucial role in the events that led up to the abolition of slavery in the state of Amazonas in 1885 and in the whole of Brazil in 1888. He later served Brazil as a diplomat, but his most important work was the transformation of Brazilian attitudes toward slavery during the 1880s. *See also* ABOLITION, BRAZIL; FREE WOMB LAWS.

NAMES. In many societies, newly introduced slaves were usually given new names to signify that a new identity had been imposed on them. The new names were often also distinctive, indicating that the person was a slave. In many societies, for example, ancient Greece and the United States, slaves had only personal names. The absence of a family name indicated their lack of kinship ties. Greek slaves were often named after gods or their country of origin. In Muslim Africa, many slaves were named after Bilali, the prophet Muhammed's slave *muezzin*. Some also received standard Muslim names like Mohammed or Abdullah, but others had distinctive names indicating, for example, the color of their skin, like "saffron" or "ink." Others were named after fruits or flowers or were given names that suggested a pleasing disposition. Derogatory names like "pig" and "torn sack" were common in Scandinavia. In the United States, about a fifth of the slaves kept their African names, but many others were given distinctive classical names like "Scipio" or "Hannibal." Of course, many slaves continued to use their original names in the privacy of their homes. After emancipation, the taking of family names was often an important statement that the slave was fully human.

NATURAL LAW. The concept of natural law involves the notion that there are certain truths valid everywhere and all the time and that they can be comprehended by reason. Both supporters and opponents of slavery often based their arguments on the idea of natural law. Many defenders of slavery used the argument made by the Greek philosopher **Aristotle** that some people lack reason and, thus, are by nature slaves. Defenders of slavery argue that it is in the best interests of these people. Different thinkers gave the idea of natural law a religious interpretation. Ibn Sina (Avicenna), the Muslim philosopher, treated pagans as Aristotle treated those lacking reason. This then justified enslaving non-Muslims. For St. Augustine, slavery was counter to natural law, but injustice could not be ended in this world, only in the next.

The first philosopher to call for the abolition of slavery because it violated natural law was the 16th-century French political theorist **Jean Bodin**. Bodin argued that the ubiquity of slavery did not prove that it was natural. The idea of natural law became essential to **Enlightenment** philosophers such as **Charles-Louis de Montesquieu, Jean-Jacques Rousseau**, and **John Locke**, who believed that all human beings are endowed with certain universal rights. These ideas informed the **American** and **French Revolutions** and inspired the American Declaration of Independence and the French **Declaration of the Rights of Man**. They were also fundamental to the British and American abolition movements, which were rooted in the Protestant churches. They often appealed to principles of justice implicit in the Bible rather than the social reality of a world described in the Bible, which involved slavery. Some, like **William Lloyd Garrison** and Henry Thoreau, went further and argued that not only could people know what was just, but that they were justified in resisting a morally unjust law like the **Fugitive Slave Law** of 1850. The philosophy of civil disobedience, later important to 20th-century social movements, was rooted in the resistance of abolitionists to laws they believed were unjust.

NAZI SLAVE LABOR CAMPS. The most massive use of slave labor during the 20th century was the slave labor system used by the Nazi regime in Germany during the Second World War. At peak, there were eight million foreign workers in Germany. Some of these were voluntary migrants from countries allied to or conquered by the Germans and some were prisoners of war, but most were either concentration camp prisoners or workers forcibly recruited from conquered countries. Slave labor was also made available to German enterprises in concentration camps scattered over the conquered countries. Many leading German companies set up factories in the camps to take advantage of the labor made available to them.

The concentration camps were originally set up for Jews, Gypsies, homosexuals, political prisoners, and Jehovah's Witnesses slated for either reeducation or extermination, but Germany suffered from a severe shortage of labor, particularly after the war took 13 million able-bodied men out of the labor force. After the German victory in Poland, 300,000 prisoners of war were put to work on German farms. By the summer of 1944, about 1.7 million had been forcibly recruited.

In German planning, there was often a conflict between brutality and exploitation. When Adolf Hitler's German armies swept into the Soviet

Union, they expected a swift victory and the return of German soldiers to the labor force. At first, there was no effort to recruit Soviet laborers. Of the 3.3 million Soviet soldiers captured in 1941, about two million died because of poor housing, inadequate food, and disease. When Soviet resistance stiffened, the Germans began recruiting Russian labor. By 1944, there were almost three million Russian laborers in Germany.

Nazi policy was shaped by racist ideology. By 1942, Nazi policy was to exterminate the Jews. In many camps, there was a careful separation of those capable of productive labor and those scheduled for the gas chambers. Many of the workers were also eventually killed, but some survived the war. Racist ideology also led the Nazis to treat Western Europeans differently from the Slavic peoples of the East who were seen as racially inferior people fit only for labor. Workers from Western Europe were generally paid the same wages as their German counterparts. Those from the East were paid less and were subjected to severe discrimination. They had to wear special badges indicating their inferior status and could be executed for having sexual relations with German women.

NEGRO CONVENTION MOVEMENT. The Negro Conventions were the first effort of the African-American community to come together to exchange ideas on political and social action. The first convention was convened in 1830 by Hezekiah Grace, a free black from Baltimore, in response to race riots in Cincinnati. Its purpose was both to give an organized voice to African-American abolitionists and to struggle against discrimination and the denial of basic political rights in the North. At the time, most African-Americans could not vote and faced strong racial discrimination. The early meetings were marked by an optimism that self-help and material progress would lead to the elimination of barriers to full citizenship. With time, the conventions began to exclude white supporters and become more militant. In the 1850s, there was a split between a faction that clung to the hope of social and political equality within the United States and another which was convinced that their rights would only be fully recognized in a black-run state. Though a few leading figures like **Alexander Crummell** did migrate to **Liberia**, most of the African-American leadership clung to the hope that they could receive equality in the United States.

NEW LAWS. These were laws proclaimed by Charles V of Spain in 1542 prohibiting Indian slavery in the Americas. *See also* HISPANIC AMERICA.

NEWTON, JOHN (1725-1807). John Newton was the captain of a slave ship who underwent a religious conversion, renounced the trade, and became an abolitionist. He is best known as the author of the hymn "Amazing Grace."After working in the Mediterranean trade, he served briefly in the Royal Navy. He first went to **West Africa** as a first mate on a slaver sailing to **Sierra Leone**. He then received his own command and sailed three times to Africa between 1750 and 1755. His account of these years, *Journal of a Slave Trader* (1788), was one of the most vivid descriptions of the way the slave trade corrupted both its African and European participants. After leaving the **slave trade**, Newton spent nine years as a customs officer before becoming ordained as a clergyman. As the abolition movement developed, Newton became particularly important to **Thomas Clarkson** and **William Wilberforce** because of his personal experience of the trade. His testimony before parliamentary committees was important in persuading many members of Parliament to oppose the trade. *See also* ATLANTIC SLAVE TRADE.

NIEBOER, HERMANUS J. (1873-?). A Dutch ethnographer, Nieboer was the author of *Slavery as an Industrial System* (1910), one of the few truly cross-cultural studies of slavery. For his research, he surveyed much of the ethnographic data available at his time. He defined the slave as property and as someone whose labor was coerced. An evolutionist, he noticed several patterns. First, slavery existed only where there was a surplus and slavery could give a return. Slavery is extremely rare in hunting and gathering societies. It is found largely in agricultural societies. For Nieboer the mode of subsistence was very important in making slavery possible. Second, he noticed that slavery was most important where there was a free land frontier and land was freely available. In such a society, labor was in short supply and control of labor was clearly a more important source of wealth and power than land. Where land was rare, landowners could get labor without coercion, but where land was freely available, coercion was necessary. Nieboer has influenced many subsequent students of slavery.

NOBREGA, MANUEL DA (1517-1570). A Portuguese Jesuit missionary, Manuel da Nobrega tried to convert the **Amerindians** of Brazil to Christianity and to protect them from enslavement. Soon after he arrived in Brazil in 1549, he petitioned the governor to free Amerindians unjustly enslaved. He asked clergy to deny confession to settlers guilty of unjust enslavement and advocated a system under which Amerindians would be gathered in villages, where they would be converted and work under Jesuit supervision. He was opposed to the Spanish system by which indigenous people were assigned to settlers as workers. In 1567, he published *Caso de Consciência* which attacked the exploitation and enslavement of native peoples. This book led to Portuguese legislation protecting indigenous peoples. Nobrega's efforts did not extend to Africans. In fact, he acquired African slaves to work on Jesuit lands in Brazil. *See also* BRAZILIAN SLAVERY; CATHOLIC CHURCH.

NORRIS, ROBERT (?- 1791). Robert Norris was an important defender of the **slave trade**. A merchant, he traded with **West Africa** from the 1750s to the 1780s. When the slave trade came under attack, Norris wrote *Short Account of the African Slave Trade Collected from Local Knowledge, from Evidence at the Bar of Both Houses of Parliament, and from tracts written on the Subject* (1787). He also represented the slave traders before parliamentary committees investigating the trade. He had visited Dahomey in 1772 and described Dahomey as such a brutal place that enslavement provided a more humane existence for its subjects. He also argued that the West Africa trade contributed to British security by training skilled sailors who were useful to the Royal Navy in time of war.

NORTHWEST ORDNANCE. In 1787, Congress passed the Northwest Ordnance to organize government in the territories ceded to the United States by Great Britain in the Treaty of Paris (1783), which ended the **American Revolution**. Article VI prohibited slavery in the territories except in cases of criminal punishment. When the adoption of the United States **Constitution** that same year voided all previous acts, the ordnance was reenacted. Of the states formed from the Northwest Territory, only Illinois and Indiana had serious debates about whether to allow slavery. Slavery in those states was eventually extinguished by court cases and legislation. The Indiana Constitution of 1816 freed slaves who were living there. In Illinois, slavery was not definitively abolished until 1848. Ohio, Michigan, Wisconsin, and Minnesota all entered the Union as free states. The Northwest Ordnance also contained a clause providing for the return of fugitive slaves, which was to be contested in later years. *See also* COLES, EDWARD; FUGITIVE SLAVE LAWS.

NOTT, JOSIAH CLARK (1804-1873). Josiah Nott was an influential doctor and racial theorist whose ideas provided much of the scientific justification for racial segregation in the United States. Born in South

Carolina, he received his medical degree from the University of Pennsylvania in 1827. In 1836, he settled in Mobile, Alabama, where his practice included running an infirmary for slaves. He wrote about the greater resistance of people of African descent to tropical diseases like yellow fever and their weaker resistance to smallpox, typhoid, and cholera. He is, however, best known for his writings defending slavery and arguing for the racial inferiority of people of African and Amerindian descent. He argued for polygenesis, the now discredited theory that the racial groups evolved separately and were separate species. He expounded his racial theories in a series of books, of which the best known was *Types of Mankind* (1854), written with George Gliddon. His ideas were very influential in the South.

-O-

OBERLIN-WELLINGTON RESCUE (1858). In 1858, a former slave named John Price was arrested under the **Fugitive Slave Law** near his home at Oberlin, Ohio. When a crowd of African-Americans and abolitionists freed him and sent him to Canada, the federal government indicted 37 of the rescuers. The subsequent trials drew national attention and inspired many demonstrations. When a county grand jury indicted the federal marshal and others for kidnapping Price, both sides reached an agreement to drop all charges.

OGÉ, JACQUES VINCENT (c. 1750-1790). Vincent Ogé was one of the leaders of an abortive revolt by the **people of color** (mulattoes), which was a precursor of the **Haitian Revolution**. The son of a white merchant, Ogé had been educated in France, and on his father's death, took over the family business. By 1789, when the National Assembly convened in France, the people of color formed an important group in Haiti that included many wealthy property owners. When the assembly voted to extend citizenship to all men in the colonies who owned property and paid taxes, it left application of this act to the colonial assemblies. The all-white assembly in **Saint-Domingue** refused to extend citizenship to people of color. Ogé went to France to campaign for the rights of people of color, and when not successful, went to Great Britain and bought arms. On his return home in 1790, he and **Jean-Baptiste Chavanne**, a wealthy mulatto landowner, led an armed band, who seized a town in northern Haiti. When their rebellion failed, they were executed along with many of their followers. In 1791, a massive slave insurrection broke out. This was the beginning of the Haitian Revolution. Ogé was not opposed to slavery and did not try to recruit slaves to his movement, but it contributed to unrest and helped bring on the revolution.

OGLETHORPE, JAMES (1696-1785). James Oglethorpe was a British parliamentarian and humanitarian who founded the colony of Georgia. First elected to the House of Commons in 1722, he attacked impressment and was interested in conditions in British prisons, particularly, debtors' prisons. Oglethorpe proposed Georgia as a colony to which poor English men and women could be sent in order to start their lives anew. In 1733, he accompanied the first settlers to Georgia. Though he owned stock in a major British slaving company, the **Royal African Company**, he opposed slavery because he feared its effect on the white settlers. Though an effective leader, he was seen by many colonists as despotic, particularly because of his opposition to slavery. He was forced to return to England in 1743 to defend his conduct of military operations and never returned. In 1750, the colony's trustees voted to permit slavery. A **plantation** sector quickly developed around Savannah and Georgia eventually became a major slave-using state. In his later years, Oglethorpe was a supporter of **Granville Sharp** and the abolitionist movement.

OSU. Among the **Igbo** of Nigeria, the *osu* were people or the descendants of people who were given to shrines to serve those shrines as slaves. In more recent times, they have had no obligations to the shrine, but remain a separate status group. *See also* TEMPLE SLAVERY.

OTTOMAN SLAVERY. Turks first entered the Arab world primarily as slave soldiers, but from the 13th century they entered as conquerors. The Ottoman empire eventually defeated the Byzantine empire and conquered most of the Arab world. Slaves came into the Ottoman empire either as prisoners of war or were purchased in slave markets. Until the expansion of Tsarist Russia closed off markets there in the 18th century, most were **Slavs**. The most high-priced slaves were Circassian and Georgian women from the Caucasus, who were sought as **concubines**. Those who became the mothers or favorites of Sultans or high officials could exercise great power. There were also black slaves from Ethiopia and elsewhere in Africa. Most of them were used as domestic labor, though many also worked in industry, particularly in the textile industry. Many were involved in public works, and in the early years of the empire, some were agricultural workers, particularly in frontier areas or areas with low population. Slaves never seem to have numbered more than 5 percent of the population because of the high rate of **manumission**.

The Ottoman Empire is best known, however, for its **elite slaves**. During the 14th and 15th centuries, when the empire was short of skilled officials, it used a form of levy called *devshirme,* which took boys from Christian areas of the Balkans. The boys were converted to **Islam** and became *kul,* privileged slaves. Some were raised by high-ranking officials, often themselves of slave origin. The official would train boys in his household and the ablest would move into government service and advance according to their abilities. Others entered the **Janissaries**, the elite military force. The *devshirme* system declined in the 17th century, as free Muslims entered government service and ended in the 18th century. Many *kul* slaves became wealthy and powerful.

The slave market in Istanbul was closed in 1846, and then the trade in black slaves was abolished in 1857. During the last years of the empire the trade was abolished throughout the empire. With the abolition of the empire and nationalist reforms of Kemal Ataturk during the 1920s, slavery essentially was ended. *See also* EMANCIPATION, MIDDLE EAST.

OVERSEERS. Any large enterprise using slave labor depended on men who could direct and control the labor of the slavers. In ancient Rome, the management of slave labor was much discussed. In the modern industrial plantation, many of these people were **drivers**, experienced slaves who organized the labor of the fellow slaves and supervised their work. Generally, however, in any plantation with over 30 slaves, there was a white overseer. The planter generally gave the overseer careful instructions about the organization of work and the treatment of the slaves. Overseers were usually warned about excessively harsh discipline, but they were generally judged by the size of the crop they brought in and thus had a tendency to drive slaves hard. Unlike the drivers, who worked under their control, the overseer never actually worked himself, but was constantly present directing the work. The overseer generally dispensed discipline.

The overseer was often a difficult employee. On most plantations, there was tension between planter and overseer. They were frequently fired, either for excessively harsh treatment of slaves or for failing to meet quotas. Few remained for long periods with the same planter. Some planters chose to hire free blacks or to rely on a head driver for control of work.

OYO. A slave-trading kingdom in West Africa known for its cavalry and its high slave exports. *See also* YORUBA.

-P-

PACIFIC ISLANDS SLAVERY. Slavery was not highly developed on the Pacific islands. It did not exist at all in Melanesia, though "big men" often had a network of clients and dependents, who provided labor and services. Where slavery existed, it originated in war. Among the Maori of New Zealand, prisoners of war could be killed, but some were spared. They did menial tasks like cooking, fetching water and paddling canoes, but they could marry and generally were well fed. Powerful chiefs always had numerous slaves. In Tahiti and on the Easter Islands, captured enemies were also often made into slaves. In Hawaii, there was an outcast population called *kauwa*. Though this word is often translated as slave, the *kauwa* did not serve anyone. They lived apart and took care of their own sustenance. They could be asked to provide human sacrifices. Micronesian societies were frequently very hierarchical. The lowest groups were often seen as impure, but cannot be seen as slaves.

After contact with Europeans began, slaves were increasingly put to work in productive ways. The Maori put their slaves to work logging, growing food crops and raising pigs. They also sent slave women off to work for whaling ships as prostitutes. During the 19th century, Pacific island societies found themselves caught up in the demands of tropical **capitalism** for labor. Particularly important were guano islands of Peru and **sugar plantations** in Australia and Fiji. **"Blackbirding"**, a form of slave-raiding existed for a while, but it proved an inefficient way of recruiting labor. With time labor was recruited by contract within the islands for plantation labor in the Pacific and in Australia.

PADDY-ROLLERS. *See* SLAVE PATROL.

PAINE, THOMAS (1737-1809). Tom Paine was a radical journalist and pamphleteer, who played a role in both the American and **French Revolutions**. Born in England, he arrived in Philadelphia a few months before the outbreak of the **American Revolution** and became the editor of the *Pennsylvania Magazine*. He believed in the cause of the rebels and articulated their goals in clear direct prose. One of his first articles was entitled "African Slavery in America." He argued for the total abolition of slavery and for grants of land to freed slaves that would make it possible for them to support themselves. He did not believe that the colonists could be free while denying freedom to others. Paine was clerk of the Pennsylvania Assembly when it passed the world's first abolition law. After the War, he returned to Great Britain, where he wrote *The Rights of Man* (1791–92) and continued to call for abolition of slavery. He was a supporter of the French Revolution and served in the Convention. In 1802, he returned to the United States, but his ideas were by then seen as too radical. Though a friend of **Thomas Jefferson**, he had little influence in his last years.

PALMARES. Palmares was the most important **Maroon** community or **quilombo** in the history of Brazil. Founded about 1605 by slaves fleeing the **sugar plantations** of Pernambuco, it grew after 1630 when slaves were able to take advantage of the instability caused by the Dutch conquest of northern Brazil. The population was probably between 10,000 and 20,000 people. They lived in small settlements, each surrounded by strong palisades. Made up largely of men, they regularly raided plantations to get women, who were less likely to run away. Most of the *palmaristas* were originally from the Angola region of central Africa. It is believed that its political and military organization was similar to that of a warrior initiation society found among the Imbangala of central Angola. The king seems to have been chosen by the leaders of the separate settlements. Religion and cultural life were also very African. The best known ruler was known as Ganga Zumbi

The lands around each settlement were carefully cultivated and often irrigated. They produced a surplus, which was used in a clandestine trade with Brazilian communities that brought in arms and ammunition. Palmares regularly repulsed Portuguese attacks. Finally in 1678, Ganga Zumbi signed a treaty with the Portuguese in which he promised to be loyal to the Portuguese crown and return any fugitive slaves. The treaty divided the *palmaristas*, and eventually, Ganga Zumbi was deposed by his nephew, Zumbi, who opposed the settlement with the Portuguese. In 1694, the Portuguese brought in *bandeirantes*, hardened frontiersmen from São Paulo who captured Palmares. Zumbi escaped, but was caught and killed the following year. Over 500 *palmaristas* were captured and returned to slavery. *See also* BRAZILIAN SLAVERY.

PARDO. The Spanish had different terms to describe different shades of racial mixture. The *pardos* were mulattoes. *See also* HISPANIC AMERICA; PEOPLE OF COLOR.

PATTERSON, ORLANDO (1940–). Orlando Patterson is a sociologist and historian who has written a number of major studies of slavery. Born in Jamaica, he graduated from the University of the West Indies and did his Ph.D. at the London School of Economics. In 1976, he published a study of Jamaican slavery, *Sociology of Slavery*. He is best known, however, for his *Slavery and Social Death* (1982). This is the first book since H. J. Nieboer's *Slavery as an Industrial System* (1910) to look at slavery in a broad cross-cultural perspective. In a wide-ranging analysis rooted in comparison between all regions of the world, he argued that the slave originated as a captive who was spared instead of being killed. Slavery was thus a form of "social death." He thus stresses the absence of kinship ties more than the property relationship. "Slavery," he argued, "is the violent domination of natally alienated and generally dishonored persons." If the slave master became honorable through his control of slaves, the slave was by definition without **honor**.

In 1991, Patterson came out with *Freedom in the Making of Western Culture*. While his earlier work stressed the mutual dependence of slave and master, *Freedom* stressed the idea that freedom is defined and given value by the existence of slavery. He is also the author of *Rituals of Blood: Redefining the Color Line in Modern America* (1998).

PAWNSHIP. Pawnship was a form of **debt slavery** common in Africa. Though there were different variants in different parts of Africa, it usually involved children or slaves of the debtor who worked for the creditor until the original debt was repaid. Where the pawn was a girl, as it usually was, the debt might be cancelled if she married into the creditor's family. The pawn was not considered a slave. She kept her own name and remained a member of the family into which she had been born, but if the debt was not repaid, she sometimes became a slave. Pawns were probably a significant source of slaves for the **Atlantic slave trade**. Once a pawn was moved out of the community in which she had been pawned, she did not have any protection.

PECULIUM. In ancient Rome, the *peculium* was property that the slave controlled with his master's permission. It was often a sum of money given to a slave to enable him to develop a business. Technically, the *peculium,* like all of the slave's belongings, was property of the master.

It could consist of some cattle in the countryside, a shop in the city or simply some money that could be used for trading or it could be money the slave earned when not serving his master. A slave could even own another slave. Some slaves used the *peculium* to build up businesses or to buy their own freedom. When freed, the slave usually kept his *peculium* The *peculium* was important because it encouraged hard work and stimulated the slave to work within the system to better himself. It thereby contributed to social stability. *See also* ANCIENT ROMAN SLAVERY.

PENNINGTON, JAMES (1809-1870). James Pennington was born in slavery on the eastern shore of Maryland, but escaped to Pennsylvania in 1830 and eventually became a minister, teacher, and writer. As a slave, he was a stone-mason and blacksmith. After escaping, he went to school and became a teacher in black schools in New York and Connecticut. He then studied theology and became pastor. In 1841, he became President of the Union Missionary Society, which advocated a boycott of products produced by slave labor. In the same year, Pennington published *A Textbook of the Origin and History of Colored People*, which attacked racist ideas on the history and abilities of people of African descent. In 1849, he published his autobiography, *The Fugitive Blacksmith*. He also lectured in the United States and Europe. In 1843, he represented Connecticut at the World Anti-Slavery Convention. When the **Fugitive Slave Law** was passed in 1850, he fled abroad until supporters arranged his **manumission**. After his return to the United States in 1851, Pennington was active in efforts to obstruct enforcement of the Fugitive Slave Law and in the fight against racial discrimination in New York. After the American **Civil War**, he served as pastor of a Presbyterian Church in Jacksonville, Florida until his death.

PEONAGE. Where slaves were freed, the former slave masters sought ways to force the former slaves to continue to work at low wages. Peonage was one way that they did this. It involved using debt to force people to work. In the United States, it was banned in 1867 by the Anti-Peonage Act, but after the end of **Reconstruction**, southern states brought in legislation on debt and vagrancy which deprived many workers in agriculture and rural industries of their freedom. In a major case in 1911, the Supreme Court threw out a peonage statue, but cases of peonage have recurred intermittently throughout the 20th century. Peonage was also common in Latin America, where it originated as a way of circumventing the Spanish Crown's protection of native people.

Employers would hire black or Indians and loan them money. When they could not pay these debts, the peons were then forced to continue working at disadvantageous terms. Peonage usually co-exists with illiteracy and rural poverty. *See also* BONDED LABOR; DEBT SLAVERY.

PEOPLE OF COLOR. The term "people of color" was used in the West Indies for mulattos. In most of the slave societies of the Americas, sexual relations between male slave-owners and female slaves were common. The offspring were often, but not always freed. There were also a significant number of marriages between white men and black women, particularly in the French Caribbean, Hispanic America and Brazil. In the West Indies and Latin America, the people of color were often seen as a separate racial group. In parts of Hispanic America, they were called *pardos*. Some of them became land-owners and came to own slaves. Many of them were also artisans or merchants. They also often faced racial discrimination and had to fight for the respect of the White community. In French **Saint-Domingue**, the struggle of the people of color, many of them quite wealthy, to be recognized as citizens was the first stage of the revolution that destroyed slavery there. In Hispanic America, many *pardos* were quite poor and often allied to slaves. *See also* SEXUAL EXPLOITATION; HAITIAN REVOLUTION.

PERSIA. See ANCIENT MIDDLE EASTERN SLAVERY.

PERSONAL LIBERTY LAWS. A personal liberty law was first passed in Pennsylvania in 1788 to protect both free blacks and former slaves from capture by slave-catchers. Eventually, such laws were passed in 14 northern states. Generally they made a distinction between free blacks and runaway slaves, but in setting up procedures for slave-owners to reclaim their human property, they protected the rights of the slave being claimed. Some of them also imposed long prison terms for kidnapping. The enforcement of these laws made it more and more difficult for southerners to reclaim fugitive slaves. When the Supreme Court in **Prigg v. Pennsylvania** (1842) held that state officials could not interfere with efforts to reclaim runaway slaves, many northern states responded with laws forbidding state officials to cooperate with efforts to reclaim fugitive slaves. This meant that slaves could not be held in local prisons while their cases were being adjudicated.

This second wave of personal liberty laws led Southerners to seek passage of the **Fugitive Slave Act** (1850). This led to a third set of personal liberty laws which limited the cooperation of state officials, appointed attorneys to defend the runaways, mandated jury trials, set up cumbersome procedures, and insisted that the burden of proof was on the claimant. Slave owners and federal marshals were often prosecuted for attempting to seize fugitives. In 1859, the Supreme Court in **Ableman v. Booth** held that the personal liberty laws were unconstitutional. The legislatures of Wisconsin and Ohio responded by announcing their intention to defy the decision, but before anything further happened, the nation was engaged in the **Civil War**.

PHILLIPS, ULRICH BONNELL (1877-1934). Ulrich Phillips was the most prolific and the most influential historian of slavery in the United States during the first half of the 20th century. Born in Georgia, he studied at Columbia University. He wrote nine books, of which the best known were *American Negro Slavery* (1918) and *Life and Labor in the Old South* (1929). Based on very solid research in primary sources, the best done up to that point, his books were very well written, but his analysis was essentially racist. He saw slavery as a benign paternalistic institution that protected, took care of, and "civilized" the slaves. He was convinced that slavery was unprofitable but necessary. His books were marked by a sympathy for the masters and a condescension toward the slaves. They represented the values of a time when Americans were interesting in healing the wounds of the **Civil War** and restoring white unity and were willing to ignore the aspirations and experience of African-Americans to do this. His works were strongly attacked by African-American historians like Carter Woodson and **W. E. B. Du Bois**, but were widely accepted by white scholars until **Kenneth Stampp**'s *The Peculiar Institution* (1956). Today, his research is respected by many but his interpretations are widely rejected.

PHILLIPS, WENDELL (1811-1884). An outstanding orator, Wendell Phillips first attracted attention with a speech in 1837 attacking the murder of abolitionist **Elijah Lovejoy** in that same year. Like **William Lloyd Garrison**, he advocated the total emancipation of slaves and the repeal of the federal union. He saw the federal government as a protector of slavery, but he differed from the pacifist Garrison in his defense of the use of violence by slaves trying to obtain their freedom. When the **Civil War** began, Phillips changed from a critic of the federal union to a supporter. During the war, he campaigned for abolition of slavery and for the use of black troops. When Lincoln agreed to use black troops,

Phillips helped to recruit them. He also campaigned for the protection of those freed and the extension of citizenship and civil rights to them. After the war, he became active on labor issues and in urban reform.

PIAR, MANUEL (1782-1817). During the wars for independence that broke out in Hispanic America in 1810, Manuel Piar was at first one of **Simón Bolívar**'s generals and later, a rival. Venezuela was a colony that was only about 10 per cent slave, but about 50 per cent of the population was made up of *pardos* (mulattos) and free blacks, many of them locked into dependent economic relations with the great Creole landowners. Bolívar came from a Creole family. Piar was a *pardo*, proud, ambitious and very race conscious. Though Bolívar eventually freed his own slaves and, after 1816, offered freedom to all who joined the struggle, the mass of the slaves and *pardos* were more interested in freedom than in independence from Spain. As their leader, Piar was committed to their priorities and not always willing to follow Bolívar. In 1816, when the war was not going well for him, Bolívar was forced to join up with Piar. Not long afterwards, when unhappy with decisions made by Bolívar, Piar resigned his command in order to return to his eastern Venezuelan base and lead the struggle for emancipation and equality. Bolívar had him arrested and executed by a firing squad. *See also* EMANCIPATION, HISPANIC AMERICA.

PIPA TSAI. Pipa tsai were slave girls in China who played an instrument called the *pipa*. Like the *mui tsai*, they were often sold by their families because of extreme poverty. They were usually owned by female entrepreneurs and often also worked as high class prostitutes. *See also* CHINESE SLAVERY.

PLANTATION. Plantations are large estates, where the labor is done by agricultural workers who live on the estate. Though workers often have private plots, plantations are usually worked by gang labor or by a highly organized task system. They often involve production for market and specialize in crops, where coercion can produce a higher profit. Much of the labor is routine, unskilled and harsh. Over a period of thousands of years, plantations have been the site of the most systematic development of slavery. Generally, the slave plantation was profitable not because slave labor was more efficient, but because more labor could be extracted from the slave.

Most Roman slaves worked on the large **latifundia**, which became common from the second century BCE, when Roman conquest brought back large numbers of slaves. With many farms empty because ordinary farmers had gone off to war, land was available for purchase and slaves could be profitably exploited growing wine, olive oil, grain and wool. In early years, they were often housed in barracks called *ergastula*. Plantations were also found in China, India and in many parts of Asia, especially after periods when conquest made large numbers of slaves available. In most slave systems, barracks-type accommodations gave way to villages of small huts where the slaves could enjoy family life.

The modern capitalist plantation originated with the Crusades and the beginning of **sugar** cultivation by entrepreneurs from Venice and Genoa on the island of Cyprus. Fuelled by an increased European taste for sweets, the plantation system spread first to the western Mediterranean. Then, Genoan entrepreneurs brought Italian technology and methods of estate management to the Atlantic islands discovered in the 14th and 15th centuries by Portuguese and Spanish navigators. Here, they found fertile volcanic islands either lacking people or rapidly decimated by European diseases and slave-raiding. The Portuguese found a regular source of slaves on the African mainland. By the end of the 15th century, Madeira was the world's largest producer of sugar in the world. By 1520 **São Tomé** had passed it. The Canaries were also major producers. The Portuguese then took the plantation system to **Brazil**, from whence the Dutch introduced it the West Indies in the 17th century. As better equipment was devised for pressing and boiling the sugar, plantations increasingly required a substantial capital investment. The Dutch provided capital, technology, methods of estate organization, and slaves to planters from Great Britain, France and Scandinavia.Such was the demand in Europe for sugar that a majority of the slaves taken across the Atlantic were destined for sugar plantations.

The rapid growth in the European economy during the 17th and 18th centuries created markets for other products. **Tobacco** was grown on small slave-worked plantations around the Chesapeake Bay, rice and indigo in the South Carolina lowlands, and after the invention of the cotton gin in 1793, **cotton** plantations spread out over the southern United States. By 1860, two of every three slaves in the United States lived and worked on cotton plantations. Elsewhere, slave plantations produced coffee in Brazil, cloves on **Zanzibar**, copra on the East African coast, and grain in the West African savannah. In many areas, plantation systems survived the end of slavery or were developed where industrial crops required a large capital investment and an efficient organization of labor. *See also* BRAZILIAN SLAVERY; CARIBBEAN SLAVERY; DUTCH SLAVE TRADE.

PONTY, WILLIAM (1866-1915). William Merlaud-Ponty was the most important liberator of slaves in French West Africa. He originally went out to Africa as the civilian secretary of General Louis Archinard, who conquered much of the Western Soudan between 1888 and 1895. After serving briefly elsewhere, he was put in charge of Upper Senegal-Niger (Mali) in 1899 and moved quickly to end slave raiding and trading. By 1903, he insisted that the colonial state could no longer support slave owners, essentially adopting the formula first used in India in 1843 of depriving slave masters of the coercive power of the state.

By the end of 1903, Governor-General Ernest Roume endorsed this approach when a new law code was issued. In 1905, the French issued a new law which prohibited any transaction in persons: sale, gift, exchange, or bequeathal. This law did not actually abolish slavery, but slaves were leaving their masters. In the spring of 1906, faced with massive resistance in the major market town of **Banamba**, Ponty told the local administrator to let the slaves leave. When the exodus spread to other places and Ponty realized that it was peaceful, he encouraged local administrators to facilitate slave departures. In 1908, he became Governor-General. By this time, he realized that most slaves either went home and became productive peasants or joined the labor force. He thus continued to urge local administrators to tolerate the process. All in all, as many as a million slaves in French West Africa left their masters. *See also* EMANCIPATION, AFRICA; EMANCIPATION, INDIA.

PORT ROYAL. One of the sea islands of Georgia, Port Royal was the site of an experiment in the transition from slave labor to free labor that Willie Lee Rose referred to as a "rehearsal for **Reconstruction**." When it was seized by Union troops late in 1861, most of the white families fled, leaving behind about 10,000 slaves. Most of these slaves wanted nothing to do with the **cotton** they had been forced to grow. Instead, they fed themselves by subsistence agriculture, hunting and fishing. Some of the missionaries who came in wanted to distribute land, but the federal government saw the **plantation** system as the source of the area's wealth and wanted to maintain it.

The first method introduced by the government maintained the gang labor and tight supervision of the plantation system, but used the profits to provide subsistence and education to the workers. When that did not work well, an entrepreneur named Edward Philbrick tried a system in which the slaves received small plots to cultivate their own food and received wages for work on the plantation. Many other plantations were auctioned off in 1863 and 1864 and sold to northern speculators. By 1865, Philbrick realized that his system had failed because of reluctance of the freed slaves to work the cotton fields. In January of that year, General William Tecumseh Sherman issued an order that all freedmen in a strip of coastal land from Charleston to Jacksonville had the right to a 40-acre plot of land. Later that year, the order was nullified when President Andrew Johnson decreed the return of all confiscated lands to their former owners. *See also* CIVIL WAR.

PRIGG v. PENNSYLVANIA. In 1793, after the United States Congress passed a **Fugitive Slave Law**, which required the return to their owners of all runaway slaves, many northern states responded to this law with **personal liberty laws**, which made the recovery of fugitives more difficult. A Pennsylvania statute of 1826 required a slave catcher to obtain a "certificate of removal" before he could take a slave back south. In 1842, a slave catcher named Edward Prigg requested a certificate for Margaret Morgan and several of her children, one of whom was born in Pennsylvania and therefore free under state law. Although Prigg was denied the certificate, he took Morgan and her children back to Maryland by force. He was then convicted of kidnapping. He appealed his sentence to the United States Supreme Court, which held that the 1793 law was constitutional and that slave owners and slave catchers had the right to recapture a fugitive privately and return that fugitive to the South. It therefore held that the Pennsylvania statute was unconstitutional. Justice Joseph Story, who wrote the majority opinion, added at the end that state officials were obligated to enforce the 1793 law, but that the federal government could not force them to do so. In a concurring opinion, Chief Justice **Roger Taney** took issue with this, arguing that many northern judges and other officials would continue to refuse to cooperate with southern slave catchers. This happened. The continuing difficulties Southerners faced in recovering their slaves led to the Fugitive Slave Law of 1850 and eventually to the **Civil War**.

PRINCE, MARY. Born a slave in Bermuda, Mary Prince was the daughter of a house servant and a carpenter. She was an infant when her master died. She was then separated from her parents when the slaves were sold off separately. Before she was an adult, Mary had been sold several times, and experienced some of the harshest forms of slavery. She worked, for a while, for example in a salt marsh, which caused sores all over her legs . Eventually, she was taken to the island of Antigua. There she became involved with the Moravian Church and learned to read and write. Her new master refused to let her purchase her freedom, but soon after, he took her to England, forcibly separating her from her husband. She eventually left her master and sought help from the Moravian Church. Her master was then asked again if he would let her buy her freedom so she could return to Antigua and live with her husband. He refused again. In 1831, her account of her experiences was published as *The History of Mary Prince, A West Indian Slave (Related by Herself)*. In it, she described her own life and the cruelties that she was submitted to. It was an important anti-slavery document.

PRIZE COURT. Courts established under international law that decided on the disposition of ships seized on the high seas. The most important one for the slave trade was the court in Freetown, **Sierra Leone**, to which the anti-slavery squadrons working on the 19th-century West African coast had to take the slave ships they seized. *See also* AFRICAN SQUADRON.

PROSTITUTION. See SEXUAL SLAVERY.

-Q-

QUACO WALKER CASES. Slavery was never important in Massachusetts and the colony early became a center of anti-slavery sentiment. In 1778, a proposed constitution for the newly independent state was voted down in part because it did not have an anti-slavery clause. The 1780 constitution, which was approved, provided that "All men are born free and equal, and have certain natural, essential and unalienable rights; among which may be reckoned the right of enjoying and defending their lives and liberty." The Quaco Walker cases tested the meaning of this.

Walker was originally a slave on the Caldwell farm. When Walker's master died and his master's wife married Nathaniel Jennison, Walker became Jennison's slave, or at least, so Jennison thought. When Walker returned to the Caldwell farm, Jennison arrived with a group of cronies, beat him, and returned him to slavery. The surviving Caldwell brothers hired a lawyer to pursue assault and battery charges on Walker's behalf. The jury awarded Walker £50 and proclaimed him a free man. Jennison then sued the Caldwell brothers on charges that they had seduced Walker from his service. This time, Jennison won and was awarded £25. In the third case, in 1783, the state accused Jennison of assault and battery and found Jennison guilty because he had no authority to beat a free man. Quaco Walker was thus a free man and slavery was ended in the Commonwealth of Massachusetts. *See also* EMANCIPATION, UNITED STATES.

QUAKERS. The Quakers, or as they are properly called, the Society of Friends, were the first religious community to oppose slavery. Founded in about 1650, they differed from other Protestants in their belief that the "inner light" of the Holy Spirit could enter any person who lived without sin and that it was oblivious to differences of gender, social class, race, and education. The Quakers were opposed to violence and rituals of deference and were committed to a simple hard-working life. It was their belief in the sanctity of all human beings and their resolute egalitarianism that made the sect a source of opposition to slavery. They were particularly important in Pennsylvania, which had been founded by a Quaker, William Penn, to provide a place where religious dissidents could live in peace.

Freed from discrimination in Pennsylvania, many Quakers became successful merchants and entrepreneurs. Though many criticized slavery, others traded with the West Indies and owned slaves. In 1688, four members petitioned the Germantown Meeting to take measures against slaveholding. While they had little success, the debate within the various Quaker meetings was intense throughout the 18th century, but seldom went beyond petition or censure. It did, however, put pressure on members to free their slaves, and finally, in 1774, the Philadelphia Yearly Meeting voted to exclude from leadership roles any persons owning slaves. Two years later, they excluded slave owners from membership.

In both Great Britain and the United States, many Quakers played a leadership role in the abolition movement. Anthony Benezet, **John Woolman**, and **Benjamin** and **Sarah Lay** were important early leaders. In North Carolina, many Quakers left the state because North Carolina law prohibited **manumission**. Quaker persuasion led Pennsylvania to become the first state to abolish slavery in 1780. In Britain, Quaker abolitionists often supported leaders from the Anglican Church like **William Wilberforce**, but they provided much of the funding and organizational skill for the abolition movement. In the United States, Quakers ran stores that sold the produce of free labor, were involved with the **Underground Railroad**, and after 1850, tried to prevent southern bounty hunters from kidnapping free blacks and runaway slaves. Quakers were often deeply divided, not over the question of slavery, but over the tactics to be used in fighting it. There was much support for **William Lloyd Garrison**, but others feared that his tactics would lead to violence, which Quakers abhorred. *See also* MOTT, LUCIA; WHITTIER, JOHN GREENLEAF.

QUILOMBO. The *quilombos* were **Maroon** communities in **Brazil**. Slaves often fled to mountainous or forested areas where they formed small communities. They were also called *mocambos*. The largest *quilombo*, **Palmares**, which resisted Portuguese and Dutch attacks for almost a century, had between 10,000 and 20,000 people. Most of the *quilombos* were much smaller and often maintained themselves for years in areas close to cities and **plantations**. They usually combined subsistence agriculture with highway robbery and raids on plantations. They needed not only food, but women since their communities were usually founded by male runaways. For the smaller groups, this kind of banditry often exposed them to attacks Portuguese security forces. Few of them lasted long, but those in more protected locations were often able to defend themselves for a while. After their experience with Palmares, which fell only in 1694, the Portuguese organized special bands of slave-hunting troops made up of frontiersmen called *bandeirantes*, that attacked *quilombos* and destroyed most of them. The problem persisted, however, until the end of slavery in 1888. Some *quilombos* integrated with indigenous communities, but most were made up of people only recently arrived from Africa. They preserved African languages, religion, music, political structures and child-rearing methods. Some of them became centers for the observance of African religions like *candomblé See also* BURACO DO TATU.

-R-

RACE AND SLAVERY. In most societies, slaves did not differ radically in physical shape and color from the free born. Rome enslaved people from the elsewhere in the Mediterranean and then later from north of the Alps. In the Arab world, slaves could be blonde-haired people from the Slavic world or black people from south of the Sahara. The word for slave in most European languages comes from the word **Slav**. Most medieval slaves came from eastern Europe. Both **Christianity** and **Islam** banned the sale of co-religionists. They both enslaved each other and felt free to enslave peoples seen as pagan or barbaric, that is to say, different from themselves. In the 15th century, when the Portuguese began bringing increasing numbers of slaves from **West Africa**, these people could not at first be interrogated and were seen as barbarians, thus enslaveable.

From the 15th century, Western enterprise opened for exploitation fertile areas that were underpopulated or became underpopulated as result of new diseases and harsh policies. In Hispanic America, with its large indigenous population, Catholic missionaries like **Bartolomé de las Casas** and **Antonio de Montesinos** were horrified by the treatment of native people and persuaded the Crown to ban their enslavement. Europeans were not willing to enslave each other and lacked the military capacity to massively enslave Arabs. It was only in Africa that they could find the labor they needed to open up commercial agriculture on the Atlantic islands, **Brazil**, and the West Indies.

The question they asked was how could Christians justify enslaving other human beings. They could argue that they were justified in enslaving Africans because they were not Christians, but that still left them with the problem of justifying the continued captivity of such people once they converted. They could only do so if they could argue that Africans were inferior, that they needed the discipline of a slave master if they were to be productive, that somehow, they were better off in slavery. If European racism originated in observation of difference, it developed as a justification of exploitation. Racist ideologies were spun out by slavers and slave-owners. Professional men from the U.S. South like **Josiah Nott** were among the first "scientific" racists in the 19th century. These racial thinkers tried to classify the world's populations according to visible characteristics like skin color, hair texture and eye shape. They then attributed differences in intellectual endowment and moral qualities to the groups they identified.

Most 20th century scientists question the science involved in that racist thought and, in fact, question the very idea of race. Skin color is only one of many characteristics that divide people, and certainly not the most important. The more traits a scientist uses, the harder it is to divide people into groups. Not only is it impossible to classify most people in neatly divided groups, but a mixing of peoples has taken place in all parts of the world. There is also no evidence to link visible physical characteristics with moral, temperamental or intellectual differences. Slavery provided few opportunities for slaves to develop their intellectual faculties. In spite of this, some slaves became successful entrepreneurs even under conditions of slavery and freed persons have often provided ample demonstration of their talents once removed from the limits of slavery. Nevertheless, once developed, racist ideologies provided a justification for racial discrimination, for systems of segregation and for colonial rule. In many modern societies, racial classifications are still used to separate people and to provide a basis for discrimination in employment, housing and access to education and jobs. They are part of slavery's enduring legacy. *See also* AFRICAN SLAVE TRADE.

RAMSAY, JAMES (1797-1884). James Ramsay was an apologist for slavery who advocated the reopening of the slave trade to the United States. Born and raised in Tennesee, Ramsay was doctor and a businessman. In numerous letters and newspaper articles, he argued that the market for labor in the South could only be met by the importation of African slaves. He also argued that slavery was humane and in the Southern climate, a natural policy. He insisted that southern slavery was benevolent and in the interests of both slaves and masters.

RAYNAL, GUILLAUME-T.-F. (1713-1796). Raynal was an **Enlighten ment** writer and the most influential abolitionist in 18th century France. Though a priest and a member of the Jesuits, he left the order to devote himself to writing. He was the editor and partial author of the six-volume *Philosophical and Political History of the Settlements and Trade of the Europeans in the East and West Indies* (1770). This included a lengthy discussion of slavery, which argued that slaves were overworked, harshly treated, poorly fed and scantily clothed. He called on slave owners to ameliorate the treatment of their slaves and on the rulers of Europe to abolish both slavery and the **slave trade**. He also urged them to provide better food, clothing, and a better gender balance so they could enjoy the pleasures of family life. He predicted that if the treatment of slaves were not improved, there would be a violent revolution. In 1780, the third edition of the book was banned because of its hostility to the **Catholic Church** and the French Monarchy. This only increased demand for it.

RECAPTIVES. When the British abolished the **slave trade** in 1807, they stationed a squadron of the Royal Navy in West African waters to enforce the new law. The slaves on board the slave ships were then taken to Freetown in **Sierra Leone**, where the British Admiralty Court was the only **prize court** in West Africa with the authority to approve confiscation of the slave ships and their cargoes. Though freed, they could not be returned to their places of origin or they risked being enslaved again. The slaves on board the ship were called recaptives or

liberated Africans. On their release in Freetown, they were often
entrusted to mission societies, which educated them and helped them to
find land or work. The recaptives became the largest component of a
Creole community centered in Freetown. Christian and usually literate,
they played a major role in the administration and government of all
British West African colonies. *See also* AFRICA SQUADRON.

RECONSTRUCTION. Reconstruction was the period after the American
Civil War, when Republicans in the Congress sought to establish
Republican hegemony in the South and in the process, reconstructed
the social order in the southern states. In some ways, Reconstruction
began with the flight of slaves across Union lines throughout the war
and the necessity of organizing these freed slaves to enable them to
support themselves and contribute to the Union cause. The **Emancipation Proclamation** of 1863 freed slaves in areas in revolt against the
Union, and at the end of the war, the **Thirteenth Amendment** abolished slavery. When **Abraham Lincoln** was assassinated at the end of
the war, his Vice-President, Andrew Johnson from Tennessee, gave an
amnesty to the defeated Southerners, restored confiscated lands and
moved to also restore local government. Southern legislatures immediately responded by passing **Black Codes** that controlled the activity of
freed people and often forced them to work for their former masters.
Parallel to this, the Ku Klux Klan was organized to terrorize and intimidate the freed people.
    When the newly elected Southern congressmen arrived to take their
seats, Southern delegations looked much like the ones that supported
secession in 1861. Congress voted not to seat them. They then passed
the **Civil Rights Act of 1866**, which made all African-Americans
citizens and guaranteed them equality before the law. Then, to prevent
the Supreme Court from nullifying the act they passed the **Fourteenth
Amendment** to add most of the provisions of the act to the **Constitution**. In 1867, they passed the Reconstruction Acts, which sent the army
back into the South to run elections. They also guaranteed the voting
rights of African-Americans and denied the franchise to the Confederate elite. The result was the appearance of so-called radical governments in the South, which were supported by African-American votes
and included African-Americans at all but the top levels of government.
White Southerners gradually regained control of the southern states,
and then, in 1876, the Reconstruction ended when Rutherford Hayes
agreed to withdraw the army from the remaining radical states in ex-

change for Southern support for his election to the Presidency.

Reconstruction involved many important progressive reforms. The **Freedmen's Bureau** helped freed slaves cope with the transition to freedom. Both black and white teachers set up schools all over the South. While the freed slaves did not receive the lands many of them hoped for, Reconstruction affirmed their freedom and prevented their former masters from regaining control over them. Radical legislatures set up the first free public schools in many southern states and abolished brutal punishments like flogging and branding. The former slaves could move freely and had won the right to control their own family life. Reconstruction was not, however, able to prevent the eventual return to power of the Confederates. For most of the freed people, the full promise of Reconstruction did not come until a century later, when new legislation confirmed their civil rights, and most important, their right to vote under the **Fifteenth Amendment**.

REDEMPTIONIST ORDERS. From Middle Ages to the 18th century, the Mediterranean was a battleground between Christian Europe and Muslim North Africa. Coastal areas were often raided and ships fought for ascendancy. The price of defeat or capture was enslavement. The Redemptionist Orders were Catholic orders, which collected money in Spain and southern France and sought to ransom Christian captives in North Africa. Members of these orders travelled to North Africa and sought to find Christian slaves, particularly members of families that had given money. If they could not pay the amount demanded, the monks offered themselves as hostages in exchange for these slaves. Some were killed, but many were well received and were successful in their mission. The Trinitarians claim to have freed 140,000 slaves since their foundation in 1198. The Mercedarians, founded in 1218, claim to have freed about 70,000. Some Mercedarians travelled with **Christopher Columbus**. They became involved in missionary work and on occasion, redeemed captives taken prisoners by Indians. Neither order became involved in the abolition movement or was concerned about Muslims held as slaves by Christians in Europe. *See also* BARBARY WARS; MEDIEVAL EUROPE.

ROUSSEAU, JEAN-JACQUES (1712-1778). Rousseau was a French philosopher who influenced abolitionist thought. Born in Geneva, the son of a clock-maker, Rousseau left home early and was largely self-educated. Both his personal life and his philosophy were a struggle against authority. His criticism of slavery was part of a broader rejection of different forms of authority. He began his most important work, *The Social Contract* (1762) with the words "Man is born free, but is everywhere in chains." Freedom was thus a natural right, which people were born with. In *The Social Contract* and his *Discourse on the Origin of Equality* (1755) he argued that since all political authority was based on voluntary contracts and the association of equals, a person could not voluntarily become a slave nor did any person have the right to hold another person in slavery. No person had the right alienate his or her freedom. Liberty, he argued in *Discourse*, is a gift children "receive from nature in virtue of being men." Rousseau's argument that all forms of domination were unjust made him an anathema to the rulers of absolutist France. He therefore lived an itinerant life and did most of his writing in various provincial retreats far from the salon life of Paris. *See also* ENLIGHTENMENT; NATURAL LAW.

ROYAL AFRICA COMPANY. During the 17th century, many European countries set up chartered companies with monopoly rights to some part of the nation's commerce. The Royal Africa Company was England's major entry in the slave trade. It was a joint stock company, which was given the exclusive right to trade with the West African coast and between Africa and the first **sugar** islands, **Barbados** and Jamaica. As such, it played a major role in making Great Britain the world's largest slave-trader. It also traded in gold, ivory, dye woods, and hides. The company built a number of trading stations in Africa, of which the largest was Cape Coast Castle on the **Gold Coast**. It also provided credit for planters getting started in the West Indies. The company's heavy capital costs made it difficult for it to compete with interlopers, ships that traded illegally within the company's zone. It also suffered losses during periods of conflict, sometimes paying stockholders out of new share issues. In 1698, an act of parliament ended the company's monopoly, but gave it the right to levy a 10 per cent tax on the interlopers. The Company continued operating until its charter expired in 1750. It carried over 100,000 Africans to the plantations of the West Indies. *See also* ATLANTIC SLAVE TRADE.

RUSSIAN SLAVERY. Throughout the Middle Ages, the most important source of slaves for both the Christian Mediterranean and the Muslim Middle East was Eastern Europe. **Viking** traders crossed the area that is now Russia via the Dnieper River and purchased slaves, furs, wax and honey, which they carried down to the Black Sea. This trade stimulated warfare and probably contributed to the development of states in this area. There was a major slave market at Kiev, which became the center of the largest state in the area. Another slave market at Novgorod provided slaves for the Baltic area. The conquest of Kievan Russia in the 13th century by the Mongols led to even more enslavement and the transport of Slavic slaves to Mongol centers in Asia. Slavic areas were also regularly raided by the Turks.

Slaves had by this time also become important in Eastern Europe. The emergence of landownership in the 12th century often involved the working of land by servile agricultural workers. **Debt slavery** also developed when people could not pay debts or fines levied for criminal acts. A new form of limited service contract slavery emerged with the rise of Muscovy in the 15th century. Poor men would contract their labor in exchange for loans. When these debts were not paid off, temporary slavery often became permanent. A form of **serfdom** developed in the late 16th century, when the Muscovite state restricted the rights of peasants to change landlords. The serf was thus tied to the land while the slave was owned by a person. The limited service slaves were often better off than the newly enserfed peasants because they did not pay taxes. The state thus sought ways to limit their numbers. In the late 17th century, the agricultural slaves were converted into serfs, and during the early 18th century, the same change was decreed for household slaves.

Slaves were better off than serfs in many other ways. As serfdom developed in Muscovite Russia, slaves were preferred as servants and dependents. Estate managers were often slaves and merchants often depended greatly on their slave retainers. Slaves also worked in government, often as aides to their masters and were most of the household servants. Russian slavery was also unusual in that slaves were not foreigners, but rather poor fellow Russians who were pressed into service. This was largely because with population low, labor was difficult to find. Wealth and power depended on the ability of the lord to find labor to work his fields. In the 1720s, Peter the Great abolished slavery, but at the same time, the modernization program he launched increased the need for labor. He required military or government service from the nobility, and in exchange, gave them greater control over their serfs. By the late 18th century, serfs could be sold or given away independent of the land to which they were supposedly attached. Serfs in Russia had thus become the same as slaves. By this time, serdom had become a form of social organization that was inhibiting economic growth. Serfdom was not abolished until 1861, when 22 million serfs were freed..*See also* EAST EUROPEAN SLAVE TRADE; SCANDINAVIAN SLAVERY; SLAVS.

-S-

SACO, JOSÉ ANTONIO (1797-1879). José Antonio Saco was a writer, editor, historian, and liberal political reformer. For over a half century, he was one of the most important Cuban abolitionists. After studies of philosophy, he taught at San Carlos Seminar in Havana. In 1828, he travelled to New York, where he edited a strongly anti-slavery periodical, *Mensagero Quincenal* (Quarterly Messenger). He was back in Cuba in 1832, but exiled two years later. Saco was three times elected as a Cuban representative to the Spanish Cortes, but never allowed to take his seat. He remained throughout his life a supporter of independence and an opponent of slavery. His major historical work was his two-volume *Historia de la esclavitud* (1875-1879). Much of his life was spent in exile. He died in Barcelona. *See* CUBAN SLAVERY.

SAHARA. The Sahara was the site of an important slave trade. The Sahara was a grassland, which began to dry out about 2500 BCE, leaving some populations isolated on oases. About the beginning of the common era, camels were introduced in North Africa. By the fourth century, there was a regular trade across the Sahara. Camels also facilitated the resettlement of the Sahara, as nomadic groups were able to move deeper and deeper into the desert. From the seventh century, Arab armies inspired by the new faith of **Islam** created a new empire in the Middle East and North Africa. The dynamism of the Arab economy stimulated demand for products of sub-Saharan Africa and its richness aroused the interests of African rulers. The Arabs were most interested in gold, but from the beginning slaves were an important item of trade. Within the Islamic world, the prohibition on Muslims enslaving other Muslims forced Arabs to seek slaves outside the Muslim world. The major sources were eastern Europe and sub-Saharan Africa. In some years, the number of slaves crossing the Sahara was as high as 10,000. They walked across and many died from the heat and from thirst. Women desired as **concubines** and servants were a majority of those traded, though men were sought both as soldiers and as servants.

The trans-Saharan trade also stimulated the growth of the Saharan economy. Nomads conquered the oases and brought in new slaves. Slaves worked the date palm groves in the oases. They **mined** for salt and copper, and they tended herds for the desert nomads. Nomads often had slaves in their camps and in villages scattered across the desert-side grasslands. In these grasslands, slaves produced grain and cloth, which desert-side people traded for salt and livestock. There were also large groups of freed slaves called *haratin* in the western Sahara and **bella** in the central Sahara. Desert society was hierarchical. No freed slave was every completely free. **Mortality** was high in the desert, which meant that slaveholdings were constantly being replenished. *See also* MIDDLE EASTERN SLAVERY.

SAID IBN SULTAN (1791-1856). Said was the sultan of Oman who was the principal creator of the **East African slave trade** of the 19th century. Inhabiting a poor desert area, the Omanis early turned to the sea, and by the 18th century, controlled much of the trade with East Africa, where **Zanzibar** island was their principal base. Said seized power in Oman in 1806, killing his cousin and rival. He early proved himself a shrewd diplomat, establishing ties with both the British and French and fending off hostile neighbors. He also saw the economic potential of Zanzibar and made it the key to his plans for Omani expansion. He encouraged Omanis to establish themselves on Zanzibar and the neighboring island of Pemba as clove producers. He owned 45 clove **plantations** himself.

Said also established a loose control over the coast from southern Somalia to northern Mozambique. In 1837, his last major rivals, the Mazruis of Mombasa submitted. He invited Indian financiers to establish themselves in the major cities of the coast as tax farmers. These financiers provided trade goods, for both Arab traders and their African rivals. As a result, caravans snaked into the far interior, bringing back ivory and slaves and establishing a Zanzibari presence in the interior. By 1840, Zanzibar had become so much wealthier than Muscat, the capital of Oman, that Said shifted his capital there. He also sought recognition of the major trading powers. By the time of his death in 1856, the United States, Great Britain and France had consulates there. Said was always particularly careful to maintain good relations with the British. *See also* TIPPU TIP.

SAINT-DOMINGUE. Saint Domingue was the French name for the island that **Christopher Columbus** had called Hispaniola. It was at first the major Spanish base in the Caribbean. The Spanish later called the capital Santo Domingo and that eventually became the name for the island. From the 17th century, it was divided between the French and Spanish. The French colony of Saint Domingue was in the late 18th century the largest single **sugar** producer in the world. Saint-Domingue was also the site of the largest ever revolt by slaves against slavery. After the victory of the former slave armies in 1803, **Jean-Jacques Dessalines** renamed the French part of the island Haiti. Part of the island remained Spanish and is today the Dominican Republic. *See also* CARIBBEAN SLAVERY; HAITIAN REVOLUTION.

SAINT PAUL (10 C.E.?-62 C.E.?). Saint Paul was the most important of Christ's apostles in shaping the theology of the early Christian church. He travelled indefatigably through Greece and Asia and corresponded with many of the early Christian churches. Thirteen letters attributed to him have become part of the New Testament. Paul often dealt with slavery, which is not surprising considering how important slavery was in the Roman empire and how attractive Christ's message was to slaves. Slavery figures in his letters in two very important ways. First, he stressed the equality of all in the eyes of God: "There is no longer Jew and Greek; there is no longer slave or free, there is no longer male and female; for all of you are one in Christ Jesus." (Galatians 3:28) He was saying here that Christianity transcends all social distinctions. At the same time, he repeatedly advised servants and slaves to be obedient to their masters: "servants, be obedient to them that are your masters according to the flesh, with fear and trembling, in singleness of your heart, as unto Christ." (Ephesians 6:5) The true reward for the faithful slave would come in the afterlife. Such passages were popular with pro-slavery preachers in the Americas. *See also* CATHOLIC CHURCH.

SAMBO. Sambo and Samba were common African names which remained important in North America. The name Sambo was often used to indicate the prototypical slave, who was lazy, easy-going, subservient, and musical. In his major study, *Slavery: A Problem in American Intellectual and Institutional Life* (1959), **Stanley Elkins** suggested that slavery contributed to the creation of a docile, malleable personality which he called Sambo. Elkins model of Sambo was widely criticized by other scholars. Many have suggested that Sambo was a role that slaves often assumed to deal with their masters.

SANDIFORD, RALPH (1693-1733). Born in **Liverpool**, England, Ralph Sandiford was an early abolitionist. He became a **Quaker** as a young man and migrated to America, eventually becoming a successful merchant in Philadelphia. Though wealthy enough to own slaves, he was convinced that trading in slaves and owning them was immoral. When the Pennsylvania Assembly reduced the duty on the import of slaves and the number of slave imports rose, he wrote a tract entitled *A brief examination of the Practice of the Times* (1729), which attacked Quakers involved with the trade. When he was expelled from the Philadelphia meeting, he published a revised version entitled *The Mystery of Iniquity; in a Brief Examination of the Practice of the Times* (1730). His efforts inspired other Quakers and led to some Quaker meetings calling for more stringent restrictions on the import of slaves.

SANDOVAL, ALONSO DE (1576-1652). A Jesuit missionary, Alonso de Sandoval ministered to the needs of African slaves in Hispanic America. From 1605, he boarded slave ships in the port of Cartagena. He baptized, administered last rites, and catechized slaves on the boats and in holding pens where they awaited sale. In 1627 he published *De instauranda Aethiopium salute,* which condemned the harshness of the trade, though it accepted the legitimacy of slavery. After correspondence with Portuguese missionaries in Angola, he accepted the idea that most of the slaves were justly enslaved, but he also argued that Africans had immortal souls. Sandoval was for a while rector of the Jesuit college in Cartagena, but he eventually lost favor. He continued his dockside mission until his death. *See also* CATHOLIC CHURCH.

SAN MARTÍN, JOSÉ DE (1778-1850). José San Martín was one of the most successful generals in **Hispanic America**'s struggle for independence from Spain. San Martín was born in Argentina, but served many years in the Spanish army. In 1812, he returned to Buenos Aires and enlisted in the army. San Martín's forces defeated the Spanish in 1813 and then crossed the Andes and in victorious campaign ended Spanish rule in Chile. From Chile, his Army of the Andes marched north to liberate Peru in 1820. San Martín was at first a reluctant supporter of slave emancipation, but in both Argentina, and Peru, he offered freedom to slaves who enlisted in his army. Argentina abolished the slave trade in 1812 and the following year, passed a **"free womb law."** Of the 5,000 soldiers in his Army of the Andes, 1500 were former slaves. In 1821, he was made the Protector of Peru with supreme military and civil authority. One of his first acts was to proclaim the freedom of all Peruvian slave children born after 28 July 1821. In 1822, San Martín resigned and went back to Europe. While the Constitution of 1823 proclaimed that no one could be born a slave in Peru, this clause was dropped from the 1826 Constitution and slavery was not finally abolished in Peru until 1854. *See also* BOLÍVAR, SIMÓN; EMANCIPATION, HISPANIC AMERICA.

SANTERIA. Santeria was an African religious cult in Cuba, which was similar to **vodun** in Cuba. It involved divination, music, spirit possession, and worship of African gods. *See also* SLAVE RELIGION.

SÃO TOMÉ. As Portuguese navigators moved out into the Atlantic and along the African coast, they discovered a series of islands. These islands became both bases for the **slave trade** with the African coast and centers of **sugar** production. As the slave-sugar complex was moved out of the Mediterranean, these Atlantic islands were the first places they were introduced. In the later 15th century, Madeira was the most important producer of sugar. São Tomé was discovered in 1471 and the neighboring island of Principe the following year. The climate was hot, the islands were well watered, and they were unpopulated. The only problem sugar planters had was acquiring labor, but they were soon bringing slaves in from nearby coastal areas of the Gulf of Guinea and from **Kongo**. The islands were very close to what is now Nigeria and Gabon and lay on the shipping route to the mouth of the Congo River. By 1520 São Tomé replaced Madeira as the world's leading sugar exporter. On Madeira and São Tomé, Italian capitalists and Portugese planters developed more better presses and more efficient ways of organizing **plantation** labor. São Tomé also became an entrepot for the slave trade from **Central Africa**. São Tomé traders became major factors in the politics of the Kongo , often intercepting messages between the Kings of Portugal and Kongo and undermining Portuguese policy when it did not serve their interests. By the middle of the 16th century, the technology and ways of organizing slave labor were taken to Brazil. *See also* AFRICAN SLAVE TRADE.

SCANDINAVIA. From the eighth to the 11th century, the **Vikings** had an impact on many parts of Europe as daring seamen, enterprising traders and feared raiders, who were the scourge of western Europe and the British isles. A major purpose of these raids was the taking of slaves and booty. Many of the slaves were sold, but most were brought back to Scandinavia, particularly from nearby areas like Ireland. Called **thralls**, they do not seem to have made up more than 10 per cent of the population, but they were an important source of labor on the larger estates. Most of Scandinavia was divided into small farms worked by free peasants.

Most thralls were farm laborers. Some males served as messengers, guards, and retainers of wealthy men. Females cooked, made cloth, and prepared fish and dairy foods. They could also be **concubines**. We know something of slave status from law codes that were written down in the 13th century and made many distinctions between slave and free. When wrongs were done to a thrall, for example, the thrall did not have the right to the compensation a free person would receive. The law codes also provided for relatively easy **manumission**, though freed slaves often remained dependents of their former masters. Slavery seems to have died out in the 13th and 14th century. Later law codes do not refer to it. The end of raiding was a factor, but even more important was probably population growth, which made rural labor available to richer landowners. It was no longer necessary to seek labor elsewhere. In the long-run, most thralls merged into the free rural population.

SCHOELCHER, VICTOR (1804-1893). Victor Schoelcher was the most important French abolitionist of the 19th century. Born the son of a Parisian merchant, Schoelcher inherited enough wealth to devote himself to travel and writing. In 1829 he made the first of several visits to the Americas. In 1840 he published the first of several books critical of slavery and race prejudice. When the revolution of 1848 took place, he entered the government as undersecretary of state for colonies. In this capacity he wrote the law that abolished slavery in all areas under French rule. It was proclaimed 27 April 1848. When Louis Napoléon seized power in 1852, Schoelcher went into exile, only to return in 1870 after the collapse of the second empire. A hero in the French West Indies, he was elected first as deputy from Martinique in 1871 and then, in 1875, as senator. In that capacity he defended the interests of former slaves and attacked the continued existence of slavery in Africa and Brazil. He played a major role in pressuring the French colonial regime in West Africa to take action against slavery.

SEA ISLANDS. Over a thousand islands stretch along the coast of South Carolina, Georgia and northern Florida. Though many are too small to be habitable, others are fertile. On them, slaves were used to cultivate rice, indigo and the highly-valued Sea Island **cotton**. Many of the slaves on the islands were brought from **Sierra Leone** and Guinea to cultivate rice, which they had grown at home. Because of the malarial nature of the climate, the white presence on the islands and along the coast was limited. This enabled African culture and languages to persist here more than in other parts of the United States. The languages spoken are known as Gullah and Geechee and are related to the languages of the Sierra Leone area. Most of the slaves were freed by Union troops under the command of William Tecumseh Sherman. Many northern abolitionists flocked to the area and developed programs to help slaves adapt to freedom. The best known was the **Port Royal** experiment.

SEASONING. One of the major problems in any **slave society** was getting slaves to adapt to their new environment. Seasoning was the process by which slave masters tried to get slaves to accept their subjection. The slaves had often been torn by violence from their native societies, marched long distances and sometimes subjected to brutal conditions on sea voyages. They were often in bad health and despaired of ever receiving humane treatment. A large part of seasoning was adapting physically to a new disease environment, a new climate, new foods, and a new work regime. The first problem was simply restoring their health. **Mortality** was usually high in the slave's first years in a new environment. In **Brazil**, for example, it was almost 50% during the first four years.

Escape was also a great problem during the seasoning process. In Africa, the newly enslaved were often forced to sleep in chains during their first years. In both Africa and America the newly enslaved were those most likely to run away. In all slave societies, the biggest problem was getting the slave to accept his or her subjection. In Africa, they were often given new **names** and sometimes were forced to undergo rituals in which they pledged not to run away. Often countrymen were used to help them forge new bonds within the slave community.

SELF-PURCHASE. In many slave societies, slaves were able to accumulate wealth and buy their freedom. This encouraged the more ambitious to work hard in order to free themselves. Often, this involved a series of payments. In ancient Rome, the slave was allowed to accumulate a **peculium** and could use that *peculium* to become free. In Cuba, there was a process called **coartación** by which a slave could ask the court to set a price for his or her liberty. In northern Nigeria, there was a similar procedure called *murgu*. In many of the United States, it became illegal for slaves to purchase their freedom. The freed slave often remained a client of his former master. In many societies, his social isolation limited the value of his freedom. The slave, after all, had no family. In parts of **West Africa**, the absence of kinship ties was such a constraint that some slaves chose to purchase slaves – or a male slave could take a second wife – rather than purchase their own freedom. *See also* MANUMISSION.

SEMINOLES. Seminole Indians originally inhabited Georgia and north Florida, but were gradually pushed south into the Everglades. Slaves fleeing white planters in Georgia and South Carolina often sought refuge among them and merged with slaves Seminole chiefs purchased from the Spaniards. These black communities established a tributary relationship with the Seminoles and became part of the Seminole nation. The former slaves were more familiar with agriculture and often became wealthier than the original Seminoles. They also served as advisors and interpreters, having firsthand knowledge of white society. The Seminoles fought two wars against the Americans. The first, during 1817 and 1818, resulted from raiding across the frontier and led to Spain selling Florida to the United States. The second Seminole war (1835-1842) resulted from American efforts to move the Seminole to what is now Oklahoma. It was one of the most bitter Indian wars fought by the Americans, largely because the black Seminole feared reenslavement and used the woods and swamps effectively to force the conquerors to pay a high price for their victories. The Americans were, however, determined to eliminate the slave refuge and eventually prevailed, though some Seminoles remained in the Everglades. Many of the Blacks were reenslaved, but others were given the right to move west with the Seminoles. *See also* AMERINDIAN SLAVERY; MAROONS.

SERFDOM. Many writers use the term serf only for the bound agricultural laborers of **medieval Europe**, but the term can be extended to farmers in other parts of the world who were tied to the land and subject to the authority of a lord. The difference between a serf and a slave lies in the nature of their subjection. The serf was attached to the land, but the slave's person was owned. The serf could not move, but had rights and lived within a community. The serf had family. The slave was kinless, an isolate who could be used as the master wished. The rights of serfs to their land were subject to clearly defined obligations to their lord.

The transition from slavery to serfdom or another form of tenancy often began when slaves were no longer being produced. With the growth of population, different forms of tenancy became more productive than slave labor as the slaves sought to expand their private plots. In Europe the transition took place gradually between the sixth and 11th centuries. The particular form that transition took was shaped by the decline of the urban and mercantile economies. Rural Europe, particularly northern Europe, gradually shifted to an economy dominated by largely self-sufficient manors. Three groups merged as tenancy became more attractive than gang labor and the distinction between slaves, tenants (*coloni*), and free peasants disappeared. The insecurity of medieval life also made the protection of a lord attractive.

The nature of the rights and obligations of serfs varied according to time and place. Sometimes the distinction between serf and slave was unclear. The Latin word for slave, *servus*, became the word for serf in the later Middle Ages as a new word, based on the root *slav*, took its place. In Russia, slavery was replaced by serfdom, but the status of slaves was so sharply reduced in the 18th century that many were sold or given away, and thus, were treated as if they were slaves. *See also* RUSSIAN SLAVERY.

SEWALL, SAMUEL (1652-1730). Samuel Sewall was a diarist, a judge, a merchant, and early abolitionist. Sewall was one of the judges in the Salem witch trials, a role which he later regretted. He was also a commissioner of the Society for the Propagation of the Gospel in Foreign Parts, which sought to convert both Native Americans and African slaves. In 1700, he published a pamphlet entitled *The Selling of Joseph*, in which he challenged the biblical sanction for the enslavement of Africans. Sewall was unhappy about the increasing number of slaves in Massachusetts and the participation of Puritans in the slave trade. His attitude was influenced by the frequency of slave flight and of petitions by slaves for their freedom. He remained a spokesman for equality and against slavery. Sewall also kept a detailed diary, which has given historians a vivid picture of Puritan society.

SEXUAL EXPLOITATION. In most slave systems, a slave has no rights. He or she is a thing, to be used as the master wishes. Female slaves, and in some cases, young male slaves, had no choice but to submit to their master's sexual desires. This was true, among other areas, in ancient Rome, ancient Greece, and China. In most **slave societies**, a master could have sexual relations with his slave, assign her to another man, and in many, could insist that she entertain his guests. Marriage was often prohibited.

In Muslim law, the position of a slave **concubine** was better because it was protected by law. A man had the right to as many concubines as he could support. The position of the concubine in the house was recognized. If she bore her master a child, the child was free under Muslim law and had equal right of inheritance with the children of wives, and she was freed when her master died. In the West Indies, there were very few white women. Planters, overseers, merchants, and accountants often took slave concubines, and sometimes, slept promiscuously with all of the women under their authority. It was common to provide a sexual partner for male guests. The slave concubine in the West Indies had few rights. In some cases, on the death of a free man, his slave lover was freed along with her children under his will, and even given a generous financial settlement. In others, she was discarded when her man tired of her and their children were ignored.

Any effort to limit sexual relations between masters and slaves was generally futile. The French **Code Noir** of 1685 prohibited sexual relations with slave women, but the **Saint-Domingue** census of 1724 found that 5,000 of 7,000 mulatto women on the island were concubines. In the United States, society was monogamous. Most planters had wives. Christian ministers generally condemned extramarital unions and state law often banned interracial sex. Nevertheless, it was difficult for a slave woman to reject her master or a member of his family and there are almost no cases of white men charged with having sexual relations with their slaves. In other cases, unmarried men or widowers had consensual and loving relations with slave women. **Thomas Jefferson**, for example, is believed to have begun a lengthy relationship with a slave named **Sally Hemings** after his wife died. She bore a number of children, two of whom he freed. Both claimed to be Jefferson's sons.

The clandestine and sometimes transient nature of these relationships in the United States meant that males rarely recognized their slave partners or acknowledged their offspring, though some had their lovers and children freed, and others, like **James Henry Hammond**, had their slave children trained as artisans. When a master died, his slave mistress was often subject to retribution from his wife. Some women did resist. **Harriet Jacobs**, author of *Incidents in the Life of a Slave Girl* (1861), resisted her master, but formed a relationship with a white lawyer, and still was eventually forced to flee to escape the importuning of her master.

The price of pretty young slave women was in most societies higher than that of any other category of slave. In the Americas, mulatto "fancy women," sold to be concubines or prostitutes, were the highest priced. Concubinage was widespread in Brazil and Spanish America, and attractive slave women were much valued. In Africa, the price of women was always higher than that of men even though the export trade preferred men. In the Ottoman Empire, the highest prices were paid for Circassian slave women from the Caucasus, who became the wives and concubines of powerful men and the mothers of other powerful men. In some areas, for example, ancient Greece and Rome, male slaves, particularly young boys, were also purchased for sexual use.

SEXUAL SLAVERY. Sexual slavery differs from other forms of slavery in that the person is only purchased for sexual services and is discarded when no longer of value. Most sexual slaves have been women, but in some cases, boys and young men are sought. In ancient Rome, there were bordellos staffed by slave women. In the cities of many slave-owning societies, slave women were put to work as prostitutes, and often purchased for that purpose. The slave prostitute either worked in a brothel, where her labor was controlled, or she worked as a freelancer and was required to return a part of her earnings to her master.

Improvement of transportation in the 19th century made the traffic of women for prostitution an international affair at a time when chattel slavery was being abolished. In the late 19th century, Singapore became a center of distribution for Chinese and Japanese women and east European women were brought to South Africa, South America, and the United States. This has been one of the most persistent forms of slavery. Today, clandestine networks are particularly active in moving prosti-tutes from Southeast Asia, Eastern Europe, and Africa to wealthier parts of the world. Poverty-stricken parents sell their children, often believing their children will be able to better themselves. Sometimes, young women are fraudulently recruited by the promise of well-paid jobs in a distant area or a foreign country. Once away from home, they often find themselves prisoners and are forced to work as prostitutes or strippers. Frequently, they are kept locked up. Sometimes, debt is used to keep them bound to the criminal syndicates that control their activity. Often, they are sold and moved from one jurisdiction to another, where their ignorance of the law and fear of arrest keeps them dependent.

In wartime, conquered or subject women have often been pressed into service as prostitutes. Military brothels were often used to maintain the morale of soldiers. The most systematic such operation in recent years was the "**comfort women**" recruited by the Japanese during World War II. While some of them were volunteers, 80 percent of them were Korean women from poor families forced into prostitution.

SHADD, MARY ANN (1823-1893). Born a free black in Wilmington, Delaware, Mary Ann Shadd became the first black female editor in North America. Her family moved to Pennsylvania in 1833 because there was no schooling available for black children in Delaware. Shadd became a teacher and like her father, an active abolitionist. In 1850 passage of the **Fugitive Slave Law** convinced her that African-Ameri-cans had a better chance to be accepted as equals in Canada. The African-American community in Canada divided between a majority, led by **Henry Bibb**, that favored separate institutions for Blacks and a group led by Shadd, which sought integration. She opened a school and in 1853, created a newspaper, the *Provincial Freeman*, to publicize her views. She advocated self-help and insisted that black people should demand their rights. After the paper folded, she returned to teaching and in 1863, returned to the United States to help recruit black troops for the Union Army. After the war, she returned to teaching and then studied law, but she remained an active campaigner for racial and gender equality until her death.

SHADRACH MINKINS CASE. The Shadrach Minkins case was the first successful rescue of a runaway slave detained under the **Fugitive Slave Law** of 1850. Minkins was a slave owned by a naval officer stationed in Norfolk, Virginia. In May 1850, he escaped to Boston, where he took work as a waiter in a restaurant in the port area. Though he used a false name, he was tracked down by a detective hired by his owner. During hearings mandated by the law, a crowd of several thousand African-Americans pushed into the court-room, grabbed him and ushered him away. The attack had been carefully organized and was successful. Within several days he was safely in Canada. The case angered the South and the federal government. Under instructions from President Millard Fillmore, eight abolitionists were indicted for their role in the rescue, but five were soon released because of inadequate evidence and the other three were eventually acquitted. It was the first case to prove that it was difficult to get a conviction in the North under the Fugitive Slave Law.

SHARP, GRANVILLE (1735-1813). Granville Sharp was a founder of the British abolition movement. Though the son and grandson of Anglican bishops, Sharp was apprenticed as a boy to a linen draper. He was largely self-educated, having mastered Greek and Hebrew in order to better understand the Bible. On the streets of London, in 1767, he found Jonathan Strong, a slave who had been badly pistol-whipped and thrown out by his master, a Barbadian sugar planter named David Lisle. Sharp got the boy medical attention and helped him regain his strength. Two years later, Lisle saw Strong and recognizing that his health was restored, sold him to a Jamaican planter. When Strong was jailed pending departure of the ship, Sharp appealed to the Lord Mayor of London and got him released. When Sharp was sued by the purchaser, he bought a set of law books and prepared to argue the case. Sharp won the case when the plaintiff chose not to pursue it. Sharp was convinced by this time that he could challenge the right of masters to own slaves in England and sought a case he could bring to the courts. He helped several slaves claimed by slave masters, but the cases never came to court. Finally, in 1772, in the case of James Somerset, Chief Justice Mansfield ruled that slaves brought to England from the West Indies could not be forced to return there.

Sharp remained an important figure in the abolition movement. He published a number of tracts on slavery and was involved in a series of legal cases, including the **Zong case** and a number of attempted kidnaps. He was one of the founders of the colony of **Sierra Leone** and of the **Society for the Abolition of the Slave Trade**, both events in 1787. He was one of the leaders of the campaign organized by the society against the slave trade and eventually persuaded the British Parliament to abolish it. *See also* ABOLITION, GREAT BRITAIN; SOMERSET V. SOMERSET.

SHARPE, SAM. *See* JAMAICAN SLAVE REVOLT (1831-32).

SIERRA LEONE. The British colony of Sierra Leone was founded as a settlement for freed slaves resettled in Africa, but it became the base for Great Britain's struggle against African slavery. The area was a center of the **slave trade**. It was a source of slaves who were preferred on the rice plantations of South Carolina. In spite of this, or perhaps because of this, it was chosen in 1787 as the site for an experiment in repatriation. Set up by British abolitionists, its first settlers in Sierra Leone came from three groups: the black poor of London, **black Loyalists** settled in Nova Scotia after the **American Revolution**, and **Maroons** from Jamaica. All three groups were former slaves. The original settlement was named Freetown and was one of the few good harbors on the West African coast.

In 1808, after Britain abolished the slave trade, the British government took over the colony and Freetown became the base for the **Africa Squadron** of the Royal Navy, which struggled for a half-century to stop the export of slaves. It also became the location of the **prize court**, the only court on the African coast that could authorize the confiscation of ships seized at sea and the liberation of their slave cargoes. This meant that when a slave ship was seized, it had to be taken to Freetown. The slaves, called **recaptives**, could not be returned to areas where they might be re-enslaved. The result was the freeing of 3,000 to 4,000 slaves a year at Freetown, which led to the city also becoming a major base for missionary activity. Most of the newly released recaptives were received by the missions, who taught them English, helped them to adapt and, in the process, converted most of them to Christianity.

Though the community came from diverse sources, they eventually merged into the **Krio** community, strongly Christian and grateful to Great Britain. Though colonial policy originally called for them to become farmers, they had important skills. The Freetown Krio population had a higher literacy rate than Great Britain. At a time when tropical diseases still killed many European settlers in tropics, the Krio were invaluable to Britain. They held a range of posts in the nascent colonial administrations, they were agents of British commerce, and Krio ministers served as missionaries. They spread out over **West Africa**, some returning to earlier homes, others going where they could earn a living. Among them were an elite of doctors, lawyers, ministers, journalists, and businessmen. *See also* ABOLITION, GREAT BRITAIN.

SIETE PARTIDAS. The *Siete Partidas*, or "Seven Divisions," was a law code adopted in the Iberian kingdom of Castile in the 13th century. It incorporated much of Roman law into Spanish law, including Roman law on slavery. The law code was particularly concerned to regulate slavery in a nation divided between three religions, **Christianity**, **Islam**, and Judaism. It limited slave-holding by **Jews**, whose slaves could become free by becoming Christians. It also determined who could be enslaved. Spanish law was concerned that the slave was justly enslaved, though Muslims were often considered enemies of Christianity and thus, automatically eligible to be enslaved. Warfare between Christians and Muslims was a frequent source of enslavement in late medieval Spain. When Spain built an empire in the Americas, the *Siete Partidas* provided a legal framework for the import of slaves to the colonies and regulated their treatment.

Siete Partidas provided that slaves could be bought, sold or loaned, but it also considered slavery an unnatural condition. It granted slaves a legal personality and offered them ways out of slavery. They had the right to purchase their freedom and a slave who was abused could appeal to a court and either be freed or sold to a less abusive owner. Slaves could be freed for service to the state such as military service, acts of heroism or betrayal of a conspiracy. Slaves were guaranteed the right to marry, to choose their own spouses and to inherit property. Masters could free slaves in their wills. This became important, especially to slave **concubines** and their children. One effect of Spanish law was that there was from early times a large free black and mulatto population in Spanish America, particularly in the cities. *See also* HISPANIC AMERICA; LAW OF SLAVERY.

SIMMS, WILLIAM GILMORE (1806-1870). William Gilmore Simms was a leading southern man of letters and a prominent defender of slavery. By 1830, Simms had produced four books of poetry and was the editor of the short-lived *Southern Literary Gazette*. He also was a successful novelist, probably one of the few men in the United States to earn his living from writing.

In 1837, in response to a book by an English critic of slavery, Harriet Martineau, Simms wrote an essay entitled "The Morals of Slavery." This and other subsequent proslavery writings were published in 1852 as *The Pro-Slavery Argument, as Maintained by the Most distinguished Writers of the Southern States*. His argument was that slavery was divinely ordained and involved a moral contract to help slaves better themselves. His novels present a highly idealized and romanticized picture of slave-master relations. They frequently describe affectionate relations between masters and "good" slaves.

SLAVE-CATCHING. In all societies where slaves were numerous, slave flight was a problem and measures were taken to pursue and catch runaway slaves. This was particularly important in places where there were potential refuges: the swamps of Florida, the mountainous "cockpit" of Jamaica, the free states of the northern United States, the frontier regions of Brazil. In ancient Rome, the slave catchers were called *fugitivarii*. In earlier Near Eastern societies there were laws regulating slave catchers. In the United States, the West Indies and Brazil, there were professional slave catchers. In Brazil, they were called *capitães do mato* or bush captains. Expert at tracking runaway slaves; these slave catchers knew the routes these slaves were likely to use and often used dogs to pick up their trail. It was a very risky occupation, so much so that insurance companies often refused to cover such men, but the bounties paid by masters could make such work lucrative. The Brazilian bush captains made use of large bands of frontiersmen called ***bandeirantes*** because they often had to deal with entrenched **maroon** settlements.

Other slave catchers specialized in tracking runaways in free states of the Northern United States. Where they could, they used the law to reclaim the slaves they pursued. From 1793, there were Fugitive Slave acts that required federal and state officials to assist southerners in their efforts to recover runaway slaves, but gradually, northern legislatures placed barriers in the way of their efforts, for example, **personal liberty laws**. Many of the slave catchers chose to kidnap runaways they were pursuing and smuggled them back into the southern states. The passage of the **Fugitive Slave Act of 1850** facilitated their activities, but led to conflict as anti-slavery groups and Northern legislatures tried to limit their activities and to physically block the return of runaways. To avoid the slave catchers, abolitionists hid slaves or helped them move north into Canada on the **Underground Railroad.** *See also* BURNS, ANTHONY; PALMARES; PRIGG V. PENNSYLVANIA; SHADRACH MINKINS CASE.

SLAVE COAST. Many parts of the West African coast were known by products Europeans expect to be able to buy there. The Slave Coast was a densely populated area which stretched from modern Togo to Cameroun and included the **Bights of Biafra** and Benin. By the late 17th century, this area was the largest source of slaves for the Atlantic slave trade. Powerful kingdoms like Oyo and **Dahomey** produced slaves with their annual military campaigns. The **Aro** developed trade routes in the **Igbo** country that lay behind the Bight of Biafra. European traders knew they could find large numbers of slaves at ports like **Whydah**, Porto Novo, Badagry, Bonny and Calabar. Trade routes centred on these ports stretched deep into the interior. The area may have provided as many as 2 million slaves for export. Whydah alone often provided 20,000 a year.

SLAVE CODES. Wherever slavery was important, law codes were needed to regulate relations between slave owners and between slave and master. A commercial law was necessary to regulate the **slave trade** and the hiring out or loan of slaves. Slave laws always defined slaves as property, but they also had to deal with fact that the slave was a person, particularly in matters of sexual relationships and the children these produced. Other perennial questions included whether a slave could be a witness, whether legal penalties from criminal acts were the same for slave and free and procedures for **manumission**. Some codes encouraged manumission. Others prohibited it. Some slave codes regulated what a slave could or could not wear.

A major question for slave codes was the maintenance of the author ity of the masters over slaves. Many **slave societies** in the Americas had a slave majority, or a large slave minority. In these, there was often an obsessive fear of slave insurrection, flight, and insubordination. In some matters, the law could be gentle with the slave because it did not want to infringe the master's property rights. In many southern states, masters could sue for damages done to their slaves. Southern slave codes made it illegal to teach slaves to read, prohibited large gatherings, and required slaves to carry passes when off the plantations.

Where authority was in question, the law was firm and its administration ruthless. Most slave codes affirmed the master's right to punish a slave, and if the slave died in the course of brutal punishments, the master was rarely tried for his excesses. Slave codes were most severe with acts of rebellion, often providing cruel punishments and insisting that these punishments be carried out as quickly as possible. Once a slave engaged in rebellion, it was no longer simply a question of the master's property rights. It was a question of the authority of the slave system. **Slave patrols** often had the right to act arbitrarily in apprehending fugitives or suspected fugitives. Rebels were subject to summary execution, were tortured, drawn and quartered, or subjected to other slow or painful means of execution. West Indian slave codes were particularly harsh. *See also* CODE NOIR; LAW OF SLAVERY; *SIETE PARTIDAS*.

SLAVE GRACE CASE. Grace was a slave on the island of Antigua who was taken to England by her mistress and lived there for many years. After returning voluntarily to Antigua, she sued for her freedom, arguing that she was freed by her long residence in England. In 1827, Justice William Scott, Lord Stowell, ruled that Grace was not free. He recognized that if she had remained in England, she could have claimed her freedom, but by returning to a colony where slavery was legal, she became a slave again.

SLAVE MODE OF PRODUCTION. In Marxist thought, the mode of production is considered basic to the understanding of how a society functions. Historic change is often defined as a movement from one mode of production to another. There are two components to a mode of production. The first is the forces of production: land, tools, and technology. The second is the relations of production. Are those who produce the same as those who own the means of production, and if not, how do they relate to each other? During the early 20th century, Marxist thinkers often saw the slave mode of production as part of a fixed evolutionary sequence, but during the second half of the century, the concept was used more flexibly. A slave mode of production was one where slaves did all or most of the productive labor. Thus, a slave mode of production could also be capitalistic, but differed from other forms of capitalist agriculture in that much of the capital was tied up in the ownership of slaves.

Some writers, like Cambridge historian, **Moses Finley**, disliked the rigidities of Marxist thought and preferred the concept of **slave society**. Others, like the French anthropologist, **Claude Meillassoux**, found the Marxist concepts powerful and going back to Marx's original ideas, have used the concept flexibly. In any case, slave modes of production and slave societies are similar in that in both, slavery is the basis of the economic system and the major source of labor in it. Both approaches accept that this shapes the social and ideological superstructure of society. *See also* MARXISM.

SLAVE MUSIC. Slaves have probably taken their musical traditions with them in many societies, though in most societies, slaves also learned the music of their masters. This is most striking with African slaves, who have often taken their music with them. When they were constrained by law, for example, by laws which prohibited drumming for fear that "talking drums" would be used to spread plans for rebellion, they found other ways to express themselves and adapt their musical heritage. Africans re-created or devised a variety of musical instruments: many kinds of drums, rattles, concussion sticks, bull-roarers, flutes, xylophones, and the banjo. They also continued things that had been done in Africa, for example making up work songs, which eased the burden of labor.

African musical traditions are most vividly seen in various kinds of religious observances,. In North Africa, it was spirit possession cults, *bori,* and *gnauwa*, which used rhythmic music and dancing to create religious ecstasy and bring on possession. There were different influences, but *candomble* in Brazil and *santeria* in Cuba preserved **Yoruba** ritual and music. Fon music was important to *shango* in Trinidad and *vodun* in Haiti. In the United States, where slaves made up a smaller percentage of the population, Africans also preserved their music, but eventually, there was a merging of traditions within a Christian context. Slaves sang hymns, but replaced the harmonizing of British music with a strong rhythmic line and an African call-and-response pattern. This marriage of traditions eventually produced spirituals, which often presented a distinctively African-American interpretation of Christian tradition, and work songs. This is a music that articulates both the hopes and sorrows of slaves. A similar marriage of traditions, but in a more secular form took place with the Brazilian *capoeira* and with the emergence of Afro-Cuban music, and in particular, the rumba. After emancipation, African-Americans elaborated their spiritual traditions, but also developed more secular forms like jazz and blues. In music one of the most profound African contributions to modern culture can be found. It is at the same time the most vivid expression of slave humanity.

SLAVE PATROLS. Slave patrols, called "paddy-rollers" by slaves in the southern United States, were common in any society where slaves were numerous and slave flight a problem. As early as 1530, there were such patrols in Cuba. All of the slave states in the United States except Delaware created citizen patrols that had the authority to stop suspicious blacks. There were also regular slave patrols on all of the West Indian **sugar** islands. The difference between the **slave catchers** and slave patrols is that the slave catchers were free agents working for planters while the patrols were sanctioned by law and often paid.

Slave patrols were voluntary organizations policing their own communities, while slave catchers ranged far from home. Slaves travelling abroad at night had to carry a pass signed by their owner and indicating where they were going. Some also had badges indicating their rights. The patrols were made up mostly of non-slave-owning whites and sometimes included free blacks or native Americans, but each patrol usually included at least one slaveowner, probably to prevent the patrols from brutalizing slaves, who were valuable property. Some of the people stopped were runaways, but others were simply slaves who did not have permission to visit spouses or friends on other **plantations**.

Slave patrols were also used to prevent gatherings of slaves and thus, to prevent revolts. They often broke up night-time religious meetings. Patrols some times entered the slave quarters to search for items slaves were not allowed to own such as guns. In the cities, they often enforced local curfews. Because of their violence and intimidation, they were much feared by slaves. In African-American lore, there are many stories of the "paddy rollers," who were used, for example, as bogeymen to threaten young children. The patrols were so detested that many slave-owners would not allow them onto the plantations. In most slave-owning societies, patrols ended with emancipation, but in the southern United States, their methods were taken up by the Klu Klux Klan, which sought to create a climate of fear among freed slaves to prevent them from exercising their rights. *See also* LAW OF SLAVERY.

SLAVE RELIGION. When a **slave society** contains large concentrations of slaves from a single area, those slaves usually take many of their religious beliefs and practices with them. They often continue to practice their own religion and, when they accept the religion of their masters, they infuse it with characteristics of their traditional beliefs. These beliefs and practices then often influenced the masters' religion. We see this most vividly with the African diaspora. In North Africa, possession cults called *bori* in Tunisia and *gnauwa* in Morocco were common. At night slaves would gather and dance to rhythmic music, which led to some practitioners being possessed by spirits. *Bori* was a pre-Islamic Hausa cult from Nigeria, but in North Africa it was often assimilated to Islamic mystical traditions of Sufism. We see a similar phenomenon on the East African coast, where people from the Congo basin carried their own music and religious practices, or in Iran and Turkey, where slaves from northeast Africa carried their *zar* cults.

In Brazil and the West Indies, African cults remain important up to the present day. These cults are marked by ancestor worship, spirit possession, divination, faith healing, and the use of music. There was often an element of syncretism between Catholicism and African religion. African cults assimilated Catholic saints to their traditional gods and used statues, holy water, and rosary beads in their rituals. Conversely, the **Catholic Church** introduced black saints the slaves could identify with and created black religious **confraternities** that preserved elements of African religious practice. New World cults often merged elements from different areas, though *candomblé* in Bahia and *santeria* in Cuba were predominantly **Yoruba** in inspiration, *vodun* in Haiti was Dahomean, and *macumba* in Rio de Janeiro was Congolese. With large gatherings banned under slavery, these cults operated at night and in secret. With the end of slavery, they became more public and often attracted people of European descent.

In all areas, the cults have been influenced by the dominant religion, but none more than in the United States. The major difference between mainland North America, the Caribbean, and Brazil was that on the mainland there were fewer slaves on each plantation and, in most areas, a white majority. Both **Islam** and African religions were practiced in secret, but gradually gave way to the "invisible church." Though many slave masters did not want their slaves to convert, others saw Christianity as a force that could teach obedience and submission. In the 18th century, there was a movement to convert slaves, which achieved large-scale conversion only during the religious revivals of the revolutionary era.

The slaves, however, gave Christianity a strongly African flavor. This included dances called "ring shouts," spirit possession, and immersion during baptism. The spiritual music of the slave community and the slave preachers sought their own interpretations of the **Bible**. Much of their religious music offered hope of freedom and a reward for suffering in the afterlife. They identified with the Hebrews wandering in the desert bolstered by hope of a promised land of milk and honey. Black preachers, many of them slaves, became important in slave communities.

Many slave religions perpetuated themselves even after the end of slavery. Yoruba shrines in the Americas reestablished contact with the Yoruba homeland in Nigeria. Yoruba *babalao* conduct religious rites in many parts of the world. African religious ideas also shaped new religions that emerged after emancipation, like the Rastafarians of Jamaica. But most important, African religions had an impact on the dominant religions. These influences are particularly striking in Muslim Sufism and in American Baptism. They include ecstatic practices, full immersion baptism, and a deeply emotional religiosity. Christianity in the United States was for long highly segregated, but the religious practices of many American Protestant churches have been strongly shaped by African religious practices.

SLAVE REVOLTS. Revolt was difficult in all **slave societies** and usually rare. Slaves were social isolates, usually unarmed and far from home. The social system kept them divided and the law usually threatened severe punishments. The most common form of resistance to slavery was not revolt but flight. Flight was often futile and desperate, but slaves regularly sought to flee, even newly purchased slaves for whom flight was a voyage into the unknown.

Flight was most successful when there was someplace a slave could flee to, either a mountainous retreat like the "cockpit" of mountainous central Jamaica or the **Seminole** communities of forested southern Florida, or an anti-slavery society like the northern United States or Canada. Many American slaves followed the **Underground Railroad** to freedom. In mountainous areas of Guinea in **West Africa**, there were Muslim reformers who received runaway slaves. In war, slaves could often flee to the enemy and sometimes be well received. The most successful fleeing slaves were able to gather together to form **Maroon** communities. Most Maroon communities were small and were eventually broken up, but **Palmares** in Brazil lasted for almost a century and the Maroons of Jamaica were never defeated by the British. The flight of the Hebrew slaves from Egypt is depicted as such a revolt. Flight has often been particularly massive in slave systems under threat. Examples would be the massive movement across Union lines by slaves during the American **Civil War**, the **Banamba** exodus in French West Africa, and the flight from the plantations in Brazil just before abolition was approved in 1888.

Slaves did take arms from time, sometimes in massive revolts like that of **Spartacus** who held out against the Romans for two years. Slave revolts were most likely under two circumstances. The first is when there were large numbers of the newly enslaved, uncertain about their future and willing to risk death to avert it. This would be true of the Spartacists and the **Stono Rebellion** in South Carolina. The second is when things seem to be getting better and there is hope for change. Thus, between British abolition of the slave trade in 1807 and of slavery in 1833, the **Jamaican Slave Revolt** of 1831 and **Bussa's Rebellion** in Barbados in 1815 were influenced by expectations of change. The same was true of revolts shaped by the **French Revolution**. The **Haitian Revolution** was the most massive and most successful slave rebellion in modern history, but unsuccessful slave revolts on Martinique, Guadeloupe, Antigua and in Venezuela were shaped by expectations of change.

Slave revolts often brought on periods of harsh repression. Societies with slave majorities or even those in the United States with large slave minorities have often been afraid of slave revolts. All slave revolts in the United States were put down quickly, usually within days, but each revolt was followed by repression and by efforts to exercise tighter control over both slaves and free blacks. Revolts usually led to the execution not only of rebels, but also of those thought to have been involved in conspiracy. Slave rebels were often killed in cruel ways and their bodies displayed in public places to instill fear in slave populations.

SLAVE SOCIETY. Slave societies are societies in which slaves provide most of the productive labor, in which slavery defines the characteristics of social organization and in which slavery permeates all aspects of life. The concept was used by Frank Tannenbaum and Elsa Goveia to describe societies in the New World, but it was most precisely defined by **Moses Finley**. Finley argued that slavery existed in many societies, but was basic to the structure of society only in ancient Greece and Rome, Brazil, the West Indies and the Southern United States. The slave society concept is similar to the Marxist notion of a **slave mode of production** in that it stresses a link between the system of production and the culture of the slave society. Some writers have added other societies to the list, in particular, African societies like the **Sokoto Caliphate, Zanzibar** and the Futa Jallon, which had slave majorities and were totally dependent on slave labor. *See also* ANCIENT GREEK SLAVERY; ANCIENT ROMAN SLAVERY; BRAZILIAN SLAVERY; CARIBBEAN SLAVERY; MARXISM; WEST AFRICA.

SLAVE TRADE. Many slave-owning societies could not find slaves close to home. Others felt that slaves close to home were of limited value if they could easily escape. Muslims and Christians were forbidden to enslave their own co-religionists. For all of these reasons, slave users have often sought slaves from far away. Slaves thus had to be moved. This was particularly true where slave-owning societies became **slave societies,** that is to say, societies dependent on slave labor for much of their production. These were usually expanding societies with a hunger for slave labor. In these societies, specialized merchants emerged. The slaves were increasingly provided by specialized slave producers, militarized states that systematically made war and raided their neighbors for slaves. The merchants connected the slavers and slave users.

There were many ancient trade routes. Egypt imported slaves from the shores of the Red Sea in what is now the **Sudan,** but the most long-lived routes are probably those from Eastern Europe and the Black Sea regions down to ancient Greece and the Mediterranean. That trade continued during Roman times and later supplied Byzantium and the Arab world. During the Middle Ages, the **Vikings** developed a trade route down the Dnieper River into the Black Sea. The Vikings also carried Irish and English slaves to **Scandinavia.** Other medieval traders carried slaves overland from eastern Europe down to the Mediterranean.

By the 15th century, Africa replaced the Slavic regions of Eastern Europe as the most important source of slaves and since that time, Africa has been the most systematically and most brutally enslaved part of the world. Slave trade routes early developed across the **Sahara** and by water from the Horn of Africa. Slaves from **West Africa** were brought first in the 15th century to Portugal and the Mediterranean, then to the Atlantic islands, and finally during the 16th century, to America. The **Middle Passage** saw the export of at least 11 to 12 million slaves from Africa. Other trade routes took African slaves by water to the Persian Gulf, to India, and to the islands of the Indian Ocean. There were also overland routes in the United States, where the opening up of **cotton** lands in Alabama and Mississippi during the early 19th century led to a massive movement from the **tobacco**-producing states of Virginia and Maryland. Similarly, the development of **mining** in the Brazilian state of Minas Gerais led to movement of slaves from the **sugar**-producing areas of northeastern Brazil. In Southeast Asia, there was a trade supplied by pirates in the Sulu archipelago who raided coastal areas and sold slaves to Chinese and European entrepreneurs and a trade from Bali and eastern Indonesia to Java, Sumatra and Malaya.

These slave trades were large businesses. Merchants depended on credit and had to carry merchandise that slave producers were interested in. Their biggest problem, however, was moving the slaves, an act that was all the more difficult because slaves had to be coerced and had to be kept alive. Slaves were often in poor health and always hostile. Often they suffered a despair so deep they wanted to die. The overland trade generally involved slaves being walked long distances, usually chained, and carefully watched so they did not escape. Traders had to be careful to have sources of food. The sea trade, especially across the Atlantic, was in some ways even harsher. Boats were often overcrowded. Male slaves were frequently kept in chains to prevent both revolt and suicide. Feeding the slaves, giving them exercise, and getting rid of the vomit and human waste were difficult tasks. Slave ships could usually be detected from afar by their smell. For the slaves, it was the most traumatic part of the long bitter voyage into slavery.

At the end of most trade routes, or at key points where one route joined another, where slaves could be displayed and sold, there were slave markets. Sometimes, slaves arrived in such ill health that they needed a period of recuperation if they were to be sold at a profitable price. They were generally examined to make they had no diseases, much as animals would be. The treatment the slave received while being traded and sold was generally the most impersonal and dehumanizing aspect of any slave system. *See also* ATLANTIC SLAVE TRADE; EAST EUROPEAN SLAVE TRADE; INDIAN OCEAN; IRANUN; RUSSIAN SLAVERY; SULU SULTANATE.

SLAVERY CONVENTION (1926). In 1926, the Slavery Convention was approved by the **League of Nations**. In it signatory nations agreed to work to end slavery, which was defined as the "status and condition of a person over whom any or all of the powers attaching to the right of ownership are exercised." It also prohibited "the capture, acquisition or disposal of a person with intent to reduce him to slavery." The convention did not actually abolish slavery and it had no provisions for enforcement. It did however require each signatory to submit laws and regulations involving slavery to the League. In 1953, the convention was approved by the **United Nations**. As of 1986, 67 nations had adhered to the convention.

SLAVS. The Slavic peoples, who inhabit most of Eastern Europe, were from the decline of the Roman Empire until the 15th century the major source of slaves for various societies of the Middle East and the Mediterranean and for the nomads of the Asian steppes. Slavs so dominated the slave trade that the word "slav" became the basis of the word for slave in most languages of the area, replacing the Latin *servus*, which came to mean serf. In Arabic, it is *sakaliba*. In French it is *esclave*, in Italian *schiavo*, in Spanish *esclavo*, in Portuguese *escravo and* in German, *Sklave*. Many slaves from Eastern Europe rose to high office as slave officials in Byzantium and in the Ottoman empire. Others became soldiers, workers and artisans. Many Slavic women became **concubines**.

Nomads from Central Asia regularly raided Slavic areas for slaves until states developed. **Vikings** developed a trade route down the Dnieper River to the Black Sea, where they sold slaves, furs, and wax to Byzantium, where many were used as soldiers or palace slaves. During the ninth and 10th centuries, there was also an important overland route from Bohemia and Poland to Spain and southern France. There were also overland routes through Serbia to Dubrovnik on the Adriatic coast, which supplied Venice with slaves. The Mongol and Ottoman empires also raided regularly into Slavic areas. Many of the boys recruited as **Janissaries** were collected by the **devshirme**, a levy of Christian children in Slavic provinces of the Ottoman empire. Slave-raiding was gradually restrained by the growth of powerful states in Poland, Lithuania and Russia capable of protecting their subjects. Enslavement persisted on a smaller scale in frontier areas into the 18th century. The conquest of the Tartar Crimean khanate by Russia in the 18th century finally ended the victimization of Slavic peoples. *See also* EAST EUROPEAN SLAVE TRADE; RUSSIAN SLAVERY.

SMALLS, ROBERT (1839-1915). Born a slave, Robert Smalls became one of the heroes of the struggle of American slaves for freedom and eventually served in the United States Congress. Smalls was brought to Charleston, South Carolina in 1851 by his master, who hired him out for different kinds of work. Smalls became an adept pilot and when the

Civil War began, he became a crew member on a Confederate transport ship. On 13 May 1862, while white members of the crew were on shore, Smalls smuggled his family and a number of other slaves on board, and with the help of other slave crewmen, sailed the ship out of the harbor to join the Union navy, which was blockading the coast. He became a pilot in the Union navy and eventually rose to the rank of captain, the only African-American to hold that rank.

After the war, Smalls was one of the African-Americans who took advantage of the opportunities offered by **Reconstruction**. He was elected first to the South Carolina House of Representatives, then the state senate, and finally in 1874, to the United States Congress, where he served for 10 years and was an advocate for freed slaves, health care and public education. After his political career ended, he became Collector of Customs at Beaufort, South Carolina.

SMITH, ADAM (1723-1790). Adam Smith was a Scottish philosopher and one of the founders of modern economics. He also had a major influence on anti-slavery thought. He first criticized slavery in *The Theory of Moral Sentiments* (1759), in which he suggested that enslavement subjected decent human beings to the hegemony of the most corrupt elements of society. Smith's most important work was his *Inquiry into the Nature and Causes of the Wealth of Nations* (1776), which criticized the intervention of the state into the economy and extolled the virtues of a free market economy. In it he argued that free labor was more productive than slave labor because free men had more motivation to work hard. He also argued that where slavery was important, slave masters had little incentive to modernize because that would reduce the value of their slaves. Smith's belief in the greater productivity of market economies was very influential during the 19th century. His argument that free labor was more productive than slave labor was important in winning broad support to the anti-slavery cause in Great Britain and the United States, and eventually, elsewhere. *See also* CAPITALISM; ENLIGHTENMENT.

SMITH, GERRIT (1797-1874). Born in western New York, Gerrit Smith was the heir to a large fortune, much of which he spent as a philanthropist and a reformer. He was an evangelical Christian, a supporter of temperance and schools for the poor. He tried for many years to reconcile support for abolition and for the movement to send black people back to Africa. By 1837, however, he rejected the colonization movement and for the rest of his life, devoted himself not only to the cause of abolition, but to the cause of racial equality. In 1840 he helped found the **Liberty Party** and in 1852 was elected to Congress, but he soon resigned out of disgust with the **Kansas-Nebraska Act**. In 1846, he gave 3,000 poor blacks land in the Adirondack Mountains so that they could become self-sufficient. He also abandoned his earlier commitment to nonviolence. In 1851, he participated in the liberation of a fugitive slave in the hands of federal marshals. He also supported the use of violence by **John Brown** in Kansas and at Harper's Ferry. He remained until his death a supporter of gender and racial equality.

SMITH, VENTURE (1729-1805). Enslaved as a child in Guinea, Venture Smith eventually freed himself and wrote his autobiography. He was captured by slavers who killed his father in 1737, sold him for four gallons of rum and a piece of calico and transported to him America. He ended up in Connecticut. His master allowed him to hire himself out and earn extra money. After many years in slavery, he was able to purchase his freedom, and then over a number of years, his wife, two sons, and a daughter. A frugal man, he eventually had his own farm and owned several slaves. In 1798, he published *A Narrative of the Life and Adventures of Venture, A Native of Africa, But Resident above Sixty Years in the United States of America.* It described both his enslavement and his life in the United States. When he died, he left to his heirs a 100 acre farm and three houses.

SOCIETY FOR THE ABOLITION OF THE SLAVE TRADE. See ABOLITION, GREAT BRITAIN.

SOCIETY FOR THE PROPAGATION OF THE GOSPEL. In 1701, the Society for the Propagation of the Gospel was organized by the Anglican Church to evangelize in England's colonial domains. Major missions were sent to the American colonies. The Society owned slaves, who were taught reading and religion and encouraged slave owners to do likewise. Most slave owners feared the effect of religious instruction; in particular, they feared that literacy would lead to disobedience. Many colonies made it illegal to teach a slave to read. Some slave owners did allow religious education, but in spite of the opposition of the Anglican Church to abolition, the Society experienced only limited success.

SOCIETY OF THE FRIENDS OF BLACKS (SOCIÉTÉ DES AMIS DES NOIRS). The Society of the Friends of Blacks was the major

French abolitionist organization during the **French Revolution**. Founded in 1788, it included the Marquis de **Condorcet**, the Marquis de Lafayette, and Abbé **Henri Grégoire**. It advocated an immediate end to the **slave trade** and gradual emancipation of slaves. An elite organization, it lacked the ability to mobilize sentiment that its British counterparts had. Based in the Protestant churches, the British abolitionists created a more broad-based popular movement. The society was, however, responsible for many anti-slavery grievances being submitted to the National Assembly in 1789 and played a major role in keeping the question of slavery alive during the French Revolution. It also unwittingly contributed to discontent and revolution in **Saint-Domingue** and other slave colonies. Many of the leaders of the society, including Condorcet, were members of the moderate Republican Gironde faction and were eliminated by Maximilien Robespierre during the reign of terror. *See also* ENLIGHTENMENT.

SOKOTO CALIPHATE. The Sokoto Caliphate in northern Nigeria was the most powerful state to come out of a series of Muslim religious revolutions that took place in West Africa during the 18th and 19th centuries. Led by Usman dan Fodio, the Muslim forces overthrew the Hausa states between 1804 and 1810 in a jihad, or religious war, and took over what was already a productive urban civilization. The success of the jihad was that it created a large, stable, and populous area within which there was substantial economic growth. It was probably the wealthiest and most powerful state in sub-Saharan Africa. The cities of Sokoto Caliphate were major producers of leather and cloth goods and the foci of important trade routes. War also brought back to the caliphate large numbers of slaves, and as the century went along, the market for labor within the caliphate absorbed most of the slaves that its armies produced. The most important use of slaves was in large agricultural estates controlled by merchants and members of the new Muslim artistocracy. The slave population at the end of the century has been variously estimated at between one and 2.5 million slaves. Palace slaves also played an important role in running the highly developed bureaucratic system. In 1903, the caliphate was defeated by British forces under **Frederick Lugard**. See also ISLAM; WEST AFRICA.

SOLON (c. 620-560 BCE). Solon was a lawgiver and the author of the constitution which was the basis of Athenian democracy. His reforms also made Athens a **slave society**. In early fifth-century Athens, there was a great deal of social unrest. Wealthy persons were accumulating land and the poor were increasingly being enslaved because of debts. When Solon was given the authority to create a new constitutional order, he cancelled all debts and prohibited **debt slavery**. He is supposed to have returned land to the dispossessed and redeemed those sold into slavery elsewhere. He also granted citizenship to all Athenians. Solon's reforms made Athens democratic, but forced Athenian landowners and merchants to seek labor elsewhere. The stability created led to a period of growth and a large-scale importation of slaves. The poorer citizens worked in the Athenian navy, which established Athenian hegemony over a large area. Thus, Solon's reforms resolved tensions within the Athenian population, but led to Athens becoming a slave society. The freedom valued by Athenian citizens was based on the labor of slaves. *See also* ANCIENT GREEK SLAVERY.

SOMERSET v. STEWART (1772). James Somerset was the subject of the law case that freed slaves in England. He had been brought to England from North America by his master, Charles Stewart. In 1771, he ran away from his master, but was subsequently captured and put on board a ship destined for Jamaica, where he was to be sold. The abolitionist **Granville Sharp** was then looking for a case that could test whether a person could be held in slavery on English soil. Somerset's friends alerted Sharp, who brought a petition for habeas corpus. The courts had up to that point avoided making a decision on whether a person could be held as property in England, but both sides pushed hard in the Somerset case, Stewart's side for the right of property and Sharp's for the position that persons could not be property. The chief justice of the Court of King's Bench, Lord Mansfield, avoided the larger question, but held that a slave could not be forced by his master to leave England. It reversed a 1729 decision that slaves could be returned to their masters and removed from the country. The decision did not completely end slavery in England, but it did make it difficult for masters to maintain their authority over slaves brought to England. *See also* ABOLITION, GREAT BRITAIN.

SOUTH AFRICAN SLAVERY. Slaves were part of the settlement built by the Dutch East Indies Company at Capetown in 1652 to supply ships on the five-month voyage between Java and the Netherlands. Slavery remained important to the Cape Colony. In order to have supplies, the company authorized settlers to develop farms near Capetown to provide meat, grain, and wine for the company's ships. Slaves provided the labor on these farms and were also used as artisans, unskilled workers, and domestic servants in the town. The slaves were imported from Indonesia, India, Madagascar, and East Africa. The population of the Cape Colony had a slave majority from early in its history up to the British abolition of slavery in 1833. At the end, there were about 36,000 slaves.

The slaves can be divided into three groups. In the city of Capetown, slaves were mostly artisans and casual workers, though females owned by the company also provided sexual services for sailors temporarily in port. These slaves were the best off, especially those who were skilled craftsmen from Asia. Immigrants from Asia also brought **Islam** with them. In the area around Capetown, there was an intensively farmed area that produced grain and wine for sale to the ships. This area depended heavily on slave labor. On the frontier, there were very few slaves. The frontier farmers were poorer and depended for labor on the local Khoisan, who they reduced to servile dependents. Slaves in these areas were very isolated and often harshly treated. Rural South Africa had a problem with flight of slaves to the frontier and to mountainous areas.

Slaves were not allowed to marry, and those who cohabited could be separated from spouses and children. Slaves had to carry passes and were subject to harsh punishments. Rebellion was difficult because slaves lived in small units and often far apart, but flight was common. There was a male majority among both the settlers and the slaves, which led to a competition for women. It also meant that the easiest road out of slavery for a woman was to marry a free male, preferably a white settler. Many slaves were owned by the company and housed in a slave lodge in the heart of Capetown. The company's male slaves built many of the public works. The women in the lodge were often expected to provide sexual services for sailors. In 1806, Capetown was taken over by the British, and in 1833 the British abolition of slavery applied to the Cape Colony. *See also* CAPE COLOUREDS; DUTCH SLAVE TRADE.

SPARTACUS (?-71 BCE). The late Roman republic experienced three great **slave revolts**, all based in southern Italy. The probable root of these revolts was that Roman armies were accumulating slaves in large numbers. Over a million slaves were introduced to Italy over a short period of time and many were placed on large farms in Sicily and southern Italy, where there was thus, for many years, large numbers of the recently enslaved. These were always the people most likely to rebel. The first two slave revolts took place in 136-132 BCE and in 104-

100 BCE, but the most successful was led by Spartacus.

Spartacus was a slave from Greece who was being trained to be a **gladiator**. In the summer of 73 BCE, Spartacus and about 70 followers broke out and set up camp at the base of Mount Vesuvius. They may have intended to form a **Maroon** community, but they quickly gathered a force of about 70,000, a force so large that they had little choice but to fight. Four armies sent against Spartacus from Rome were defeated. Spartacus proved himself brave and an able military strategist. In the course of these victories, Spartacus marched to the north of Italy and could have left Italy, but it would have been unsafe for his army to disperse. They would simply have been hunted down. As a result, they turned back south, where they had to face two large Roman armies. In the winter of 71 BCE, Spartacus was finally defeated and killed. Six thousand of his soldiers were crucified along the road to Rome. *See also* ANCIENT ROMAN SLAVERY.

STAMPP, KENNETH (1912-   ). Kenneth Stampp was the author of *The Peculiar Institution: Slavery in the Ante-Bellum South* (1956). This book was a rethinking of much American historiography on slavery and opened up a great outpouring of revisionist historiography on the subject. In the 90 years after the American **Civil War**, there was a tendency for American historians to present an idealized and sometimes racist picture of slavery. This tendency found its most sophisticated expression in the work of **Ulrich Bonnell Phillips**, who pictured slavery as a benevolent institution in which planters served as tutors to "uncivilized" Africans. Writing at a time when the civil rights movement was just beginning and Americans were rethinking ideas of race and the history of race relations, Stampp denied Phillips's image of slavery as a paternalistic institution. He described it as harsh, dehumanizing, and profitable, and argued that slaves perceived it as such. For Stampp, slavery was based on rigid discipline and demanded total submission by slaves to the will of their masters, which was often enforced by brutal punishments. Stampp also argued that slaves were a "troublesome property," who resisted the authority of their masters in many ways. Stampp's argument that slavery was both profitable and morally indefensible has remained a consistent theme of subsequent historical scholarship. In other ways, historians have amended and elaborated on his approach.

STATE v. MANN (1829). State v. Mann was a case that illustrated the magnitude of the power of a master over a slave. It involved a slave named Lydia, who had been rented to John Mann. When Lydia ran away to avoid a whipping, Mann shot her. Lydia's owner could have sued for damages to her property, but instead, she filed charges of assault and battery. Mann was convicted in the lower court, but on appeal, Chief Justice Thomas Ruffin of the North Carolina Supreme Court held that Mann, as a renter, had all of the rights of a slave owner. This meant that he could punish a slave in any way he wished short of killing her. He explained that "the power of the master must be absolute to render the submission of the slave perfect." The power of the master could in no way be brought into question. Furthermore, the slave had to be made aware of that power. *See also* LAW OF SLAVERY.

STEWART, MARIA (1803-1879). A black female abolitionist author and lecturer, Maria Stewart was born free in Hartford, Connecticut. Stewart was raised by a clergyman and went to work as a domestic servant at 15. Though she had no formal education, she had clearly been exposed to learning in the clergyman's home and at church. A born-again Christian, she believed that Christians had an obligation to oppose all forms of injustice. Her first tract, *Religion and the Pure Principles of Morality* (1831), was printed by **William Lloyd Garrison**, and soon afterwards, she began speaking in public. She denounced slavery and claimed for African-Americans the right to fully participate in American political life. She stopped public speaking in 1833, but for much of the rest of her life, taught school in New York, Baltimore and Washington. During the last years of her life, she was matron of Washington's Freedman's Hospital, which served ill and destitute former slaves.

STILL, WILLIAM (1821-1902). William Still was an African-American abolitionist who was a key figure on the **Underground Railroad**. Born free, Still was the son of a mother who had fled slavery and a father who had purchased his freedom. In 1847, he joined the Pennsylvania Anti-Slavery Society and several years later, became the head of its Vigilance Committee. In that capacity, he assisted more than 800 fugitive slaves moving through Philadelphia. One of those he helped was his own brother, who had been left behind when his mother ran away. In 1855, Still visited Canada to talk to former slaves who had fled there. On his return, he described their success in answer to those who claimed that African-Americans could not survive freedom. During Still's years with the Vigilance Committee, he interviewed many fleeing slaves about their experiences in slavery and in their escapes. His notes became useful when he published *The Underground Railroad* in 1872.

This was an account which placed as much stress on the ingenuity and heroism of the fugitives as on the white abolitionists who helped them. It served as a corrective to the accounts of many white abolitionists.

STONE, LUCY (1818-1893). Lucy Stone was a leader in the struggles both against slavery and for women's rights. Though from Massachusetts, Stone studied at Oberlin College in Ohio, a center of the moderate anti-Garrisonian wing of the abolition movement. In spite of this, she became a Garrisonian and after graduation became a lecturer for the **American Anti-Slavery Society**. A very effective orator, she sometimes faced the criticism of male abolitionists unhappy with her mixing of the causes of slaves and women. In 1863, she joined Susan B. Anthony and Elizabeth Cady Stanton in founding the Women's National Loyal League to campaign for a **Thirteenth Amendment** to the United States Constitution to guarantee the freedom of slaves. She became its president, and after the war helped form the American Equal Rights Association to campaign for the **Fourteenth** and later, the **Fifteenth Amendments**. She devoted most of the rest of her life to the struggle for women's rights. *See also* GARRISON, WILLIAM LLOYD.

STONO REBELLION (1739). The Stono rebellion was one of the most important revolts against slavery in Great Britain's American colonies. In September 1739, a group of slaves working on a road repair crew broke into a general store, killing two persons and seizing weapons. Then shouting "Liberty" and beating drums, they headed toward Florida, led by a slave named Jemmy. In Florida, the Spanish were then freeing slaves of their British enemies. As they marched, they burned plantations, killed more than 20 whites and added slave recruits. Before they reached their destination, they were attacked by a white posse, who killed or hung 44 of them, placing their heads on posts along the road.

The Stono rebellion aroused fear among Whites in South Carolina, where Blacks outnumbered Whites by almost two to one. The import of slaves was temporarily suspended, a very rigid **slave code** was passed, and patrols were introduced to control the movement of slaves. Many of the slaves involved were from Angola, which led to the reduction of imports from Angola. *See also* SLAVE PATROLS; SLAVE REVOLTS.

STOWE, HARRIET BEECHER (1811-1896). Harriet Beecher Stowe was the author of *Uncle Tom's Cabin* (1852), a powerful anti-slavery novel. The daughter of Lyman Beecher, an important clergyman, she married Calvin Stowe, a biblical scholar. She lived an itinerant life, moving from place to place, first with her father and then with her husband. While living in Cincinnati as a young woman, Stowe first confronted the reality of slavery. She visited a **plantation** in Kentucky and met slaves who had fled across the Ohio River to freedom. She also began to write, and after the passage of the **Fugitive Slave Law** (1850), turned to writing an anti-slavery novel. *Uncle Tom's Cabin* captured the imagination of the reading public as no other anti-slavery literature had done. It described the experiences of a slave family. While several members of the family escaped to Canada, Uncle Tom is sold down river to Louisiana, where he is oppressed by Simon Legree and eventually beaten to death.

Uncle Tom's Cabin was important because it vividly depicted the horrors of slavery and presented black slaves as sympathetic and heroic individuals. The book was translated into 37 languages and is estimated to have sold three million copies in the United States alone. It was also a best-seller in Europe. It created such intense feelings both in the North and the South, that **Abraham Lincoln** is reported to have greeted her when he met her as the woman responsible for the **Civil War**. In 1853, Stowe published *The Key to Uncle Tom's Cabin*, a collection of documents describing the evils of slavery. In 1856, she published another anti-slavery novel, *Dred: A Tale of the Great Dismal Swamp*. About an unsuccessful attempt at slave rebellion, it had none of the impact of the earlier novel. Though Stowe did more than any other person to win the Northern middle classes to the cause of abolition, she was never active in the abolition movement.

STURGE, JOSEPH (1793-1859). Born the son of a prosperous farmer, Joseph Sturge was a successful corn merchant who became a **Quaker** philanthropist and social activist. The son of a prosperous farmer, he early became a successful corn merchant. In 1826, he became the secretary of the Birmingham Anti-Slavery Society. He was part of the more radical wing of the abolition movement and opposed the idea of apprenticeship for freed slaves. Convinced that **apprenticeship** was merely an extension of slavery, he took a six-month trip to the West Indies in 1837. The account of this trip was published as *The West Indies in 1837* (1837). It helped persuade parliament to end apprenticeship. He also publicized laws passed by colonial assemblies in the West Indies, which limited the freedom of ex-slaves or imposed harsh penalties on them. Although, the abolitionists had achieved their major goal, many were convinced that the struggle would not be over until slavery no longer existed anywhere. In 1839, they organized the British and Foreign Anti-Slavery Society. This was to remain the major British anti-slavery organization. Sturge was the dominant figure of this organization into the 1850s. He was also active throughout his life in the education of freed slaves, temperance, peace and community betterment. *See also* ABOLITION, GREAT BRITAIN; ANTISLAVERY INTERNATIONAL

SUDAN. The Sudan is the strip of savannah that stretches across Africa south of the Sahara from the Atlantic to the Nile River. It has long had contact with the Mediterranean world, but that trade with the Mediterranean increased only after the introduction of the camel into the Sahara early in the first millenium. Slaves were an important item in this trade, but nowhere more than in the upper Nile basin, which had the earliest known and longest continuing slave trade. Ancient Egypt was not a large-scale exploiter of slave labor, but it did raid and trade with Nubia for slaves. The frontier at any given point was a center of both commercial and military activities. One result of the growth of the slave trade is that kingdoms in the Sudan both used slaves and sold them. The Christian kingdoms of Nubia provided slaves as tribute to Muslim Egypt. Further south in the middle Nile, the sultanate of Sennar raided and received slave tribute from areas yet further south. Slaves were incorporated as soldiers and bureaucrats and worked agricultural estates. The export of slaves was a major source of revenue. Kanem in the central Sudan and Ghana in the western Sudan also provided slaves for the Saharan trade and used slave labor.

During the 19th century, there was a dramatic increase in the slave trade, in slave use and in slaving. Egypt was a province of the Ottoman empire, but its viceroy, Muhammed Ali, wanted to assert his independence from the Turks by copying economic and technological changes then taking place in Europe. In 1820, he invaded and occupied the Sudan, partly to acquire slaves for his army. His government encouraged trade and introduced better means of communication. This facilitated penetration of what is now the southern Sudan. The peoples of this area had hitherto been untouched by long-distance trade and lacked the technology and the organization to effectively resist the invaders. The traders were based in *zaribas*, fortified bases staffed by slave soldiers and fed by slave workers, all taken from neighbouring peoples. These *zaribas* originally exported mostly ivory, but soon specialized on slave exports, some of them going into the Middle East, but most used in the Arab areas of the middle Nile, many as agricultural workers. As the use of modern rifles spread further west, a series of highly predatory states emerged, not only in the Nile basin, but in what is now Chad and the Central African Republic. With the international slave trade almost over, they served mostly markets within Africa.

The slave trade only declined when the rise of the Mahdist state after 1881 isolated the Sudan. The Mahdists were conquered by the British in 1898, but slavery was by this time so basic to the social and economic system that the British were hesitant to take action against it. The slave trade was reduced and eventually exterminated, but slavery was only abolished in 1936. One heritage of the slaver's activity is a continuing civil war between the north, overwhelmingly Muslim and the south, today Christian or traditionalist. During the 1980s and 1990s, slaving resumed as government troops and local militias fighting southern rebels captured and enslaved women and children. *See also* AFRICAN SLAVE TRADE.

SUGAR. More than any other crop, it was sugar that created a demand for slaves in the Americas. It was sugar that most slaves produced. And it was sugar that produced the harshest regime and the highest mortality of any slave-produced crop.

The Crusades led to Europeans discovering cane sugar, which was already being grown by Arabs. At the time, the only sweetener in the European diet was honey. Entrepreneurs from Venice and Genoa started growing sugar on Crete and Cyprus. In the subsequent centuries, as Europe grew more prosperous, so too did its taste for sugar, which was useful in sweetening other imports from the non-Western world: tea, coffee and chocolate. Sugar was from the first a **plantation** crop because of the importance of processing. As the market grew, the planters developed better technology and more efficient methods of estate management, and European navigators discovered tropical areas capable of producing sugar. In the 15th and 16th centuries, Genoan capital developed sugar plantations on Madeira, **São Tomé** and other Atlantic islands. Madeira was the world's largest sugar producer in the early 16th century and Brazil at the end. In the mid-17th century, the Dutch, British and French opened up sugar production in the West Indies.

During the 17th and 18th centuries, European mercantilist ideology stressed the accumulation of silver and gold. Sugar was an ideal crop for that. It could no longer be grown competitively anywhere in Europe, but the market was large and constantly growing as Europeans added tea, coffee and chocolate to their diets. European nations were interested in producing sugar to meet domestic demand, and thus, to avoid the loss of specie, and to export to nations that lacked tropical colonies. The problem that European entrepreneurs faced is that the areas best suited for sugar were either unpopulated islands like Madeira, or were areas like the West Indies where population had been decimated by European diseases and harsh labor policies. Workers brought in from Europe as **indentured labor** had a high mortality. European planters soon looked to the **African slave trade** to meet the demand for labor.

Sugar had another problem. The work was very harsh. The biggest problem was that the harvest season was long, sometimes as long as seven or eight months. Furthermore, it was important to get the sugar into the presses and the boiling room as soon as possible. The longer it took, the less sugar could be extracted from the cane. Sugar planters were trying to make money and were often in debt. They often planted more than they could process. They thus used force and pushed their laborers as hard as possible, sometimes forcing them to work 18- and 24-hour shifts. Men pushed to the limits of human endurance by threats of violence were prone to injury. Many were killed or mangled by the presses. Slaves were often in poor health and prone to disease. These conditions were not favorable to family life and reproduction. Sugar planters preferred adult male slaves, often calculating that it was cheaper to buy a slave than to raise one. In no sugar-producing area did the slave population reproduce itself until after the slave trade was ended, and then, only a few reached a replacement rate. The failure to reproduce meant that sugar colonies always needed slaves to replace those who died. *See also* BARBADOS; BRAZILIAN SLAVERY; CARIBBEAN SLAVERY; DEMOGRAPHY OF SLAVERY; DUTCH SLAVE TRADE; MORTALITY.

SULU SULTANATE. Based at Jolo in the southern Philippines, the Sulu Sultanate was base of operations for slave-raiding pirates called **Iranun** and Balangingi during the 18th and 19th centuries. Sea-based slave-raiding had been important in the area from the 16th century. By the 18th century, the raiding was being done by the relatively autonomous Iranun, who ranged through the island seas of Southeast Asia preying on isolated communities. The Sulu elite put the slaves to work and traded them or the commodities they produced. The biggest market was China, which wanted sea creatures called *tripang,* bird's nests valuable for Chinese soups, wax, camphor, mother of pearl and tortoise shell. Slaves were farmed out to communities on the Borneo coast which gathered these products. Slaves were also used to make salt and to grow rice and other agricultural products. Trade goods were brought in by the British country traders from India, who provided the Sulu Sultanate with cloth, opium, guns and gunpowder.

Slaves were also used by the Sulu elite and were sold to Dutch and Chinese males who wanted **concubines** and servants. Jolo, the sultanate's capital was a market for slaves and for commodities sought by the slavers. The prices received for women were always higher than the prices for men. The number of slaves in Jolo was several times the number of free persons. They included concubines, slave officials, artisans and peasants. **Manumission** was common in Sulu, though more for women than for men. The Sulu Sultanate was conquered by the Spanish in 1870s. *See also* CHINESE SLAVERY; INDONESIAN SLAVERY.

SUMERIANS. See ANCIENT MIDDLE EASTERN SLAVERY.

SUMNER, CHARLES (1811-1874). For 22 years, Charles Sumner was the most eloquent and uncompromising voice defending slaves and freed persons in the United States Senate. After graduating from Harvard College and then studying law, Sumner became a lawyer, but he was primarily concerned with social and political issues. During the 1840s, he opposed the **Mexican-American War**, supported racial integration of the Boston schools, and was a member first of the **Liberty Party**, then of the **Free-Soilers**, and finally, a Republican. In 1851, he was elected to the U.S. Senate. In 1852, he gave a four hour speech that marked him as the most resolute anti-slavery voice in Congress. In May 1856, he gave a speech entitled "The Crime against Kansas." Two days after this, while working at his desk, he was beaten so badly by Preston Brooks, a South Carolina congressman, that he was unable to return to the Senate for three years, but when he did, it was with a speech entitled "The Barbarism of Slavery." During the war, he pushed **Abraham Lincoln** to emancipate the slaves, and then, to use black troops. After the war, he became one of the architects of the **Reconstruction** policy which was imposed by the Union Army on the South. *See also* KANSAS-NEBRASKA ACT.

-T-

TACKY'S REBELLION (1760-1761). One of the largest **slave revolts** in Jamaican history, Tacky's rebellion involved primarily Akan slaves, known as Coromantee, from southern Ghana. It began on Easter Sunday, 1760, when a band of 150 slaves led by a slave named Tacky, attacked the fort at Port Maria and seized gunpowder and muskets. They then marched south, gathering new recruits as they went.

The rebellion took place at a time when Jamaican **sugar** cultivation was expanding rapidly. Some120,000 slaves had been imported during the previous 20 years. In addition, Great Britain was involved in the Seven Years War with France, which meant that security was not as strong as usual. The rebellion broke out in St. Mary's parish which had the highest percentage of Akan and the lowest percentage of whites on the island. The rebels wanted to expel all whites and create an independent state. One of the leaders was an African religious specialist called an *obeah* man, who prepared amulets for the rebels. Tacky was captured during the early days of the revolt and was executed. The *obeah* man was captured soon afterwards, but the bands dispersed and continued a guerilla war for many months afterwards. The final suppression of the revolt was not announced until October 1761.

Retribution was harsh. Nearly 400 slaves died in the fighting. About a hundred were executed. Another 500 were transported to other colonies. Only about 60 whites and 60 free blacks were killed. The rebellion led to a tightening of security on the island. *Obeah* was forbidden, slave access to weapons was restricted and the right of slaves to hold meetings was limited. Fortifications were also built so the colony would not be so vulnerable.

TANEY, ROGER B. (1777-1864). Roger Taney was the Chief Justice of the United States Supreme Court, whose pro-slavery decisions helped to bring on the **Civil War**. This was in spite of the fact that he had reservations about slavery. Born the son of a Maryland tobacco farmer, he inherited several slaves, whom he freed. Though he was critical of slavery, he did not believe that whites and blacks could live equally in the same society. He was thus a supporter of repatriation of free slaves to Africa. In 1831, he was appointed Attorney-General by Andrew Jackson and in 1836, he became Chief Justice. Throughout his long career, he was a supporter of state's rights, in particular, believing that only states could act against slavery. He also consistently defended the rights of slave owners to their human property. His most important case involved a slave named **Dred Scott**, who claimed his freedom because his master had taken him into a free territory. Taney held that he could not sue because the **Constitution** did not grant citizenship to blacks. He also argued that Congress did not have the power to make slavery illegal in any of the territories, which nullified the **Missouri Compromise**. In another case, **Ableman v. Booth**, he overruled a Wisconsin court that held the **Fugitive Slave Law** unconstitutional. He insisted that no state authorities could interfere with federal marshals seeking to enforce federal law.

TANNENBAUM, FRANK (1893-1969). Professor of history at Columbia University, Frank Tannebaum is best known for a brief book entitled *Slave and Citizen: the Negro in the Americas* (1946). In it, he argued that the creation of new societies in the Americas was as much an African accomplishment as a European one. He also argued that the difference between the United States and Catholic Latin America lay in the assimilation by Latin countries of Roman law and the insistence by the **Catholic Church** that slaves had a right to the sacraments, most importantly, the sacrament of marriage. This meant, Tannenbaum argued, that slavery was less harsh in the Latin countries and that there was more miscegenation and more **manumission**. In later work, Tannenbaum again raised the question of miscegenation and the different roles of mulattoes.

Tannenbaum's work was important because it stimulated a lot of research on comparative slave systems. His work was a precursor of the outpouring of research on slavery that developed during the 1950s and 1960s. Many of his ideas have been disproven or amended. Carl Degler argues in *Neither Black nor White: Slavery and Race Relations in Brazil and the United States* (1971) that the Catholic Church had too little manpower and depended too much on the planters to effectively limit the harshness of slavery. The church tried to protect the slave family, but it had limited success. *See also* BRAZILIAN SLAVERY; HISPANIC AMERICA; RACE AND SLAVERY; *SIETE PARTIDAS*.

TAPPAN, ARTHUR (1786-1865) AND LEWIS (1788-1873). The Tappan brothers were major figures in the American abolition movement. Born in Massachusetts, both were strongly influenced by their mother's evangelical Christianity. They remained active Christians and uncompromising supporters of abolition and of the rights of African-Americans all of their lives. As young men, the brothers moved to New York, where they prospered in the silk business. They were thus able to support both Christian and abolitionist causes. They gave to missionary activity, to interracial Oberlin College, and to the **American Colonization Society**. In 1830, they left the colonization movement to become supporters of **William Lloyd Garrison**, only to split with Garrison a decade later over his support for the women's rights movement. In 1839, both were involved in the *Amistad* case. They were also involved with the **Liberty Party** and supported its candidate for president, James Birney, in 1844. They underwrote an abolitionist newspaper, the *National Era,* and founded the **American Missionary Association**, which provided employment for many African-American radicals. During the 1850s, Lewis became a key supporter of the **Underground Railroad**.

TEMPLE SLAVERY. In many societies, slaves were given to temples or to shrines to serve the gods. Temple slaves were particularly important in the civilizations of Mesopotamia, where temples were centers of great wealth and power. They were also common elsewhere in the Middle East, in Greece and Rome, among the Hindu and Buddhist societies of Asia and at shrines in Africa. Slaves were often given by persons who wanted the god's favor or by victorious generals who wanted to thank a god for their victories. Abandoned children were often given to temples to be cared for. Slaves did very different kinds of work at the temples. Temples were in many societies wealthy institutions, controlling lands and much economic activity. In cases, where the temple controlled lands, slaves worked the lands. Other slaves assisted priests in running temples, serving as custodians, assisting priests in sacrifices, or working as clerks and messengers. In Buddhist Burma, for example, there were three groups of slaves: those who maintained the temple and its grounds; those who took care of the libraries and copied sacred texts; and those who served the monks as cooks and servants. In some cases, for example, the temples of Aphrodite in ancient Greece, slaves worked as sacred prostitutes. Among the **Igbo** of Nigeria, slaves given to shrines were called *osu* and were very much set apart from other social groups. Among the Ewe of Togo and eastern Ghana, there are still girls called *trokosi*, who are given to shrine priests. In many cases, slaves did harsh labor. In others, they did tasks important for the religion, for example, copying sacred texts. Such slaves tended to be well treated. *See also* BUDDHISM; HINDUISM.

THAI SLAVERY. Slavery is an old institution among Thai peoples. The earliest written sources, from the 13th century, mention different forms of slavery. Slavery probably resulted from warfare and natural disasters and certainly existed long before our earliest records. Slavery was also widespread. In the 19th century, one European observer suggested that a third of population was made up slaves. The principal reason that slavery was important was that population densities were low. The land was fertile and there was a lot of it. Wealth and power came not from control of land, but from control of people. Wars were fought not so much to control territory as to control people. Conquered communities were often physically moved to the conqueror's territory and distributed by the king to those who served him. Captives and their descendants were probably the most numerous kind of slave.

Because land had little value, people could only use their persons or those of their dependents as security for loans. Many people became slaves through debt, sometimes because they could not repay loans, sometimes because of gambling debts. The war captives were enslaved in communities. The **debt slaves** were enslaved individually, and in most cases, could redeem themselves by paying their debts. Some people voluntarily put themselves in slavery to have the protection of a powerful man. As a result, homes of the wealthy and powerful were largely staffed by slaves. Government was staffed by slaves. Buddhist monasteries and temples depended on slaves to provide maintenance and to feed the monks. The status of different kinds of slaves was carefully defined by law, which regulated the rights and obligations of slave and master, and by contract. For example, if a female debt slave bore her master's child, the birth of that child cancelled her debt.

The conditions that made for slavery gradually changed during the 19th century. Chinese migrants poured into Thailand and hired themselves out for wages. Thailand became a major rice exporter and was increasingly dependent on wage labor. While slave labor was becoming less important, the Thai kings were also anxious to preserve the nation's independence and afraid that Great Britain or France would use Thai slavery as an excuse for intervening. King Mongkut gradually began to restrict the control men exercised over women. In 1868, he decreed that neither a woman nor her children could be enslaved without her consent. In 1874, King Chulalongkorn decreed that the price of slave children born after 1868 would decrease year by year until they were free at age 21. His hope was that they would buy the freedom of their parents. A series of other measures restricted slavery even further until in 1905, slavery was abolished. With little protest, Thailand had gradually done away with slavery. *See also* BUDDHISM; EMANCIPATION, SOUTHEAST ASIA.

THIRTEENTH AMENDMENT. Abraham Lincoln's Emancipation Proclamation did not end slavery in the United States. Slavery had collapsed in Maryland and had been abolished by Unionist governments in Louisiana and Arkansas and in the new state of West Virginia, but it still existed in Delaware and Kentucky. The definitive abolition came with the Thirteenth Amendment to the U.S. **Constitution**. It provided that "Neither slavery nor involuntary servitude, except as a punishment for a crime whereof the party shall have been duly convicted, shall exist within the United States, or in any place subject to their jurisdiction." It also gave Congress the right to pass appropriate laws to enforce this prohibition. The amendment was passed by Congress after Lincoln's re-election and was approved by three-fourths of the states in less than a year. By this time, slaves in both rebel and loyal areas had freed themselves and most states had taken action against slavery.

The amendment proved difficult to enforce. Some southern states ratified it reluctantly, but then also passed "**Black Codes**," which limited the rights of freed slaves to contract, to own property or to participate in public life. Many forced slaves to continue working for their former masters, effectively perpetuating slavery. Congress responded by passing the **Civil Rights Act** of 1866 and the **Fourteenth Amendment**, which made the Black Codes illegal, gave the freed slaves citizenship and prohibited the states from enacting any law that would deny the freed slaves their rights without due process of law. The **Fifteenth Amendment** prohibited the denial of voting rights by race, guaranteeing the freed slaves the right to vote. *See also* RECONSTRUCTION.

THRALLS. Thralls were slaves in **Scandinavia**. Taken as prisoners in raids all over northern and Western Europe, they worked mostly as agricultural laborers. Males were also servants and females were often taken as **concubines**. Thralldom died out during the 13th and 14th centuries.

TIPPU TIP (c. 1837-1905). Hamed bin Muhammed el-Murjebi, who was better known as Tippu Tip, was the most powerful of a series of Swahili traders who penetrated the Great Lakes and upper Congo region of **Central Africa**. These traders brought cloth, beads, guns and other goods into the interior and bought ivory, slaves and copper. During the late 1850s, Tippu Tip first began trading into Katanga. About 1870, when ivory was becoming scarce, he shifted further north into the Maniema area of the upper Congo and built his capital at Kasongo. Using slave warriors and slave officials, he created a state and gradually extended his trade routes further into the Congo basin and down river to Stanley Falls. In Maniema, he appointed officials, set up courts, maintained peace and introduced new crops, using slave labor to produce food. He was recognized by Sultan Barghash of **Zanzibar** as the governor of the Upper Congo and Maniema. In 1876, Tippu Tip met the British explorer, Henry Morton Stanley. When Stanley took service with the Congo Free State being built by King Leopold of the Belgians, Tippu Tip became Leopold's representative at Stanley Falls. By 1889, however, Leopold was convinced that he had to link himself to the anti-slavery movement to win support for the Congo Free State. Tippu Tib, recognizing that his time was up, returned to Zanzibar in 1891, leaving his Congolese army to resist the Congo Free State by itself. He remained a wealthy planter until his death, controlling at peak 10,000 slaves. *See also* EAST AFRICAN SLAVE TRADE; BRUSSELS CONFERENCE.

TOBACCO. The first slave economy to develop in what is now the United States developed around tobacco in Virginia. Tobacco was first planted within a decade of the establishment of Virginia in 1607. With smoking becoming increasingly popular in Europe, the tobacco economy grew steadily. Until 1680, it was grown largely by small farmers, often assisted by indentured servants and sometimes a slave or two. Maryland was founded in 1634 and it too found in tobacco a profitable commercial crop. Toward the end of the century, larger units began to appear and rising wages in Great Britain made it harder to find indentured servants. Slave-worked plantations expanded dramatically during the 18th century. In 1810, Virginia's population was 40 per cent slave and Maryland was almost half slave.

Tobacco does not have the economies of scale that led to large units in the **sugar** colonies. It also does not require the same kind of harsh gang labor. Most tobacco farmers had fairly small holdings, worked often with three or four slaves, and even large plantations tended to be divided into small units of production. Few farms had more than 20 slaves. Virginia and Maryland also had a more diversified agriculture. Wheat was grown commercially. Many farmers raised livestock, corn and vegetables. Slaves were often farmhands rather than laborers. By about 1720, the slave population was growing naturally in Virginia and Maryland, the first slave population in the Americas to do so. There were probably a number of different factors: healthier diet, a more beneficent disease environment, an equal number of men and women, and a less onerous work regime. Virginians began to worry about the large slave population. In 1778, Virginia ended slave imports. With the decline in the tobacco economy and the rise of **cotton** early in the 19th century, Virginia and Maryland planters began selling slaves or migrating with them. Most of them moved into growing cotton. *See also* DEMOGRAPHY OF SLAVERY.

TONJON. The *tonjon* were slave warriors in the Bambara kingdoms of Segou and Kaarta in what is now western Mali. Actually, the tonjon were slaves of the *ton*, the male hunting society which was the nucleus of the state. As the *ton* began imposing itself on surrounding areas, it began incorporating young males as slaves of the *ton*. They became an elite group of slave warriors, who used their horses to raid widely in the savanna and to provide slaves for the French in the Senegal River and the British in the Gambia River. The *tonjon* remained slaves in theory, but were powerful enough to make and break rulers. *See also* AFRICAN SLAVE TRADE; CEDDO; MILITARY SLAVES.

TOUSSAINT-LOUVERTURE (1743-1803). Toussaint-Louverture was the leader of the largest and most successful **slave revolt** in history. Born in the French sugar colony of **Saint-Domingue**, Tousssaint was the son of slave imported from the Dahomey area of West Africa. He worked on a **plantation**, probably as a coachman and stockman, but by 1791, when the revolt broke out, he had been free for many years and grew coffee on a plot of land that he rented. In the beginning, there were several different rebellions. Toussaint joined the slave rebellion and soon became one of its most effective military leaders. He was briefly allied to Spanish forces, which invaded the area, but refused to sell prisoners or non-combatants to the Spaniards. By 1793, the French were forced to abolish slavery. By 1794, Toussaint allied with them and became the most effective general on the island. At this time, he took the name "Louverture," the opening, which suggested a new birth of freedom. With French armies confined to Europe, Toussaint was effectively in charge of Saint-Domingue by 1796. He even seized the Spanish part of the island and negotiated treaties with Great Britain and the United States.

　　Toussaint's forces often lacked food, clothing and ammunition, but he eventually created the most effective fighting force on the island. By 1800, he had defeated his major rival, the mulatto, André Rigaud, and a year later, the French recognized him as Captain-General. Many of the island's plantations had passed into the hands of his officers. At this time, Toussaint tried to revive the plantation economy by forcing former slaves to work on plantations in exchange for a share of the produce. Afraid that he would have no revenue to support his army, he used the army to force peasants to work. He encouraged the return of white planters and in 1801 proclaimed a constitution which made him Governor-General for life. He shied away from declaring the island's independence from France, but in 1802, Napoleon invaded. The French armies re-established slavery, defeated Toussaint, and deported to him to France, where he died in prison a year later. Others carried on the fight, expelled the French and founded the state of Haiti. *See also* DESSALINES, JEAN-JACQUES; HAITIAN REVOLUTION.

TRIANGULAR TRADE. The triangular trade was the trade in slaves and sugar. Boats would leave Great Britain and other trading nations with a cargo of commodities popular on the African coast. They would buy slaves on the African coast and carry them to the West Indies. There, they would load a cargo of sugar for European markets, paying for it with the revenues from the slave trade..

In fact, most ships in the West India trade did not sail the triangle. The trade between Brazil and Angola involved a direct back-and-forth voyage as did some of the voyages from the mainland colonies. More important, there was a large direct trade between Europe and the West Indies because the trade in sugar was larger than the trade in slaves and West Indian elites were a market for European goods. Slaving ships were also not as well equipped for a bulk commodity as those designed to carry sugar. Some of them sailed back to Great Britain and France relatively empty. Finally, there was a large trade between the British and French colonies of the mainland and the West Indies, which depended on the mainland for fish, grain and timber. And yet, the triangle involving industrial goods, slaves and sugar was at the heart of the whole process because slaves were essential to the development of sugar production. Everything else was derivative.

TROKOSI. Among the Ewe people of Ghana and Togo, the *trokosi* are girls given to shrine priests to serve them and the shrines. *See also* TEMPLE SLAVES.

TRUTH, SOJOURNER (c.1797-1883). Born as a slave in New York, Sojourner Truth became a preacher, abolitionis,t and civil rights activist. She left her New York owner in 1826 and took refuge with another white family, who bought her to keep her out of prison. A year later, she was freed under New York's gradual emancipation statute. She then went to court to have her son freed. Soon after that, she had a religious conversion, changed her name from Isabella to Sojourner Truth, and became an itinerant preacher. Though illiterate, she was a colorful and witty speaker, who travelled around southern new England, campaigning for Christianity, anti-slavery, and women's rights. When the **Civil War** began, she campaigned for the use of black troops, and when the first Michigan Colored Infantry Regiment was organized, she collected food and clothing for them. In 1864, she moved to Washington, D.C., where she worked for the **Freedmen's Bureau**, helping to find jobs for former slaves from Virginia and Maryland. She helped desegregate the streetcars in Washington and campaigned for land to be given to freed slaves in the West.

TUBMAN, HARRIET (c. 1821-1913). Born a slave on the eastern shore of Maryland, Harriet Tubman became one of the heroines of the struggle against slavery. In 1849, she fled a life of hard field labor, and headed North. She travelled only at night, following the North Star until she reached Philadelphia. In 1850, she became a conductor on the **Underground Railroad**, the clandestine network of paths and abolitionist sympathizers, that helped slaves flee to the North, and thence often to Canada, where they would be beyond the reach of the **Fugitive Slave Act.** At least 15 times, she went back into the South, ushering from 200 to 300 slaves to freedom. Among them were her own parents. Between expeditions, she worked as a cook, using the money she saved for subsequent expeditions. The groups she led usually left on Saturday because Sunday was the slaves' day off and they would not be missed right away. Her trips were always carefully planned. Though there was a price on her head, she was never caught. Her strength and endurance often inspired her charges to carry on when tired. No one knows exactly how much she did because she remained reticent to talk about her expeditions.

During the American **Civil War**, she went to the South Carolina coast, where she worked among recently freed slaves and occasionally served the Union Army as a scout or a spy. A deeply religious Christian, she remained an activist after the war was over. She helped set up schools for freed slaves, and then returned to the home she had purchased in Auburn, New York, where she opened her home to orphans and the elderly indigent.

TUCKER, ST. GEORGE (1752-1857). St. George Tucker was a Virginia jurist and soldier, who published a plan for the abolition of slavery. Born in Bermuda, he came to Virginia in 1774 to study law at the College of William and Mary. When the **American Revolution** began, he enlisted in the colonial army and rose to the rank of Lieutenant Colonel. After the war, he became a lawyer, a law professor and then a judge and is best known for his edition of *Blackstone's Commentaries* (1803). Tucker believed that the introduction of slavery into the United States was a tragic error and an anomaly in a nation that had just fought for its liberty. In 1796, after corresponding with other leaders of the time, he wrote *Dissertation on Slavery: with a Proposal for the Gradual Abolition of it in the State of Virginia*. Tucker proposed a very gradual process that would have taken almost a century. As a judge he proved even more cautious. When presented with an argument that Virginia's constitution abolished slavery when it declared that all men were equal, he disagreed. Slaves had become too valuable a form of property.

TURNER, NAT (1800-1831). Nat Turner led one of the most important **slave revolts** in United States history. Born a slave in Southampton County Virginia, Turner was a bright child who taught himself to read and write. His father escaped from slavery, but Nat found himself as a child working for a harsh master. When his master died in 1822, Turner and his wife were sold to separate masters. He began to have visions and started preaching on Sundays. He taught that on Judgment Day, God would raise the slaves above the masters. On 21 August 1831, Turner and six followers entered the home of his master and killed all five members of the family. They then moved from house to house, killing whites and attracting supporters. Within two days, militia units were on the scene and Turner's force had been destroyed.

Turner hid out for two months, but finally was captured, tried and executed. At peak, Turner had between 60 and 80 supporters. They killed almost 60 whites. In the suppression, approximately two dozen of his men were killed in skirmishes or hung. At least 120 African-Americans were killed by white mobs or by the militia. While in prison, Nat Turner told his story to his lawyer, Thomas Gray, who published them as *Confessions of Nat Turner* (1832). The *Confesssions* give an insight into the mind of a slave rebel that has fascinated American thinkers for a century and a half. The most important immediate effect of the rebellion was the tightening of control by the state of Virginia over free blacks and over African-American religion. It also led to a debate in the Virginia legislature over whether slavery should be abolished.

-U-

UNDERGROUND RAILROAD. The term Underground Railroad refers to a system of assistance to fugitive slaves seeking freedom in the Northern United States and in Canada. It has been the subject of many stories, which have often exaggerated its accomplishments, but it did exist. In both free and slave states, there were individuals willing to help escaped slaves, both free African-Americans and sympathetic whites. Some abolitionists made organizing contacts a speciality. **Levi Coffin** organized a network, first in Newport, Indiana and then in Cincinnati, Ohio. Thomas Garrett did the same thing in Wilmington, Delaware. Such networks were regional rather than national and usually based in the North.

The passage of the **Fugitive Slave Act of 1850** gave a great stimulus to anti-slavery activity. Abolitionists organized vigilance committees, provided food, housing, transport and travel instructions to fleeing slaves. After 1850, much of the underground activity was in the North, where the goal was often to get the runaway slaves to Canada. Vigilance committees also often blocked efforts by slave catchers and federal authorities to return captured slaves to the South. They failed to stop the return of **Anthony Burns** from Boston, but succeeded in other cases. Though aiding a slave to run away was illegal, Underground Railroad activists like Levi Coffin operated quite openly in the North. Coffin was never arrested. Those caught aiding runaways in the South often spent years in prison. When **Henry "Box" Brown** became famous for his ingenious escape from slavery, the white friend who mailed the box was arrested.

Many abolitionist accounts of the Underground Railroad talked of "stations"and "conductors" and often described the "passengers" as passive participants in their own escapes. Most slave narratives make clear the ingenuity and courage of fugitives, who either used clever disguises or who hid out by day and travelled by night. When they received help, it was often after the most dangerous part of their journey was over. The most remarkable stories involve **Harriet Tubman**, an African-American woman, who went into the South many times, leading 200 to 300 slaves to freedom. Both abolitionist and pro-slavery propaganda made much of the Underground Railroad. For the abolitionists, it provided heroic and romantic tales, many published after the **Civil War.** For Southerners, such activity was a violation of their right to protection of their private property. *See also* ABOLITION, UNITED STATES.

UNITED NATIONS. Soon after its founding in 1945, the United Nations indicated its intention to continue the work of the **League of Nations** on slavery. The Universal Declaration of Human Rights, adopted in December 1948, included a provision that "No one shall be held in slavery or servitude; slavery and the **slave trade** shall be prohibited in all their forms." The following year, the General Assembly asked the Secretary-General to set up a committee to investigate slavery and the slave trade in the world. In 1956, the United Nations adopted the Supplementary Convention on Slavery, the Slave Trade and Institutions and Practices Similar to Slavery. These institutions include debt bondage, forced marriage, **serfdom** and the exploitation of child labor by persons other than the child's parents. Many of these institutions have been the subject of subsequent United Nations conventions, and subsequent U.N. bodies have included other institutions like forced labor, forced prostitution, and the conscription of children for military service.

Since 1970, slavery has been illegal everywhere in the world, though in some countries, like Mauritania, people remain in slavery, and in others, like the **Sudan,** enslavement has become an important tactic in civil wars. This means the United Nations is primarily concerned with institutions that do not meet classic definitions of slavery. Since 1975, the Working Group on Contemporary Forms of Slavery has met annually. It has no powers of enforcement, but it meets publicly and takes evidence from non-governmental organizations. These hearings place pressure on countries that tolerate institutions "similar to slavery." Probably the most common are those that involve children forced into prostitution or to work in rug factories or as camel jockeys. *See also* BONDED LABOR; CONTEMPORARY FORMS OF SLAVERY; SEXUAL SLAVERY.

URBAN SLAVERY. Over the years, most slaves have been agricultural laborers, but slavery has also been common in cities. Urban slaves were important in the ancient Middle East, in Rome, in the cities of the medieval Mediterranean world, in Spanish America and in the United States. In the Mediterranean cities of the Middle Ages, slaves were not much used in agriculture except for such specialized kinds of agriculture like vineyards. Some slaves were owned by and worked with artisans. Many, probably a majority, were servants. Most of the population of 19th century African towns and cities was servile. They were the artisans, they manned the boats, and they were the servants of the rich. The same thing is true of many of the European colonial cities of Asia.

Urban slaves have often done a wide variety of tasks. Rich house holds in **slave societies** have always had many servants and often recruited them largely from among slaves. Many slave-owners in different urban contexts rented their slaves out. The slave would work for a wage and give part of that wage to his or her master. Such slaves often had much more personal freedom than rural slaves and the opportunity to accumulate money. In Capetown, for example, many urban slaves worked on a hire-labor basis. They lived in their own quarters and had a vibrant slave culture centered around **Islam**. In rural South Africa, slaves were part of the slave-owner's household and worked under his close supervision. In the United States, slaves could also take advantage of the relative anonymity of urban life. For **Frederick Douglas** and **Robert Smalls**, it was useful in preparing an escape from slavery. For **William Ellison** and **Simon Gray**, it provided an opportunity to become wealthy.

During the 19th century, urban slavery declined dramatically in the United States. In the North, it disappeared in cities like New York, where it had been important, as slavery itself declined and free labor proved preferable. In the South, it declined because of the high prices being paid for plantation labor. Still, 19th century entrepreneurs found they could use slave labor profitably in textile factories, iron forges, on railroads, and as stevedores. Slaves remained important in Richmond, Charleston, and New Orleans. When the Civil War ended, a major source of leadership for the African-American community was urban slaves, who were often literate and already had experienced a measure of autonomy. Similarly, in West Africa, urban slaves became a major source of the merchant class and of the first groups educated in European languages. *See also* HOUSEHOLD SLAVES; SOUTH AFRICAN SLAVERY.

-V-

VESEY, DENMARK (C.1767-1822). A former slave, Denmark Vesey was the author of an elaborate plot for a **slave revolt** in Charleston, South Carolina. As a slave, Denmark Vesey had travelled widely with his master, a slave trader named Vesey. He was literate and able to speak several languages. After winning $1,500 in a lottery in December 1799, Vesey bought his own freedom for $600, but did not have the money to free his whole family. He set himself up as a carpenter in

Charleston and became a leader in the **African Methodist Episcopal Church**. He briefly considered moving to **Sierra Leone**, but decided instead to organize a revolt and lead the successful rebels to Haiti, whose President, Jean-Pierre Boyer, had invited African-Americans to settle in his country.

From 1818 to 1822, he visited **plantations** around Charleston to conduct religion classes for slaves, but also to identify potential collaborators. The plan called on slaves to rise on Bastille Day, 14 July, slay their masters, seize control of the city of Charleston and then sail for Haiti. One of Vesey's collaborators, Jack Pritchard, claimed that he had 6,600 slaves ready to revolt. The plan was betrayed less than a month before it was to take place. The mayor called up the city militia and immediately arrested many of the plotters. After a quick trial, Vesey and 35 slaves were hanged. Forty-two slaves were sold outside the United States. The **African Methodist Episcopal Church** was demolished and its leaders banished. The state assembly banned the entry of free blacks to the state, though it did nothing about those already there. The city of Charleston tried to prevent anyone teaching African-Americans to read.

VIEIRA, ANTONIO (1608-1697). Antonio Vieira was a Jesuit preacher and critic of slavery. During Vieira's lifetime, the use of slave labor was expanding dramatically in Northeast Brazil. When Vieira took his first vows in 1625, he secretly pledged to do missionary work among Indian and African slaves, but he became instead a teacher of theology, a court preacher, and an advisor to King John IV. In 1652, he got his wish and was sent to Brazil, where he became the Jesuit Superior in the Amazon. Vieira's job included the distribution of Indian labor to the settlers. He tried to stop slaving expeditions in the backlands. Unable to do so, he returned to Lisbon and to ask King John to stop the enslavement of Indians. These laws, issued in 1655, provided that enslavement of Indians was legitimate only when ordered by the King, when Indians stopped the preaching of Christianity, or in a just war. When Vieira returned to the Amazon, his efforts to enforce these laws led to the expulsion of the Jesuits from the Amazon in 1661.

Though the Jesuits were allowed back two years later, Vieira was excluded. He asked in later years for the Indians to be placed in communities under Jesuit control and totally separated from the settlers. He never developed a similar position for African slaves. He believed that under economic conditions in Brazil, slavery was inevitable, that Africans were better suited to slave labor than Indians, and that the introduction of African slaves was the best way to limit the need for Indian labor. *See also* BRAZILIAN SLAVERY; CATHOLIC CHURCH

VIKINGS. For three centuries, the Vikings were the most feared people in Europe. The eighth to the 11th century were a period of great Viking expansion. Viking longboats ranged across the North Atlantic, reaching as far as Newfoundland and leaving settlements in Iceland and Greenland. Viking raiders wrecked havoc over much of the British isles and western Europe and even penetrated the Mediterranean. In some areas, like Normandy in northern France, they settled. Iceland became an important center of Scandinavian culture. There were also Viking settlements in Great Britain and Ireland, but in most of Europe the Vikings were feared as raiders who ravaged, took booty and enslaved. Many of these slaves were brought back to Scandinavia. Others were sold. Vikings also developed overland trade routes that passed along the rivers of what is now Russia to the Black Sea. They traded for slaves, fur and wax with indigenous people and sold these products to the Byzantines. The Viking trade routes were a major source of slaves for **Byzantium** and the Mediterranean world, both Christian and Muslim. *See also* EAST EUROPEAN SLAVE TRADE; RUSSIAN SLAVERY; SCANDINAVIA.

VODUN. *Vodun,* or Voodoo as it is more popularly known, is an African religion popular in Haiti and wherever Haitians have migrated. It is predominantly Dahomean, but contains elements of **Yoruba** and Catholic religion. Though slave owners tried to suppress African religions, they persisted and were a factor in the Haitian revolution. *Vodun* practitioners believe in a high God, several lesser gods and spirits called *orisa.* They believe that every person has a soul and that there is a large guardian angel concerned with all of us and a lesser guardian angel for each person. Believers pray alone or in groups and make sacrifices to the gods in trying to contact them to influence human events and prevent possession by evil spirits. *See also* SLAVE RELIGION.

-W-

WALKER, DAVID (1785-1830). A free black, born in Wilmington, North Carolina, David Walker grew up in the South, but in 1825, he moved to Boston, Massachusetts, and rapidly became active in African-American organizations. In 1827, he opened a clothing store that catered to seamen, and which he used to smuggle abolitionist literature into the South. He put pamphlets in the pockets of garments he sold, knowing that they would find their way into the hands of African-Americans in the South. He also mailed his own writings to the South.

In 1829, he published *Appeal to the Coloured Citizens of the World*, which called on masters to free their slaves and called on the slaves to revolt and kill their masters. He had little hope of racial harmony, insisting that African-Americans must have a nation of their own and urging them to defend themselves and to follow only African-American leaders. It was the most radical manifesto of the abolitionist movement and an early expression of black nationalism, but there is no evidence that it had any impact on subsequent events. It was cited by Southerners who were hostile to African-American churches and wanted to prohibit anyone from teaching slaves to read. There is evidence that it also led several Georgians to put a price on his life. In 1830, his body was found near his store. The cause of death was never determined.

WARD, SAMUEL RINGGOLD (1817-1866). Samuel Ward was born as a slave on the eastern shore of Maryland and became an influential Black abolitionist. In 1820, the Wards fled Maryland, eventually settling in New York. Samuel was educated and became first a teacher and then a Congregationalist minister. In 1840, he joined the **Liberty Party** and became active in the abolition movement. When the **Fugitive Slave Law** was passed in 1850, he spoke against it and was involved in the freeing of Jerry, a runaway slave, from a Syracuse, New York, jail in 1851. Fearing arrest, he fled to Canada, where he became the Canadian agent of the **American Anti-Slavery Society**, founding local chapters and assisting runaway slaves who made it to Canada. He also made a fund-raising tour of Great Britain. In 1855, he published *Autobiography of a Fugitive Negro: His Anti-Slavery Labours in the United States, Canada and England*. He spent the last years of his life as a minister in Jamaica.

WELD, THEODORE DWIGHT (1803-1895). The son of a small-town pastor, born in Connecticut and raised in New York, Theodore Weld early moved to Ohio, where he became one of the leaders of the western branch of the abolition movement. Though he and his friend **James G. Birney** were briefly involved in the colonization movement, they early became advocates of immediate and total abolition and helped found the **American Anti-Slavery Society**. While working at Lane Theological Seminary, Weld became involved in educational efforts in Cincinnati's large black community, which contained many people who had fled slavery or purchased their freedom. He taught theology, but also learned from his students what slavery was really like. After marrying fellow abolitionist **Angelina Grimke** and moving to Oberlin College, he published *The Bible against Slavery* (1837) and *American Slavery As It Is* (1839) . The latter included many stories told by his students at Lane and Oberlin and vividly depicted the brutality and harshness of slavery. It was the most popular book on slavery, until **Harriet Beecher Stowe**, one of Weld's students, wrote *Uncle Tom's Cabin* (1852).

WEST AFRICA. Slavery has long existed in West Africa. The area was the center of powerful states, which developed in the savanna regions and in western Nigeria during the first millenium. The first slaves were probably war captives. The empires of Ghana, Mali, Kanem, Songhai, and Bornu, all traded with the Arabs, and while Arabs were most interested in gold, there was a steady stream of slaves across the **Sahara**. During the 15th century, when Portuguese navigators sailed along the West African coast, they often kidnapped people, who were taken back to Portugal to be trained as interpreters. They soon found, however, that in most areas, they could buy slaves, usually in small numbers.

West Africa soon became the major source of slaves for the growing European **slave trade**. It was near the Atlantic islands, and the closest source of slave labor for the western Mediterranean and the developing markets in the Americas. The result was a steady growth in slaving within West Africa, the development of supply routes into the interior, and the increasing availability of large numbers of slaves on the coast. During the 17th century, when the northern European states moved into **sugar** production in the West Indies, the demand for slaves increased as did the prices Europeans were willing to pay. The result was the formation of a series of powerful states in West Africa capable of supplying large numbers of slaves and often using slave warriors: Oyo, **Asante, Dahomey**, Segou, and Futa Jallon. All of them were formed or rose to power between 1660 and 1725.

One by-product of the slave trade routes that crossed West Africa was the increasing market for slaves within the region. Slave-based production increased in the desert-side regions and in some of the more important Muslim states. Great Britain abolished the slave trade in 1807, and then, one by one, so did other European states. European demand was at this time increasing for African products. More and more slaves were exploited within Africa to produce peanuts, palm oil, and other goods for European markets. The result is that the slave trade remained important until the early colonial period. *See also* AFRICAN SLAVERY; AFRICAN SLAVE TRADE; ATLANTIC SLAVE TRADE; EMANCIPATION, AFRICA; YORUBA.

WHEATLEY, PHILLIS (c. 1753-1784). Born in West Africa, enslaved and brought to Massachusetts as young girl, Phillis Wheatley became a well-known poet. She was owned by John Wheatley, a merchant tailor. Phillis Wheatley learned to speak English quickly and her master's family taught her to read the Bible. She soon also taught herself to write and as a teenager, was already writing poetry. In 1767, she published her first poem. In 1773, she visited England with Nathaniel, her master's son. In the same year, she brought out *Poems on Various Subjects, Religious and Moral* with financial help from an English patron. Most of Wheatley's poetry dealt with religious subjects. Her poetry was as good as any being written in the colonies, but there was doubt that a black slave could write such poetry. Some 18 leading Bostonians supported her by signing a letter that they believed she had written the poetry. Her last years, however, were spent in poverty. By 1779, most of the Wheatleys were dead. She married a free Black named John Peters, but their three children all died young and they had financial difficulties. Sick and poor, she died in 1784. During her lifetime and later, she was often cited as an example in debates about the intellectual capacities of African-Americans.

WHITTIER, JOHN GREENLEAF (1807-1892). Though his education was limited, John Greenleaf Whittier became one of the most popular poets of 19th- century United States. Born a **Quaker** in Massachusetts, Whittier was a voracious reader and began as a teenager to write poetry. In 1826, his sister sent a poem he wrote to a newspaper edited by **William Lloyd Garrison**. Garrison published it and much of Whittier's later literary production. He also found Whittier a job as the editor of the *American Manufacturer* in 1829. Whittier earned his living for many years as an editor, but also wrote prolifically and worked for the temperance and anti-slavery movements. He even ran for the Massachusetts legislature in 1835.

WHYDAH. Europeans began buying slaves at Whydah in the Bight of Benin during the late 16th century and Europeans had forts there by

1670. Originally a small kingdom, Whydah was conquered by **Daho mey** in 1727 and became Dahomey's preferred port. Already an important slave port, it was for most of the 18th century, the most important single port for the West African **slave trade**. The major European slavetrading companies had forts there. The king of Dahomey was represented by an official called the *yevogan,* who traded the king's slaves and collected customs. Over the years, at least a million slaves were shipped out of Whydah.

WILBERFORCE, WILLIAM (1759-1833). William Wilberforce was the parliamentary leader of the struggle to end the **slave trade**. The son of a merchant from Hull, Wilberforce was first elected to the House of Commons in 1780. After a conversion to evangelical Christianity in 1784, he was convinced that Christian ideals should be implemented in everyday life. He became the leader of the anti-slave trade bloc in the House and in 1787 was one of the founders of the Society for Effecting the Abolition of the Slave Trade. To a movement dominated in its early years by **Quakers**, he was valuable because he was a member of the more established Anglican church. He was also charming, an eloquent orator and a fine propagandist.

Wilberforce started by trying to introduce antislavery clauses into a treaty being negotiated with France. During the next decade, he introduced abolition bills five times, and each time, there were bitter and acrimonious debates. The **French** and **Haitian Revolutions** aroused fears and the opposition of King George. His allies, however, were perfecting the techniques of using petitions and mass meetings to bring pressure on parliament. In 1807, both houses of parliament finally approved the bill, which went into effect on 1 January 1808. This victory did not end slavery. Nor in spite of the efforts of the **Africa Squadron** of the Royal Navy did it end the slave trade. Wilberforce and his colleagues were convinced that the trade would end only when there was no market for slaves. In 1823, they created the Antislavery Society and launched a campaign to end slavery. Wilberforce was once again the leader, but by 1825, ill health forced him to yield to **Thomas Fowell Buxton**. He lived long enough to see the third reading of the abolition bill passed shortly after his death in 1833. *See also* ABOLITION, GREAT BRITAIN.

WILLIAMS, ERIC (1911-1981). A historian and politician, Eric Wil liams spent most of his adult life as Prime Minister of Trinidad. As a historian, he is best known for his controversial doctoral dissertation, published as *Capitalism and Slavery* in 1944. Born in Trinidad, the son of a postal clerk, he was an outstanding student and received a fellowship to Oxford, where he completed his Ph.D. in 1938. From 1939 to 1955, he taught at Howard University in Washington, D.C., but when the process of decolonization began, he returned to Trinidad, organized the People's National Movement and was elected Chief Minister in 1956. He was Prime Minister from independence in 1962 to his death. He also wrote *From Columbus to Castro: the History of the Caribbean* (1970).

In *Capitalism and Slavery*, he made three arguments: that American slavery resulted from economic interests and thus that racism was a consequence of slavery and not a cause of it; that the English Industrial Revolution was financed by profits from the American plantation economy; and that the **slave trade** was ended not because of British humanitarianism, but because important economic interests opposed it. *Capitalism and Slavery* provoked a great deal of debate and much further research. This research has disproved some of Williams's detailed statements, but much of his broader argument is accepted. Thus, most writers would agree that slavery is an economic institution. Racism is seen not as a cause, but as a result of slavery. Most writers would accept that the plantation economy was central to the development of the Americas and to European industrialisation, though not necessarily in the direct way pictured by Williams. His argument on the roots of abolition, however, is weak. Many scholars have presented persuasive evidence that at the time of abolition, the slave economies were very prosperous, though few would go back to earlier arguments that abolition was a triumph of human decency. *See also* ABOLITION, GREAT BRITAIN.

WILMOT PROVISO. In 1846, during the **Mexican-American** War, a Pennsylvania Congressman name David Wilmot moved an amendment to a military appropriations bill that slavery should be prohibited in all territories acquired as a result of the war. Almost all Northerners voted for the amendment. Almost all Southerners opposed it. It passed the House of Representatives, but was defeated in the Senate. The Wilmot Proviso was supported by Northern congressmen who had not previously been responsive to abolitionist appeals, but who were alienated by President James Polk's expansionism and his pro-slavery agenda. For the next 15 years, the extension of slavery to new territories was a central issue in American political life, and the polarization that marked the discussion of the Wilmot Proviso deepened and grew more intense. *See also* COMPROMISE OF 1850; MEXICAN-AMERICAN WAR.

WOOLMAN, JOHN (1720-1772). John Woolman was an early **Quaker** abolitionist. Born to a Quaker farming family, Woolman turned early to shop-keeping, tailoring, and teaching school. He prospered in business, but he was from very young a pious man and a believer in putting Christian ideals into practice. He became a lay minister when only 22 and spent much of his life travelling in the service of the Quakers. He writes in his *Journal* that he was troubled when an employer asked him to write a bill of sale for a slave woman. Visits to the South further aroused his conviction that slavery was incompatible with Quaker beliefs in equality. At a time when many Quakers had slaves, he advocated a prohibition against Quakers owning slaves. In 1754, he submitted to the Philadelphia Annual Meeting an essay entitled "Some considerations on the Keeping of Negroes; Recommended to the Professor of Christianity of Every Denomination." He was a key figure in the Quakers eventually closing membership to slave owners. Another essay, "A Plea for the Poor," published posthumously, argues that monetary compensation should be paid to former slaves or their heirs. He also wrote on many other issues: conscription, injustice toward the Indians and taxation for military purposes. In 1772, he died of smallpox on a visit to New York.

WRIGHT, FRANCES (1795-1852). Frances Wright was reformer and abolitionist born in Scotland, who tried to develop an alternative to slave labor in the South. She visited the United States and described her visit in *Views of Society and Manners in the United States* (1821). Conversations about the book with the Marquis de Lafayette persuaded her to try to put her ideas into practice. In 1825, she bought land near Memphis and eight slaves and with them, founded Nashoba **plantation**. To earn their freedom, slaves had to perform enough labor to reimburse the plantation for their purchase price plus 6 per cent interest and the cost of food and clothing. The slaves were all taught a trade, how to read, do arithmetic, and write. Children were to receive a full education. While Wright was on the plantation, there was no corporal punishment. When Wright left the area in 1827, her managers abandoned her ideas about corporal punishment and began using harsh punishments. Wright also wanted equality between men and women on the plantation, but it soon ran into trouble. The soil was poor and the area was malarial. By 1830, the plantation had failed, but Wright kept her promise to the slaves, freeing them and taking them to Haiti. Wright continued to lecture about the emancipation of women and slaves and to advocate the ideas that led her to create Nashoba.

-Y-

YEVOGAN. The Yevogan was the official who represented the King of Dahomey in the slave trading port of **Whydah**. He was also known as the "chief of the white men." The custom was that the king's slaves were sold first. The Yevogan traded for the king and collected customs on the rest of the trade. After the ascension of King Ghezo in 1818, his power was superseded by a Brazilian merchant, **Francisco Felix De Souza**, who held the office of *chacha*. Other slave-trading kingdoms had similar institutions, which were important if the rulers were to maintain control of the trade.

YORUBA. The Yoruba of western Nigeria are one of the largest ethnic groups in **West Africa**. The Yoruba were never united before colonial rule, but the powerful kingdom of Oyo was one of the most powerful slaving kingdoms in West Africa and controlled northern Yorubaland. The origins of Oyo are shrouded in myth, but in the 17th century, it expanded, using cavalry to impose tribute on its neighbors to both North and South. The Oyo cavalry were widely feared, but not able to conquer areas in the forest not suitable to horses. Oyo was, however, able to collect slaves through warfare and tribute and to send large numbers of slaves to different coastal ports.

In the 19th century, the Oyo empire broke down in a series of civil wars. While different Yoruba factions struggled for power, northern Yorubaland fell under the ascendancy of the Muslim **Sokoto Caliphate**. The Caliphate failed in its efforts to extend itself into the forest zone. As a result, the Yoruba went from being predators to being the major source of slaves during the last half-century of the transatlantic **slave trade**. One result was the importance of Yoruba religious movements in the Americas: *Candomble* and *shango* in Brazil and *Santeria* in Cuba. After the end of the slave trade, Yoruba shrines in the Americas often re-established contact with those in the Nigeria. *See also* SLAVE RELIGION.

-Z-

ZANJ. Zanj is a word that is used by both Arabs and Iranians for the East African coast and for black slaves coming from that area. Zanj slaves were responsible for one of the greatest slave revolts in history. During the period from the seventh to the ninth centuries many slaves from that area were imported into southern Mesopotamia. Drainage canals in the area had silted up in previous centuries and what had been fertile farmland became swamps and salt flats. Large slave gangs were used to re-dig drainage canals, eliminate saline soils and prepare the land for cultivation. Life for the slaves was harsh and brutish, and not surprisingly, there were a series of slave revolts. There were two during the seventh century, but the most important began in 869 and was led by an Arab known as Ali ben Sahid al-Zanj (Master of the Zanj). The Zanj armies occupied the Iraqi port of Basra and the Iranian port of Abadan and came within 70 miles of Bagdad. Finally, in 881, the armies of the Abbasid Caliphate began pushing the Zanj back and blockaded the Zanj in their capital Mukhtara, which fell in 883 after a three year siege. Tens of thousands of Zanj soldiers were massacred. One effect of the revolt was a limitation on the import of Africans. The revolt ended efforts to restore the fertility of the southern Iraqi salt flats. African slaves were henceforth used more as household slaves than as agricultural labor. The term Zanj is still used within the Arab world to refer to blacks. *See also* INDIAN OCEAN; MIDDLE EASTERN SLAVERY.

ZANZIBAR. Lying off the coast of East Africa, Zanzibar and Pemba were long popular anchorages for ships in the **Indian Ocean** trade. During the 19th century, they became a major center of clove production and the base for trade with the interior of East Africa for slaves and ivory. Zanzibar became a preferred port for Arab traders from Oman during the 18th century. In 1806, **Said ibn Sultan** became Sultan of Oman. Said had a three-pronged development program. First, he gradually extended his control over most of the Swahili-speaking towns on the East African coast. Second, he encouraged his fellow Arabs to develop clove plantations on the islands of Zanzibar and Pemba. They were so successful that by 1840, Zanzibar was the world's largest clove producer and the most important market for slaves from the interior of East Africa. Third, he also encouraged Omani Arabs to develop trade with the far interior. Since most of the Arabs lacked capital, he encouraged Indian financiers to settle in the towns along the coast, often giving them lucrative contracts to collect taxes. The caravans that penetrated into central Africa, traded in both ivory and slaves.

Said's program was dramatically successful. By 1840, Zanzibar was so much wealthier than Oman that Said relocated there. Zanzibar controlled a coastal strip, within which slave-worked **plantations** produced grain, copra, and sesame, and bases as far inland as Lake Tanganyika. The British, Americans, French, and later, the Germans established embassies there. When Said died in 1856, the British controlled the succession and blocked the efforts of Omani Arabs to re-establish control over the islands. Dependant on the British, one of Said's sons, Sultan Barghash, abolished the **slave trade** in 1873, though slave labor remained the basis of the plantation economy. In 1885, the Germans claimed Zanzibar's mainland domains. In 1890, Great Britain proclaimed a protectorate over Zanzibar and in 1897, they abolished slavery, though they tried to help the planters to maintain control over their labor supply. *See also* EAST AFRICAN SLAVE TRADE; TIPPU TIB.

ZAR. Northeast Africa spirit possession cult taken by slaves to the Middle East and Iran. *See also* BORI; SLAVE RELIGION.

ZARIBA. The *zaribas* were fortified bases for slave traders operating in the southern **Sudan**. They were inhabited by traders and their slave soldiers who lived off the land and were generally fed by slaves, who worked the land around each of the *zaribas*. *See also* ZUBAYR PASHA.

ZONG CASE. The *Zong* was a slave ship that left West Africa in 1781 with a cargo of 470 slaves. On its passage to America, the ship was struck by an epidemic which killed 60 slaves and 17 crew members. Running low on water, Captain Luke Collingwood decided to throw the sick slaves over board. Some 131 slaves drowned after being thrown into the sea, many of them jumping into the sea with their shackles to end their suffering. Collingwood assumed that the insurance would pay for the lost slaves. By the time the ship made it back to England, Collingwood was dead, but the owner, Gregson, sought to collect his insurance. The insurance underwriter refused to pay. His lawyers argued that there was no crisis and that Collingwood had the slaves tossed overboard because he was afraid he would have a hard time selling them. Gregson won in the original court, but the case was appealed. Chief Justice Mansfield, who had been judge in the **Somerset Case**, decided to order a new trial. It is not known how that trial turned out, but the case was much publicized and gave a strong boost to the abolitionist cause. **Granville Sharp** unsuccessfully asked that murder charges be brought against those responsible. In 1791, Parliament prohibited reimbursal of insurance costs in cases where slaves were thrown overboard.

ZUBAYR PASHA (1830-1913). Zubayr Pasha was a soldier and slave trader in the southern **Sudan**. Born in the Sudan and educated in Khartoum, he served as an officer in the Turco-Egyptian army. After leaving the army, in 1856, he moved to the southern Sudan with other Khartoum-based traders looking for profits from the ivory trade. The local people often had little interest in trading with the newcomers. Many traders responded by raiding and incorporating some of the men they took as soldiers in their private armies. Within a short time, Zubayr controlled Bahr al-Ghazal and began extending his control over adjacent areas. Operating out of fortified bases called *zaribas,* his power was based on use of slave soldiers armed with the latest rapid-firing rifles. Other slaves produced the food that fed his army. He traded both slaves and ivory. In 1872, Egypt accepted his power by recognizing him as Governor of Bahr al-Ghazal. In 1874, he conquered the powerful emirate of Darfur, but a year later, when he went to Egypt for political discussions, he was not allowed to return.

BIBLIOGRAPHY

Reference

Drescher, Seymour, and Stanley L. Engerman, eds. *A Historical Guide to World Slavery*. New York: Oxford University Press, 1998

Finkelman, Paul, and Joseph C. Miller , eds. *Macmillan Encyclopedia of World Slavery*. 2 vols. New York: Simon & Schuster, 1998.

Miller, Randall M., and John David Smith, eds. *Dictionary of Afro-American Slavery*. Westport, Conn.: Greenwood, 1988.

General

Bales, Kevin. *Disposable People: New Slavery in the Global Economy*. Berkeley: University of California Press, 1999.

Barry, Boubacar. *Senegambia and the Atlantic Slave Trade. Tr.* Ayi Kwei Armah.. Cambridge: Cambridge University Press, 1998.

Berlin, Ira. *Many Thousands Gone: The First Two Centuries of Slavery in North America*. Cambridge, Mass.: Harvard University Press, 1998.

Blackburn, Robin. *The Making of New World Slavery: From the Baroque to the Modern*. London: Verso, 1996.

———. *The Overthrow of Colonial Slavery, 1776-1848*. London: Verso, 1988.

Blassingame, John. *The Slave Community: Plantation Life in the Antebellum South*. New York: Oxford University Press, 1972.

Chatterji, Indrani. *Gender, Slavery and Law in Colonial India*. New Delhi: Oxford University Press, 1999.

Cooper, Frederick. *Plantation Slavery on the East Coast of Africa*. New Haven, Conn.: Yale University Press, 1978.

Curtin, Philip. *The Rise and Fall of the Plantation Complex: Essays in Atlantic History*. Cambridge: Cambridge University Press, 1990.

———. *Economic Change in Precolonial Africa: Senegambia in the Era of the Slave Trade*. Madison: University of Wisconsin Press, 1975.

Davis, David Brion. *The Problem of Slavery in the Age of Revolution*. Ithaca, N.Y.: Cornell University Press, 1966.

————. *Slavery and Human Progress*. New York: Oxford University Press, 1984.

Drescher, Seymour. *Econocide: British Slavery in the Era of Abolition*. Pittsburgh: University of Pittsburgh Press, 1977.

Dunn, Richard. *Sugar and Slaves: The Rise of the Planter Class in the English West Indies*. Chapel Hill: University of North Carolina Press, 1972.

Elkins, Stanley M. *Slavery: A Problem in American Institutional and Intellectual Life*. Chicago: University of Chicago Press, 1959.

Eltis, David. *Economic Growth and the Ending of the Transatlantic Slave Trade*. New York: Oxford University Press, 1987.

————. *The Rise of African Slavery in the Americas*. Cambridge: Cambridge University Press, 2000.

Ennaji, Mohammed. *Serving the Master: Slavery and Society in Nineteenth Century Morocco*. Tr. by Seth Graebner. Houndsmills, Basingstoke, Hampshire: Macmillan, 1999.

Finley, Moses. *Ancient Slavery and Modern Ideology*. New York: Viking, 1980.

Fogel, Robert. *Without Consent or Contract: The Rise and Fall of American Slavery*. New York: Norton, 1989.

Fogel, Robert and Stanley Engerman. *Time on the Cross: The Economics of American Negro Slavery*. 2 Vol. Boston: Little Brown, 1974.

Foner, Eric. *Nothing but Freedom: Emancipation and Its Legacy*. Baton Rouge: Louisiana State University Press, 1983.

Genovese, Eugene. *Roll, Jordan, Roll: The World the Slaves Made*. New York: Pantheon, 1974.

Gomez, Michael. *Exchanging Our Country Marks: The Transformation of African Identities in the Colonial and Antebellum South*. Chapel Hill: University of North Carolina Press, 1998.

Gutman, Herbert. *The Black Family in Slavery and Freedom, 1750-1925*. New York: Pantheon, 1976.

Hopkins, Keith. *Conquerors and Slaves*. Cambridge: Cambridge University Press, 1978.

Jordan, Winthrop. *White over Black: American Attitudes toward the Negro, 1550-1812*. Baltimore, Md.: Penguin, 1968.

Klein, Herbert S. *African Slavery in Latin America and the Caribbean*. New York: Oxford University Press, 1986.

————. *The Middle Passage: Comparative Studies in the Atlantic Slave Trade*. Princeton, N.J.: Princeton University Press, 1978.

Lewis, Bernard. *Race and Slavery in the Middle East*. London: Oxford University Press, 1990.

Lovejoy, Paul. *Transformations in Slavery*. Cambridge: Cambridge University Press, 1983.

Meillassoux, Claude. *Anthropology of Slavery: The Womb of Iron and Gold*. Tr. Alide Dasnois. Chicago: University of Chicago Press, 1991.

Miers, Suzanne, and Igor Kopytoff, eds. *Slavery in Africa: Historical and Anthropological Perspectives*. Madison: University of Wisconsin Press, 1977.

Miers, Suzanne, and Richard Roberts, eds. *The End of Slavery in Africa*. Madison: University of Wisconsin Press, 1989.

Miller, Joseph C. *The Way of Death: Merchant Capitalism and the Angolan Slave Trade, 1730- 1830*. Madison: University of Wisconsin Press, 1988.

Morgan, Philip D. *Slave Counterpoint: Black Culture in the Eighteenth-Century Chesapeake and Lowcountry*. Chapel Hill: University of North Carolina Press, 1998.

Patnaik, Utsa, and Manjari Dingwaney, eds. *Chains of Servitude: Bondage and Slavery in India*. Madras: Sangam, 1985.

Patterson, Orlando. *Slavery and Social Death*. Cambridge, Mass.: Harvard University Press, 1982.

Raboteau, Albert.J. *Slave Religion: The "Invisible Institution" in the Antebellum South*. New York: Oxford University Press, 1978.

Rawick, George P. *From Sunup to Sundown: The Making of the Black Community*. Westport, Conn.: Greenwod, 1972,

Rawley, James A. *The Transatlantic Slave Trade*. New York: Norton, 1981.

Reid, Anthony, ed. *Slavery, Bondage and Dependency in Southeast Asia*. St. Lucia, Australia: University of Queensland Press, 1983.

Schwartz, Stuart. *Sugar Plantations in the Formation of Brazilian Society: Bahia, 1550-1835*. Cambridge: Cambridge University Press, 1985.

Scott, Rebecca. *Slave Emancipation in Cuba: The Transition to Free Labor, 1860-1899*. Princeton, N.J.: Princeton University Press, 1985.

Sheridan, Richard B. *Sugar and Slavery: An Economic History of the British West Indies 1623-1775*. Baltimore, Md.: Johns Hopkins University Press, 1974.

Solow, Barbara, ed. *Slavery and the Rise of the Atlantic System*. Cambridge: Cambridge University Press, 1991.

Stampp, Kenneth. *The Peculiar Institution*. New York: Random House, 1956.

Stuckey, Sterling. *Slave Culture. Nationalist Theory and the Foundations of Black America*. New York: Oxford University Press, 1987.

Thornton, John. *Africa and Africans in the Making of the Atlantic World, 1400-1680*. Cambridge: Cambridge University Press, 1992.

Toledano, Ehud. *Slavery and Abolition in the Ottoman Middle East*. Seattle: University of Washington Press, 1998.

Vogt, Joseph. *Ancient Slavery and the Ideal of Man*. Tr. by Thomas Wiedemann. London: Oxford University Press, 1975.

Williams, Eric. *Capitalism and Slavery*. Chapel Hill: University of North Carolina Press, 1944.

Wood, Peter. *Black Majority: Negroes in Colonial South Carolina from 1670 through the Stono Rebellion*. New York: Norton, 1974.

Some Narratives by Slaves, Slave-Owners and Slave Traders

Andrews, William L., ed. *Black Women's Slave Narratives*. New York: Oxford University Press, 1987.

Bassett, John Spencer, ed. *The Plantation Overseer as Revealed in His Letters*. Northampton, Mass.: Smith College, 1925.

Berlin, Ira et.al., eds. *Free at Last: A Documentary History of Slavery, Freedom and the Civil War*. New York: New Press, 1992.

Blassingame, John W., ed. *Slave Testimony: Two Centuries of Letters, Speeches, Interviews and Autobiographies*. Baton Rouge: Louisiana State University Press, 1977.

Conneau, Theophilus. *A Slaver's Log Book, or 20 Years Residence in Africa*. Englewood Cliffs, N.J.: Prentice-Hall, 1976.

Curtin, Philip. *Africa Remembered: Narratives by West Africans from the Era of the Slave Trade*. Madison: University of Wisconsin Press, 1968.

Douglass, Frederick. *My Bondage and My Freedom*. New York: Miller, Orton, 1855.

Equiano, Olaudah. *Equiano's Travels*. Portsmouth, N.H.: Heinemann, 1996 (1789).

Gates, Henry Louis, ed. *The Classic Slave Narratives*. New York: Penguin, 1987.

Mellon, James, ed. *Bullwhip Days: The Slaves Remember. An Oral History*. New York: Avon, 1988.

Wright, Marcia. *Strategies of Slaves and Women: Life Stories from East/Central Africa*. New York: Lilian Barber Press, 1993.

ABOUT THE AUTHOR

Martin A. Klein (B.S., Northwestern University; M.A. and Ph.D., University of Chicago) is a professor emeritus at the University of Toronto, where he taught African History from 1970 to 1999. He has also taught at the University of California in Berkeley and at Lovanium University in Kinshasa. He has lectured at universities in Africa, Asia, Europe, and the United States.

Professor Klein is the author of *Islam and Imperialism in Senegal: Sine-Saloum, 1847-1914* and *Slavery and Colonial Rule in French West Africa,* which was given an honorable mention in the competition for the Herskovits Prize, given by the African Studies Association for the best book on Africa published in the United States. He has edited *Women and Slavery in Africa* (with Claire Robertson), *Breaking the Chains: Slavery, Bondage, and Emancipation in Modern Africa and Asia,* and *Slavery and Colonial Rule in Africa* (with Suzanne Miers). He has also written numerous articles on Islam, colonial rule, slavery, and the slave trade. He is now working on a comparative study of slavery in world history.

Professor Klein has received numerous research grants and has served as president of the Canadian Association of African Studies and the African Studies Association (U.S.). In 2001, he was given the Distinguished Africanist Award of the African Studies Association.